Public–Private Partnerships in Sub-Saharan Africa

Public–Private Partnerships in Sub-Saharan Africa

The Evidence-Based Critique

JAMES LEIGLAND

OXFORD
UNIVERSITY PRESS

OXFORD
UNIVERSITY PRESS

Great Clarendon Street, Oxford, OX2 6DP,
United Kingdom

Oxford University Press is a department of the University of Oxford.
It furthers the University's objective of excellence in research, scholarship,
and education by publishing worldwide. Oxford is a registered trade mark of
Oxford University Press in the UK and in certain other countries

First Edition published in 2020

Published in the United States of America by Oxford University Press
198 Madison Avenue, New York, NY 10016, United States of America

British Library Cataloguing in Publication Data
Data available

Library of Congress Control Number: 2019954821

ISBN 978–0–19–886182–9

Preface

This book focuses on a current issue of widespread concern for the international development community—whether or not private sector investment in infrastructure will benefit what Paul Collier calls "the Bottom Billion" residents of the world's poorest nations.[1] At the time Collier's book was published in 2007, the development community—International Monetary Fund (IMF), bilateral donors, multilateral development banks (MDBs), non-government organizations (NGOs), etc.—was beginning to acknowledge that the poorest countries were not actually growing and developing as expected. It was becoming clear that the delivery of infrastructure services in these countries (water, power, transport, etc.) was still deteriorating rather than improving. The G20 began promoting the use of PPPs for use in "transformational" megaprojects in poor countries, to rapidly scale up the size and impact of private investment in regional infrastructure. The G20 also started to pressure the IMF and MDBs to do more to facilitate these kinds of projects. When the Sustainable Development Goals (SDGs) were agreed on in 2015, infrastructure-related targets played a major role in the SDG framework. It was obvious that the poorest countries and their development partners would need huge amounts of additional support to be able to finance the achievement of these ambitious new goals. The development community immediately looked to the private sector for that additional investment. So, the international development orthodoxy began to consolidate around the idea that scaled-up private investment, particularly via PPP projects, would help get development back on track in low-income countries (LICs). Publications by development banks and academicians provided best-practice advice regarding how, when, and where to do such projects to maximize development impacts.

Meanwhile, civil society groups, like organized labor and NGOs, continued their long-standing criticism of all forms of privatization, including PPPs. These groups tend to view PPPs as irresistible opportunities for the private sector to exploit poor people by making profits from the monopoly control and sale of essential services like water and electricity. But because this criticism has always been largely ideological in nature, it has been mostly ignored outside the civil society community.

The timing of this book relates to the fact that the widespread use of infrastructure PPPs in developing countries is relatively recent, beginning only in the 1990s

[1] Paul Collier. 2007. *The Bottom Billion: Why the Poorest Countries Are Failing and What Can Be Done About It*. New York: Oxford University Press.

under the structural adjustment lending programs of the multilateral development banks. For the last 30 years, the debate about PPPs has been characterized by a lack of hard evidence on both sides. Advocates as well as critics have been dogmatic about PPPs, appealing more to conflicting interpretations of "common sense" than empirical evaluation. Academic scholars have generated insights about PPPs but have mostly concentrated on developed countries where the population of PPPs has been large and information on projects accessible. However, compelling evidence about PPP performance in the poorest countries has been quietly accumulating in working papers, project evaluations, and industry publications. Because much of this evidence documents the existence of PPP shortcomings, it has largely been ignored by PPP advocates, who tend to assume that the case in favor of PPPs has already been made convincingly. And this evidence is only just beginning to find its way into civil society critiques. This body of evidence is reaching a kind of critical mass, but neither of the principal sides in the PPP debate has yet fully captured the details and subtleties of what the evidence says about how and where PPPs are used, and what makes these projects sustainable or not in poor countries. Thus far, there has been no decisive winner in the PPP debate.

The purpose of this book is to summarize and consolidate what this critical mass of evidence-based research is saying about PPPs in LICs and thereby help to resolve the argument about the value of these mechanisms and their likely developmental role going forward. The focus of the book is on Sub-Saharan Africa (SSA), home to most of Collier's Bottom Billion, although insights from other regions and more affluent developing countries are also included. This book organizes this research into categories like PPP project popularity and prevalence, project costs and profits, preparation expenses, the ability to leverage private finance and investment, poverty impacts, and governance issues. The results are then used to explain shortcomings with specific types of PPPs, like brownfield concessions, management contracts, and greenfield power projects. Case studies of many of the best-known PPPs in Africa are used to illustrate these findings. The likely ability of PPPs to have impacts on transformational megaprojects and SDGs are also assessed, and emerging alternatives to PPPs considered.

What the evidence is telling us is that PPPs clearly have not met expectations in the poorest countries, but not for reasons having to do with private sector exploitation or a failure to follow best-practice project guidelines. The fundamental problem with these projects in impoverished countries is that they are simply not commercial in nature. They are expensive to prepare properly, do not generate expected profits, and cannot attract adequate levels of private investment. These projects tend to be sustainable only when they are done as hybrids that compromise on many of the original defining characteristics of PPPs. The biggest compromise involves the need for large amounts of public finance to pay for preparation and cover substantial portions of capital investment. In fact, the concept of "blended finance"—the use of public money to catalyze private finance—is now beginning to dominate discussions of how infrastructure in developing countries is most effectively financed. But the question becomes, how much public finance is too much? How do we guard against so much public subsidization of these projects that they are no longer worth doing as complicated and expensive PPPs, and the public money better used in some other way? Experiments are now underway in some developing countries to identify what those other ways might be. The ultimate judgment of this evidence-based critique is that PPPs have a role to play, but only if expectations remain realistic, based on evidence, and projects are subject to transparent evaluation and competition. However, it seems highly unlikely that PPPs will be effective in implementing transformational megaprojects or achieving the SDGs. Unfortunately, there is no compelling evidence that the private sector, through PPPs, will play a significant role in the rescue of Collier's Bottom Billion.

Contents

List of Figures

List of Tables and Boxes

Tables

Boxes

List of Acronyms and Abbreviations

ADB	Asian Development Bank
AfD	Agence Française de Développement (French Development Agency)
AfDB	African Development Bank
AICD	Africa Infrastructure Country Diagnostic
ANC	African National Congress
APEC	Asia-Pacific Economic Cooperation
AUC	Africa Union Commission
AVRL	Aqua Vitens Rand Ltd.
BAMWSP	Bangladesh Arsenic Mitigation Water Supply Project
BIDE	Boston Institute for Development Economics
BLT	Build-lease-transfer
BOO	Build-own-operate
BOOT	Build-own-operate-transfer
BOP	Base of the pyramid
BOT	Build-operate-transfer
BROT	Build-rehabilitate-operate-transfer
BRWSSP	Bangladesh Rural Water Supply and Sanitation Project
BWSSP	Bangladesh Water Supply Program Project
CAPEX	Capital expenditure
CBO	Community-based organization
CDC	Commonwealth Development Corporation (UK)
CDM	Clean Development Mechanism
CER	certified emission reduction
CIE	Compagnie Ivoirienne d'Electricite
COI	Conflict of interest
CSR	Corporate social responsibility
CTF	Clean Technology Fund
CWS	City Water Services
DAC	OECD Development Assistance Committee
DANIDA	Danish International Development Agency
DAWASA	Dar es Salaam Water and Sewerage Authority
DBSA	Development Bank of Southern Africa
DCA	Development Credit Authority (USAID)
DCD	Department for Constitutional Development
DEG	Deutsche Investitions und Entwicklungsgesellschaft
DFI	Development finance institution (e.g., AfD, CDC, OPIC, Proparco, DBSA)
DFID	UK Department for International Development
DPHE	Department of Public Health Engineering
DRC	Democratic Republic of Congo

DTW	Deep tube well
EAIF	Emerging Africa Infrastructure Fund
EBRD	European Bank for Reconstruction and Development
ECA	Europe and Central Asia
ECA	Export credit agency
EECI	Energie Electrique de Côte d'Ivoire
EIA	US Energy Information Administration
EIB	European Investment Bank
EPC	Engineering, procurement, construction
ESMAP	Energy Sector Management Assistance Program
FiP	Feed-in premium
FiT	Feed-in tariff
FMO	Netherlands Development Finance Company
G20	Group of Twenty
GEF	Global Environment Facility
GET FiT	Global Energy Transfer feed-in tariff
GHG	Greenhouse gas
GIF	Global Infrastructure Facility
GNUC	Greater Nelspruit Utility Company
GoB	Government of Bangladesh
GoI	Government of India
GoL	Government of Liberia
GPOBA	Global Program for Output-Based Aid
GWCL	Ghana Water Company Ltd.
HAM	Hybrid annuity model
HH	Household
HIPC	Heavily Indebted Poor Country
IA	Implementation agreement
IBRD	International Bank for Reconstruction and Development
ICA	Infrastructure Consortium for Africa
ICAI	Independent Commission on Aid Impact
ICED	Infrastructure and Cities for Economic Development
ICR	Implementation completion report
ICSID	International Centre for Settlement of Investment Disputes
ICT	Information and communication technology
IDA	International Development Association
IDB	Islamic Development Bank
IEA	International Energy Agency
IEG	Independent Evaluation Group (World Bank Group)
IFC	International Finance Corporation
IFI	International finance institution
IMF	International Monetary Fund
IPO	Initial public offering
IPP	Independent power producer
IPS	Industrial Promotion Services (Aga Khan Fund for Economic Development)

IRS	Interest rate subsidies
JICA	Japan International Cooperation Agency
KenGen	Kenya Power Company
KFW	Kreditanstalt für Wiederaufbau (German Development Bank)
KPI	Key performance indicator
KPLC	Kenya Power and Lighting Company
LAC	Latin America and the Caribbean
LEC	Liberia Electricity Corporation
LIC	Low-income country MAGAMaterial adverse government action
M&E	Monitoring and evaluation
MDB	Multilateral development bank (e.g., World Bank Group, ADB, AfDB, EIB, IDB)
MDC	Maputo Development Corridor
MDG	Millennium Development Goal
MDRI	Multilateral Debt Relief Initiative
MEMD	Ministry of Energy and Mineral Development
MENA	Middle East and North Africa
MHI	Manitoba Hydro International
MIC	Middle-income country
MIGA	Multilateral Investment Guarantee Agency
MIS	Management information system
MOU	Memorandum of Understanding
MSA	Municipal Systems Act
MTR	Mid-term review
MW	Megawatt
NEPAD	New Partnership for Africa's Development
NERSA	National Energy Regulator of South Africa
NGO	Non-governmental organization
NPCA	NEPAD Planning and Coordinating Agency
NTLC	Nelspruit Transitional Local Council
O&M	Operations and maintenance
OBA	Output-based aid
ODA	Official development assistance
OECD	Organisation for Economic Co-operation and Development
OPEX	Operational expenditure
OPIC	Overseas Private Investment Corporation (US)
PAD	Project appraisal document
PAP	Priority Action Plan (PIDA)
PCG	Partial credit guarantee
PFI	Private Finance Initiative (UK)
PHRD	Policy and Human Resources Development
PID	Project information document
PIDA	Program for Infrastructure Development in Africa
PIDG	Private Infrastructure Development Group
PMU	Project management unit

PPA	Power purchase agreement
PPI	Private participation in infrastructure
PPIAF	Public–Private Infrastructure Advisory Facility
PPP	Public–private partnership
PRG	Partial risk guarantee
PROPARCO	Group Agence Française de Développement
PSC	Public sector comparator
PSEDP	Private Sector Energy Development Project
RDA	Rural Development Academy
REC	Regional economic community
REFIT	Renewable energy feed-in tariff
REIPPPP	Renewable Energy Independent Power Producer Procurement Program
RFP	Request for proposals
RSA	Republic of South Africa
SADC	Southern Africa Development Community
SAPP	Southern African Power Pool
SDF	Social Development Foundation
SDG	Sustainable Development Goal
SDI	Spatial Development Initiative
SECO	Swiss State Secretariat for Economic Affairs
SIDA	Swedish International Development Agency
SIPP-1	Social Investment Program Project
SME	Small and medium enterprise
SODECI	Société de Distribution d'Eau de Côte d'Ivoire
SOE	State-owned enterprise
SPV	Special-purpose vehicle
SSA	Sub-Saharan Africa
STAP	NEPAD Short-Term Action Plan
T&D	Transmission and distribution
UETCL	Uganda Electricity Transmission Company Ltd.
UNCDF	United Nations Capital Development Fund
UNCTAD	United Nations Conference on Trade and Development
UNDP	United Nations Development Program
UNECA	United Nations Economic Commission for Africa
UNEP	United Nations Environment Programme
UNICEF	United Nations Children's Fund
UPs	Union Parishads
USAID	US Agency for International Development
VFM	Value for money
VGF	Viability gap funding
VIP	Ventilated improved pit
WAPDA	Water and Power Development Authority
WBG	World Bank Group
WBI	World Bank Institute
WEF	World Economic Forum

WSA	Water Services Act
WSP	Water and Sanitation Program
WSS	Water supply and sanitation
WTO	World Trade Organization

1
Introduction
The Evidence-Based Critique of PPPs

1.1 The Emerging Critique

In a largely unnoticed working paper published in 2015 by the World Bank, former Bank official Michael Klein shared some unusually frank observations about infrastructure public–private partnerships (PPPs) (Klein, 2015). Now a professor at the Frankfurt School of Finance and Management in Germany, Klein retired from the World Bank in 2009 after a 17-year career that ended with a dual position as Vice President for Financial and Private Sector Development at the Bank and Chief Economist at the International Finance Corporation (IFC). During Klein's leadership in the World Bank Group, the institution was a strong advocate of the idea that private participation in infrastructure was a highly positive force for improving service delivery in developing countries. Under Klein's direction, the Bank published its first recommendations regarding the best ways to do infrastructure concessions and other kinds of PPPs in developing countries (Kerf et al., 1998; Klein, 1998a, 1998b; Klein and Hadjimichael, 2003).

This work was being done against a backdrop of World Bank concern about whether or not it should continue lending to heavily indebted, poorly managed state-owned infrastructure enterprises. This was an urgent issue in the 1990s, especially in low-income regions like Sub-Saharan Africa (SSA), where most water, electricity, and transport utilities were close to financial collapse. During this period, the Bank also set up the private participation in infrastructure (PPI) Project Database, established the Public–Private Infrastructure Advisory Facility (PPIAF), and helped fund the creation of the Private Infrastructure Development Group (PIDG), a multi-donor trust fund headquartered in London and dedicated to facilitating PPI, mostly via PPPs. As the Director of the joint Bank/IFC Private Sector Advisory Department, Klein oversaw the transformation of IFC's PPP advisory services into a dedicated PPP transaction team that continues to help complete PPPs across the developing world. Klein and his colleagues were instrumental at the time in reshaping the development finance architecture to support PPPs globally.

But after more than 25 years as one of the principal thought leaders in this field, Klein's 2015 paper offers a less than ringing endorsement of the PPP

Public–Private Partnerships in Sub-Saharan Africa: The Evidence-Based Critique. James Leigland, Oxford University Press (2020). © James Leigland.
DOI: 10.1093/oso/9780198861829.001.0001

concept. He noted that, despite two decades of use and refinement of the mechanism, there were still no consistent geographical patterns of usage: "The general picture is one of waves of enthusiasm for PPPs followed by some disenchantment and consolidation. Different countries were caught up in the waves at different times" (Klein, 2015, 5). What accounts for this lack of sustained enthusiasm? Klein recognized that PPPs could outperform public sector firms, and were "useful tools for reform of service delivery" (Klein, 2015, 15). But it was no longer clear that PPPs were consistently better run than public firms. For Klein, the evidence suggested that well-run public firms tended to match the performance of private firms in regulated sectors (Klein, 2015, 13).

Coming at a time when global support for PPPs seems stronger now than ever before, Klein's disenchantment with the mechanism warrants serious examination. This support has taken a number of different forms. Discussions in G20 meetings over the last several years have increasingly focused on the need for a huge scale-up in infrastructure investment in developing countries, particularly in low-income countries. G20 pronouncements talk continuously about the advantages of realizing this scale-up via "transformational" projects involving private sector participation. By this they mean large, regional, or cross-border infrastructure projects involving private investment and management, which are expected to have positive, far-reaching impacts on entire countries or regions. From time to time over this period, the G20 has considered efforts to modify the mandates of national and international development banks so that these institutions would take the lead on such initiatives.

A number of development banks, like the World Bank, the Asian Development Bank, and the African Development Bank (AfDB), have already adjusted their business models to give more attention to large-scale regional infrastructure PPPs. During the IDA17 negotiations in 2013, for example, the World Bank proposed using concessional funding to develop transformational PPP projects. Those proposals have since evolved into the Bank's Global Infrastructure Facility (GIF), an entity aimed at coordinating the efforts of development finance institutions (DFIs), multilateral development banks (MDBs), bilateral donors, private investors, and governments to prepare and structure PPPs. Similarly, and as a competing initiative, the BRICS countries (Brazil, Russia, India, China, South Africa) at their March 2013 summit in Durban, South Africa, announced that they were creating a new development bank, later called the New Development Bank, to focus on infrastructure in a way that would make up for the deficiencies they perceived in the existing Bretton Woods and regional financial architecture. As described in a report published by the Republic of South Africa (RSA), this BRICS development bank would catalyze the private sector investments needed in rapidly growing BRICS economies (RSA, 2014). But, perhaps the most ambitious and concrete commitment to date was the decision by the AfDB in July 2013, to create a billion-dollar preparation and financing facility targeting large infrastructure projects in Africa, referred to as "Africa50." Its stated purpose was "to unlock private financing sources... and... accelerate the speed of infrastructure delivery in Africa" (AfDB, 2013). The G20 continues to consider new strategies for using development banking institutions to stimulate much larger levels of private investment in infrastructure than has been the case historically, especially in Africa (G20 Eminent Persons Group, 2018).

Global support for PPPs in infrastructure surged again with the Sustainable Development Goals (SDGs), set by the UN General Assembly in 2015 as a blueprint for addressing poverty in the developing world by 2030. Infrastructure appears as an explicit goal (SDG 9), as well as a means to implement and achieve other SDGs, particularly universal access to water and electricity services. One of the SDGs (SDG 17) specifically recommends using PPPs as one of the key mechanisms for implementing the SDG agenda. To the development community it was clear immediately that private finance would be essential in achieving the SDGs. Public aid flows would continue to be important, along with domestic resource mobilization. But both of these sources were already beginning to stagnate. The SDG challenge would involve unlocking commercial finance, transforming billions of dollars of development finance into the trillions needed for sustainable growth and poverty reduction in the developing world (World Bank, 2015). PPPs were expected to play a principle role in this transformation of "billions to trillions."

However, Klein's 2015 paper reminds us that a significant amount of evidence-based research on PPPs has been generated by PPP practitioners since the early 1990s. And much of this research, particularly that focusing on PPPs in the poorest countries, has not been uniformly positive about PPPs, at least not in the manner suggested by the promotional literature issued by the development community during the 1990s and early 2000s. These later studies are based on non-ideological empirical reviews of existing projects, are often focused on discrete aspects of these PPPs, and usually do not claim to be "PPP evaluations" or express opinions on the overall value of PPPs. Some of this research has been conducted by academicians, but most of the large existing body of academic literature on PPPs deals with PPPs in Organisation for Economic Co-operation and Development (OECD) countries, where the population of completed projects is substantial and project information is readily available (Leigland, 2018).[1] Most of the evidence that has accumulated on PPPs in low-income countries remains buried in collections

[1] The most compelling examples of academic research on PPPs have focused on projects in the UK, Australia, Europe, and North America. Examples of research by leading scholars in different fields include: economics—Boardman and Vining (2012); Geddes and Reeves (2017); Bel, Bel-Pinana, and Rosell (2017); accounting—Stafford and Stapleton (2017); public policy and management—Verhoest et al. (2015); Klijn and Koppenjan (2016); Hodge and Greve (2007); urban geography—Siemiatycki (2015); public and private finance—Hellowell and Vecchi (2012); development studies—Brinkerhoff and Brinkerhoff (2011).

of working papers, project evaluations, project databases, and reports by donors and non-government organizations (NGOs). Klein's 2015 working paper is probably the most notable recent example of this growing body of criticism because of his prominent role in leading the World Bank's efforts to justify and guide private sector participation in infrastructure in the developing world. But Klein's paper, like much of this emerging evidence-based research, has had little impact on public policy.

So, taken together, a powerful, evidence-based critique of PPPs in the poorest countries is emerging largely from the practitioner-generated literature on these projects. This critique is more measured than much of the censure of PPPs by organized labor and civil society groups over the previous two decades. This emerging critique recognizes that there may be situations in which PPPs can generate value for money, but it also highlights numerous cases where PPPs have not been successful.

Some of this research, for example, by retired World Bank infrastructure economist (and former colleague of Klein's) Antonio Estache, is now being used to bolster PPP criticisms prepared by civil society groups (e.g., Alexander, 2013). Such groups have produced a broad collection of critical PPP studies, including: International Rivers (Bosshard, 2012), Public Services International (Hall, 2015), Heinrich Boell Foundation (Alexander, 2013), CEE Bankwatch Network (2008), Oxfam (Marriott, 2014), and the Bretton Woods Project (2016). These and other organizations have long criticized the use of PPPs for the delivery of infrastructure services in developing countries. These criticisms have found their way into the global press, where in extreme forms they characterize PPPs and privatization as tools of a global "neoliberal" conspiracy to make "stupendous fortunes" for private investors (Monbiot, 2016). The view among PPP advocates traditionally has been that these criticisms are mostly strident, ideological polemics that mix opinion with selected but often misinterpreted facts.

Now, however, the growing use of evidence-based research, which is being reported on by former practitioners like Estache and others, has added weight to these civil society arguments. As a result, these criticisms are increasingly becoming more rigorous and less ideological. While more careful consideration of these criticisms by PPP advocates is now warranted, the reality is that they are largely still being ignored. The emerging evidence-based critique is having no obvious impact on PPP discussions in organizations like the G20.

The primary objective of this book is to identify, summarize, and consolidate the kinds of PPP criticism that are emerging from the work of PPP practitioners after three decades of implementation. What does the criticism say about the likely success or failure of types of PPP projects, such as brownfield concessions, management contracts, and independent power producer projects? Are PPP mechanisms likely to be successful in implementing large, regional, transformational infrastructure projects? Can PPPs play a significant role in transforming billions of dollars in development finance into the trillions needed to achieve the SDGs? What do case studies of high-profile PPPs reveal about the practical relevance of this kind of criticism? What are the public policy implications of this research?

While the primary focus in this book is on projects in SSA, home to most of the world's low-income countries, the experience with PPPs will be assessed taking into consideration insights gained from PPP-related research in other developing regions and in countries representing a variety of socio-economic circumstances.

1.2 An Overview of PPPs in Developing Countries

In undertaking this inquiry, it is necessary first to explain what PPPs are and to interrogate how they differ from other kinds of projects that are financed or managed by public or private sector entities. Klein broadly defines PPPs to cover a broad range of mechanisms through which the private sector can participate in infrastructure sectors such as telecoms, transport, water and sanitation, waste management, and electricity (Klein, 2015). But for the purposes of this discussion, a more precise breakdown is required of the types of PPPs that have been studied and evaluated since the early 1990s. The World Bank's PPI Project Database provides a useful taxonomy as part of its effort to track the progress of a large variety of projects identified under the general heading of "private participation in infrastructure" (PPI) (World Bank, 2018). PPPs make up the largest proportion of that data base. They are defined as risk-sharing relationships in which a legal contract assigns public service delivery responsibilities to a private entity. The PPP contract allocates risks and rewards associated with the delivery of these public services between the private entity and the public owner or sponsor of the project. Among other things, "risk sharing" usually means that the compensation received by the private entity for delivery of this service will vary depending on their performance.

1.2.1 Types of Projects

The best-known form of PPP involves investment by the private entity in the assets needed for service delivery, as well as operation of the assets over a long period of time. In other words, the provision of public service is expected to improve as a direct consequence of both the private sector's efficiencies in managing service provision, as well as the latter's expertise in financing and constructing (or rehabilitating) public assets. Usually, these kinds of PPP contracts, often referred to as concessions, are long-term in order for the private entity to recoup its investments via the sale of the services. An example of this type of contract would be a water utility concession, where a private company takes over management of a water utility, then rehabilitates and extends the assets, and manages distribution of water to customers while recouping its costs via user fees.

An example of a slightly different kind of concession, which is typical in the power sector, is the so-called independent power producer (IPP) project. An IPP project involves the development of a new power generating facility by a private company that then sells the power on a wholesale basis to government utilities that distribute the power to individual customers. With IPP projects in low-income countries, the assets may belong to the private company, but the power is normally sold to the government (or a government power utility) for retail distribution as a public service to customers. For IPP projects generally, the critical form of PPP contract is usually the power purchase agreement (PPA), concluded between the private power generator and the government purchaser of the wholesale service.

A less widely used form of PPP involves a contract that requires management of public services by a private entity, but does not require any major capital investments. Usually, these contracts are shorter in term because the private entity does not need a long period to recoup investments. An example of this kind of contract is a management contract in the water sector, pursuant to which a private entity would manage (but not necessarily invest in) a government-owned water distribution utility. In most cases, the private entity would be compensated via annual payments from the government rather than from revenues generated by sales to customers.

PPPs may be either brownfield, meaning that they involve rehabilitation or extension of existing assets (e.g., an existing power transmission line or distribution system), or greenfield, meaning that they involve the design and construction of new assets (e.g., a new water treatment plant or a new power generation plant).

It is also worth keeping in mind the two principal ways in which a private partner in a PPP is paid for its services: either through the commercial retail sale of services to customers, or via payments by governments or government utilities on a periodic basis (usually annually or semi-annually) for the wholesale sale of services by the private entity. These government payments may be referred to in a number of ways, for example, “unitary” or “annuity” payments.

Finally, two additional kinds of infrastructure projects involving private participation should be distinguished from PPPs as defined earlier. The first is divestiture or sale of government assets, where a government relinquishes ownership of assets by selling them to a private company (either by selling the collections of assets as a functioning company or by liquidating the assets). The sale itself is not a form of PPP as defined here, but the subsequent use of those assets in public service delivery might qualify, as in the case of a power plant sold to a private company that in turn signs a PPA to sell the power back to the government for retailing to customers through a government-owned distribution utility (this would be a brownfield IPP project). The second form of non-PPP private participation is the merchant project, involving the ownership, construction, and operation of assets by a private company at its own risk, without a government commitment to buy the services. In the telecommunication or energy sectors, merchant projects normally operate in liberalized markets, mostly in middle-income countries, where the sale of services is unrestricted by a PPP contract with government. In other words, the private entity is free to sell the services to anyone who can pay.

Divestitures and merchant projects have grown in popularity since the mid-1990s because in many cases they are less risky for private companies than traditional forms of PPP. Both of these additional kinds of PPI are important and valuable ways in which the private sector can be involved in infrastructure service provision. But neither are usually defined as PPPs as the term is being used here, and therefore these kinds of projects are not included in this study.

1.2.2 The Historical Context: the PPP Rollercoaster

The World Bank's PPI Project Database confirms Klein's claim that infrastructure PPPs in developing countries have experienced "waves of enthusiasm" followed by "disenchantment and consolidation." The following sections trace this rollercoaster effect, which is represented graphically in Figure 1.1.

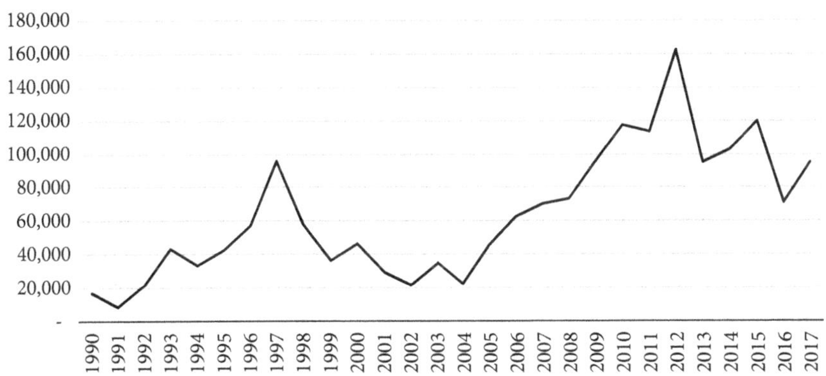

Figure 1.1 PPP Investment in Developing Countries by Sector, 1990–2017, in 2018 US$ millions[2]

Source: World Bank, 2018.

[2] The World Bank's PPI Project Database includes non-PPP projects like privatizations and merchant projects in addition to traditional PPPs such as brownfield concessions, greenfield concessions, and management contracts. When this study refers to "PPI," it means the full range of private participation covered by the database. When this study draws information from this database in reference to "PPPs," as in Figure 1.1, data on privatizations and merchant projects has been excluded.

In the late 1980s, the growing popularity of PPI service delivery was to a large extent a reaction by the development community against what seemed like excessive and inefficient government management of these services, either directly by government enterprises or indirectly with the help of government subsidies. Traditionally, governments in developing countries tended to assume that markets could not deliver beneficial public services and opted to provide goods and services themselves. The result of this intervention often was to distort markets and "crowd out" the private sector. Because government and donor resources were limited, these direct interventions either failed to meet public service needs or generated temporary and unsustainable supply. In the worst cases, the supply of the goods and services became a form of patronage. By the end of the 1980s, widespread problems with poorly conceived state involvement in basic service delivery provided the justification for a return, driven by donors, DFIs, and MDBs, to an economic policy framework with much more of an emphasis on market-based private provision of these services.

In the early 1990s, the development community sometimes took this promotion of market-based service provision to an extreme, advocating for private participation in a large variety of infrastructure service situations as workable on a self-sustaining basis with customer tariffs set at full cost-recovery levels (Kerf et al., 1998). Government subsidies were considered an inefficient tool that in most cases could be scrapped. It was assumed that costs of services provided to poor customers could on the whole be covered by cross-subsidization if necessary, with wealthier customers charged more to cover these costs. By the mid-1990s, the World Bank Group (under the intellectual leadership of Michael Klein and his colleagues) began sharply cutting back its lending, believing that the private sector would largely fill the needs for infrastructure investment and more efficient service delivery in many developing countries.[3]

The 1997 Asian financial crisis triggered a long period of decline in all forms of PPPs, by demonstrating among other things that the private sector could not be expected to always take on and mitigate the commercial risks associated with basic service provision. Furthermore, assigning project risks to the public sector did not automatically mean that those risks would be effectively managed. Although measures like cross-subsidization proved to be useful, they were by themselves often inadequate to generate sufficient additional revenue to fill the gap between actual costs of provision and what poor customers were willing and able to pay. A growing body of research documented that, even in most developed countries, customers did not pay the full cost of basic services. It became

[3] In a 1998 publication that asked authors to speculate on the future of development banks like the World Bank and EIB, Klein "looked back" from a 2044 vantage point and noted that "the private provision of most economic and social services rendered the funding and guarantee functions of the World Bank group largely superfluous" (Klein, 1998c, 34).

clear that more meaningful government risk sharing was warranted and even essential in most cases.

The global PPP market started to rebound in 2004 as mechanisms were developed for reducing risks for private partners or finding more effective ways of shifting risks to public partners, via capital grants, subsidies, political risk insurance, and other measures. PPI also began to change structurally after the Asian financial crisis, with a growing percentage of transactions taking the form of less risky divestitures and merchant projects, fewer brownfield projects (which turned out to be much riskier in developing countries than expected), as well as fewer large-scale projects, perhaps in recognition of the high costs of preparing sustainable, large-scale PPPs in developing countries.

Different regions of the developing world have had very different experiences with PPPs, largely due to differing levels of GDP, size and depth of local capital markets, and proximity to project finance banking institutions in Europe and North America. For example, Latin America, as a mostly middle-income region, was by far the most active in terms of PPPs in the late 1990s, and remains a leading region. PPPs in Eastern Europe and Central Asia began to slowly grow in 2004, as European banks started to finance investments associated with EU accession—but the proximity to these banks led to a severe cutback in investment with the onset of the global financial crisis in 2007. South Asia—led by massive private investments in India—exhibited tremendous PPP growth beginning in 2005, but experienced a sharp decline in investment starting in 2010. In the early to mid-1990s, East Asia was a leading PPP region, but was slow to fully recover following the 1997 East Asian crisis. The region has surged in the aftermath of the global financial crisis and since 2017 has become the most active region in concluding PPP transactions. Historically, the Middle East and SSA have been the least active regions in terms of PPPs, with numbers of projects far below those of other regions.

A major shortcoming of PPPs, and a central focus of the evidence-based critique, is that these projects do not generate many benefits in low-income countries. Arguably these countries need the most help with infrastructure improvements, but collectively they have attracted only about 4.5 per cent of total PPP investment since 1990. Figure 1.2 distinguishes PPP investment levels in countries eligible for support from the International Development Association (IDA), that is, countries whose Gross Net Income per capita is below US$1,215, from levels in non-IDA developing countries ("blend" countries have been excluded).

1.2.3 Sectoral Concentration

Tables 1.1 and 1.2 indicate the sectoral role of PPPs and non-PPP private investment projects in developing countries, in terms of numbers of projects and amount of investment. Across the developing world between 1990 and 2017, PPP

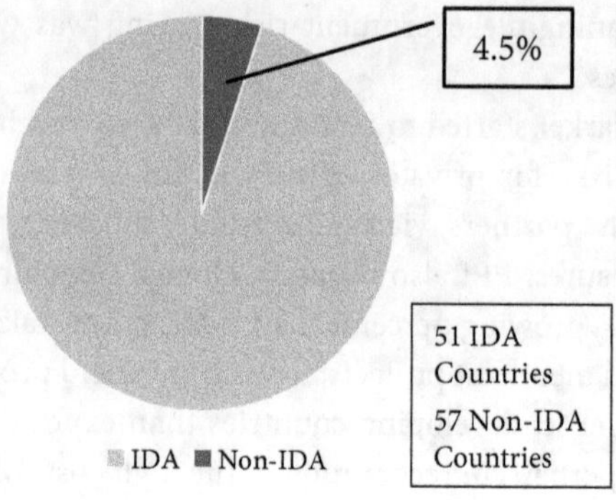

Figure 1.2 PPP Investment by IDA Status, 1990–2017
Source: World Bank, 2018.

Table 1.1 PPPs in Developing Countries, 1990–2017, in US$ millions (nominal values)

Sectors	Public–Private Partnerships						Totals	
	Brownfield PPPs				Greenfield Concessions			
	Concessions		Mgmt Contracts*					
	US$m	No.	US$m	No.	US$m	No.	US$m	No.
Power	133,662	233	592	48	652,898	2,945	787,153	3,226
ICT	2,605	9	276	10	14,747	108	17,627	127
Transport	305,616	1,009	7,245	93	255,480	546	568,341	1,648
WSS	51,346	385	1,666	153	24,460	436	77,471	974
Totals	493,228	1,636	9,779	304	947,585	4,035	1,450,593	5,975

* Including leases
Source: World Bank, 2018.

Table 1.2 Other Private Participation Projects (non-PPPs), All Developing Countries, 1990–2017, in US$ millions (nominal values)

Sectors	Other Private Participation Projects						Totals	
	Divestiture—Full		Divestiture—Partial		Merchant Projects			
	US$m	No.	US$m	No.	US$m	No.	US$m	No.
Power	38,650	137	104,506	304	28,932	117	172,088	558
ICT	28,072	23	53,393	171	20,295	199	101,760	393
Transport	1,528	11	15,850	60	2,486	15	19,864	86
WSS	436	3	3,020	20	0	0	3,457	23
Totals	68,686	174	176,769	555	51,713	331	297,169	1,060

Source: World Bank, 2018.

investments were focused primarily on two sectors: power and transport. The total investment in these sectors has accounted for over 93 per cent of all PPP-related investments (Table 1.1).

Power: Power dominates, with 54 per cent of total investment and 54 per cent of the total number of projects. Nearly 75 per cent of all power projects exclusively involve power generation (Figure 1.3). The vast majority of these are IPP projects, discussed earlier. These projects are normally "project financed," meaning that they are heavily financed with debt, where most of the financing comes via limited- or non-recourse loans to special purpose project vehicles (SPVs), and are backed by project payment streams. PPAs are highly technical documents that usually serve to confirm for lenders that power will be purchased at specified prices under a variety of circumstances. The definition of an IPP project is usually limited to greenfield projects, although privatized (or concessioned) brownfield generating facilities can also operate in this fashion. In most developing countries, including almost all IDA countries, the purchaser (or "off-taker") of the power is a monopolistic state-owned electricity utility, referred to as the "single buyer" of power, which carries out retail power distribution to customers.

Brownfield concessions exclusively focused on electricity distribution are rare in the developing world, accounting for only about 8 per cent of total sector investment. The private sector views such projects as extremely risky, particularly in IDA countries. Concessionaires must invest capital to rehabilitate and extend distribution networks, then recoup their investments via the retail sale of power to thousands of customers under price regimes that are normally pre-determined by government regulators. Although "independent" regulation is becoming the

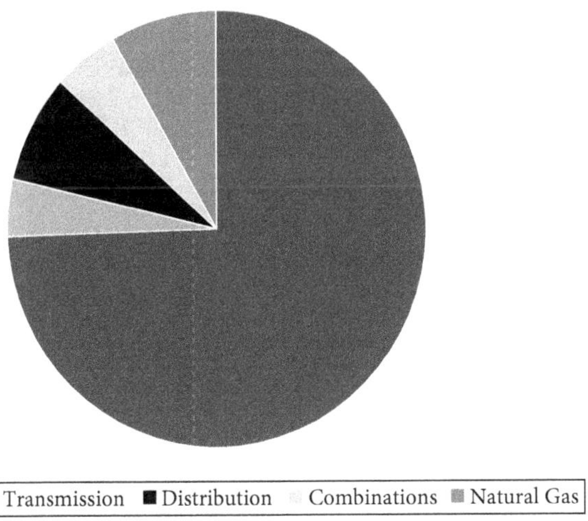

Figure 1.3 PPP Investment in Power Sub-sectors, All Developing Countries, 1990–2017

Source: World Bank, 2018.

norm across the developing world, this rarely means that price-setting will not be influenced by highly contentious political circumstances, or that prices will allow cost recovery by the concessionaire.

Transportation: Transport ranks second to power in terms of total PPP investment (39 per cent) and number of projects (28 per cent). Road projects, mostly toll roads, dominate this sector with over 47 per cent of total global investment (Figure 1.4). Toll roads are widely used in non-IDA countries, but the sharp decline in toll road investments in South Asia in 2013 and in Latin America in 2015, has had a major impact in terms of reduced total private infrastructure investment in developing countries. The usefulness of toll roads in IDA countries is severely limited by a lack of vehicular traffic. The World Bank's Africa Infrastructure Country Diagnostic study estimated that only 7–8 per cent of the total continental road network in SSA had the traffic density required to support the development of traditional user-pay toll roads (Foster and Briceno-Garmendia, 2010). It is not necessary for drivers to pay directly for the use of roads; governments can pay via shadow tolls or other payment mechanisms and collect whatever they can in the form of tolls or fuel taxes. But most governments in IDA countries do not have the requisite cash flow to take on such liabilities.

Rail concessions have been less popular than toll roads, accounting for just under 21 per cent of all transport PPP investment. The viability of these projects often depends on transport regulation. The private sector is attracted to rail projects focused on profitable freight services (rather than passenger services, which often must be subsidized). Rail concessions are also much more attractive when a

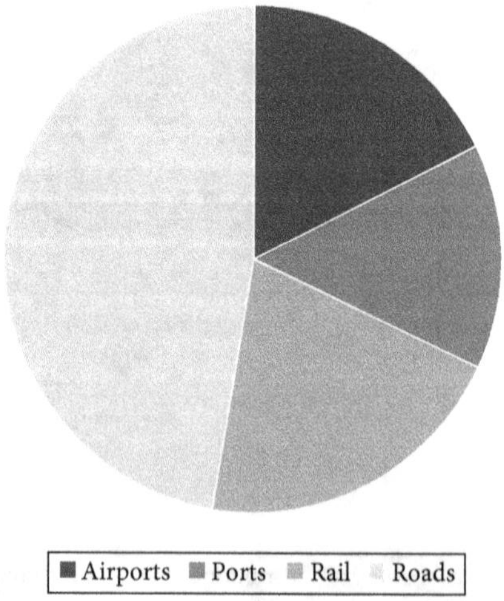

Figure 1.4 PPP Investment in Transport Sub-sectors, All Developing Countries, 1990–2017

Source: World Bank, 2018.

government regulates heavy vehicle road transport, because unregulated road traffic tends to take freight business away from rail, usually at the expense of road quality.

Globally, seaport container handling concessions have accounted for the smallest percentage of total transport PPP investments, at just over 14 per cent. But in IDA countries, these projects have dominated PPP activity in this sector, and may be the most commercially viable PPPs in Africa. Ports are relatively attractive targets for the private sector because of their ability to generate hard currency revenues. The landlord port model, now generally regarded as the preferred PPP model for the sector, is gradually spreading in IDA countries.[3] Cancelled or distressed projects are relatively rare, and performance improvements have been the norm, particularly with concessioning of container facilities.

Telecommunications: Over 85 per cent of the total private investment in telecommunications has come via merchant projects or divestiture of telecom companies—in other words, non-PPP arrangements that do not involve contractual risk sharing agreements between public and private partners. Tables 1.1 and 1.2 indicate that ICT (information and communication technology) is the only one of the four basic infrastructure sectors in which far more investment (almost six times) is generated via types of private participation other than PPPs. Projects in the ICT sector typically involve robust revenue streams, even in low-income countries, because they are often secured by prepayment systems. Such projects involve relatively inexpensive, mass produced technology, comparatively low capital costs, and mostly benefit from unregulated tariffs.

PPPs were once the only kind of contracting mechanism legally available to facilitate private sector participation in ICT in countries that allowed only state-owned telecommunication operations. But it has become increasingly clear that there is little benefit from state ownership or operation of ICT service providers. PPPs in this sector are increasingly seen to be inconsistent with the promotion of liberalized ICT markets and competitively neutral regulation and policies.

There are still situations in IDA countries where it makes sense to use ICT PPPs. For example, where there is a need to promote universal service coverage for various ICT services that state-owned monopoly ICT utilities are unable to finance. But generally, the role of PPPs in the telecoms sector should continue to decline as sector investment becomes less about PPPs and more about stimulating competition among private service providers, by increasing the number of mobile operators and liberalizing access to international gateways (Williams, Mayer, and Minges, 2011).

[3] "The landlord port model" refer to PPPs in which a government port authority owns the basic port infrastructure, but leases it out to a private operator who administers port operations on a long-term concession basis. The port authority retains regulatory functions; the operator usually builds and maintains port superstructure such as buildings and cargo handling equipment. For early examples of the model in Africa, see Leigland and Palsson (2007).

Water and sanitation: Although investment needs in water and sanitation are significant, this sector is by far the worst performing and least active in terms of privately financed capital investment, accounting for only 0.5 per cent of PPP investment and 1.6 per cent of projects. The latter are mostly greenfield projects involving water treatment or storage facilities. In the early 1990s, the development community had high hopes for traditional brownfield concessions in the water sector, involving substantial private investment. But such projects have been relatively rare since the Asian crisis, and no longer frequently attempted in IDA countries. Only a handful of these projects have had some success in SSA, but only in middle-income countries like Gabon and South Africa.

Greenfield concessions, for example, for water treatment facilities, and management or lease contracts that aim at operational efficiency and service quality rather than private investment, continue to be used in the sector, but often fail to meet expectations of governments or customers. Investment is sometimes linked to management or lease contracts, but paid for with government and donor funding, as in the case of the *affermage* contracts in West Africa (where investment is implemented by government asset-holding companies), or from annual cash flows, as in projects in Mali and Côte d'Ivoire. Of all the infrastructure sectors, water and sanitation has proved to be the most difficult for PPPs, especially in terms of generating private capital investment (Marin, 2009). This is especially true in African countries. It is likely that government ownership, financing, and even management will remain the norm in these countries for the foreseeable future.

1.3 Scope of This Study: PPPs in SSA

PPPs in developing countries have, in general, not met the expectations articulated by experts like Michael Klein and his World Bank colleagues when they first began overseeing the implementation of infrastructure PPPs in the 1990s. While PPPs have not disappeared, and probably will not do so for the foreseeable future, they have not achieved what was expected of them—and particularly they have not generated significant benefits in low-income countries.

As noted earlier, this book evaluates the PPP experience in SSA, home to most of the world's low-income countries. The latter are defined in this study as countries eligible for support from the IDA, that is, countries whose Gross Net Income per capita is below US$1,215. But SSA is also home to several middle-income countries with valuable PPP experiences and lessons learned, such as South Africa. The PPP track record in SSA is assessed using insights from research conducted in Africa and across the developing world. Some of this research has been published by academicians, but much of it has been conducted by practitioners and still appears mainly in working papers and project evaluations. However, the intention here is to use only research that can be characterized as evidence-based and non-ideological.

One growing challenge for the development community is that after 25 years of experience, this empirical research is now finding its way into the criticisms of PPPs prepared by civil society organizations. The use of evidence to bolster dogmatic beliefs, makes the civil society criticism more important and worthier of attention, but also more difficult to assess. This book attempts to review the evidence without the dogma. It does so by organizing the discussion around several key themes:

- **Precisely how have PPPs under-performed?** Following this introduction, Chapter 2 reviews global evidence relating to: (i) how widely PPPs are actually used in developing countries; (ii) the commercial profitability associated with these projects; (iii) the costs and complexities of project preparation; (iv) the ability of such projects to generate private investment finance; (v) the pro-poor benefits of these projects; and (vi) the institutional and political problems that limit project success. In light of this evidence, how practical are recent efforts by international organizations to promote increases in the number and size of PPPs in developing countries. The G20's recent advocacy of "transformational" PPPs as mechanisms for dealing effectively with infrastructure challenges in low-income countries is an example of this kind of PPP promotion.
- **Case study: SSA's first transformational PPP.** Chapter 3 presents a case study of the Maputo Corridor toll road concession. As the first cross-border transport PPP in SSA, this project is the first PPP in the region with a claim to "transformational" status. However, this is still the only cross-border toll road concession ever completed in SSA. Why have no similar projects ever been completed? What makes the Maputo toll road a unique project? What lessons can we learn from the Maputo project about the likely success of cross-border transformational PPPs in SSA?
- **Why did the private sector lose confidence in brownfield concessions?** Chapter 4 examines the fate of brownfield concessions. In the early 1990s, these PPPs served briefly as the flagship of the global PPP movement, and were highly recommended by the development community as ideal "privatization" solutions to many of the problems facing infrastructure utilities in low-income countries. These concessions involve the construction of certain new infrastructure assets to improve or extend existing facilities, but mostly focus on rehabilitation of existing assets. Theoretically such projects should be relatively easy to do because risks associated with initial financing and construction are largely eliminated by the time a PPP contract is signed. But since the 1997 Asian Crisis, relatively little investment has been generated by these projects. In IDA countries, very few of these projects have been

attempted and much of the related investment has actually come from governments or their development partners. What accounts for the rise and fall in popularity of brownfield concessions?

- **Case study: SSA's last brownfield water concession.** Chapter 5 presents a case study of the Nelspruit water concession completed in South Africa's Mpumalanga Province in 1999. This is generally considered to be the third "classic" brownfield water concession in SSA, involving capital investment in system assets as well as commercial operation of the system by the private partner. The Nelspruit project exhibits most of the risks and shortcomings that helped account for the precipitous decline in private sector interest in such projects after the Asian financial crisis, as documented in Chapter 4. How did these risks and shortcomings materialize in Nelspruit? How were they dealt with and in what manner does the project continue to function after two decades? Why have there been no other prominent examples of similar "classic" water concessions in South Africa or in other SSA countries since 1999?
- **Does disappointment with management contracts result from poor performance or misunderstood objectives?** In Chapter 6, the discussion turns to management concessions as they have been used in the water and power sectors of developing countries. Because these arrangements are typically short term and involve little or no private investment, they considerably reduce the normal PPP risks faced by private partners. But despite the apparent potential of such contracts for improving the operational efficiencies of infrastructure service systems, as well as the reduced risks of such projects for private partners, these kinds of PPPs have rarely met the expectations of local stakeholders, especially in IDA countries. Governments in Africa have often refused to renew such contracts once their initial terms have been completed because, although the contracts are introduced with great fanfare and sometimes achieve contract performance targets, the general perception is that they have failed to solve important sector problems. Is this criticism fair, or are the objectives of these contracts misunderstood? Hybrid forms of these contracts seem to be emerging in response to disappointment with traditional models. Will these hybrids be successful in achieving the original aims of management contracts?
- **Case studies: Searching for successful management contracts in SSA.** Chapter 7 presents a series of short case studies of the best-known management contracts for water and electricity services in SSA. The studies attempt to identify projects that successfully met the expectations of a wide variety of key stakeholders. But the review finds very few contracts that have achieved this standard of success. What do these case studies tell us about the factors that help these contracts meet stakeholder expectations?
- **The IPP policy dilemma.** Chapter 8 focuses on IPP projects, by far the most successful kind of PPP in the developing world. These projects generate

more investment in developing countries than all other forms of PPP combined. However, the development community exhibits ambivalence toward IPP projects. These projects are supposed to work best in power sectors that are being reformed, where user tariffs are cost reflective and off-taker utilities are creditworthy, where necessary investments and management improvements are being made in transmission and distributions, and governments are moving away from monopolistic "single buyer" models. Yet, in practice, many influential MDBs, DFIs, and donors are encouraging the use of IPP projects virtually everywhere in the developing world, whether or not sector reforms are taking place. What are the implications in terms of project benefits of this single-minded effort to promote these projects without the requisite supportive policy framework? This raises a dilemma: most low-income countries desperately need more generating capacity, but should the development of IPP projects be delayed until progress is made on broader sector reforms? To make matters worse, there is some supporting evidence that the introduction of IPP projects actually reduces the pressure on host governments to move forward with reforming existing sector policies and institutions. How can these policy dilemmas be resolved? Who can make that happen?

- **Case studies: IPP tender programs in SSA.** Chapter 9 assesses three recent renewable energy IPP tender programs in SSA, in Uganda, Zambia, and South Africa. Using competitive tenders to select IPP projects is rare in Africa, but is generally viewed as an effective way of lowering project costs. And with the rapid reductions in the equipment costs associated with wind and solar projects, renewable energy IPP projects may represent the power sector PPPs of the future. These case studies detail the role of development partners in designing and implementing the first two of these programs and compare the performance and development value of these programs with that of the South African program. The latter was a completely "home grown" program, designed and managed almost exclusively by South African officials and their advisers. What are the lessons that can be learned from these two distinct approaches? What impact do these kinds of programs have on the "IPP policy dilemma" described in Chapter 8?
- **The future of PPPs in low-income countries: Blended finance.** While PPPs have not been as successful as expected, the various kinds of hybrid PPP project forms that have emerged may suggest ways in which PPPs can sustainably generate some value and meet some stakeholder expectations. These hybrids may indeed be successful, but in what ways do they represent significantly reduced expectations regarding the benefits of PPPs, as these projects were conceived in the 1990s? Chapter 10 discusses what is perhaps the most dramatic compromise, the dominating role now played in most of these projects by "blended" or subsidized finance. Governments and their

development partners pay for and manage most basic project preparation work, contribute to the capital costs of these projects, and provide guarantees and other risk-mitigation mechanisms insisted on by private sponsors and financiers. How should blended finance like this be justified and managed to ensure against market distortion and wasted resources that could be used more productively elsewhere?

- **Case study: How much blended finance is too much?** Chapter 11 presents a final African case study assessing a recent water PPP in Rwanda, which has many of the hybrid features discussed in earlier chapters, including the use of blended finance. This project is widely recognized as an important achievement for the country and likely to be successful (although it does not yet have a significant operating track record). But the extensive use of blended finance needed to make this PPP commercially viable raises questions about how that blended finance was justified. How much subsidy in support of private finance is too much? Is it possible that a project like this may exceed a threshold beyond which it would be less expensive and more sustainable if implemented as a public project supported by concessional lending, rather than as a PPP with a relatively small measure of private finance (but all the costs and complexities that come with PPPs)? If so much grant and concessional (or near concessional) debt is available for a project like this, are there more traditional contracting mechanisms that might work better than PPPs? Countries like India are experimenting with such alternatives to PPPs for less commercial projects in poorer regions.
- **Appendix: A cautionary case study from South Asia.** The focus of this book is on PPPs in SSA, but the evidence-based critique of these projects derives from experiences across the developing world, particularly from experience with PPPs in low-income countries. In this respect, probably the most dramatic case that best illustrates the lessons generated by this critique comes from South Asia. This is the 15-year effort by the World Bank to conclude PPPs for rural water schemes in Bangladesh—an effort that was dramatically unsuccessful. In terms of almost every important evaluation category discussed in this book, the Bangladesh BOT (build-operate-transfer) program reflects the shortcomings that have plagued PPPs in developing countries worldwide since the beginning of their global popularity in the early 1990s.

References

African Development Bank (AfDB). 2013. "Africa50: Questions and Answers." Memorandum to the AfDB Board of Directors from Secretary General, C. Akintomide (July 16).

Alexander, N. 2013. *Responsible Investment in Infrastructure: Recommendations for the G20*. Washington, DC: Heinrich Böll Foundation North America (October). Accessed at: https://us.boell.org/sites/default/files/responsible_investment_in_infrastructure.pdf

Bel, G., P. Bel-Pinana, J. Rosell. 2017. "Myopic PPPs: Risk Allocation and Hidden Liabilities for Taxpayers and Users." *Utilities Policy* 48(4): 147–56.

Boardman, A.E., A. Vining. 2012. "The Political Economy of Public–Private Partnerships and Analysis of their Social Value." *Annals of Public and Cooperative Economics* 83(2): 117–41.

Bosshard, P. 2012. "Infrastructure for Whom? A Critique of the Infrastructure Strategies of the Group of 20 and the World Bank." International Rivers (May). Accessed at: https://www.internationalrivers.org/sites/default/files/attached-files/infrastructure_for_whom_report.pdf

Bretton Woods Project. 2016. "World Bank Rolls Out the Carpet for "Troubled Megaprojects" and PPPs" (April). Accessed at: http://www.brettonwoodsproject.org/2016/04/world-bank-rolls-out-the-carpet-for-troubled-megaprojects/

Brinkerhoff, D.W., J.M. Brinkerhoff. 2011. "Public–Private Partnerships: Perspectives on Purposes, Publicness, and Good Governance." *Public Administration and Development* 31(1): 2–14.

CEE Bankwatch Network. 2008. "Never Mind the Balance Sheet: The dangers posed by public-private partnerships in central and eastern Europe." CEE Bankwatch Network (November). Accessed at: http://bankwatch.org/documents/never_mind_the_balance_sheet.pdf

Foster, V., C.M. Briceno-Garmendia. 2010. *Africa's Infrastructure: A Time for Transformation. AICD Flagship Report*. Washington, DC: World Bank.

G20 Eminent Persons Group. 2018. *Making the Global Financial System Work for All*. Report of the G20 Eminent Persons Group (October). Accessed at: https://www.globalfinancialgovernance.org/report-of-the-g20-epg-on-gfg/

Geddes, R.R., E. Reeves. 2017. "The Favourability of U.S. PPP Enabling Legislation and Private Investment in Transportation Infrastructure." *Utilities Policy* 48(C): 157–65.

Hall, D. 2015. "Why Public–Private Partnerships Don't Work: The many advantages of the public alternative." Public Services International Research Unit (February). Accessed at: file:///C:/Users/JL/Documents/Q&A/PSIRU.David%20Hall.%202015-03-PPP-WhyPPPsdontworkEng.pdf

Hellowell, M., V. Vecchi. 2012. "An Evaluation of the Projected Returns to Investors on 10 PFI Projects Commissioned by the National Health Service." *Financial Accountability and Management* 28(1): 77–100.

Hodge, G.A., C. Greve. 2007. "Public–Private Partnerships: An International Performance Review." *Public Administration Review* 67(3): 545–58.

Kerf, M., R.D. Gray, T. Irwin, C. Levesque, R.R. Taylor. 1998. "Concessions for Infrastructure—A Guide to Their Design and Award." Technical Paper No. 399. Washington, DC: World Bank.

Klein, M. 1998a. "Bidding for Concessions," World Bank Policy Research Working Paper No. 1957. Washington, DC: World Bank.

Klein, M. 1998b. "The Case for Periodic Rebidding of Concessions." Public Policy for the Private Sector, Viewpoint Note 161. Washington, DC: World Bank.

Klein, M. 1998c. "One Hundred Years After Bretton Woods: A future history of the World Bank Group." *In EIB Papers: International Financial Institutions in the 21st Century* 3(2): 30–59.

Klein, M. 2015. "Public–Private Partnerships: Promise and Hype." World Bank Policy Research Working Paper, No. 7340. Washington, DC: World Bank.

Klein, M., B. Hadjimichael. 2003. *The Private Sector in Development: Entrepreneurship, Regulation, and Competitive Disciplines*. Washington, DC: World Bank.

Klijn, E.H., J. Koppenjan. 2016. "The Impact of Contract Characteristics on the Performance of Public–Private Partnerships." *Public Money and Management* 36(6): 455–62.

Leigland, J. 2018. "Public–Private Partnerships in Developing Countries: The Emerging Evidence-based Critique." *The World Bank Research Observer* 33(2): 103–34.

Leigland, J., G. Palsson. 2007. "Port Reform in Nigeria: Upstream Policy Reforms Kick-Start One of the World's Largest Concession Programs." Gridline No. 17, Public-Private Infrastructure Advisory Facility (PPIAF). Washington, DC: World Bank.

Marin, P. 2009. *Public–Private Partnerships for Urban Water Utilities: A Review of Experiences in Developing Countries*. PPIAF Trends and Policy Options Series No. 8. Washington, DC: World Bank. Accessed at: www.ppiaf.org

Marriott, A. 2014. "A Dangerous Diversion: Will the IFC's flagship health PPP bankrupt Lesotho's Ministry of Health?" Oxfam Briefing Note, Oxfam International (April). Accessed at: https://www.oxfam.org/sites/www.oxfam.org/files/bn-dangerous-diversion-lesotho-health-ppp-070414-en.pdf

Monbiot, G. 2016. "Neoliberalism—The Ideology at the Root of All Our Problems." *The Guardian*, 15 April. Accessed at: https://www.theguardian.com/books/2016/apr/15/neoliberalism-ideology-problem-george-monbiot

Republic of South Africa (RSA). 2014. "BRICS and Africa: Partnership for Development, Integration and Industrialization." Papers of the Fifth BRICS Academic Forum, South African Department of International Relations and Cooperation. Pretoria: Madiba Communications.

Siemiatycki, M. 2015. "Public–Private Partnership Networks: Exploring Business-Government Relationships in United Kingdom Transportation Projects." *Economic Geography* 87(3): 309–34.

Stafford, A., P. Stapleton. 2017. "Examining the Use of Corporate Governance mechanisms in Public–Private Partnerships: Why Do They Not Deliver Public Accountability?" *Australian Journal of Public Administration* 76(3): 378–91.

Verhoest, K., O.H. Petersen, W. Scherrer, R.M. Soecipto. 2015. "How Do Governments Support the Development of Public Private Partnerships? Measuring and Comparing PPP Governmental Support in 20 European Countries." *Transport Reviews* 35(2): 118–39.

Williams, M.D.J., R. Mayer, M. Minges. 2011. *Africa's ICT Infrastructure: building on the Mobile Revolution.* Washington, DC: World Bank.

World Bank. 2015. *From Billions to Trillions: Transforming Development Finance.* Document prepared jointly by the African Development Bank, the Asian Development Bank, the European Bank for Reconstruction and Development, the European Investment Bank, the Inter-American Development Bank, the International Monetary Fund, and the World Bank Group for the April 18, 2015 Development Committee meeting (April 2). Washington DC: World Bank. Accessed at https://siteresources.worldbank.org/DEVCOMMINT/Documentation/23659446/DC2015-0002(E)FinancingforDevelopment.pdf

World Bank. 2018. PPI Project Database. Accessed at: http://ppi.worldbank.org/customquery?mode=1

2

The Performance of PPPs in Developing Countries

The Evidence

2.1 Introduction

Bilateral donors, development finance institutions (DFIs), and multilateral development banks (MDBs) have been actively supporting PPP projects and issuing PPP guidance materials for 30 years. But the 2030 Agenda for Sustainable Development has re-emphasized the need for more infrastructure finance to accelerate transformational change, especially in low-income countries. And this need has drawn new attention by international development organizations to the potentially "critical" role that public–private partnerships (PPPs) can play in this kind of financing (UNCTAD, 2014). Even before the Sustainable Development Goals (SDGs) were published, the G20 was expressing enthusiasm for regional or "transformational" PPP projects—the term is normally used to refer to large, regional, or cross-border infrastructure projects involving private participation. Various prioritized lists of such projects have been compiled by several interlocutors, including the World Bank (2011), the G20 MDB Working Group (2011), and the African Union Commission (2012).

All of this has been happening in the face of increasingly vocal criticism by civil society groups. By the end of 2017, 152 civil society organizations had issued a "global manifesto" calling on the World Bank to halt its "aggressive support of PPPs" (Bretton Woods Observer, 2017). But civil society criticism of PPPs is usually dismissed as uninformed or ideological. Yet, at the same time, research by respected social scientists (many of them former employees of MDBs) has been quietly accumulating evidence regarding the track record of PPP performance. Much of this research has been critical of PPPs, but at the same time, much of it seems clearly non-ideological in character.

This chapter summarizes some of the most compelling examples of the emerging evidence-based critique of PPPs by organizing them into several key themes: (i) how prevalent is the usage of PPPs in the developing world; (ii) the costs and profits associated with these projects; (iii) the significant outlay involved in preparing these projects; (iv) their struggle to attract commercial financing; (v) how

Public–Private Partnerships in Sub-Saharan Africa: The Evidence-Based Critique. James Leigland, Oxford University Press (2020). © James Leigland.
DOI: 10.1093/oso/9780198861829.001.0001

developmental they are; and (vi) the institutional and political problems that limit their success. The discussion of each key theme also attempts to extract insights about some of the efforts to deal with these criticisms and establish conditions under which PPPs are likely to provide value for money (VFM).

Finally, this chapter uses this summary to assess the practicality of the G20's ongoing promotion of "transformational" PPPs as mechanisms for dealing effectively with infrastructure challenges in low-income countries.

2.2 PPP Prevalence

The foundation of the argument expressed by Michael Klein, discussed in Chapter 1, is that although many countries use PPPs at least occasionally, the prevalence of usage surges in waves, often driven by fiscal problems or other ways in which the public system has "run into trouble" (Klein, 2015). But the waves inevitably recede, "in seemingly random patterns" (Klein, 2015). Klein attributes the shallowness of PPP popularity to a lack of clear and consistent evidence that PPPs perform better than public sector organizations. He estimates that as of 2015, while PPPs account for a share of the total infrastructure investment in low and especially middle-income countries, it is normal for a country to use PPPs for only about 15–25 per cent of total infrastructure investment.

Other sources of data suggest even lower levels of PPP prevalence. The World Bank's Africa Infrastructure Country Diagnostic study (AICD), published in 2010, found that in total the private sector accounted for an impressive level of infrastructure investment in sub-Saharan Africa (SSA) by contributing about 29 per cent of total capital spending (Table 2.1).

But the AICD further qualified this data in several important ways. First, it demonstrated that private investment was heavily skewed in terms of countries, with about 60 per cent of total SSA private sector investment shared equally by just two countries—Nigeria and South Africa. Second, private investment was heavily skewed in terms of sectors, with 77 per cent of SSA's private investment since 2000 going to telecommunications, mostly via build-own-operate (BOO) projects. According to the AICD, the energy sector, which is arguably the most in need of urgent major capital investment, attracted only 10 per cent of total private investment.

Other studies tend to support lower usage figures. Burger and Hawkesworth (2011) surveyed 22 countries (19 OECD countries and three middle-income countries) regarding VFM issues associated with PPPs. Of these, 18 countries reported that less than 10 per cent of public sector infrastructure investment took place via PPP arrangements. From 2000 to 2010, the UK's Private Finance Initiative (PFI) probably averaged a higher annual percentage of total infrastructure

Table 2.1 Sources of Annual Financial Flows to SSA Infrastructure, 2010, in US$ billions

Operations & Maintenance	Capital Investment						All Spending
Public Sector O&M	**Public Sector Capex**	**Non-OECD Financiers**	**Official Development Assistance**	**Private Households**	**Private Sector**	**Total Capex**	**All Sources**
20.4	9.3	2.4	3.7 J	2.1	7.3	24.8	45.2
Percentage of Total Capex	38%	10%	15%	8%	29%	100%	

Source: Foster and Briceno-Garmendia, 2010.

investments via PPPs than most other OECD countries, at about 12 per cent. The only two non-OECD countries surveyed, Mexico and Chile, reported that over 20 per cent of their infrastructure investment occurred via PPPs. A number of the countries surveyed admitted informally that they did not foresee PPPs exceeding 15 per cent of total public investment (Burger and Hawkesworth, 2011).

Across the developing world, PPPs play a relatively small role in infrastructure investment, averaging 15–20 per cent according to the Independent Evaluation Group of the World Bank (Independent Evaluation Group, 2014). In low-income developing countries, the use of PPPs has been even more negligible. Figure 2.1 demonstrates this, using data from the World Bank's PPI Project Database to show PPP-related investments in countries eligible for support from the International Development Association (IDA; i.e., countries whose gross net income per capita is below US$1,215), and contrasts these against data from non-IDA developing countries ("blend" countries have been excluded).[1] In a review of private participation in infrastructure in IDA countries since 2011 (including non-PPPs like merchant projects and divestiture), a World Bank report remarks: "The market for PPIs has not been expanding" (Ruiz-Nunez, 2016).

In the developing world, a share of infrastructure investment in the range of 15–20 per cent does not mean that PPPs have failed to play a significant role in infrastructure. But it is far less than what was expected of PPPs in the 1990s when Klein and his colleagues at the World Bank were considering sharp reductions in infrastructure lending because they expected the private sector to eventually play

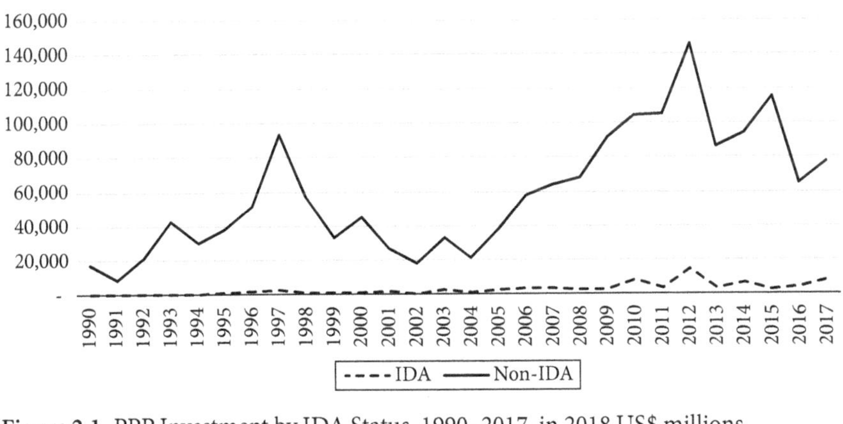

Figure 2.1 PPP Investment by IDA Status, 1990–2017, in 2018 US$ millions
Source: World Bank, 2018.

[1] This database defines "PPI projects" to include non-PPP projects like utility privatizations and merchant projects, but Table 2.1 omits data on those projects to focus on PPPs as they are defined in this study.

a more dominant role in financing and managing infrastructure services in developing countries.

What does this information about PPP prevalence tell us about the conditions under which PPPs are likely to provide VFM? The message is simple: PPPs work much better in middle-income economies than they do in low-income countries. This means that in most cases a complex, long-term, brownfield concession for retail water distribution, for example, requiring significant capital investment, should not be the first choice as the service delivery solution in a low-income country (as such contracts often were in the early 1990s). This review suggests that low-income countries can usually benefit more from traditional technical assistance and capacity building, or from hybrid projects that mix elements of PPP contracts with those of consulting or engineering, procurement, and construction (EPC) contracts to reduce risks for the private partners. Reforms to legal and regulatory frameworks within which PPPs eventually would be structured are also critical in these countries, along with help in improving government procedures for things like procurement and construction management.

2.3 Costs and Profits

PPPs involve multiple stakeholders, all of whom have interests in how the project performs. The conventional view of PPPs is that, when compared with typical public projects, they should provide better service at lower costs. The private partner needs to make a profit, but the return should be reasonable. Projects that do not meet these expectations can be subject to public criticism from government, the news media, user groups, civil society, etc. But getting the balance right in a way that satisfies all key stakeholders is not an easy task, as the recent history of PPPs indicates.

The profitability of private firms involved in PPP projects, and the resulting costs for governments and end users, has long been a controversial subject in industrialized countries like the United Kingdom, where the government's PFI became one of the OECD's best-known PPP programs starting in the early 1990s. Studies of the profitability of PFI deals in the UK health sector have found rates of return as high as 60 per cent (Shaoul, 2008).

Whether or not the cause is high profits, PPPs have often tended to be more expensive than traditional public procurement. A 2006 report by the European Investment Bank (EIB) reviewed the costs of 227 road projects in 15 European countries and concluded that projects structured as PPPs (65 of the total) were 24 per cent more expensive than those done via traditional public procurement (Blanc-Brude, Goldsmith, and Välilä, 2006). In a 2015 review of effective interest rates on private finance projects, the UK's National Audit Office found that these rates, at 7–8 per cent, were double the rates on normal government borrowing, at

3–4 per cent (UK National Audit Office, 2015). In a 2016 review of PPP literature sponsored by the UN Department of Economic and Social Affairs, the authors concluded that "Overall, the evidence suggests that PPPs have often tended to be more expensive than the alternative of public procurement" (Jomo et al., 2016).

Most industrialized countries try to anticipate project benefits and costs, including private profits, by requiring a VFM analysis of PPP projects as part of project preparation. VFM analysis involves estimating project costs, including profits for the private partners, and measuring them against project benefits, including service quality, quantity, and prices for governments or end users. Quantitative VFM assessment typically involves comparing the chosen PPP option against a "public sector comparator" (PSC). The PSC allows a comparison of the risk-adjusted cost to government of procuring the project through traditional procurement (the PSC), with the expected cost to government of the PPP (pre-procurement) or the actual PPP bids (post-procurement).

The survey by Burger and Hawkesworth (2011) found that 17 of 22 countries used "public sector comparators" to assess the VFM of PPPs. But ever since the technique was first refined and pioneered as part of the UK's PFI program in the1990s, it has been criticized for being inaccurate and subject to manipulation. A UK Audit Commission report (2003) concluded that "the PSC has lost the confidence of many people, and risks being seen more as a hoop to jump through on the way to government funding than a valuable exercise that can help ensure better VFM." Early research concluded that PSCs were often an expensive way of endorsing the pre-selected choice of private participation (Leigland and Shugart, 2006). Research in developed countries has found that the use of PSCs and similar VFM techniques is consistently biased in favor of PPP options (Boardman and Hellowell, 2016).

Engel, Fischer, and Galetovic (2014) noted that in some countries PPPs are attractive to government not necessarily because they are expected to be less expensive, but simply because accounting rules allow project costs to be moved off government books in order to give the appearance of lower debt levels. Klein also mentions this and notes that when the United Kingdom changed its accounting rules in 2009, PFI projects became less attractive as a result. If true, this may account for some of the well-documented failures of the PSC to accurately forecast PPP project costs.

Of course, other kinds of quantitative comparisons can be done on an economic cost–benefit basis, using a wide variety of VFM methodologies (World Bank Institute and Public–Private Infrastructure Advisory Facility, 2013). It is also true that regardless of the method used, huge mistakes are routinely made in the estimation of financial costs and benefits associated with infrastructure projects—whether or not PPPs are involved. In a survey of 58 rail projects (a mixture of public and private projects), Flyvbjerg (2005) found that costs were underestimated by an average of 45 per cent and demand forecasts were overestimated by an average of 51 per cent. Flyvbjerg concluded that such consistently large mistakes in cost–benefit estimations must be attributed to a combination of faulty techniques, as well as causal effects like "optimism bias" and "strategic misrepresentation." Doing an infrastructure project as a PPP does not lead to any more accurate estimation of costs and benefits. Vassallo (2007) and Bain (2009) investigated the forecasting performance of privately financed toll roads; their findings were similar to Flyvbjerg's. These authors found that PPP toll road traffic forecasts were typically characterized by large errors and considerable optimism bias.

However, in the developing world, VFM techniques like PSCs are arguably even more unreliable than in OECD countries. Even industrial countries have little objective relevant data upon which to base cost estimates. Without such data, which is virtually non-existent in low-income countries, calculating with any accuracy how much a project will cost over 25–30 years of operation is almost impossible. As noted by Estache and Philippe (2012), officials in these countries often find out, after contracts have been signed, that original forecasts of project costs and profits were inaccurate. Indeed, projects frequently turn out to be unprofitable for private partners, triggering renegotiations:

> Experience has shown that besides the short-term subsidies sometimes needed to support privatization processes, the public sector often has eventually had to commit subsidies for the long-term as well–usually as one of the outcomes of a renegotiation. (Estache and Philippe, 2012)

A widely cited study by Sirtaine et al. (2004), examined the profitability of PPP projects in Latin America during the late 1990s using a sample that included both brownfield and greenfield projects. The Sirtaine study suggested that, on average, projects demonstrated profitability only after about ten years. Up to that point, project shareholders earned negative returns on their investments, even when adding in management fees, estimated accumulated capital gains, and potential investment markups. The study further found that 40 per cent of the sampled concessions did not have the potential to ever become profitable, with that proportion increasing to 50 per cent for concessions in the energy and transport sectors. Indeed, Sirtaine estimated that over the history of these projects, on average they were unable to generate sufficient annual operating income after taxes to cover all of their financial obligations. Only by adding in "indirect forms of dividends" like investment markups, transfer fees, and payments for capital appreciation paid at the end of the contract period could these concessions generate reasonable remuneration for their private partners. The study suggested that, at a minimum, these PPPs face constant cashflow problems over at least the first decade of their existence.

Another study, by Guasch (2004), reached conclusions consistent with Sirtaine's findings. Guasch found high rates of PPP contract renegotiation after only a few years of operation, that is, long before Sirtaine says that private partners are able to confirm their projects' long-term profitability. Using a sample that also included brownfield and greenfield projects in Latin America, the study concluded that PPP projects in that region registered a high incidence of renegotiation, about 42 per cent, coming on average after only 2.2 years of operation. The results of renegotiation tended to favor operators, mostly with improvements to cash flow and profitability via compromises such as permitted delays in investment obligations (69 per cent), reductions in investment obligations (62 per cent), tariff increases (62 per cent), and increased passthrough to tariffs of cost items (59 per cent). Again, this suggested that PPP cash flow problems tended to be severe, generating stresses that operators and investors had to live with over the long term, and which were critical in precipitating many renegotiations.

Estache and Philippe (2012) concluded that sectors like telecommunications and electricity generation in which cost-reflective tariffs seem less controversial have proven to be reasonably profitable and largely free of subsidies. But most other sectors in the developing world—electricity distribution and transmission, transport, and water and sanitation—often require subsidies to sustain cash flows or bring the rate of return close to the cost of capital. If the subsidies are not built into the initial contracts, they are likely to result from renegotiation of those contracts. In the latter event, renegotiation increases the risk of a less than optimal reduction in the fiscal benefits that governments care most about, that is, the size and pace of investment. Renegotiations also tend to increase the most politically painful costs—tariffs or off-take payments—sometimes to unaffordable levels for governments.

How are governments and their development partners coping with the fact that PPPs are costlier and less profitable than assumed in the 1990s? One way is to rely more heavily on "blended finance" approaches to PPPs. Since the launch in the early 2000s of the multi-donor trust fund for output-based aid (the Global Partnership on Output-Based Aid), "blended finance" has become increasingly popular as a way of using concessional finance to catalyze private sector investment, particularly in infrastructure PPPs. The International Finance Corporation's (IFC) Blended Finance Unit, launched in 2007, and the EU's regional blending finance facilities, such as the EU–Africa Infrastructure Trust Fund, have all used subsidies to bring down the costs of various kinds of infrastructure PPPs (IFC, 2012). The use of blended finance in this way creates a hybrid approach that combines PPP elements with those of more traditional public projects.

But blended finance involves subsidies, and the use of subsidies requires justification to ensure that it is really crowding in private finance rather than crowding it out. Economists typically recommend the use of cost–benefit analyses for such justifications to clearly identify any obstacles that reflect market failure and help determine whether subsidized finance can solve the problem. Theoretically, cost–benefit analyses can confirm that the likely development impacts of using subsidized finance far outweigh the distortions that may result. When this kind of analysis can be done, it almost certainly leads to more developmental projects. But the difficulties involved in this should not be underestimated. The World Bank's Independent Evaluation Group found in 2010 that the use of cost–benefit analysis dropped from 70 per cent of all World Bank projects in 1970 to 25 per cent in 2008, largely because of problems with data and the difficulties in quantifying costs and benefits (Independent Evaluation Group, 2010). (For a more extensive discussion of blended finance, see Chapter 10.)

2.4 Preparation Costs

The OECD (2008) has indicated another important reason for the high costs associated with PPPs in many countries—the high cost of PPP project preparation, especially when compared with the costs of traditional public procurement. Preparation costs include the legal, financial, and technical costs incurred by both public and private sector actors in developing a PPP for commercial operation, and so include "transaction costs" associated with PPP procurement processes and contract negotiation, as well as (especially in some developing countries) "upstream" legal, regulatory, and policy preparation tasks that go well beyond normal transaction costs.

In their review of the PPP literature, De Schepper, Haeqendonck, and Dooms (2015) noted widespread agreement among practitioners and academics that PPP preparation costs are higher than preparation costs associated with traditional public procurement. In many cases, these costs are so high that they discourage potential bidders from competing for projects, and in some cases undermine the basic cost effectiveness rationale of PPPs and negatively impact on the economic and financial viability of projects. De Schepper et al. (2015), in their study of 172 public infrastructure projects in Belgium, found much longer and more complex bidding processes associated with PPPs than with projects procured via traditional public methods.

There are several reasons why PPP preparation costs are so much higher than the costs of preparing projects involving traditional public procurement. The survey by Burger and Hawkesworth (2011), which found widespread use of "public sector comparators" to ascertain VFM of PPPs, also noted that the process of preparing a PSC and requiring each bidder to prepare a projected PPP model is costly and time consuming. Complex PSCs can take several months to finalize, and the resulting reduction in net benefits for potential private partners may cause them not to bid on projects that are deemed to be too small, with potential revenues not high enough to compensate for preparation costs. On the other hand, some projects are avoided because they seem too large and complex, leading to expensive bid preparation and time and cost overruns resulting from protracted contract negotiations. This may explain the findings of Zitron (2006), which showed that on average only three bidders competed for each PPP contract in the United Kingdom, and that there were fewer than three bidders on one-quarter of the contracts. Governments can partially or completely compensate firms for their bidding costs, but of course this increases the cost of the PPP option relative to the traditional public procurement option.

Twelve of the countries in the Burger and Hawkesworth (2011) survey said they used some form of cost–benefit analysis to assess VFM for projects involving traditional public procurement, but these appear to be much less rigorous tests than PSCs and do not constitute the public sector equivalent of "private sector comparators." Only a few countries applied criteria to all prospective projects to establish which mode of procurement would result in the highest VFM. In other words, for many countries traditional public procurement remains the lower cost, less complicated, default option for procurement, and the PPP choice depends on the discretion of departmental officials.

There is no single widely accepted metric for infrastructure project preparation costs. Costs may be measured as a percentage of initial capital costs, construction costs, or even the total net present value of the deal over its entire lifetime. Most published work has focused on "transaction" costs, usually synonymous with "downstream transaction costs," and mostly procurement-related costs incurred by governments or their MDB partners. A sampling of different metrics follows:

- In a widely cited study of the procurement phase costs of bidding and negotiating contracts for 55 infrastructure PPPs in six sectors of the UK economy, Dudkin and Valila (2005) concluded that total transaction costs of this type averaged over 12 per cent of the capital value of the projects, with the public sector cost at about 3.5 per cent, the winning bidder's cost at about 3.8 per cent, and costs to losing bidders totaling about 5 per cent.
- The World Bank (Lin and Doemeland, 2012) estimated that MDB and government preparation costs for the Nam Theun 2 hydropower project in Lao PDR (total investment: US$1.4 billion) amounted to US$124 million at project close in 2005, or 9 per cent of total project investment.
- Farajian (2010) found lower average transaction costs in several case studies of large transport PPPs in the United States, but concluded that the transport agencies involved were not reporting all relevant costs. He also found that some individual state departments of transportation were requiring that project managers budget up to 10 per cent of total investment for procurement and contract negotiations managed by state officials.
- Castalia Strategic Advisors (2010) estimated government transaction costs of PFI school projects in Australia and New Zealand to be 10–11 per cent of total project construction costs, with significant premiums to be expected for first-time projects in either country.

- Bhattacharya, Romani, and Stern (2012) found that for projects in developing countries involving limited experience with the type of project or technology, or in a low-capacity country, preparation costs, including costs of design and arranging financing, "can constitute up to 10 percent of overall investment costs."
- The AfDB (2013) estimated that their preparation costs for large infrastructure projects in Africa can reach 10–15 per cent of project capital costs.
- These kinds of studies suggest that PPP project preparation costs in developing countries are much higher than they are in OECD countries because of the need to include costs for things like upstream preparation and premiums for new or particularly complicated sectors like hydropower. These costs are also considerably higher than for projects involving traditional public procurement because of the need in many cases to carry out VFM analyses (which are typically less onerous for public procurement) and use more complex bidding processes.

Under what conditions can governments and their development partners deal effectively with the time and costs involved in project preparation? For many years, the default solution was to make as much of this preparation as possible the responsibility of the private sector. This attitude was an outgrowth of the notion that implementing a PPP meant handing over government problems with infrastructure to private companies for solution. Probably the first notable example of this approach was the Buenos Aires water concession, signed in December 1992. This was one of the first, large brownfield infrastructure concessions. A "defining feature" of the tender process was a lack of information about the water system and its problems (Alcazar, Abdala, and Shirley, 2000). Bidders were required to do all of their own due diligence, and the winning bidder had to refine its implementation plan in the first few months after signing the contract. A protracted series of contract renegotiations would follow because latent defects made the project much more expensive than anticipated.

That approach has been frequently copied over the years (see Chapter 5), but by the early 2000s, donors, DFIs, and MDBs began to recognize that: (i) private partners cannot by themselves fully prepare PPP projects in a way that optimizes economic benefits; and (ii) a much more substantial effort by donors, DFIs, and MDBs to pay for and supervise preparation *before* private partners become involved can result in more effective, sustainable, and pro-poor projects. The stronger role for governments and their development partners in identifying problems and designing solutions for private partners to implement is a characteristic of hybrid management contracts being developed or implemented in countries like Benin, Liberia, and Sierra Leone (Republic of Sierra Leone, 2015). These contracts shift risks away from private partners, toward governments, donors,

DFIs, and MDBs, who are, theoretically, better able to mitigate those risks. Ultimately, this should make the contracts more productive and sustainable.

On a broader scale, a number of multi-donor project preparation facilities were established in the 2000s to deal with the high costs of preparation, but evaluations later showed that these facilities were too small and too bureaucratic to have much of a substantial impact (Cambridge Economic Policy Associates, 2012). As noted in section 2.1, much larger preparation platforms have been created more recently to try to address the problem, but they have not yet had a chance to show results in terms of sustainable PPPs.[2]

2.5 Finance and Investment

PPP advocates expect, and sometimes promise, that such contracts will lead to improved efficiency and increases in investment from private sources, consequently leading to greater service capacity and coverage. But again, the evidence suggests that this is not consistently the case. As various studies demonstrate, private sources of finance have not played as strong a role in infrastructure PPPs in developing countries as hoped. In Africa, the long-standing practice in some sectors of government on-lending concessional finance to private concessionaires illustrates this fact. Many of the rail concessions in SSA benefited from this kind of debt, sourced as relatively inexpensive sovereign guaranteed loans from bilateral donors, DFIs, or MDBs. These concessions often needed financial help because concessionaires could not or would not borrow to finance assets like rail lines, with operational lifespans being much longer than the terms of the concession contracts. Governments themselves often filled this gap by providing a large share of project financing. In the 1990s, this kind of on-lending was usually done with an interest rate markup to the concessionaire to cover government administrative costs and loan loss liability, but was still lower than the commercial rates that the concessionaire could obtain. As commercial lending for all kinds of brownfield concessions began to diminish following the Asian crisis, the markups were slashed to compensate for diminished global project finance lending, and by the mid-2000s, in some cases the markups disappeared entirely (Pozzo di Borgo et al., 2006).

A study by Gassner, Popov, and Pushak (2009), examined whether water and electricity utilities involving private participation outperformed those managed by governments. The study used a data set of more than 1,200 utilities in 71 developing countries. The results of the study showed that the private sector delivered

[2] Examples are Africa50, established by the African Development Bank, and the World Bank Group's Global Infrastructure Facility (GIF), both of which address project preparation as well as financing.

higher labor productivity and operational efficiency, convincingly outperforming comparable companies that remained state owned and operated. But the study found mixed evidence regarding increases in investment and could not conclude that investment usually increases with private participation.

Gassner et al. addressed the investment question in terms of different sectors and types of private participation. For electricity divestitures, investment per worker increased with private participation, as economic theory predicts. For lease and management contracts, for water and sanitation or electricity, private partners were usually not obligated to make major capital investments, but their results suggested that even if private participation generated operational improvements, the public utility companies involved did not increase investment. And for concession contracts, which also tend to generate improvements in operational efficiency, "there is no conclusive evidence that investment increases," (Gassner et al., 2009). If efficiency improves but is not supported by increases in public or private investment in the maintenance and expansion of utility networks, Gassner et al. asked how operational improvements could be sustained over the long term.

A second study, by Marin (2009), undertook a global review of public–private partnerships for urban water utilities in developing countries. The study focused on 65 large urban water PPPs in operation for at least five years. Marin concluded that the principal benefit of these projects was operational efficiency rather than their ability to supply private sector finance. The author also acknowledged that private investment was the main attraction of PPPs in the water sector in the 1990s, but added that "experience has shown that this was largely the wrong focus" (Marin, 2009).

A host of other studies have found PPP-related efficiencies generated under different conditions, in different sectors, including electricity distribution, telecommunications, and water distribution (Estache and Rossi, 2004; Andrés, Schwartz, and Guasch, 2013), and transport (Perelman and Serebrisky, 2012). Estache and Philippe (2012) surveyed many other studies showing some measure of PPP efficiency in different sectors. But again, these studies do not consistently show a corresponding increase in investment.

Government on-lending to PPPs accelerated in some countries after the onset of the 2008 global financial crisis, which caused a collapse of the syndication market, inactive bond markets, and unusually high costs of funding. Governments and government-owned development banks used concessional lending to meet funding shortfalls resulting from projects unable to raise sufficient commercial debt finance on acceptable terms. The UK government attempted to salvage its PFI program with a proposed investment fund that would provide up to 100 per cent of the financing needed for projects to reach financial closure (Farquharson and Encinas, 2010). In developing countries such as Brazil, India, Mexico, and South Africa, government-owned DFIs provided funding or guarantees to kick-start PPP projects. Because countries like Brazil and India accounted for such a large share of private investment activity in developing countries, their use of government-owned banks and local public banks to fund large projects kept global PPP market investment numbers from declining as much as expected from 2008 to 2009 (Izaguirre, 2009).

The global financial markets have still not fully recovered from the financial crisis and resultant increased financial regulation, at least not in the sense of returning to earlier levels of high liquidity, substantial risk appetites, and low cost of project finance debt provided by commercial banks. Governments, especially those in larger middle-income countries, continue to replace scarce commercial finance with public money from government budgets or donors, DFIs, and MDBs. Recent efforts by the World Bank's PPI Project Database to collect detailed information on PPP financing sources in developing countries confirm that the private sector plays even less of a financing role in low-income countries. In 2015, 57 per cent of PPP funding in IDA countries came from governments, multilaterals, and bilateral institutions, with the balance coming from commercial sources. For all developing country regions in 2015, the percentage was 41 per cent (Table 2.2). In her analysis of this data (which in this case included information on merchant projects and divestiture), one World Bank staff member noted that, "One of the prevailing notions about PPPs is that upfront costs are wholly paid for by the private sector... However, this is a myth" (Chao, 2016).

What does this critique say about the conditions under which affordable private financing can be accessed for infrastructure PPPs? There clearly are factors that make a difference in terms of financing costs, which involve the particulars of a project like country, sector, type of contract, risk mitigation features of the contact, and the mix of financiers. The stronger a country's sovereign credit ratings, the easier it seems to be for infrastructure PPPs to raise affordable private finance (IMF, 2006). In terms of sectors, power generation is probably the easiest in which to raise private finance, largely because the supply of power is relatively commercial, with cost-reflective end-user tariffs being less controversial for power than for services like water supply. Electricity generation PPPs can also be purely private operations, often structured as Independent Power Producer (IPP) projects involving ownership of the assets by the private sector rather than by government as in traditional concessions. Private financing for power generation can also be

Table 2.2 Breakdown of PPI financing by Developing Country Region, 2015, in US$ billions

Region	Total Investment	Public Money	Donors/MDBs	Private Sector
Latin America	17.3	39%	14%	46%
East Asia	10.1	13%	4%	83%
SSA	6.2	13%	21%	64%
South Asia	5.4	30%	21%	49%
All Regions	39.0	27%	14%	59%

Source: Chao and Saha, 2016.

relatively affordable because generation is not a natural monopoly service in the same way that some other infrastructure services are, such as water supply—multiple facilities can be built to feed power into national grids, so generation can be relatively competitive. This puts some downward pressure on financing costs.

IPP projects may be popular, but affordable private finance for all kinds of large PPPs usually requires a host of risk mitigation mechanisms. Most IPP power purchase agreements (PPAs) must be backed by security arrangements such as escrow accounts, letters of credit, targeted subsidies, budget commitments, etc. In countries without domestic capital markets that can finance PPP projects, PPAs often must be denominated in hard currencies such as US dollars or euros, indexed to currency baskets, or backed by foreign exchange liquidity facilities. Sovereign guarantees are also usually required to back various aspects critical to PPP project cash flows and profitability, including off-take commitments, fuel supply availability, currency convertibility and transferability, interest rates, exchange rates, tariff rates, and revenue levels. Donors, DFIs, MDBs, as well as private institutions also provide guarantees or insurance products to cover risks that private lenders or investors are unable or unwilling to take. Finally, governments, donors, DFIs, and MDBs have all increased their financing shares in large PPPs to reduce the size of private project finance and help make it affordable.

But when governments assume or share project investment risks, they need to manage conflicts of interest. For example, can governments act simultaneously as financiers interested in the financial sustainability of projects, as well as regulators charged with protecting the interests of end users? Will a government allow a concession company in which it has invested substantial amounts of capital to declare bankruptcy?

Does it ultimately matter if private participation leads to operational efficiency, but not more investment? If services become less costly and their availability increases, why should a lack of investment be a concern? The problem is that PPPs tend to involve complex contracts that are difficult and costly to prepare. Most of the time this effort and expense is justified on the basis that more investment will be forthcoming. The absence of such investment substantiates Klein's point that very little separates PPPs from well-run public companies and argues for more attention to basic management improvements and better regulation before considering private participation.

2.6 Poverty Impacts

If a PPP generates investment, or even if it achieves only efficiency gains, it can make possible a host of other benefits like improved service quality, affordable tariffs, or expanded service access. In low-income countries, these kinds of benefits are usually cited as justification for involving the private sector in infrastructure service delivery. But Estache and Philippe (2012) note that there is relatively little empirical evidence that focuses on the development impacts of small or large-scale PPPs. What evidence there is suggests that such projects do not provide poor households with enough affordable access to services.

The study by Gassner et al. (2009) shows why this topic can generate so much controversy. They compared average annual values for indicators measuring performance before and after private sector involvement in water and electricity utilities. Private involvement (via PPPs or privatization) generated a number of impressive efficiency gains, but they were not associated with an equitable distribution of project benefits. For example, the labor productivity gains were associated with reductions in staff numbers for both water and electricity. Employment fell by 24 per cent in electricity and by 22 per cent in water following the introduction of private participation. Utilities operated by governments used considerably more employees than privately operated utilities to achieve the same level of service. Moreover, the efficiency gains were not associated with changes in investment or average residential tariffs. Because the gains would normally translate into lower costs for the operator, Gassner et al. (2009) speculated about reasons why there was no sign of the lower costs translating into greater investment or lower prices. One possible explanation was that services were already so underpriced that even huge efficiency gains could not justify price reductions. Another possibility was that the private operators took advantage of weak regulatory oversight to simply retain all of the gains as profits, passing on nothing to customers or to cover operations and maintenance (O&M) costs. This latter possibility raises questions about the long-term sustainability of PPP efficiency gains.

In their survey of PPP research, Estache and Philippe (2012) concluded that investment and efficiency gains in the telecommunications sector (resulting mostly from technological advances) have generally contributed to the wide distribution of benefits like increased access, improved affordability, and better service quality. But in most other sectors, even when benefits result from improved efficiency or investment, they were not always shared with customers or governments. This is because regulation is not typically designed to pass on such gains to other stakeholders like residential users: "For the most successful projects, unless regulation works, efficiency gains become rents which fuel conflicts between government, users and operators" (Estache and Philippe, 2012).

How can PPPs be structured in such a way that the likelihood of developmental benefits is strongly increased? PPPs that successfully generate benefits for low-income residents of developing countries usually begin with the realization that such benefits do not automatically result from increased private investment or improved efficiency. And as long as private partners are mostly responsible for developing work plans, as part of the bid process and later during early stages of implementation, there is no reason to expect effective measures for benefit distribution. This is not a particularly new problem. PPP contract designs and tariff structures that fail to benefit—or even disadvantage—major constituencies of stakeholders have led to renegotiations and project collapses from the early days of infrastructure concessions in the early 1990s. Many recommendations have been made about the need to undertake stakeholder analysis by modeling the distribution of project benefits before a contract has been awarded (e.g., van den Berg, 2000). But again, this kind of preparation requires financial resources and expertise that must be brought into play before PPP contracts are signed.

2.7 Governance Issues

Governance refers to the various ways in which governments' institutional capacity or lack thereof, intentionally or unintentionally affects the performance of PPPs. Political leadership is a rare but highly important way in which governments can facilitate significant infrastructure investment via PPP arrangements (Jones, Jammal, and Gokgur, 2002; Eberhard, Kolker, and Leigland, 2014). But generally, strong political support for PPPs in low-income countries is rare. A country's investment climate can also have a major positive impact on the development of PPP projects (IMF, 2006), but low-income countries typically do not have investment grade credit ratings that would reflect strong investment climates.

Engel et al. (2014) argued that the governance structure under which most PPPs operate is "usually defective." This is largely because PPPs share many of the same defects as standard public works projects, including improper design, poor procurement, and frequent renegotiations that Engel and his co-authors conclude are often opportunistic attempts by private contractors to increase profits. A recent study by the World Bank's Public–Private Infrastructure Advisory Facility (PPIAF) found that in the interests of getting projects to completion, many developing countries use limited competition and direct negotiation to procure private sponsors and operators (PPIAF, 2014). But PPIAF also found that projects procured in this manner tend to be more expensive and subject to more problems in implementation.

Eberhard and Gratwick (2010) found that few African countries have established the key legal and regulatory elements needed to guide private participation in their power sectors—a clear policy statement and supporting legislation. Some countries have passed laws permitting IPP projects, but almost none have addressed the relationship between IPP projects and state-owned energy utilities. In a more recent study, Eberhard et al. (2016) conclude that in general, Africa's power sector continues to reflect a partial approach to reforms that facilitate more private investment, with little achieved over the last 20 years in terms of unbundling, privatization, or the introduction of competition.

After "PPP units" became prominent in countries like the United Kingdom and Australia, they have become the preferred institutional tool to regulate the process of PPP project development in many developing countries. A variety of international organizations have recommended establishing PPP units, including the OECD (2010), the UN (2007), and APEC (2008). The rapid growth in the number of such units seems to have resulted from a widespread perception that well-functioning PPP units are important for the success of a country's PPP program. However, a recent literature review by Lemma (2013) concluded that "there is very little quantitative evidence of the value of centralized PPP coordination units…." There seems to be consensus that a large and growing number of such units exist, but they differ so widely by country and sector that it is difficult to generalize about their value, or even agree on how to measure their worth (Burger and Hawkesworth, 2011; EPEC, 2014).

The contribution of PPP units to achieving success may not be entirely clear, but the reasons for their ineffectiveness are more so. One of the earliest studies of these units, sponsored by PPIAF (2007), noted that they were often established due to frustration on the parts of governments with the inability of existing institutions to move PPP programs forward. But the study found that in such situations governments often overlooked the fact that the very shortcomings that made the existing institutions underperform may well undermine the new PPP units as well (PPIAF, 2007). The PPIAF study concluded that in countries where top politicians do not support the PPP program, where procurement of infrastructure and capital works is not transparent and competitive, and where the machinery of government is chronically uncoordinated, PPP units are unlikely to be effective.

One problem with PPP units that seems to have limited their usefulness is their disappointing performance in accelerating PPP deal flow. Government officials in developing countries often expect such units to speed up the process of getting PPPs to completion. But such units often produce exactly the opposite result—the flow of deals slows down because of the perceived need to carefully apply standardized procedures in project development. Better-prepared projects should be more sustainable, and that should off-set lengthy preparation periods to some degree. But this logic rarely satisfies government officials interested in getting projects done as quickly as possible.

A case in point is South Africa's PPP Unit, which was established in mid-2000 in the National Treasury. It boasted procedures and guidebooks that quickly became good practice examples used by other national agencies in Africa (Lemma, 2013). The guidelines called for over two dozen relatively elaborate preparation steps, as well as a series of National Treasury approvals of the process recommended by the Treasury's PPP Unit. The entire process (including the use of "public sector comparators") was quickly judged by the private sector to be too lengthy, too complex, very expensive, highly overregulated, and unfortunately responsible for slowing down PPP deal flow (Castalia Strategic Advisors, 2007). The PPP Unit itself admitted that its required VFM studies at the municipal level averaged about 30 months (Levinsohn and Reardon, 2007). As a result, under this regulatory regime, PPP deal flow remained stagnant in South Africa.

In 2012, the PPP Unit lost its status as a separate department within National Treasury when it was absorbed by the Government Technical Advisory Centre (GTAC), and its role changed from process regulator to the provider of PPP transaction advisory services (GTAC, 2015). The experience of South Africa's PPP Unit seems consistent with the findings of several researchers, confirming that complicated frameworks for regulating the development of PPP projects can significantly slow the process of getting projects to financial close (Zhang and Kumaraswamy, 2001; Chan et al., 2010).

PPIAF's long experience with the creation of PPP units, particularly in Africa, suggests two conditions under which these entities can add value. First, if units have no authority to require compliance with their recommendations, they tend to be quickly relegated to minor advisory roles without much influence. This is because in low-income countries governments cannot afford to employ the sort of experts whose advice is of significant value to public or private sector project proponents. Sometimes experts can be seconded to PPP units from private sector firms or recruited for limited periods with the help of donor funding. But these kinds of experts typically cannot be retained long enough to transfer significant levels of professional skills to regular staff (and if they do, regular staff members tend to leave for higher-paying jobs). To enforce government rules regarding how PPPs should be developed and structured, as opposed to just providing advice, units can function reasonably well with a small central core of expertise. The rest of the staff component can be made up of competent project managers with more general kinds of professional skills.

Second, the rules that PPP units enforce should minimize direct pre-approval of actions by senior government officials based on vague decision-making guidance, in favor of routine, post-audit reviews of actions based on clear, specific procedural guidelines or regulations. Senior officials can become involved after the fact, if the post-audit reviews reveal that proper procedures were not followed. The pre-approval approach encourages arbitrary decision making and can slow implementation to a standstill. But the post-audit approach is not easy to implement: it requires clear and complete procedural guidelines or regulations, along with consistent, reasonably high-quality auditing skills and procedures. PPP units will not work well in countries already plagued with severe governance defects affecting standard public works procurement and contracting. This is one of the reasons why PPPs are not ideal tools for every developing country.

2.8 Transformational PPPs

In light of the preceding discussion, what is to be made of the G20's enthusiasm for regional or "transformational" PPP projects? Indeed, why would such projects be any more successful than smaller and simpler PPP projects in meeting expectations regarding costs, profits, finance, investment, equity, efficiency, and governance?

Those who defend these large PPP projects point to the advantages of economies of scale and of scope. This "bigger is better" approach is also consistent with popular theories of economic development, which argue that big development challenges like poverty alleviation, energy scarcity, and urbanization can only be solved by "big push" solutions involving large projects and large amounts of aid (Sachs, 2006). However, these "transformational" projects frequently possess the size and complexity that would make them subject to what Bent Flyvbjerg refers to as the "iron law of megaprojects." According to Flyvbjerg (2014), 90 per cent of projects costing over US$1 billion, end up "over budget, over time, over and over again." This is a problem for all large projects, not just PPPs, but Flyvbjerg points out that "Private capital is no panacea for the ills in megaproject management, to be sure; in some cases, private capital may even make things worse" Flyvbjerg (2014). Part of the reason for this is that the complexity of large PPPs—with multiple players, complicated and lengthy contract negotiations, high transaction costs, forecasting uncertainties, etc.—leads to what Ansar et al. (2016) call a low "investment fragility threshold"—a high vulnerability of the projects to become unsustainable due to the impact of random events.

With large, transformational projects, economies of scale are cited as a factor that should help reduce the amount of preparation costs. But using the cost metrics discussed earlier, and even assuming some economies of scale, the costs of preparing transformational PPP projects are staggering. The average total cost of the 14 regional power sector projects in the Priority Action Plan of the Program for Infrastructure Development for Africa (PIDA) is US$2.9 billion (AUC, 2012). Preparing projects of that size could require as much as US$430 million in total development costs, with roughly one-third of that (US$140 million) being the responsibility of the government and its development partners. These development costs tend to be more expensive than costs incurred for developing conventional publicly procured projects, because, in addition to more complicated contracts and contact negotiations, they involve much more upstream preparation. Many low-income countries do not have a specific PPP legislative framework conducive to large PPPs or a single set of procedures for the award of a suitable PPP contract. Without such a legal-regulatory framework in place, project sponsors need to obtain multiple licenses, permits, and authorizations from various governmental and local authorities in order to implement the project. All of this increases the political risk for private investors, in case one or more key permissions cannot be obtained, and makes it more difficult to have these licenses, permits, and authorizations assigned to the project financiers as a form of security under the financing arrangements.

What role would private finance play in these large, regional PPPs? Inga III, a regional power project which is probably on more lists of "transformational" infrastructure projects than any other in SSA, suggests some answers to this question. When it came under serious consideration in the early 2000s, Inga III was intended to be the third and largest hydropower project in the Inga basin of the Congo River in the Democratic Republic of the Congo (DRC). Private sector participation has always been described as a requirement for the project rather than an option because the combination of the government plus donors, DFIs, and MDBs could not provide the kind of capital required for project investment (World Bank, 2014). But as the project developed, it became clear that neither could private partners be expected to be responsible for all or even most of the finance required for the project.

In a "preliminary financing feasibility study" commissioned by the World Bank (BNP Paribas, 2009), the consultants estimated the total cost of the project at about US$9 billion for a facility that would generate 4,500 MW. The debt share of total costs (US$6.7 billion) would be provided by four MDBs, six DFIs, several export credit agencies, and Chinese policy banks. Commercial banks were expected to provide no more than about 10 per cent of the total, assuming that MDB credit enhancements could be accessed from the World Bank's Partial Risk Guarantee (PRG) facility and the Multilateral Investment Guarantee Agency (MIGA). The study assumed that one-third of the equity needed for the project (about US$2.2 billion) would come from the government, sourced as loans from MDBs and DFIs. This government equity contribution (about US$730 million) would be in addition to project preparation costs that could be as much as US$400 million for a project of this size, using the metrics already discussed.

At over US$1 billion, the government contribution needed to make Inga III viable as a PPP seems untenable. In mid-2010, the government reached the completion point under the Enhanced Heavily Indebted Poor Countries (HIPC) initiative after benefiting from assistance under the Multilateral Debt Relief Initiative (MDRI). By 2013, the DRC's total outstanding central government debt owed to bilateral and multilateral creditors was US$2.9 billion (IMF, 2015). This total reflected a marked improvement over the 2009 level. But the DRC's debt sustainability rating was still assessed as "moderate" by the IMF, meaning that any sharp increase in external debt, even to MDBs, DFIs, or donors, risked the return of debt distress. The wisdom of a precipitous 30 per cent increase in such debt to support Inga III would no doubt be questioned. The conclusions regarding Inga III seem clear: it would not be predominantly financed by the private sector, leaving the government with a financing burden that it could not afford.

Is there any evidence to suggest that benefits resulting from efficiencies or investment generated by large transformational PPPs would be distributed equitably across the country's population? In terms of equity arguments, MDBs have not been consistent in their messaging. On the one hand, the World Bank (2011) argued in its infrastructure strategy update that "Large infrastructure projects have often been successful in making project affected people the beneficiaries of the project displacing them, as well as achieving development objectives, like the benefit sharing arrangements in hydropower."

But the same document acknowledged that the Bank's strategy of pursuing economic growth through such infrastructure projects, with the expectation that benefits will "trickle down" to poor households, had not been borne out by the facts, and that the results of this approach had often been "slow". Poverty impacts had proven "complex to achieve and demonstrate": "Learning from past experiences, the Group will do more to enhance the delivery of infrastructure services to the poor" (World Bank, 2011).

At least in the power sector, views on the socio-economic value of large regional projects may be changing. The International Energy Agency (IEA) has acknowledged that 70 per cent of rural areas in developing countries are best electrified with minigrid and other off-grid solutions (mostly wind and solar), and that these kinds of solutions would need to receive most of the new investments recommended for the power sector (International Energy Agency, 2011). The value of this small-scale approach seems to be supported even in the DRC, where the government's Inga III project director acknowledged that the project would not generate many benefits for rural areas, and that off-grid solutions involving wind, solar, and small hydropower would be needed to adequately serve populations in those areas (Worldfolio, 2016).

The larger the PPP, the more important it is to have knowledgeable and well capacitated partners, including governments who must play a principal role in project preparation, procurement, and post-closure performance monitoring. In low-income countries, that kind of capacity does not exist, so donors, DFIs, and MDBs try to create it, sometimes specifically for transformational projects. But how effective is this kind of just-in-time institutional development? Again, Inga III serves as an instructive example. As a condition of receiving an IDA grant for project preparation studies in 2014, the DRC Government was asked by the World Bank to adopt a key element of improved project governance. By 2015, the government agreed to create a ring-fenced development authority (*Agence pour le Développement la Promotion d'Inga*—ADEPI) to manage Inga III's development, and mobilize private participation and public financing. ADEPI was supposed to be created by law as an autonomous entity reporting to the Prime Minister's office. It was to have a board of directors representing various Inga development stakeholders. All ADEPI staff members, including the director, were supposed to be recruited competitively. In other words, ADEPI was expected to act as a kind of independent PPP unit specifically for the Inga project, combining financial resources and expertise to ensure that responsible best practice was followed in the development of the project.

The grant was made, but the government evidently did not feel compelled to meet these obligations. On September 12, 2016, the World Bank (2016b) cancelled its grant support to Inga III. The activity had already been suspended in July due to the government's decision to "take the project in a different strategic direction" to that agreed with the Bank in 2014. At the time of suspension, only 6 per cent of total preparation financing had been disbursed; most of the studies had not been completed, and many had not been started. ADEPI had not been established as an autonomous entity (World Bank, 2016a). In late 2015, President Kabila moved ADEPI into his cabinet and took personal control of the project. But this meant that the independent PPP unit functions would be lost and some of the key environmental and social studies probably would not be completed. The lesson here also seems clear: governments without a recent history of legal, regulatory, and institutional reforms are unlikely to make rapid, significant progress in these areas during the course of a single large project.

Are there ways of increasing the chances that transformational PPPs will be successful? There are very few examples of successful PPPs of transformational scale, but Ansar et al. (2016) make recommendations regarding ways of avoiding problems with megaprojects, which apply equally well to large PPPs: (i) be skeptical of the numbers presented at appraisal; (ii) seek to de-bias estimates of time to task completion, costs, and benefits by demanding more extreme stress tests; and (iii) look for evidence of meaningful cost–benefit analysis as part of appraisal.

A second way to avoid problems with transformational PPPs is to do smaller PPPs instead. This is particularly the case when transformational PPPs involve massive capital investments based on razor-thin profit margins. When possible, projects of this kind need to be broken down into smaller projects. In the case of projects like Inga III, this suggestion is more practical than it may sound. Since the last wave of work on Inga III began in the late 2000s, a change in thinking about investment in renewable power generation has occurred in Africa, thanks mainly to South Africa's Renewable Energy IPP Procurement Program (REIPPPP). Over four rounds of bidding between 2012 and 2015, South Africa's program attracted US$19 billion in private investment in 92 on-grid IPP projects, totaling 6,327 MW, with wind and solar PV prices among the lowest in the world (Eberhard, Kolker, and Leigland, 2014). Instead of being primarily about climate change mitigation, or off-grid service in rural areas, REIPPPP has shown how quickly renewable energy can add generating capacity to power grids, as compared with large hydropower or coal-fired plants. Construction times for these solar projects are typically under 12 months per facility. In other words, by 2018, South Africa will have 32 per cent more generating capacity in place than Inga III is expected to provide after ten years of construction.[3] (For more on REIPPPP, see Chapter 9.)

[3] Wind and solar power are much more variable than hydropower, and cannot provide the base load capacity that most developing countries need. Thus, this comparison between large hydropower and wind and solar is somewhat misleading. But when combined with small hydropower plants or gas-based generation, wind and solar could dramatically reduce the need for a massive hydropower investment in a country like DRC, especially if the primary objective is increasing energy access for the largely rural population.

2.9 Conclusions

The evidence presented by the studies reviewed in this chapter suggests that in most respects PPPs have not met expectations in developing countries, especially in low-income countries. The use of PPPs has never become as prevalent as expected in the 1990s, and this fact likely reflects the shortcomings of the mechanism in terms of higher than expected operating costs and lower than expected profits, expensive preparation costs, the struggle to attract commercial finance while generating benefits for poor households, as well as institutional and political problems that limit sustainability.

The evidence suggests that some PPPs have been successful, and in general PPPs are not likely to disappear. The development community continues to learn lessons about how to adjust for PPP shortcomings and to establish conditions under which PPPs are likely to provide VFM. But most of this involves blending commercial finance with different kinds of non-commercial finance, as the PPP mechanism moves further away from its original concept of pure private participation. PPPs can be expected to continue experiencing the sort of surges in popularity described by Klein, followed by waves of disappointment and declining popularity. In light of the PPP shortcomings documented in this chapter, it seems likely that the G20's recent promotion of "transformational" PPPs as mechanisms for dealing effectively with infrastructure challenges in low-income countries will lead to disappointment. In fact, Klein's description of the ebb and flow of PPP popularity is likely to be evident at the international level as well, with regard to transformational PPPs.

Chapter 3 presents a case study of the Maputo toll road concession, the first cross-border project in SSA with a legitimate claim to being a "transformational" toll road PPP. The 1997 project is widely judged to have been a success, but the project illustrates some of the reasons why such PPPs are unlikely to play a major role in the future development of the region. The project remains the first—and only—PPP of its kind in Africa.

References

African Union Commission. 2012. *Program for Infrastructure Development in Africa: Interconnecting, integrating and transforming a continent.* Africa Union Commission (AUC), African Development Bank (AfDB), UN Economic Commission for Africa (UNECA), NEPAD Planning and Coordinating Agency (NPCA) (January). Accessed at: https://www.afdb.org/en/topics-and-sectors/initiativespartnerships/programme-for-infrastructure-development-in-africa-pida/.

Alcazar, L., M.A. Abdala, M.M. Shirley. 2000. "The Buenos Aires Water Concession." Policy Research Working Paper No. 2311. Washington, DC: World Bank.

Andrés, L., J. Schwartz, L. Guasch. 2013. *Uncovering the Drivers of Utility Performance: Lessons from Latin America and the Caribbean on the Role of the Private Sector, Regulation, and Governance in the Power, Water, and Telecommunication Sectors.* Washington, DC: World Bank.

Ansar, A., B. Flyvbjerg, A. Budzier, D. Lunn. 2016. "Big Is Fragile: An Attempt at Theorizing Scale." In *the Oxford Handbook of Megaproject Management*, edited by Bent Flyvbjerg, Oxford: Oxford University Press.

Asia-Pacific Economic Cooperation (APEC). 2008. "Joint Ministerial Statement: 2008." 15th Finance Ministers' Meeting, Trujillo, Peru, 5–6 November.

Bain, R. 2009. "Error and Optimism Bias in Toll Road Traffic Forecasts." *Transportation* 36 (5): 469–82.

Bhattacharya, A., M. Romani, N. Stern. 2012. "Infrastructure for Development: Meeting the Challenge." Policy paper sponsored by The Centre for Climate Change Economics and Policy, the Grantham Research Institute on Climate Change and the Environment, in collaboration with the Intergovernmental Group of Twenty-Four on International Monetary Affairs and Development (G-24) (June). Accessed at: http://www.lse.ac.uk/GranthamInstitute/wp-content/uploads/2014/03/PPinfrastructure-for-development-meeting-the-challenge.pdf.

Blanc-Brude, F., H. Goldsmith, T. Välilä. 2006. *Ex Ante Construction Costs in the European Road Sector: A Comparison of Public–Private Partnerships and Traditional Public Procurement*. Luxembourg: European Investment Bank.

BNP Paribas. 2009. "Preliminary Financial Feasibility Study—Project Inga 3." Unpublished report prepared for the World Bank and PPIAF, December.

Boardman, A., M. Hellowell. 2016. "A Comparative Analysis and Evaluation of Specialist PPP Units' Methodologies for Conducting Value for Money Appraisals." *Journal of Comparative Policy Analysis: Research and Practice* 19(3): 191–206.

Bretton Woods Project. 2017. "CSOs Call on World bank to Halt its Aggressive Support of PPPs." December 6. Accessed at: https://www.brettonwoodsproject.org/2017/12/csos-call-world-bank-halt-aggressive-support-ppps/

Burger, P., I. Hawkesworth. 2011. "How to Attain Value for Money: Comparing PPP and Traditional Infrastructure Public Procurement." *OECD Journal on Budgeting* 2011(1): 1–56. Accessed at: https://www.oecd.org/gov/budgeting/49070709.pdf.

Castalia Strategic Advisors. 2007. "Key Challenges to Public Private Partnerships in South Africa: Summary of Interview Findings." Report to the Support Programme for Accelerated Infrastructure Development (SPAID), jointly sponsored by the Presidency of the Republic of South Africa and the Business Trust, Pretoria, April.

Castalia Strategic Advisors. 2010. "School PPPs in New Zealand: Will PPPs Provide Value for Money as a Method of Procuring Schools in New Zealand? Working Paper No. 2: Cost Benefit Analysis." Report to the Australian Department of Education and Training, Canberra.

Cambridge Economic Policy Associates. 2012. *Infrastructure Consortium for Africa (ICA) Assessment of Project Preparation Facilities for Africa*. Report to the ICA Secretariat, in Association with Nodalis Conseil, London, September.

Chan, A.P.C., P.T.I. Lam, D.W.M. Chan, E. Cheung, Y. Ke. 2010. "Critical Success Factors for PPPs in Infrastructure Developments: Chinese Perspective." *Journal of Construction Engineering and Management* 136 (5): 484–94.

Chao, J. 2016. *How are PPPs Really Financed?* Washington, DC: World Bank. Accessed at: http://blogs.worldbank.org/ppps/how-are-ppps-really-financed.

Chao, J., D. Saha. 2016. *Sources of Financing for PPP Investments 2015*. Washington DC: World Bank. Accessed at: https://ppi.worldbank.org/~/media/GIAWB/PPI/Documents/Data-Notes/2015-PPP-Investments-Sources.pdf.

De Schepper, S., E. Haeqendonck, M. Dooms. 2015. "Understanding Pre-Contractual Transaction Costs for Public-Private Partnership Infrastructure Projects." *International Journal of Project Management* 33 (4): 932–46. Accessed at: www.sciencedirect.com.

Dudkin, G., T. Valila. 2005. *Transaction Costs in Public-Private Partnerships: A First Look at the Evidence*. Luxembourg: EIB.

Eberhard, A., K. Gratwick. 2010. *IPPs in Sub-Saharan Africa: Determinants of Success. Management Programme in Infrastructure Reform and Regulation*. Cape Town: University of Cape Town, Graduate School of Business.

Eberhard, A, K. Gratwick, E. Morella, P. Antman. 2016. *Independent Power Projects in Sub-Saharan Africa: Lessons from Five Key Countries*. Washington, DC: World Bank.

Eberhard, A, J. Kolker, J. Leigland. 2014. *South Africa's Renewable Energy IPP Program: Success Factors and Lessons*. Washington, DC: World Bank. Accessed at: www.ppiaf.org.

Engel, E., R. Fischer, A. Galetovic. 2014. *The Economics of Public-Private Partnerships: A Basic Guide*. Cambridge: Cambridge University Press.

Estache, A., C. Philippe. 2012. "The Impact of Private Participation in Infrastructure in Developing Countries: Taking Stock of about 20 Years of Experience." ECARES Working Paper, 2012–043, Universite Libre de Bruxelles, Brussels.

Estache, A., M. Rossi. 2004. "Have Consumers Benefited from the Reforms in the Electricity Distribution Sector in Latin America?" Policy Research Working Paper No. 3420. Washington, DC: World Bank.

European PPP Expertise Centre. 2014. *Establishing and Reforming PPP Units: Analysis of EPEC Member PPP Units and Lessons Learnt*. Luxembourg: European Investment Bank.

Farajian, M. 2010. "Transaction Cost Model for Infrastructure Public Private Partnerships in the U.S." Master's Thesis, University of Maryland, Graduate School of Engineering, College Park.

Farquharson, E., J. Encinas. 2010. *The UK Treasury Infrastructure Finance Unit: Supporting PPP Financing During the Global Liquidity Crisis*. Washington DC: World Bank (March).

Flyvbjerg, B. 2005. "Policy and Planning for Large Infrastructure Projects: Problems, Causes, Cures." Policy Research Working Paper No. 3781. Washington, DC: World Bank.

Flyvbjerg, B. 2014. “What You Should Know about Megaprojects and Why: An Overview.” *Project Management Journal* 45 (2): 6–19.

Foster, V., C.M. Briceno-Garmendia. 2010. *Africa's Infrastructure: A Time for Transformation*. Washington, DC: World Bank.

G20 Multilateral Development Bank, Working Group on Infrastructure. 2011. “Infrastructure Action Plan: Submission to the G20 by the MDB Working Group on Infrastructure.” Washington, DC: World Bank. Accessed at: http://documents.worldbank.org/curated/en/828751468331900533/pdf/655610BR0v10Se0Official0Use0Only090.pdf.

Gassner, K., A. Popov, N. Pushak. 2009. *Does Private Participation Improve Performance in Electricity and Water Distribution? Trends and Policy Options No. 6*. Washington, DC: World Bank. Accessed at: www.ppiaf.org.

Government Technical Advisory Centre. 2015. *Government Technical Advisory Centre and National Treasury Programme 8: Technical Support and Development Finance, Annual Report 2014/15*. Pretoria: South African National Treasury. Accessed at: http://www.gtac.gov.za.

Guasch, J.L. 2004. *Granting and Renegotiating Infrastructure Concessions: Doing It Right*. Washington DC: World Bank.

Guasch, J.L. 2014. *World Bank Group Support to Public-Private Partnerships: Lessons from Experience in Client Countries, FY02–12*. Washington, DC: World Bank.

Independent Evaluation Group. 2010. *Cost-Benefit Analysis in World Bank Projects*. Washington, DC: World Bank (June).

International Energy Agency. 2011. *Energy for All, Special Early Excerpt of the World Energy Outlook 2011*. Paris: IEA. Accessed at: https://www.iea.org/publications/freepublications/publication/weo2011_energy_for_all.pdf.

International Energy Agency. 2017. *Renewable Energy Auctions: Analysing 2016*. Paris: IEA. Accessed at: http://www.irena.org/publications/2017/Jun/Renewable-Energy-Auctions-Analysing-2016.

International Finance Corporation (IFC). 2012. “Blended Finance at IFC: IFC's Approach to Blending Concessional Funds.” Report prepared for the IFC Board of Directors, IFC, Washington, DC, March 15.

International Monetary Fund (IMF). 2006. *Determinants of Public-Private Partnerships in Infrastructure*. IMF Working Paper, IMF Institute. Washington, DC: IMF Institute.

International Monetary Fund (IMF). 2015. *“Democratic Republic of the Congo: Staff Report for the 2015 Article IV Consultation – Debt Sustainability Analysis.”* Washington, DC: IMF. Accessed at: https://www.imf.org/external/pubs/ft/dsa/pdf/2015/dsacr15280.pdf

Izaguirre, A.K. 2009. “Impact of the Financial Crisis on the Closure of New Infrastructure Projects with Private Participation: A Preliminary Assessment as of January 2009.” Presentation to the Finance, Economics, and Urban (FEU) Department of the World Bank, Washington, DC, March 30.

Jomo, K.S., A. Chowdhury, K. Sharma, D. Platz. 2016. “Public-Private Partnerships and the 2030 Agenda for Sustainable Development: Fit for Purpose?” UN Department of Economic & Social Affairs, Working Paper No. 148ST/ESA/2016/DWP/148, United Nations, New York.

Jones, L., U. Jammal, N. Gokgur. 2002. "Impact of Privatization in Cote D'Ivoire." Report Prepared by the Boston Institute for Developing Economies (BIDE) for Privatization Committee, Boston, July 15.

Klein, M. 2015. "Public–Private Partnerships: Promise and Hype." Policy Research Working Paper No. 7340. Washington, DC: World Bank.

Lemma, A. 2013. "Literature Review: Evaluating the Costs and Benefits of Centralised PPP Units." Overseas Development Institute, Economic and Private Sector PEAKS, April. Accessed at: https://assets.publishing.service.gov.uk/media/57a08a49e5274a31e0000510/Evaluating_the_Costs_and_Benefits_of_Centralised_PPP_Units_24.pdf

Leigland, J. 2018. "Public–Private Partnerships in Developing Countries: The Emerging Evidence-based Critique." *The World Bank Research Observer* 33(2): 103–34.

Leigland, J., C. Shugart. 2006. "Is the Public Sector Comparator Right for Developing Countries?" Gridline No. 37, Public-Private Infrastructure Advisory Facility (PPIAF). Washington, DC: World Bank.

Levinsohn, D., D. Reardon. 2007. "Municipal PPP Projects in South Africa: Obstacles and Opportunities." IP3 Public–Private Partnership Information Series, Washington, DC.

Lin, J.Y., D. Doemeland. 2012. "Beyond Keynesianism: Global Infrastructure Investments in Times of Crisis." Policy Research Working Paper 5940. Washington, DC: World Bank.

Marin, P. 2009. "Public-Private Partnerships for Urban Water Utilities: A Review of Experiences in Developing Countries." PPIAF Trends and Policy Options Series No. 8, Washington, DC: World Bank. Accessed at: www.ppiaf.org.

Organisation for Economic Co-operation and Development (OECD). 2008. *Public-Private Partnerships: In Pursuit of Risk Sharing and Value for Money*. Paris: OECD Publishing.

Organisation for Economic Co-operation and Development (OECD). 2010. *Dedicated Public Private Partnership Units: Survey of Institutional and Governance Structure*. Paris: OECD Publishing.

Perelman, S., T. Serebrisky. 2012. "Measuring the Technical Efficiency of Airports in Latin America." *Utilities Policy* 22: 1–7 (September).

Pozzo di Borgo, P., A. Labeau, R. Eskinazi, J. Dehornoy, A. Parte, M. Ameziane. 2006. "Sub-Saharan Africa: Review of Selected Railway Concessions." Africa Transport Sector Report No. 36491. Washington, DC: World Bank.

Public–Private Infrastructure Advisory Facility. 2007. *Public–Private Partnership Units: Lessons for their Design and Use in Infrastructure*. Washington, DC: World Bank. Accessed at: www.ppiaf.org.

Public–Private Infrastructure Advisory Facility. 2014. *Unsolicited Proposals—An Exception to Public Initiation of Infrastructure PPPs: An Analysis of Global Trends and Lessons Learned*. Washington, DC: World Bank. Accessed at: www.ppiaf.org.

Republic of Sierra Leone. 2015. *Bidding Documents for a Management Contractor for Electricity Distribution and Supply Authority*. Freetown: Ministry of Energy.

Ruiz-Nunez, F. 2016. *PPI Investments in IDA Countries, 2011 to 2015*. Washington, DC: World Bank. Accessed at: https://ppi.worldbank.org/~/media/GIAWB/PPI/Documents/Data-Notes/PPI-in-IDACountries-2011–2015.pdf.

Sachs, J.D. 2006. *The End of Poverty: Economic Possibilities for Our Time*. New York: Penguin.

Shaoul, J. 2008. "Market Based Reforms in the Provision and Financing of Healthcare in the UK." *Kurswechel* 2: 47–57.

Sirtaine, S., M.E. Pinglo, J.L. Guasch, V. Foster. 2004. *How Profitable are Infrastructure Concessions in Latin America? Empirical Evidence and Regulatory Implications*. Washington, DC: World Bank. Accessed at: www.ppiaf.org.

UK Audit Commission. 2003. *PFI in Schools*. London: UK Audit Commission.

UK National Audit Office. 2015. "The Choice of Finance for Capital Investment." Briefing by the National Audit Office, HM Treasury, NAO Communications, London. Accessed at: https://www.nao.org.uk/wp-content/uploads/2015/03/The-choice-of-finance-for-capital-investment.pdf.

United Nations. 2007. *Guidebook on Promoting Good Governance in Public–Private Partnerships*. New York: United Nations.

United Nations Conference on Trade and Development (UNCTAD). 2014. *World Investment Report 2014: Investing in the SDGs: An Action Plan*. New York: United Nations.

van den Berg, C. 2000. "Water Concessions: Who Wins, Who Loses, and What to Do about It." Note No. 217, Private Infrastructure Notes. Washington, DC: World Bank.

Vassallo, J.M. 2007. "Why Traffic Forecasts in PPP Contracts are Often Overestimated?" *EIB University Research Sponsorship Programme*. Luxembourg: EIB.

World Bank. 2011. *Transformation Through Infrastructure: World Bank Group Infrastructure Strategy Update FY12-15*. Washington, DC: World Bank.

World Bank. 2014. "Project Appraisal Document on a Proposed Grant in the Amount of SDR 47.7 Million (US$ 73.1 Million Equivalent) to the Democratic Republic of Congo for an INGA 3 Basse Chute and Mid-Size Hydropower Development Technical Assistance Project." Report No. 77420-ZR, Washington, DC: World Bank.

World Bank. 2016a. *The World Bank Implementation Status & Results Report: DRC Inga 3 and Mid-Size Hydropower Development TA (P131027)*. Washington, DC: World Bank.

World Bank. 2016b. *World Bank Group Suspends Financing to the Inga-3 Basse Chute Technical Assistance Project*. Washington, DC: World Bank. Accessed at: http://www.worldbank.org/en/news/pressrelease/2016/07/25/world-bank-group-suspends-financing-to-the-inga-3-basse-chute-technicalassistance-project.

World Bank. 2018. PPI Project Database. Accessed at: http://ppi.worldbank.org/customquery?mode=1

World Bank Institute and Public–Private Infrastructure Advisory Facility. 2013. "Value-for-Money Analysis—Practices and Challenges: How Governments Choose

When to Use PPP to Deliver Public Infrastructure and Services." Report from World Bank Global Round-Table, 28 May, 2013, World Bank, Washington DC. Accessed at: www.ppiaf.org.

Worldfolio. 2016. "'Coherence & Efficiency' Define New Energy Approach: Interview with Bruno Kapandji Kalala, Project Director for the Grand Inga Development and Promotion Agency (ADPI)." *Worldfolio*, September 20. Accessed at: http://www.theworldfolio.com/interviews/coherence-efficiency-define-new-energy-approach/4178/

Zhang, X., M. Kumaraswamy. 2001. "Procurement Protocols for Public–Private Partnered Projects." *Journal of Construction Engineering and Management* 127 (5): 351–8.

Zitron, J. 2006. "Public–Private Partnership Projects: Towards a Model of Contractor Bidding Decision-Making." *Journal of Purchasing and Supply Management* 12 (2): 53–62.

3

Case Study

Maputo Toll Road—SSA's First "Transformational" Transport PPP

3.1 Introduction

The 2010 G20 summit in Seoul identified infrastructure as a key element of the international development agenda. Since that time the G20 has elaborated on the need for a huge scale-up in infrastructure investment in developing countries, particularly through large regional or cross-border projects involving private sector participation. In 2017, the G20 agreed on a "G20 Compact with Africa," the aim of which was to help meet the G20 commitment "to address key constraints to regional projects and PPPs [public–private partnerships] for transformational infrastructure projects in low income environments" (World Bank, 2017, 25).

Chapter 2 attempted to assess the G20's enthusiasm for regional or "transformational" PPP projects in light of the emerging evidence-based critique of PPPs. Using the trouble-prone Inga III hydropower project in the Democratic Republic of the Congo (DRC) as an example, the discussion concluded that "transformational" PPPs are unlikely to be any more successful than smaller and simpler PPP projects, especially in terms of costs, profits, finance, investment, equity, efficiency, and governance. If that is the case, what accounts for the confidence on the part of the G20 and other international organizations that such projects would meet expectations?

Part of the reason for the G20's enthusiasm for large cross-border infrastructure projects is that such projects have long been considered priorities by individual African governments as well as African regional political bodies, like the African Union (AU) and various Regional Economic Communities (RECs). The continent includes many landlocked countries as well as countries that are too small and poor to be able to finance adequate power and transport infrastructure without the collaboration of neighbors. A central pillar of the AU's "Agenda 2063" is their Program for Infrastructure Development in Africa (PIDA), developed in collaboration with the New Program for Africa's Development (NEPAD). PIDA produced a Priority Action Plan (PAP) of regional investment projects that was endorsed by the African heads of state in January 2012. An ongoing program of PIDA activities now exists, supported by a website and project database. As of

Public–Private Partnerships in Sub-Saharan Africa: The Evidence-Based Critique. James Leigland, Oxford University Press (2020). © James Leigland.
DOI: 10.1093/oso/9780198861829.001.0001

2018, the PIDA website identified 433 "large cross-border infrastructure projects," 95 per cent of which were in energy or transport sectors (NEPAD et al., 2018). The AU's Agenda 2063 has been recognized by the G20 as "the starting point" for its Compact with Africa (World Bank, 2017).

In a developing country region like Sub-Saharan Africa (SSA), there is very little experience with regional infrastructure PPP projects. The World Bank's PPI Project Database has recorded only seven regional (cross-border) infrastructure projects in SSA since 2000; five have been transport projects and two have been natural gas transmission projects (World Bank, 2018). However, it would be misleading to assume that large regional projects are easier to do in other regions. Since 1992, the PPI Project Database has recorded only 15 cross-border projects in all developing countries, in any infrastructure sector (World Bank, 2018).

One source of inspiration regarding the possibility of successfully developing regional infrastructure PPPs is the fact that at least some projects have been completed. These projects have been repeatedly studied to generate lessons that can be used to facilitate more regional infrastructure PPPs in the future (World Bank, 2014). One cross-border toll road appears on this list. In 1997, a 30-year concession was awarded to a private company to upgrade, construct, operate, and maintain a toll road linking South Africa's industrialized, but effectively landlocked, northern and eastern regions (Gauteng and Mpumalanga provinces) to the Mozambican port of Maputo. At the time the contract was signed, it was estimated to be worth ZAR 3 billion (about US$640 million in 1997 values).

The "Maputo toll road," also referred to as the "N4 toll road" using the South African highway designation, is now generally considered to be a pioneering project. It was SSA's first toll road concession and the first cross-border transport PPP. At the time, it was the largest limited recourse project finance deal in Southern Africa (Farlam, 2005). The project was also expected to lead the way for future regional development. Industrial and commercial projects were expected to follow along the 600 km corridor, now known as the Maputo Development Corridor (MDC). PPPs were anticipated for rail transport, port facilities, and social infrastructure. The toll road and the MDC were also expected to become models for similar developments across the continent—the kinds of transformational cross-border projects now frequently discussed in G20 meetings.

But after two decades of work by donors, DFIs, MDBs, African governments, regional political bodies, and private sector investors and operators, the success of the Maputo toll road has not been replicated. It remains the only cross-border toll road concession in SSA. Most of the other SSA economic corridors identified by the AU and NEPAD remain largely undeveloped. After the signing of the toll road concession contract, enthusiasm quickly diminished for the other PPPs expected along the corridor. Some reached financial closure, like the Maputo port concession and the Nelspruit water concession, but only after long delays and much controversy.

In order to better understand the lessons offered by the Maputo toll road concession, this chapter first conducts a short historical review of SSA's intense focus on regional infrastructure. This review covers efforts over the last 20 years to develop cross-border infrastructure PPPs, and the challenges faced by those efforts. Next, the ways in which the toll road met those challenges are explained. A concluding section of this chapter discusses the policy implications of the Maputo toll road experience by trying to identify which of its success factors are applicable today to other cross-border transport PPPs.

3.2 Cross-Border Infrastructure Projects in SSA: The Historical Background

The Maputo toll road concession was developed against a backdrop of growing regional concern about cross-border infrastructure in SSA.[1] Regional integration had already been a high priority in Africa for many years and had spawned a complex network of organizations designed to work across borders on important issues. These organizations include RECs, power pools, transport corridor authorities, river basin authorities, as well as continent-wide bodies like the AU and NEPAD (later integrated into the AU and renamed the NEPAD Planning and Coordinating Agency, or NPCA). A series of high-profile efforts had been undertaken in SSA by these entities since the end of the 1990s to identify, develop, and implement regional infrastructure projects. In 2002 NEPAD published its Infrastructure Short-Term Action Plan (STAP), which identified 40 regional investment projects. By the time of the final STAP evaluation in 2010, 18 of these projects were classified under the heading of regional transport (NEPAD, 2010).

But progress on the STAP projects was consistently disappointing over the years. A considerable number of STAP projects were abandoned as unsuccessful or simply stopped making progress. The different evaluations of STAP progress, from 2002 to 2010, highlighted a number of key problems affecting the implementation of cross-border projects. One problem was that most of the projects had been prioritized by RECs, and were selected for political reasons, with little attention to whether or not public or private financiers considered them to be viable. Often, project proposals were backed only by out-of-date engineering studies and involved no additional analysis or preparation.

[1] The following sections of this chapter are adapted from the author's contribution to an original work by The World Bank (2014). Responsibility for the views and opinions expressed in the adaption rests solely with the author and views are not endorsed by The World Bank. Also, see Leigland (2012).

A second problem was the general reluctance of national governments to support regional projects. In many cases, this reluctance arose from security concerns. In other cases, national officials felt that regional planning bodies lacked expertise in project finance, or even the ability to coordinate and monitor project progress. The final STAP evaluation found almost no information on many of the projects and even had trouble locating an official list of projects after all of the additions, deletions, and amendments since 2002 (NEPAD, 2010).

In an effort to upgrade and extend STAP, the AU, in association with NEPAD, launched the PIDA in 2010. PIDA represented a vastly better-resourced attempt to identify and prioritize regional infrastructure projects across Africa, as well as address the many challenges associated with them. The original TOR for the PIDA study emphasized the importance of the private sector for the achievement of PIDA objectives: "it should be noted that an explicit aim of PIDA is the mobilization of private sector participation in infrastructure development" (NEPAD et al., 2009, 6).

But it is still not clear how much of an improvement PIDA is compared with STAP, other than its longer list of projects and an interactive website with frequently updated information on project status. The quality of the background analysis is difficult to judge. The African heads of state approved PIDA plans in January 2012, based on a 70-page "study synthesis" and list of projects (NEPAD et al., 2011). But the details of PIDA's long-term economic forecasts and its sectoral studies—thousands of pages of analysis prepared by French consulting firm SOFRECO—have never been made publicly available, despite the fact that most of the funding for PIDA came from the UK's Department for International Development (DFID). All of the released PIDA documents stress the importance of using PPPs to make possible regional infrastructure development. But the final published reports offer no details on how PPPs will be used or what challenges must be overcome to do so.

3.3 The Toll Road Concession Structure

The Maputo toll road concession contract was awarded in 1997 to the Trans Africa Concessions consortium (TRAC), a special-purpose corporate entity created by three construction companies. The concessionaire was required to upgrade, construct, operate, and maintain the toll road for 30 years before returning control to the governments. About 380 km of road covered by the contract was already operational in South Africa, but required rehabilitation and maintenance. On the Mozambican side of the border, about 50 km of new road needed to be built, plus an additional 40 km of existing road needed maintenance.

The toll road concession is usually referred to as a build, operate, transfer (BOT) project (UNDP, 2008; PPIAF, 2009). But that term does not accurately classify this project. "BOT" normally refers to a "greenfield" project involving the construction and operation of new assets. In contrast, the Maputo concession is actually an example of a "brownfield" project, usually referred to as a "build, rehabilitate, operate, transfer" (BROT) project (World Bank, 2018). A BROT project involves private operation, maintenance, and rehabilitation of existing road assets, owned and normally operated by government (TRAC owns only the equipment used in the project). TRAC must recoup its investment and make a profit from toll revenue collected at six toll stations over the 30-year term of the contract. Figure 3.1 displays the overall structure of the Maputo toll road BROT.

3.4 How the Maputo Toll Road Met Key Challenges

There is no single body of research that focuses on cross-border toll road concessions. But there is quite a large number of studies that approach this topic from different disciplinary perspectives. A growing body of research looks at the effects of large size on the accuracy of project demand projections and the overall fragility of infrastructure projects (Flyvbjerg, 2005, 2014; Ansar et al., 2016). Credit rating agencies have published reports explaining their analytical approaches to credit ratings of large infrastructure projects (Fitch Ratings, 2009). The complexities and risks associated with large or cross-border rail projects have been the subjects of study by academicians and government auditors (UKNAO, 2014; Dimitriou and Sartzetaki, 2016). Lessons learned from cross-border projects in regions where they have been used more frequently than in SSA have been discussed in several studies (Fujimura and Adhikari, 2010; Verougstraete, 2017). Multilateral development banks have produced "tool kits" for structuring cross-border infrastructure PPPs (ADB, 2007).

The subsections that follow discuss the key challenges to the successful implementation of cross-border toll road concessions and the ways in which South Africa and Mozambique dealt with those challenges in order to complete the Maputo toll road project. In most cases the challenges were successfully met, at least in the short term. But, in almost every case, the measures for addressing the challenges were themselves plagued by shortcomings, sometimes leading to longer-term problems.

3.4.1 Political Challenges

As was apparent in STAP evaluations, a major long-term challenge for cross-border infrastructure projects in SSA has been the lack of coordinated country ownership of and support for cross-border projects (NEPAD, 2010). The high sensitivity of such projects to geopolitics is cited by a number of studies as creating project risks that are particularly difficult to manage (Fitch Ratings, 2009; Fujimura and

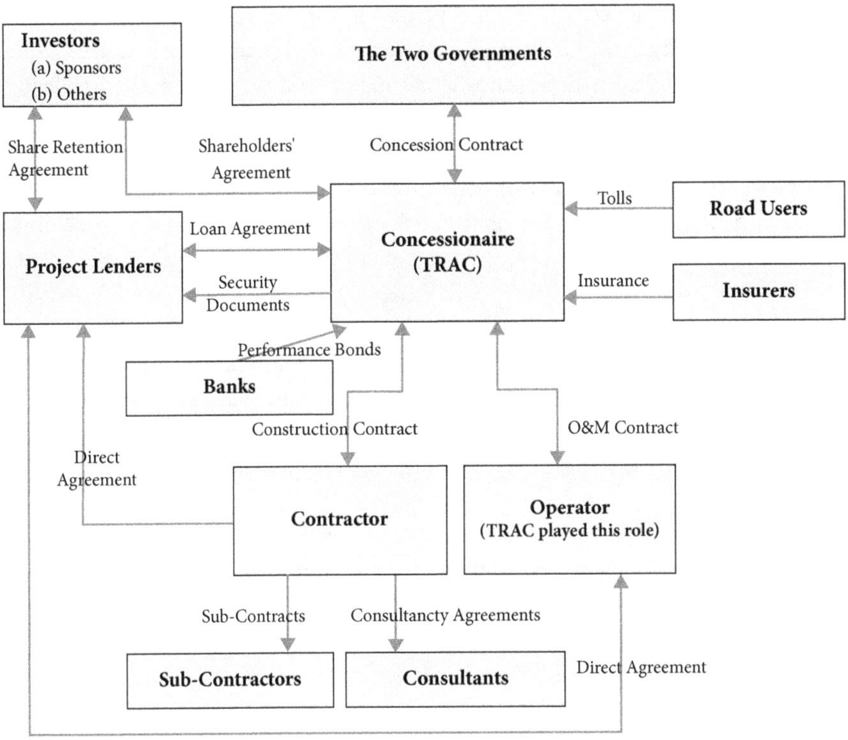

Figure 3.1 Maputo Toll Road BROT Project Structure
Source: Compiled by the author based on South African National Treasury, 2001.

Adhikari, 2010; Dimitriou and Sartzetaki, 2016). The fact that several levels of participating governments are often involved in planning and coordinating cross-border infrastructure adds to the project complexities caused by multiple constituencies (ADB, 2007).

The toll road project met this challenge with an unusual degree of high-level political support for the toll road and the MDC, of which the road was a central part.

- High-level support for the project included a who's who of South Africa's African National Congress (ANC) political elite, led by President Nelson Mandela. Mandela had long considered the Mozambique Liberation Front (FRELIMO) to be a strong ally of the ANC in its struggle against apartheid. Nothing better demonstrates the new government's commitment to the corridor and the toll road than Nelson Mandela's personal appeal to private sector investors at the launch of MDC project activities in Maputo in 1996 (Mandela, 1996).
- South Africa's newly elected ANC-led government was eager to demonstrate developmental successes, but lacked the budgets to do so immediately. To

enlist the private sector to the government's cause, senior government officials were eager to show the private sector that it had nothing to fear from the new political regime—the "white flight" and property market collapse that followed independence in Zimbabwe in 1980 were still vivid memories in the minds of many South Africans.

- Since the 1800s, the corridor between the Maputo port and the industries of South Africa's Gauteng Province had been an active trade and transport link between the two countries. The route from Gauteng to Maputo was shorter than the route south to the South African port of Durban, so Maputo port had long been the logical overseas disembarkation point for South African export industries. In the mid-1990s, the two countries were in effect trying to re-establish this link, which had made economic sense since the industrialization of Gauteng started in the 1800s, but had been disrupted by politics and war in the mid-twentieth century.

Not all officials of the new South African government were enthusiastic about working with the private sector. In the case of the toll road, the collaboration was viewed as an arrangement of convenience driven not by institutionalized policy, but by top-level ANC personalities in search of pragmatic solutions to the problematic legacies of apartheid. When it handed over power in 1994, the apartheid government left behind very little in terms of government resources required for badly needed infrastructure investment. The apartheid government's budget deficit increased dramatically in the early 1990s. During its last year in office, the apartheid government increased the country's national debt by almost one-third (Taylor, 2000). By 1997, unmet investment needs in the country's road sector totaled nearly R5 billion—about US$1.1 billion at the time (Taylor, 2000).

Mozambique's involvement in the toll road reflected another radical change in political direction in southern Africa, signaled by the appearance of the Mozambican president, Joaquim Chissano, alongside Nelson Mandela at the Maputo Corridor investors' conference in 1996. Mozambique's ruling party, FRELIMO, led the country as a one-party Marxist state from the country's independence in 1975 through a protracted civil war finally ending in 1992. After the conflict ended and the Soviet Union collapsed, FRELIMO allowed multiparty elections in 1994 and began to replace its version of socialism with a market economy. Chissano drove the reforms, which included the privatization of hundreds of state-owned companies and the removal of price controls. But enthusiasm for private participation in government service provision was not universally shared among Mozambican politicians or government bureaucrats.

The Maputo toll road concession demonstrates the value of high-level political support for such a project, but also the fragility of such support when it derives mostly from personalities and short-term pragmatism rather than some form of institutionalized policy commitment. After South Africa's 1999 national elections, most of the South African politicians who had strongly supported the toll road and the MDC had retired or taken new positions in the private sector or other government ministries or agencies.

The enthusiastic official acceptance of a major role for the private sector in the Maputo Corridor had not been widely shared by all influential government officials in the two countries or by a new generation of politicians moving into ANC leadership positions. When high-level political supporters of the project moved on, resistance to private participation began to manifest itself in a number of significant ways in the development of various other corridor projects. For example, the planned private operating concession for Maputo port was delayed for years by resistance of the Mozambican Ports and Railway Company (CFM) to the possibility of worker retrenchments by a private operator. The World Bank offered funding for retrenchment packages, but the delay persisted. Eventually, a 15-year concession for the port was signed in mid-2003.

There was never any strong South African government interest in fulfilling plans for a private rail concession along the MDC. South Africa's state-owned transport company, Transnet, demanded that its own rail subsidiary, Spoornet, handle renovation and operation of a cross-border rail line rather than a private company. A cross-border arrangement was concluded in principle after years of negotiations, but collapsed immediately as Spoornet could not agree on detailed terms with CFM, Spoornet's Mozambican counterpart. Spoornet officials were clearly less than enthusiastic about facilitating Maputo port's ability to compete for business that was benefiting the South African ports of Durban and Richards Bay, both operated by Transnet (Driver and de Barros, 2000).

The development of the MDC was also supposed to include a number of private investments in social infrastructure. The Nelspruit water concession, in Mpumalanga Province near the border with Mozambique, was identified at the Maputo MDC launch as one of the key corridor social projects. But the development of the project moved slowly, giving anti-privatization civil society groups and labor unions time to consolidate and strengthen opposition to the concession. The contract was eventually signed in 1999, but the personality-driven political support for private participation in the corridor's infrastructure had already begun to diminish and the water concession never received an endorsement from the national Department of Water Affairs and Forestry. A year later, the South African Parliament passed legislation making it all but impossible to conclude additional PPPs of this kind for basic infrastructure service delivery (Leigland, 2003). After Nelspruit, no other long-term water concessions of this nature have ever been attempted in South Africa. (For more on the Nelspruit PPP, see Chapter 5.)

3.4.2 Institutional Challenges

Even when participating governments are strongly committed to a cross-border infrastructure project, a host of institutional challenges must be overcome. How are key project design and development decisions to be made when more than one government "owner" is involved? How can differences in institutional and human capacities be overcome, especially in terms of the expertise needed for PPP projects? The importance of planning and coordination for cross-border projects makes necessary institutional and legal-regulatory frameworks that work best if they are formalized (ADB, 2007). Clear intergovernmental agreements, and regional cooperation platforms, are among the recommendations made to deal with these issues (Verougstraete, 2017). Compelling arguments for project benefits and commercial viability are needed to ensure sustained multi-institutional commitment and cooperation (UKNAO, 2014).

An important way in which the project overcame institutional changes was through the leadership of project development by the South African Department of Transport (DOT). The in-house capacity of the DOT team seems to have given the toll road advantages that South African PPPs in other sectors did not have. DOT was the first of South Africa's sectoral ministries to formalize and prioritize the use of PPPs. DOT published a white paper in 1996, which strongly endorsed the use of BOTs like toll roads as mechanisms for addressing "fiscal constraints" (SADOT, 1996). By 1997, the South African Roads Board had prepared an aggressive policy for encouraging unsolicited bids from private companies as a way to increase the use of tolling to pay for the rehabilitation of regional roads (SARB, 1997).

The toll road project team included participation of other South African institutions in addition to DOT, including the Department of Trade and Industry (DTI), the Development Bank of Southern Africa (DBSA), the Industrial Development Corporation (IDC), and the Council for Scientific and Industrial Research (CSIR). DOT engineers also had considerable experience with government-operated toll roads in South Africa. By 1996, five government tolling projects were operational. At 380 km, the total road length involved was relatively small, but DOT engineers used the projects as opportunities to learn how to estimate things like vehicle traffic flows, cost-reflective toll tariffs, and annual growth rates necessary to make long-term private toll roads bankable (Copley and Shaw, 2007).

In 1996, DOT assisted in establishing a technical unit in Mpumalanga province, providing funding for a technical support program at the provincial level. The unit was supposed to assume responsibilities for developing corridor projects prioritized by the two governments. Two additional institutional coordinating mechanisms were also established in 1996 to manage the toll road development process on a binational basis. The first was the Maputo Corridor Company (MCC), designed to represent the two countries along with the private sector in the toll road development process (de Beer, 2011). The second entity was the Implementing Authority (IA), responsible for managing the concession procurement process and designing the contract structure. The two governments recognized that contract negotiations, construction supervision, and project monitoring and evaluation would be best handled by one entity that could act as a single point of contact for the private operator.

Most of these efforts to decentralize the project development process and increase binational project coordination proved to be unsustainable. The envisioned takeover of the project by South African provincial officials never effectively took place because (i) the desire to speed the process along meant that national-level officials were uncomfortable relinquishing control to local officials; (ii) provincial officials lacked the skills and resources to take on these responsibilities; (iii) provincial political support for the corridor progressively weakened as new politicians took over the provincial government; and (iv) with even less capacitated local officials, Mozambique did not establish a similar local unit and maintained a highly centralized approach to corridor activities. This made it more difficult for South African local government officials to act effectively as counterparts (Taylor, 2000; Bek and Taylor, 2001).

Similarly, the two aforementioned binational institutions also could not be sustained for long. Within two years, the two governments concluded that the IA needed to be replaced by two separate national agencies for the administration of the toll road. The problem was that the two governments used different legal and regulatory systems that could not easily be harmonized. Tax regimes were different, as were systems for currency management and company reporting. These differences were underpinned by two fundamentally different legal systems (South Africa's Roman Dutch Law and Mozambique's Portuguese Colonial Law). South Africa created the South African National Road Agency, Ltd. (SANRAL) in 1998. In 1999, Mozambique created a SANRAL counterpart, Administracao Nacional de Estradas (ANE).

The MCC, created in 1997 to represent the interests of public and private corridor stakeholders in both countries, lasted a bit longer than the IA, but never really achieved any of its objectives. It was designed to be a not-for-profit company with shareholding by the public and private sectors, but legal restrictions in Mozambique made the non-profit status of the MCC difficult to achieve and the South African private sector was not enthusiastic about sharing ownership with the governments. A decision was taken in mid-1998 to limit the MCC to a public sector initiative with separate project managers and separate budgets. By 2000, the South African government had become disenchanted with the MCC's lack of accomplishment and in 2001 withdrew its support.

3.4.3 Technical Challenges

Most studies of cross-border transport PPPs identify as a major challenge the high transaction costs needed to deal with the complexity of such projects, because they require extensive preparation and complicated decision making (Dimitriou and Sarzetaki, 2016). The costs of preparing these projects, including feasibility studies, procurement, contract structuring, and negotiation, have hindered such projects in SSA (NEPAD, 2010). The demand forecasting track record of such projects is particularly poor (Flyvbjerg, 2005; Fitch Ratings, 2009). And the larger the project, the more important are program management skills, which are typically in short supply in government environments (UKNAO, 2014). Some experts argue that these kinds of technical challenges cannot be overcome without upfront external support in the form of subsidies (ADB, 2007).

As a way to deal with these kinds of challenges, South Africa's project managers adopted a fast-track, top-down approach to project implementation (Taylor, 2000; Roodt, 2007). The approach was facilitated by the project's high-level political support and the in-house capacity of South Africa's DOT. There were several reasons for adopting this approach. First, the ANC government was keen to achieve project success quickly, to demonstrate that its developmental agenda was beneficial and realistic. Second, both governments also wanted to reduce the overall cost of the project as much as possible because of their own budget constraints. The main reason for doing the project as a PPP was the lack of public money for infrastructure investment. Government officials assumed that one way to cut costs was to require that potential private partners do most of the project preparation work (Alexander et al., 2004). As noted in Chapter 2, this approach was fairly common in the developing world in the early 1990s as PPPs were beginning to achieve popularity (Alcazar et al., 2000; Kotze et al., 2000). Finally, by accelerating the project development process the team hoped to avoid what, in South Africa at the time, could have been crippling ideological debates about the appropriate role of the private sector in the provision of government services.

There is no doubt that DOT's approach did indeed accelerate the project development process. The approach allowed the project to move from bid invitations to financial closure at a relatively fast pace for a project of this size. The invitation to tender for the toll road was issued in March 1996. A preferred bidder was named in December of that year. The concession contract was signed three months later. The fast-track approach also seems to have shortened the construction period for such a project. The construction program was scheduled for 43 months, but was completed in 38 months, excluding a defects liability period.

However, despite its success in accelerating project development, the process led to a variety of other problems that affected the project later during implementation. One problem, admitted by DOT staff, was that bidders were required to do too much of the detailed project design work as part of their bids; the tender documentation did not include enough detail to give bidders more than a general idea of what was needed and how much it would cost (Alexander et al., 2004). And by warning bidders that mistakes in their designs or other errors in preparation would not be compensated for later with tariff increases or contract amendments, the DOT team simply made the resulting contract more fragile. No private operator would accept a major loss on a contract of this kind because of a design error, their own or the government's. Most operators would try to renegotiate the contract. If that failed, they would simply default on the agreement, then take advantage of contract termination clauses usually allowing for various kinds of financial restitution.

Another problem was that detailed proposals were difficult for the government's tender team to comparatively evaluate, due to different design assumptions. The government eventually paid for the development of its own base case for use in comparing and evaluating the private sector bids, something that should have been done in advance of the tendering. One of DBSA's senior engineers estimated that the governments had spent R32 million to prepare what was in effect its own bid for the project. This was in addition to the R50–100 million spent by each of the private bidders on their own proposals (Copley and Shaw, 2007).

The fast-track approach also led to a series of construction problems. In order to speed the construction process, the contractor was allowed to self-certify construction quality. So, decisions regarding the acceptability of the completed work were made by the contractor, and if disputes arose regarding the specifications of completed work they were typically resolved in the contractor's favor. The result of applying all of this on the Maputo toll road project was "poor quality work" in the view of South Africa's National Roads Agency. Although the construction was completed in 38 months, the correction of latent defects took an additional 25 months, far longer than anticipated (Alexander et al., 2004).

Finally, the fast-track approach meant that competitive procurement and stakeholder consultation were sacrificed to the need for speed. DOT used a desk-stop short-listing process to pre-qualify five bidders who were then invited to submit initial bids—in other words, a very limited competition process instead of a fully transparent, publicly competitive tender. Similarly, because of the need to maintain momentum, little or no effort was made to consult with local officials, much less with local residents, about many details of the project, including the toll tariff framework. Most South African and Mozambican local officials had not been involved in preparing the original list of corridor projects offered to the private sector by President Mandela at the Maputo investors' conference in 1996, and reportedly were unhappy about being left out of the process (Mitchell, 1998). Other local officials claimed that national government had denied them access to the final version of the toll road concession contract (Taylor, 2000).

3.4.4 Financial Challenges

Financing of highly capital-intensive, long-life infrastructure is of course a major challenge under any circumstances. Governments in developing countries rarely have the resources necessary to finance such large projects or are unable to agree among themselves on how financing should be shared. Governments in Africa have also often been unable or unwilling to respond to private sector financing requirements of cross-border PPPs (NEPAD, 2010). Those requirements usually include demonstrating in a compelling fashion that the project is commercially viable over the long term and helping to mitigate the private sector risks inevitably associated with such projects (Verougstraete, 2017). Even if governments help with risk mitigation some experts question whether or not the private sector can effectively manage all the remaining risks inherent in large, complex projects, and whether project finance approaches used on most PPPs are really the best financing technique for such projects (Fitch Ratings, 2009).

In post-apartheid South Africa, the decision was taken early on by senior politicians that partnership with the private sector was an essential aspect of economic corridor development policy, endorsed by the cabinet in 1995. But "partnership" did not necessarily mean a balanced sharing of responsibilities. The private sector was expected to supply at least 90 per cent of the financing needed for such projects because, due to fiscal constraints, "government's financial investment in an initiative is limited to less than 10 per cent of the total amount" (Jourdan, 1998, 718). So, the South African government was willing to help facilitate private involvement in these projects, but only in very limited fashion.

Under other circumstances, this might not have been enough government support to attract significant private investment in a project like the toll road. A decade after the concession contract was signed, a World Bank study concluded that less than 10 per cent of Africa's road network had the minimum traffic flow needed to make toll road concessions commercially viable without additional financial support (Foster and Briceno-Garmendia, 2010). On the South African side of the border at least, the targeted roadway had that kind of necessary traffic flow. But the prospective toll road also enjoyed a number of other advantages when it came to demonstrating bankability to potential private investors.

One of the first and most important of these was the fact that the toll road was intended to be the core project in a much larger economic development effort, involving strong government support for hundreds of projects that would ensure steady increases in traffic levels along the road for many years to come. After the end of apartheid in 1994, South Africa and Mozambique began a process of rebuilding their relationship as southern Africa neighbors, and in 1995 started to formally discuss a strategy for revitalizing the Maputo Corridor, which involved a variety of private investments in infrastructure (Interim Co-ordinating Committee, 1996). At the 1996 MDC investors conference presided over by Presidents Mandela and Chissano, over 180 commercial projects along the corridor, purportedly worth over US$7 billion, were identified for private investment.

In addition to being a core element of a revitalized transport and trade corridor, a second major advantage of the Maputo toll road was that most of it was located in South Africa, and most of it was already a functioning roadway, meaning that it could generate toll revenues almost immediately. Because the project emphasized brownfield rehabilitation rather than greenfield construction of new roadway, private sector operators and investors were more easily convinced of project bankability because traffic flows could be estimated with some accuracy and almost all of the major construction had been completed and construction-related risks already managed (Copley and Shaw, 2007). The project was a textbook example of what, in the mid-1990s, was considered to be the financing advantages of brownfield projects over greenfield projects (see Chapter 4 for a discussion of brownfield vs. greenfield projects). Plus, 94 per cent of the toll revenues would reflect the income per capita of South Africa (an upper middle-income country) rather than Mozambique (a least-developed country).

A third major advantage enjoyed by the toll road was South Africa's financial sector, the largest, deepest, and most sophisticated in Africa. Already in the early 1990s, the sector was highly liquid, offered long-term debt, understood project finance, had some experience with PPPs and private finance of public infrastructure, and was beginning to develop a small secondary market in bonds and syndicated paper. The sector also enjoyed the participation of public pension funds and several government-owned development financing institutions, like DBSA and the IDC. While the financial sector was perceived to be conservative and expensive from the perspective of an advanced industrial economy, in Africa, South Africa's financial sector had no equal. It was essential in helping a private investment project like the Maputo toll road reach financial closure in a timely fashion. About half of the concession's project debt had 20-year maturities; the other half came with 15-year maturities (and grace periods on principal repayment of four to ten years) (South African National Treasury, 2001). Two decades later, these kinds of loan terms are still unavailable in virtually all other SSA countries. Box 3.1 lists the project's financiers.

The two governments took an unrealistic view of the degree to which private partners were willing to take on project financing risks, and this nearly derailed the project. The South African government insisted on honoring its public promise to pass on all financing risks to the private partner in the project, and not provide any subsidies. But TRAC insisted that the governments provide revenue guarantees for the project, a widely used mechanism at the time for mitigating operator traffic risks (Fisher and Babbar, 1996). The governments resisted and delays in negotiation became a serious problem because South Africa's procurement rules at the time required a contract to be finalized within six months of appointing a preferred bidder, or negotiations would have to begin with the second-ranked bidder. A compromise was eventually reached. Revenue guarantees were not provided, but the governments provided joint and severable guarantees of the project debt and equity, under certain conditions (South African National Treasury, 2001).

The concession contract involved remarkably little government financial support, even for similar concessions signed in the mid-1990s. As the contract was signed, the Asian financial crisis was beginning to sweep across the developing

Box 3.1 TRACs Financiers

Equity (20%)	Debt (80%)
Sponsor equity	(Excluding equity investors who also provided debt)
Bouygues (Fr) }	ABSA Corporate and Merchant Bank (SA)
Basil Read (SA)40% owners of TRAC	Development Bank of Southern Africa (SA)
Stocks & Stocks (SA)100% owners of SBB	First National Bank (SA)
Non-sponsor equity	Mine Employees and Officials Pension funds (SA)
South African Infrastructure Fund (SA)	Nedcor Bank (SA)
Rand Merchant Bank Asset Management (SA)	Standard Corporate and Merchant Bank (SA)
Commonwealth Development Corporation (UK)	
South African Mutual Life Assurance (SA)	
Metropolitan Life Ltd (SA)	
Sanlam Asset Management (SA)	
SCDM (Moz)	

Source: South African National Treasury, 2001.

world and it took ten years for PPPs to regain the investment levels of 1997. When the toll road PPP market had recovered by about 2005, the projects no longer looked like the Maputo concession. They were backed with minimum traffic or revenue guarantees, availability payments, shadow tolls, partial risk guarantees, and grants. The Maputo concession was one of the few pre-1997 toll road PPPs that survived the Asian crisis (Queiroz and Izaguirre, 2008). All kinds of brownfield concessions in developing countries went into sharp decline with the Asian crisis, and regained their pre-crisis investment levels, briefly, only after another decade (see Chapter 4).

3.4.5 Legal and Regulatory Challenges

The legal-regulatory issues associated with cross-border toll roads are formidable and require a considerable amount of careful coordination between national governments as well as between national and local government entities (ADB, 2007). In the case of PPPs, participating countries need to have reasonably compatible legislation authorizing such contracts, plus procurement and contracting rules that facilitate the engagement of the same private partners for service provision on both sides of the border. Once the physical infrastructure is in place, regulation of the toll road becomes the biggest challenge to fully realizing the advantages of cross-border projects (Fujimura and Adhikari, 2010). A critical attraction for private investment in cross-border toll roads is the minimization of administrative hurdles at borders, including things like streamlining customs and visa procedures, the use of one-stop border posts, etc. (Verougstraete, 2017).

Most of the key legislation establishing frameworks within which the Maputo toll road could be developed was formalized just as the tender process to select a concessionaire was initiated. South Africa's original legislation for government-operated road tolling was passed by Parliament in 1980, and eventually facilitated the development of five toll roads. But DOT's White Paper, setting out a framework for private toll road concessions, was approved in 1996 as the Maputo toll road concession was being tendered. Mozambique decided to participate in the project before any national legislation allowing privately managed toll roads had been passed by its Parliament. But such legislation was passed ten days before the two countries agreed to establish the MDC and set rules for operation of the toll road (SADC Banking Association, 2003).

However, not all of the necessary regulatory coordination on the project was achieved in a timely fashion. Foremost among such problems was the inability of the governments to agree on how to establish a one-stop border post between the two countries. Both governments agreed early on that in order to facilitate freight and passenger flows between the two countries, a one-stop border control procedure was needed. And bidders were led to believe that such a border post would be established. By road, the distance from Johannesburg to Maputo is somewhat shorter than that from Johannesburg to Durban. But long delays at the border meant that the Johannesburg to Durban route took less time and therefore was more popular with freight haulers. Even after the toll road concessionaire had rehabilitated the roadway, analysts knew that Durban or even Richards Bay would be more attractive export harbors than Maputo unless border delays could be significantly reduced.

The design of a one-stop border post was quickly prepared while the concession was still being negotiated. But the large number of stakeholders involved made it difficult to get consensus on the design, and related systems of a single border post. In June 2006 both governments reconfirmed their agreement to move to a one-stop border post. In 2007, DBSA estimated that the Gauteng to Durban freight traffic was still five times that of Gauteng to Maputo, in spite of the fact that the latter route was somewhat shorter in terms of distance (Copley and Shaw, 2007). By 2013, the South African Parliament was still considering a bilateral legal framework for a one-stop border post. As of 2017, none of the country's planned one-stop border posts were in operation.

3.5 Conclusions

The Maputo toll road is indeed a successful, bilateral, cross-border toll road concession. Even though original estimates of initial traffic volumes were overly optimistic, those volumes have grown steadily, making the toll road a strongly commercial venture almost immediately (USAID, 2008). The MDC, anchored by the toll road, is now home to a large number of private enterprises.

But the toll road is one of a kind—the only cross-border toll road concession ever completed in SSA. What does the success of this concession say about the chances of other regional projects of this kind ever reaching completion in SSA? There are at least three kinds of reasons reviewed here why the success of the Maputo toll road is unlikely to be replicated in the near to medium term.

3.5.1 Success Factors Beyond Governmental Control

The project strongly benefited from the road configuration—the fact that the South African portion of the roadway accounted for nearly 80 per cent of the total road length, was already functioning, and would account for over 90 per cent of the toll revenue, much of which could be generated almost immediately (Copley and Shaw, 2007). The unique geographical positioning of the road between industrial areas in South Africa's Gauteng province and Maputo port, plus the long history of the road as central to a functioning if under-developed economic corridor, meant that vehicle traffic was already nearly at a level that could sustain toll road operations without operating subsidies—something very rare in SSA. The project also benefited tremendously from the fact that South Africa was already the most developed economy in SSA—only one other SSA country at the time (Mauritius) was simultaneously classified by the OECD as an upper middle-income country and given an investment grade sovereign credit rating by an international rating agency (Moody's). South Africa's financial system was by far the largest and most sophisticated in Africa.

3.5.2 Success Factors Under Governmental Control, but Difficult to Realize

The toll road had very strong, high-level political support from the two countries, and this is usually cited as critical for the project's success (Mitchell, 1998; PPIAF, 2009). But the nature of this support demonstrates how volatile and fragile such support can be in SSA. The support for the Maputo toll road was personalized and pragmatic, rather than institutionalized in policy. After key political personalities moved on, the support for private participation largely evaporated. The South African government eventually created a PPP Unit in National Treasury in 2000, but so many costly rules were imposed on project development that a robust pipeline of projects never materialized (Leigland, 2018b). In addition to political support, South Africa already had a history of building and operating toll roads as well as a cadre of engineers in DOT who had the skills and experience to manage the toll road development process without having to resort to outside consultants.

3.5.3 Success Factors Unlikely to be Realizable in the Future

The top-down, fast-track project implementation process helped the toll road become fully operational in record time. By moving quickly, DOT denied the many South African opponents of private participation in infrastructure the time to marshal ideological resistance to the project. But the top-down process meant that the toll road was developed and managed in the style of a national project rather than cross-border one. At the time the toll road concession was developed, both South Africa and Mozambique were members of the Southern Africa Development Community (SADC). Some commentators have speculated that the fact that the toll road was consistent with regional initiatives and priorities promoted by the SADC helped account for the project's success (UNDP, 2008). But SADC actually had no role in the Maputo toll road. By the mid-1990s, SADC had officially endorsed the idea of PPPs, but some of its members were still uncomfortable with private participation in such projects (Mitchell, 1998). South Africa deliberately kept the development of the toll road and the corridor under its own control in order to maintain the fast-track approach and avoid disputes around private investment in infrastructure (de Beer, 2011).

This domination of the project by South African politicians, financiers, and in-house technical expertise, meant that stakeholders, including Mozambican officials and residents, were not significantly engaged in project planning or that procurement was not transparent or publicly competitive (Taylor, 2000). The approach also had longer-term negative consequences for the cost and adequacy of project design and quality of construction. Although this top-down, fast-track approach was popular for a while in the early 1990s, it is no longer widely recommended or used.

Similarly, the government's resistance to any form of revenue guarantee for the private operator may have helped move forward contract negotiations at the time. But already by the late 1990s, in the aftermath of the Asian Crisis, governments were taking much more flexible approaches to public financial support for brownfield concessions of all kinds in order to attract and sustain private sector interest (Leigland, 2018a).

None of this means that regional roads cannot be built, rehabilitated, or tolled. But the Maputo toll road concession suggests that the idea of developing these projects as cross-border PPPs under the coordination of regional political bodies like RECs, is probably mostly a distraction. Regional projects of any kind depend on the strengths of the national partners involved—for large projects private operators and investors insist on dealing with sovereign governments, not regional entities. The PIDA Inception Report notes that regional projects are "best justified on a regional or basin-wide basis" (NEPAD et al., 2010, 5). But regional PPP projects need to be justified first and foremost on a national basis to give confidence to potential private sector partners that sovereign governments have sufficient commitment to the project. Similarly, regional policies and strategies for infrastructure projects can be useful, but again, strong national policies, plans, and regulations must be in place for infrastructure projects, even regional projects, to be viable as PPPs. The success of the Maputo toll road concession—a national project often confused as a regional one—underscores this.

References

Alcazar, L., Manuel, M.A., Shirley, M.M. 2000. "The Buenos Aires water concession." Policy Research Working Paper No. 2311. Washington, DC: World Bank.

Alexander, P., Burger, D.W., Esterhuysen, G., Smit, J.J., Taute, A. 2004. "Cost and quality issues in road concession contracts." Proceedings of the 8th Conference on Asphalt Pavements for Southern Africa, Sept. 12–16, Sun City, South Africa.

Ansar, A., Flyvbjerg, B., Budzier, A., Lunn, D. 2016. "Big is fragile: an attempt at theorizing scale." *The Oxford Handbook of Megaproject Management*, edited by B. Flyvbjerg. Oxford: Oxford University Press.

Asian Development Bank. 2007. *Cross-border Infrastructure Tool Kit*. ADB and PPIAF, Manila.

Bek, D., Taylor, I. 2001. "Evaluation of spatial development initiatives: case studies of the Maputo Development Corridor and the West Coast Investment Initiative." Working Paper No. 01/52, Development Policy Research Unit. University of Cape Town, Cape Town.

Copley, P., Shaw, A. 2007. "The evolution of road funding in South Africa, within its SADC Context." Paper presented at the International Seminar on Road Financing and Investment. Arusha, Tanzania, April 16–20.

de Beer, G. 2011. "Regional public goods in Africa: The Maputo Corridor." Paper presented at the Third Africa Policy Seminar on Regional Public Goods in Africa, sponsored by the Collaborative Africa Budget Reform Initiative (CABRI), Johannesburg, South Africa, November.

Dimitriou, D.J., Sartzetaki, M.F. 2016. "Decision framework for cross-border railway infrastructure projects." *International Journal of Industrial and Systems Engineering* 10(11): 3658–63.

Driver, A., de Barros, J.G. 2000. "The Impact of the Maputo Development Corridor on Freight Flows: An initial investigation." Working Paper No. 00/38, Development Policy Research Unit. University of Cape Town, March.

Farlam, P. 2005. "Working Together: Assessing Public-private Partnerships in Africa." Nepad Policy Focus Report No. 2. South African Institute of International Affairs, Johannesburg, February.

Fisher, G., Babbar, S. 1996. "Private financing of toll roads." RMC Discussion Paper Series 117, Project Finance and Guarantees Group. Washington, DC: World Bank.

Fitch Ratings. 2009. "Large projects, giant risks?" Report by Fitch Global Infrastructure & Project Finance. Fitch Ratings, New York, May 18.

Flyvbjerg, B., 2005. "Policy and planning for large infrastructure projects: problems, causes, cures." World Bank Policy Research Working Paper No. 3781. Washington, DC: World Bank.

Flyvbjerg, B., 2014. "What you should know about megaprojects and why: an overview." *Project Management Journal* 45(2): 6–19.

Foster, V., Briceno-Garmendia, C.M. 2010. *Africa's Infrastructure: A Time for Transformation.* AICD Flagship Report. Washington, DC: World Bank.

Fujimura, M., Adhikari, R. 2010. "Critical evaluation of cross-border infrastructure projects in Asia." Asian Development Bank Institute Working Paper Series, No. 226. ADB, Manila.

Interim Co-ordinating Committee. 1996. *A Development Perspective: Maputo Development Corridor.* Government Printer, Pretoria.

Jourdan, P. 1998. "Spatial Development Initiatives (SDIs)—the official view." *Development Southern Africa* 15(5): 717–25.

Kotze, R., Ferguson, A., Leigland, J. 2000. "Government facilitation of public-private infrastructure projects: Lessons from South Africa." *Journal of Project Finance* 6(1): 61–70.

Leigland, J. 2003. "Managing the threat of MAGA in emerging PPP markets: A case study from South Africa." *The Journal of Structured and Project Finance* 8(4): 49–54.

Leigland, J. 2012. "Regional PPP Case Studies: Johannesburg to Maputo N4 Toll Road." Case study prepared for the World Bank Institute, May.

Leigland, J. 2018a. "Changing perceptions of PPP risk and return: the case of brownfield concessions." *The Journal of Structured Finance* 23(4): 47–56.

Leigland, J. 2018b. "Public-private partnerships in developing countries: the emerging evidence-based critique." *The World Bank Research Observer* 33(1): 103–34.

Mandela, N. 1996. Speech at the Maputo Development Corridor Investor Conference, May 6. South African History Online. Accessed at: http://www.sahistory.org.za.

Mitchell, J. 1998. "The Maputo Development Corridor: a case study of the SDI process in Mpumalanga." *Development Southern Africa* 15(5): 757–69.

NEPAD. 2010. *Project implementation review of the NEPAD Infrastructure Short Term Action Plan (STAP).* African Development Bank, Tunis.

NEPAD, African Union, AfDB. 2009. *Programme for Infrastructure Development in Africa: General terms of reference.* African Development Bank, Tunis.

NEPAD, African Union, AfDB. 2010. *Programme for Infrastructure Development in Africa: PIDA inception report.* AfDB, Tunis.

NEPAD, African Union, AfDB. 2011. *Programme for Infrastructure Development in Africa: PIDA study synthesis.* AfDB, Tunis.

NEPAD, African Union, AfDB. 2018. Virtual PIDA Information Centre: PIDA Projects Dashboard. Accessed at: http://www.au-pida.org/pida-projects/

PPIAF. 2009. "N4 Toll Road from South Africa to Mozambique." *Toolkit for Public-Private Partnerships in Roads and Highways.* Public-Private Infrastructure Advisory Facility (PPIAF). Washington, DC: World Bank.

Queiroz, C., Izaguirre, A.K. 2008. "Worldwide trends in private participation in roads: growing activity, growing government support." Gridline No. 37, Public-Private Infrastructure Advisory Facility (PPIAF). Washington, DC: World Bank.

Roodt, M. 2007. "Borderlands—the impact of regional integration initiatives in a Southern African cross border region: Maputo Development Corridor." Conference paper No. 34, Conferencia Inaugural do IESE, *Desafios para a investigacao social e economica em Mocambique*, September 19.

SADC Banking Association. 2003. "Overview of regulatory and institutional PPP environment in Mozambique." Report prepared by Edward Nathan & Friedland and SAL Consultoria e Investimentos. SADC Banking Association, Johannesburg.

South African Department of Transport. 1996. *White Paper on National Transport Policy.* Pretoria, August. Accessed at: https://www.gov.za/documents/white-papers?page=2

South African National Treasury. 2001. *National Treasury PPP Manual, Version 1.* National Treasury PPP Unit, Pretoria.

South African Roads Board. 1997. *Policy of the South African Roads Board in Respect of Unsolicited Proposals.* South African Ministry of Transport, Pretoria.

Taylor, I. 2000. "Public–private partnerships: lessons from the MDC toll road." Working Paper No. 00/44, Development Policy Research Unit. University of Cape Town, Cape Town, December.

UK National Audit Office. 2014. "Lessons from major rail infrastructure programmes." Report by the Comptroller and Auditor General. NAO, London, October.

UNDP. 2008. "The N4 Toll Road, South Africa and Mozambique." *Sharing Innovative Experiences Vol. 15: Examples of Successful Public–Private Partnerships.* United Nations Development Program, South–South Cooperation Unit, New York.

USAID. 2008. "Maputo Corridor Summary report: a transport logistics diagnostic tool study." Report prepared by Nathan Associates for USAID, March.

Verougstraete, M. 2017. "Public–private partnerships for cross-border infrastructure development." United Nations Economic and Social Commission for Asia and the Pacific, April.

World Bank. 2014. *Building Integrated Markets within the East African Community: EAC Opportunities in Public–Private Partnership Approaches to the Region's Infrastructure Needs*. World Bank Studies. Washington, DC: The World Bank. Doi: 10.1596/978-14648-0227-0. License: Creative Commons Attribution CC BY 3.0 IGO.

World Bank. 2018. PPI Project Database. Accessed at: http://ppi.worldbank.org/customquery?mode=1

World Bank Group. 2017. "The G-20 Compact with Africa, A Joint AfDB, IMF and WBG Report." G-20 Finance Ministers and Central Bank Governors Meeting, March 17–18, Baden-Baden, Germany.

4
The Rise and Fall of Brownfield Concessions

4.1 Introduction

Chapter 2 explained the extent to which infrastructure public–private partnerships (PPPs) in developing countries have not met expectations, particularly in low-income countries. But why were expectations so high to begin with? And why has it taken so long for the evidence of this under-performance to accumulate to the point where it is possible to discuss the emergence of an evidence-based critique? Part of the answer to these questions can be found by understanding the somewhat mysterious rise and fall in popularity of brownfield infrastructure concessions. In the early 1990s, this kind of contract served briefly as the flagship of the global PPP movement and was highly recommended by donors, development finance institutions (DFIs), and multilateral development banks (MDBs) as an ideal solution to many of the problems facing infrastructure utilities in developing countries. In 1996 and 1997, brownfield concessions were the fastest growing form of PPP. But the Asian financial crisis in 1997 brought a sudden halt to this growth in popularity. Many contracts collapsed or had to be renegotiated. Other forms of PPP were much less dramatically affected by the crisis and recovered relatively quickly. Brownfield concessions however experienced a steep decline across the developing world after their record investment performance in 1997, and have never really recovered the momentum of the early 1990s. Why were brownfield concessions so popular in the early 1990s, and why did that popularity diminish so quickly? Why were they never able to fully recover after the late 1990s? Why did greenfield projects go on to dominate the PPP markets in all developing countries?

This chapter attempts to answer these questions by clarifying the role of donors, DFIs, and MDBs in the rise of brownfield concessions, and explaining why the risk–reward perceptions of private investors subsequently changed so rapidly in the late 1990s.

Public–Private Partnerships in Sub-Saharan Africa: The Evidence-Based Critique. James Leigland,
Oxford University Press (2020).
DOI: 10.1093/oso/9780198861829.001.0001

4.2 Greenfield vs. Brownfield Concessions

Brownfield PPPs belong to a group of private sector solutions to problems with existing infrastructure service systems, as opposed to "greenfield" solutions involving the construction of new systems (Box 4.1). Brownfield solutions include PPP and non-PPP mechanisms that involve transferring public service delivery responsibilities to a private entity. Brownfield PPPs use contracts to allocate risks and rewards associated with the delivery of these public services between the private entity and the public owner of the project. The compensation received by the private entity for this involvement can vary depending on performance. The most widely used types of these PPP contracts, often referred to as concessions, normally must be long-term in order for the private entity to recoup its investments via the sale of the services. An example of this kind of contract would be a water distribution concession, in which a private company takes over management of an existing water utility, rehabilitates and extends the assets, then manages distribution of water to customers and recoups its investments via user fees.

Brownfield solutions also include non-PPP options like divestiture or liquidation of government assets. Divestiture is the most extreme brownfield approach to using the private sector to solve service delivery problems with existing infrastructure assets. It takes place when a government relinquishes ownership of existing assets by selling them to a private company. Because there is no on-going contract-based risk sharing between public and private entities after these sales take place, they are usually not considered PPPs.

Management contracts are brownfield solutions that are usually, but not always, classified as PPPs.[1] However, they are different from other forms of PPP because they involve less risk for private partners, and typically have much shorter life-spans—they involve no investment costs that must be recouped. These contracts involve legally enforceable agreements that engage a contractor to manage a range of enterprise activities on behalf of the owner, usually for a relatively short period of time (typically two to five years).

Greenfield solutions make use of private sector actors to finance, build, and manage new infrastructure assets or systems (Box 4.2). These solutions include "build–operate–transfer" (BOT) and "build–own–operate" (BOO) projects (both also often referred to as greenfield concessions). A typical example of this kind of project in the power sector is the so-called "independent power producer" (IPP) project. This usually involves the development of a new (greenfield) power

[1] Because management contracts have much shorter life-spans than other forms of PPPs, and involve little or no capital investment, the World Bank's Independent Evaluation Group (IEG) refuses to include them in their evaluation of the Bank's work on PPPs: "these mechanisms do not induce the level of risk sharing common to the other PPPs" (IEG, 2015, xviii).

Box 4.1 Brownfield Infrastructure Solutions

1. **PPPs** – a private entity takes over the management of an existing government-owned enterprise and also assumes significant risk for performance and sometimes for investments needed to extend, complete, or rehabilitate the enterprise facilities. Varieties include:
    - Rehabilitate, operate, and transfer (ROT): a private sponsor finances and carries out the rehabilitation of an existing facility, then operates and maintains the facility at its own risk for the contract period.
    - Rehabilitate, lease or rent, and transfer (RLT): a private sponsor finances and carries out the rehabilitation of an existing facility, leases or rents the facility from the government owner, then operates and maintains the facility at its own risk for the contract period.
    - Build, rehabilitate, operate, and transfer (BROT): a private developer finances and builds an add-on to an existing facility or completes a partially-built facility and rehabilitates existing assets, then operates and maintains the facility at its own risk for the contract period.
    - Lease contracts: a private entity leases a government-owned facility for a specified period, usually paying a rental fee to the government owner, but retains system revenues over and above the rental fee; the government retains responsibility for investments.
    - Management contracts: the government owner contracts with a private entity to manage a facility for a specified period, paying a fixed management fee, sometimes supplemented with performance-based success fees; the government retains responsibility for investments.
2. **Divestiture** – transfer of asset ownership from government to private entities via liquidation, asset sale, public offering, or mass privatization programs.
    - Full: the entire enterprise or facility is sold or liquidated; the government retains no interest.
    - Partial: via partial share sale; the government maintains an ownership share.

Source: Adapted from the World Bank PPI Database (World Bank, 2018).

generating facility by a private company that sells the power on a wholesale basis to government utilities that distribute it to individual customers. In the case of IPP projects, the assets may belong to the private company, but the power must be sold to the government (or a government-owned power utility) for retail distribution as a public service to customers. For IPP projects, the critical form of PPP

Box 4.2 Greenfield Infrastructure Solutions

1. **PPPs** – a private entity builds and operates a new facility for a period of time, and under conditions, specified in a contract. Examples include:
    - Build, lease, and transfer (BLT): a private sponsor finances and builds a new facility largely at its own risk, transfers ownership to the government, leases the facility back from the government and operates it at its own risk up to the expiry of the lease, at which time the facility is transferred back to the government. The government usually provides revenue guarantees through long-term take-or-pay contracts for bulk supply facilities or minimum traffic revenue guarantees.
    - Build, operate, and transfer (BOT): a private sponsor finances and builds a new facility at its own risk, operates the facility at its own risk, and then transfers the facility to the government at the end of the contract period. The government usually provides revenue guarantees through long-term take-or-pay contracts for bulk supply facilities or minimum traffic revenue guarantees.
    - Build, own, and operate (BOO): a private sponsor finances and builds a new facility at its own risk, then owns and operates the facility at its own risk. The government usually provides revenue guarantees through long-term take-or-pay contracts for bulk supply facilities or minimum traffic revenue guarantees.
    - Rental: Utilities or governments rent service delivery facilities (e.g., mobile power plants) from private sponsors for periods ranging from 1 year to 15 years. A private sponsor owns and operates the facility at its own risk during the contract period. The government usually provides revenue guarantees through short-term purchase agreements such as power purchase agreements for bulk supply facilities.
2. **Merchant projects** – A private sponsor builds a new facility in a liberalized market, for which the government provides no revenue guarantees. The private developer assumes financing, construction, operating, and market risk for the project (e.g., a merchant power plant).

Source: Adapted from the World Bank PPI Database (World Bank, 2018).

contract is usually the "power purchase agreement" (PPA), by which the government off-taker agrees with the facility owner on the conditions under which it will purchase the wholesale services.

Another widely used form of greenfield project, which is not usually classified as a PPP, is the merchant project, involving the ownership, construction, and operation of assets by a private company at its own risk without government risk sharing in the form of commitment to buy the services. In telecommunication or energy sectors, merchant projects normally operate in liberalized markets where the sale of services is unrestricted by a PPP contract with government—in other words, the private entity is free to sell the services to anyone who can pay.

4.3 The Fleeting Popularity of Brownfield Concessions

In the early 1990s, brownfield infrastructure concessions were widely promoted by donors, DFIs, and MDBs.[2] The general argument was that these contracts were win–win arrangements with benefits for everyone involved: government assets would be rehabilitated at no cost to the government (but the ownership would not change); private companies would make profits over the long term (20–30 years) of the contracts; customers would receive better, less expensive services due to greater operational efficiency, carefully targeted and managed investments, and more realistic pricing. World Bank experts pointed out that the new arrangements would be largely self-supporting, in dramatic contrast to the huge budget deficits that had resulted from public subsidies for inefficient service provision (Kerf et al., 1998). In sum, these concessions offered a solution to one of the most difficult infrastructure problems facing the developing world—what to do with existing, but barely functioning, infrastructure service systems, such as water distribution facilities and roads, which could not be shut down or sold off.

It is sometimes assumed that by far the most urgent priority in developing countries is new infrastructure. But when the brownfield and greenfield infrastructure needs of African countries were comprehensively quantified and compared for the first time by the World Bank in 2010, the results showed that brownfield assets needed almost as much attention as greenfield ones (Table 4.1). The authors found that the size of required capital investment was massive, at about US$35.5 billion per year. The need for operations and maintenance was about one-third of that total, at US$12.6 billion. But the authors also concluded that operational inefficiencies of various kinds were costing these countries about US$17.4 billion per year. So, the total potential value of actions needed to address problems with existing infrastructure assets was almost as big as the need to build new capital assets. This fact was abundantly clear to development experts in the early 1990s and helps account for the strong endorsement of brownfield concession (and other brownfield infrastructure solutions) by donors, DFIs, and MDBs.

However, by the late 1990s, governments and the private sector came to realize that although the ideal notion of brownfield concessions seemed to work reasonably well in developed countries, it worked hardly at all in developing countries,

[2] The following sections draw (with the author's permission) from Leigland (2018).

Table 4.1 Infrastructure Investment Needs in SSA, 2010, in US$ billions

Infrastructure Needs	Electricity	ICT	Irrigation	Transport	WSS	Total
Funding Gaps:						
New Assets	22.1	0.0	2.4	1.0	10.4	35.5
O&M	7.1	0.0	0.0	1.0	3.9	12.6
Cost of Operational Inefficiencies:	6.0	1.3	0.1	3.8	2.9	17.4
Greenfield Needs:	22.1	0.0	2.4	1.0	10.4	35.5
Brownfield Needs:	13.1	1.3	0.1	4.8	6.8	30.0

Source: Foster and Briceno-Garmendia, 2010.

especially in low-income countries. After reaching an investment peak in 1997, the Asian crisis exacted a severe toll on these contracts. It took 15 years for brownfield concessions to match their 1997 investment total again in nominal values—in 2012, middle-income countries like China and Brazil used high levels of government support to substitute for private investment and briefly propelled brownfield concessions back to their record 1997 investment level. Over the two decades since the onset of the Asian crisis, greenfield projects have dominated the world of PPPs in developing countries (Figure 4.1).

The ascendancy of greenfield concessions in low-income countries has been especially dramatic. Figure 4.2 compares greenfield and brownfield concessions in IDA countries. These are countries whose gross net income per capita is below US$1,215, and which are therefore eligible for support from the International Development Association (IDA)—the soft lending window of the World Bank Group. World Bank data indicates that from 1993 to 2015, 84 per cent of private investment into IDA countries was via greenfield projects, and only 7 per cent came via brownfield concessions (the balance from divestiture) (World Bank, 2018).

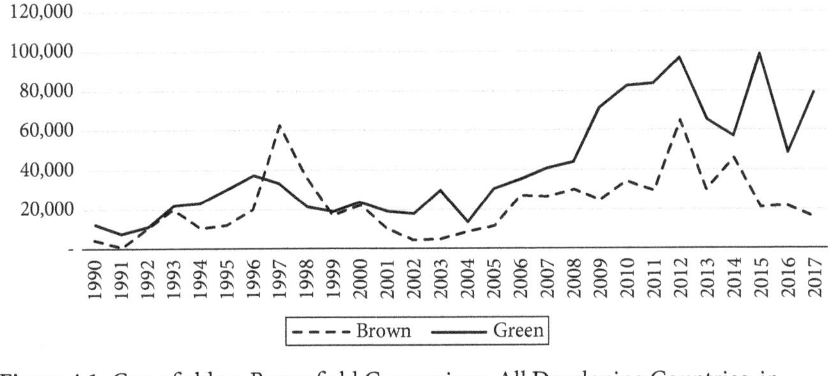

Figure 4.1 Greenfield vs. Brownfield Concessions, All Developing Countries, in 2018 US$ millions

Source: World Bank, 2018.

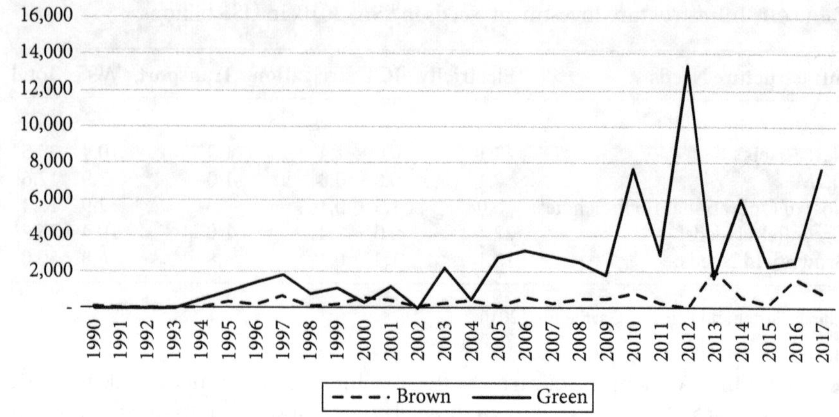

Figure 4.2 Greenfield vs. Brownfield PPPs, IDA Countries, in 2018 US$ millions
Source: World Bank, 2018.

Over the same period, in non-IDA developing countries, 58 per cent of investments came via greenfield projects and about 20 per cent from brownfield projects (the balance via divestiture).

Figure 4.2 shows that the amount of investments into both brownfield and greenfield projects in all developing countries converged between 1997 and 1998. But thereafter, greenfield projects accelerated, capturing greater investments. So, after starting out about equal in terms of investment generated in 1997, these two types of concessions diverged sharply over the succeeding two decades. The question is, why did this happen?

There are several reasons why investors dramatically changed their minds about the desirability of brownfield concessions, ranging from miscalculations regarding some of the basic risks associated with these projects in developing countries, to a misunderstanding of the MDB policy environment of the 1990s within which many of these projects were developed.

4.4 Brownfield vs. Greenfield: The Textbook Explanation

Conventional project finance wisdom is perhaps partly to blame for the misreading of the risk differential between greenfield and brownfield concessions. Textbook wisdom argues that greenfield projects are inherently riskier than brownfield ones and that unless risk-weighted returns are pegged much higher to compensate for these risks, greenfield concessions are therefore less attractive to private investors. As the name suggests, greenfield concessions are start-up projects that initially involve a significant investment of capital and the participation of multiple actors in developing the project. The involvement of these actors adds to the complexity and risks of project development—the actors must be coordinated and managed as key development activities progress (e.g., design and architecture, construction, finance, and operations). An important feature of greenfield projects is their cash flow profile. As project assets move from construction through to operational maturity, the projects typically have little, if any, income that can provide a return for investors. Once construction is successfully completed, it is usually only then that development risks have been reduced to the point where the project can be sold off or refinanced. Two of the most important development risks affecting greenfield projects are the following:

- **Completion risk.** This is mostly made up of risks that arise during construction and can involve problems such as construction cost overruns, completion delays, permitting problems, flawed technology, and design mistakes. In industrialized countries, a project developer is able to mitigate these kinds of risks by employing a competent engineering, procurement, construction (EPC) contractor to deliver a project that meets its performance objectives on time and on budget. Finding such a contractor to work in a developing country is much more challenging, and therefore these risks are amplified.
- **Demand risk.** This risk involves determining accurately the precise level of demand for the services to be offered once construction is complete and the infrastructure facility starts operation. Under traditional greenfield concession models, demand risk will stay with the project developer who will not know whether this risk has been correctly assessed until the project commences operations and demand ramps up. Therefore, the commercial success of a greenfield infrastructure concession largely depends on how quickly and how extensively demand growth is realized.

This time-honored view holds that because brownfield concessions involve existing infrastructure assets, completion and demand risks are not relevant, and operational risk can be determined with a high degree of reliability from the operating track record. In exchange for this lower risk profile, investors in brownfield concessions tend to target more modest returns than would be the case with greenfield projects. Brownfield concessionaires are often required to improve the project assets through rehabilitation, extensions, repairs, or maintenance. This may result in some level of design, construction, or technology risk. But these improvements are normally smaller and take much less time than greenfield development, and project participants can assess the likely success of the project by referencing historic demand and financial data. The assumption is that unlike greenfield projects, brownfield projects have the potential to provide investors with almost immediate cash flow, and therefore can offer investors a more certain return.

Unfortunately, governments, private investors, and their development partners discovered early on that the textbook view of the comparative risk profiles of greenfield vs. brownfield concessions did not apply very strongly in the developing world. World Bank data shows that as brownfield concessions began to proliferate during the 1990s, they were far more likely to experience contractual distress or premature contract cancellation than greenfield concessions (World Bank, 2018). In terms of the numbers of brownfield concessions reaching closure between 1990 and 1998, the percentage of cancelled or distressed projects was 41 per cent higher than that for greenfield projects, like BOTs (10.7 per cent vs. 7.6 per cent). In terms of affected investment, brownfield concessions were three times more likely to experience these problems than greenfield projects (27.9 per cent vs. 8.6 per cent). In other words, from 1990 to 1998, investments into brownfield concessions were riskier in terms of contract distress or cancellation than for other forms of long-term PPPs.

4.5 Brownfield Concession Risks in Developing Countries

The project finance principles that underlie brownfield concessions as well as other forms of long-term infrastructure PPPs were well developed and highly successful long before the PPP boom of the 1990s. Project finance was already beginning to be used extensively on infrastructure projects in the 1970s, particularly after the viability of the approach was demonstrated in British Petroleum's North Sea Forties oil field project in 1972 (De Lemos et al., 2000). The mechanism has continued to enjoy success, but mostly in the developed world. And this seems to be a key to understanding the declining use of brownfield concessions beginning with the Asian Crisis: their use in the developing world was compromised by serious misconceptions about underlying risks in these countries, perhaps because those structuring deals were overly optimistic in assuming that risk levels were closer to developed country standards than they turned out to be. When these risks materialized as serious problems, the basic PPP structure did not cope well. These projects in developing countries, especially low-income countries, often simply lack the ability to generate positive cash flows or profits, these weaknesses were not anticipated in project preparation, and risk mitigation mechanisms failed to deal with problems when they manifested themselves.

4.5.1 Too Much Non-Revenue-Generating Investment

A hallmark of brownfield concessions in developing countries has been the fact that much more investment in assets is typically made than can be adequately supported by project revenues enhanced by subsequent improvements in infrastructure service delivery. A fundamental reason for this was that the assets turned over to operators were in extremely poor condition, poorer than many of the parties to the transactions realized.

This meant that conventional investor distinctions between terms like "greenfield" and "brownfield" did not apply in most low-income countries. In a developed country context, investors often understand brownfield projects to have commercial operating track records, because they involve mature operating assets that generate revenues sufficient to cover costs. These projects are contrasted with much riskier "greenfield" projects not yet in commercial operation, involving non-recourse or limited recourse investments that depend for repayment on the future cash flows of assets only after construction is completed. But in low-income countries, "brownfield" projects typically do not involve mature operating assets, or commercial operations that fully recover costs. These are assets managed and maintained by governments, which typically require major rehabilitation and strengthened management before they can be operated commercially and generate cash flows to repay investors. Many governments became desperate enough to engage private companies for infrastructure service delivery because these facilities operated in a state of constant cash flow crisis, with revenues not even covering operations and maintenance expenses, much less capital investment liabilities or obligations. So, in this sense, the textbook distinction between brownfield and greenfield investments as it usually applies in developed countries disappears—in developing countries both kinds of projects are risky because both require that major project investment financing be dependent for repayment on future revenues generated by operations that are possible only after major construction activities have been completed.

One reason why asset disrepair was often underestimated in low-income countries was the fact that typically very little performance data was available on these systems, the status of asset repair, the age or even location of assets. Information about how well the assets provided services, or even to whom services were provided, was often missing.[3] In many cases operators learned what to fix, and in what sequence, only after months of operation. But meanwhile, with many brownfield concessions, operators were incentivized to make major investments as early as possible in the life-spans of these projects. This was done, often at the insistence of government partners, so that concessionaires could quickly begin showing positive results. Sponsors and operators also wanted the maximum amount of time allowed under the contract to recoup investment costs from operating revenues. But this meant that most of the investment was made at a time when demand risk was high, and the project was generating much less

[3] This is now such a widely understood aspect of doing infrastructure PPPs that private companies are in danger of accusations of negligence if they take at face value government data on public enterprise performance. See Lawyers' Environmental Action Team (2007).

revenue than it would be expected to do later, after investments had facilitated more robust cash flows (Estache and Strong, 2000).

To make matters worse, the most visible problems with infrastructure service provision, such as the poor condition of assets, inadequate management, generally low-quality service, etc., often were manifestations of more profound problems that brownfield concessions were not designed to directly address, such as lack of sectoral and institutional reform and corruption. In hindsight, it was a fundamental mistake to assume that these kinds of concessions—or any kind of PPP contract—could solve such problems.[4]

4.5.2 Weak Revenues

The other side of the problem of investments generating too little operating revenue had to do with the fact that basic revenues, even revenues generated by rehabilitated systems, were simply not robust enough in many infrastructure sectors to support investment without some kind of subsidization. The brownfield concession mechanism was largely associated in the early 1990s with projects involving distribution of infrastructure services to end users who would pay for the services via fees. Over two-thirds of the concession-related investment commitments made in 1997, the peak year for concessions, involved projects of this kind.[5] But we now know that proponents of the brownfield concession mechanism, as it was used in developing countries, were unrealistic in their expectations that user fees could cover the full costs of operations and investments.

In the early 1990s, mainstream economists were advocating that "prices be based on the most economically efficient way to recover total costs" (Israel 1992, 27). Subsidies, and even cross-subsidization, were discouraged as being costly and inefficient. Even as the Asian crisis was beginning to unfold, experts on concession contracts were still making the same basic arguments in favor of cost-covering tariffs, and against subsidies and cross-subsidization (Kerf et al., 1998, 34). But, as has now become evident, cost recovery in many infrastructure sectors, particularly water, has almost never been successfully achieved. Even high-income countries routinely subsidize water costs (Foster and Yepes, 2006). The belief that full cost recovery from user fees was fair and practical, was fundamental in helping to make the brownfield concession concept seem workable. A legacy of this kind of overselling is the large number of anti-privatization critics who

[4] This is one of the key lessons learned in assessments of the characteristics of well-performing water utilities. See Baietti, Kingdom, and van Ginneken (2006), 25.

[5] This is an estimate by the author, based on a review of projects included in the World Bank's PPI Project Database (World Bank, 2018).

continue to equate PPPs with full cost recovery, private operator profits, and exploitation of the poor.[6]

One would expect that this combination of too much non-revenue generating investment and inadequate revenue would result in problems with cash flow and profitability, and that is exactly what research shows. The studies by Guash (2004) and Sirtaine et al. (2004) cited in Chapter 3 were among the first to suggest that concessions (both brownfield and greenfield) commonly suffered from problems with cash flow and profitability over at least the first decade of their existence. Sirtaine's study suggested that many operators live through years of negative cash flows and constant uncertainty about long-term profitability. Guasch suggested that cash flow problems likely play a leading role in contract distress and cancellation. The fact that so many contracts are renegotiated after only a few years, long before the contracts can establish their profitability, suggests that cash flow problems may be important in precipitating renegotiation. Cash flow stresses are well documented in connection with various types of concessions, in the African rail sector for example (Pozzo di Borgo et al., 2006).

4.5.3 Too Much Debt

An important factor that exacerbated cash flow and profitability problems was the natural tendency to try to maximize the debt–equity ratios in PPP project financing—to pay for the aforementioned investments with borrowed money. This is a characteristic of all kinds of long-term PPPs. Because these are risky projects, sponsors and operators need a way to insulate themselves from the financial liabilities of their projects and to share substantial levels of risk with other parties. A project finance approach to capital financing makes this possible through the creation of special purpose vehicles (SPVs)—separate corporate entities with a legal personality that allows the company to be fully responsible for its own assets and liabilities, thus protecting the sponsor's balance sheet from those responsibilities. If the SPV defaults on debt, it is solely responsible for the consequences—the SPV's separate legal personality means that lenders have recourse to whatever assets it may own, including equity investments by the sponsors, but not to the sponsor's assets. This kind of limited recourse to the assets of sponsors and operators protects them from possible bankruptcy caused by the financial problems of their large infrastructure concession projects, and shifts a significant share of project risks to lenders who provide the debt that pays for most of the project investment.

[6] Some private sector operators have fanned the flames of this debate by arguing for the necessity of "full cost recovery" and the elimination of cross-subsidies in developing countries, even in sectors such as water supply (Martin, 2005).

This means that high levels of debt in the capital structure of a PPP have some advantages. But debt service costs are prime factors in increasing the cash flow sensitivity of an enterprise, because unlike dividends earned by equity investors, debt service payments (principal and interest on debt) must be paid according to pre-agreed schedules—they represent a constant, predictable drain on the cash of the enterprise. Dividends may be delayed as needed, for months or even years, in order to sustain the cash flow needed to allow debt service payments in support of growth-enhancing investments. This appears to have been common practice in the infrastructure concessions in Latin America referred to earlier. But debt service payments are more difficult to delay—normally they must be made in a timely fashion in order to avoid default on obligations to lenders.

Some experts have argued that a variety of factors incentivized project sponsors or operators to use higher levels of debt in PPP projects than they would have otherwise—that "too much" debt was used in the early 1990s (Estache and Strong, 2000; Ehrhardt and Irwin, 2004; de Fraja and Stones, 2004). Brownfield concessions were especially vulnerable because of unrealistic textbook notions of project risks described earlier. Lenders may have been convinced in some situations to allow "too much" borrowing because brownfield concessions were supposed to be less risky than greenfield ones, with assets and the cash flows derived from them, already in place.

A factor that adds to the potential cash flow problems faced by brownfield concessions, as defined here, is the fact that they have access to fewer of the remedies for dealing with the problem than do other kinds of business enterprises or even other forms of PPP. This is because, as Guasch points out, cash flow is the only asset "owned" by a brownfield concessionaire, and only for the lifespan of the concession contract. Unlike a privatized business or a greenfield project (like a BOO project), a brownfield concession involves transfer only of the right to use the assets and operate the enterprise. Even in cases where contracts allow concession companies to own newly created assets, disposal of these assets to help with cash flow problems almost always must be agreed to by government partners and done in a way that does not compromise service quality. Of course, for any public or private company, infrastructure assets (such as water pipes or rail or electricity lines) are usually difficult if not impossible to dispose of for cash.

This means that, practically speaking, there are no inventories, fixed assets, or intangibles to be sold to enhance liquidity or pledge for additional loans. More aggressive marketing strategies are rarely helpful in selling infrastructure services. Because service levels and quality are often stipulated in the concession contracts, these cannot be reduced without defaulting on contractual obligations. Many brownfield concessions begin with severe cost-cutting measures that governments may not be willing to take responsibility for, so it is often difficult to make additional reductions—for example, in the workforce—when cash crises occur after initial retrenchments have been made. And, of course, ultimate cash flow remedies such as selling the business or merging with another company are not available to infrastructure concession companies that do not own any company assets.

Brownfield concessions also tend to be at a disadvantage when it comes to the ability to increase normal operating revenues. Although not a defining characteristic, most of the brownfield concessions registered in the PPI Project Database (World Bank, 2018) involve facilities that distribute services (water, electricity, toll roads) to end users who pay via service fees—privatized facilities and greenfield projects are much less likely to generate most of their operating revenues in this manner. Price increases are the most powerful tools for strengthening brownfield concession cash flows, but they are unpopular during the early years of these projects and often encounter political opposition, even when they are permitted by contracts.

4.5.4 The Failure of Risk Mitigation

Whatever the vulnerability of brownfield concessions to cash flow and profitability problems, these and other risks associated with these projects should have been identified, allocated to whomever was best able to manage them, and appropriately mitigated when the time came. The Asian Crisis and the international aftershocks that followed demonstrated the failure of risk mitigation for a variety of PPP types, but particularly for brownfield concessions. The PPI Project Database (World Bank, 2018) statistics cited previously indicate that by 1998, these kinds of concessions had experienced far higher levels of distress and collapse than any other forms of PPP.

These economic shocks caused severe cash flow problems for companies, including infrastructure SPVs, which were massively overleveraged, often with foreign currency debt (Pomerleano, 1998). As the Asian crisis unfolded it underscored all of the above-mentioned weaknesses and problems, including the fragility of the concession mechanism and inadequate returns on investment, as well as debt that, under the circumstances, turned out to be "too much."

The materialization of these risks was supposed to trigger risk mitigation mechanisms, the most important of which were those provided by state-owned enterprises (SOEs) and utilities or the governments themselves, principally in the form of off-take agreements and project guarantees. But the crisis also forced many governments to realize that their understanding of how PPP contracts were supposed to work was not accurate. In the early 1990s, many governments were convinced to use these mechanisms because it seemed that they could turn over all responsibility for infrastructure provision to private partners who would cover all costs and accept all related business risks. The nature of governments' contingent liabilities associated with these contracts was often completely ignored or misunderstood (Pomerleano, 1998). Governments in fact retained considerable contingent liabilities for these operations, via off-take agreements and outright guarantees, as well as under routine early-contract-termination scenarios. But under the intense pressure of the Asian crisis, many governments simply repudiated these obligations.

A managing director of Moody's Investors Service noted that this repudiation was most clearly evident in Asia, where:

> structures set up to mitigate these economic risks unraveled almost as soon as they were put to the test. Counterparties who had accepted risk repudiated that risk when it occurred. Legal systems simply proved unable to enforce the contracts as agreed. Regulatory approvals that had been held out as straightforward proved anything but when projects moved to the operations stage. And, above all, the political will that had been so apparent getting the projects financed evaporated when the projects needed support in a time of crisis (Marshella, 2001, 31).

The off-take agreements, guarantees, and other legal protections were the risk-mitigation mechanisms that were supposed to provide sponsors, operators, and lenders with at least some protection from many of the other problems outlined in earlier sections of this chapter. Instead, the economic crisis led to hundreds of project defaults, renegotiations, restructurings, and rating downgrades. Anecdotal evidence suggests that many projects continued as partially restructured arrangements, but with unhappy private partners tolerating what they perceived to be less than satisfactory profits and cash flows rather than face penalties for default and early termination.

The failure of these backstop mechanisms meant that most private players no longer viewed brownfield infrastructure concessions—as they had been developed and implemented in the early 1990s—as a viable project type in these countries. The precipitous post-crisis drop in the use of brownfield concessions registered by the PPI Project Database seems to be, in large part, a reflection of the private sector's new perspective on these projects.

4.5.5 Poor Project Preparation

The failure of risk mitigation became widely apparent as a result of the Asian crisis. But cash flow vulnerabilities of the brownfield concession mechanism and the potential for inadequate returns on investment, should have been apparent much earlier. And risk mitigation measures should have been tailored to deal with these problems. Why were so many of these contracts completed before these weaknesses were noticed? A large part of the answer seems to be that the preparation of these projects, from conceptualization, feasibility assessment, structuring, and negotiation was incomplete or of very poor quality.

As noted in Chapter 2, one result of the notion that government problems were being handed over to private companies for solution was that governments (as well as donors, DFIs, and MDBs) often were unwilling to spend time or money preparing brownfield concessions, doing feasibility studies, assessing PPP contracting options, etc. In many of the contracts signed in the early 1990s, all of this work was assumed to be the responsibility of potential private partners; part of their normal due diligence, because if the project ultimately failed, it would be at the sole cost of the private partners. But for existing facilities that often were over 50 years old, governments needed independent, impartial assessments of the condition of the existing assets in order to be able to identify the objectives of brownfield concessions and evaluate bids. By leaving such assessments to bidders who spent different amounts of time and resources on feasibility studies and asset reviews, bids were often difficult to compare or were simply based on incomplete or inaccurate views of infrastructure investment needs. Sometimes the intense competitive pressures of lowest-cost procurement incentivized bidders to reduce preparation costs as much as possible in order to win the project, hoping to be able to identify problems and adjust the contract after a period of implementation. Occasionally, bidders purposely underbid for projects, assuming that contracts would later have to be renegotiated. Without independent assessments done by or on behalf of governments in preparing the early brownfield concessions the bidders and government officials had different opinions about how much investment was going to be needed to turn service delivery into a commercial proposition.

Even in cases where one party or another was willing and able to undertake full feasibility studies to accurately determine the condition of infrastructure assets to be concessioned and the key elements needed to make a concession viable, the task often turned out to be difficult if not impossible. As noted earlier, not only were the assets dilapidated and neglected, but management information and basic recordkeeping was also often nonexistent. Historical performance data was inaccurate or unavailable. The condition of underground pipes was impossible to evaluate. Even customer records were incomplete or missing—there was often no way to tell how many end users were connected to water systems, for example, much less how many were paying their bills.

It is likely that the preparation of concession projects was also affected by several limitations in the way in which project appraisal techniques were applied to anticipate and avoid problems with cash flows and profitability. Quantitative techniques for assessing financial and economic costs and benefits of prospective projects were in many cases simply not used. A government's decision to grant a brownfield concession, and the view that no practical alternative existed for solving problems with existing, badly maintained facilities, often made it appear unnecessary to undertake sound quantitative analysis of financial, much less economic, costs and benefits or comparisons of PPP options as compared to traditional public options for project financing and management. This was particularly true in cases where the private sector was expected to carry out project preparation as part of their normal due diligence. To the extent that techniques were used by or on behalf of government partners, they often served to justify rather than evaluate projects.[7]

To the extent that such techniques were actually used by bidders, the analysis in some cases was flawed. Bent Flyvbjerg's research documented the huge mistakes routinely made in the estimation of financial costs and benefits associate with large infrastructure projects. Flyvbjerg attributed these consistently large mistakes to faulty techniques, but also to "optimism bias" and "strategic misrepresentation" (Flyvbjerg, 2005).

In retrospect, it seems likely that many brownfield concessions were not viable to begin with, but were nevertheless accepted as win–win solutions by many politicians and policy makers, as well as some representatives of donors, DFIs, and MDBs. In the rush to confirm that already approved concessions were cost-effective solutions to huge infrastructure problems, analytical techniques were overwhelmed with project complexities, coopted to rubber-stamp political decisions, or simply not used at all.

4.6 The Development Community Involvement in SOE Reform

To explain the problem with brownfield concessions only in terms of a misunderstanding of basic project risks makes it sounds as if investors and operators were too quick to embrace these kinds of projects in the first place, somewhat recklessly, and without sufficient preparation. But investors and operators were attracted for another compelling reason, one that sometimes overwhelmed normal due diligence, or at least suggested that someone else had done it. Brownfield concessions in the 1990s did not often result from market interactions between governments and private investors. They were introduced under the auspices of the policy-based lending activities of the World Bank and International Monetary Fund (IMF), as tools for use in removing the state from economic activity and privatizing SOEs. SOE privatization was a key prescription of the MDB's "structural adjustment" lending operations of the 1980s and 1990s.

The SOE reform priorities of structural adjustment were driven by the degree of government intrusion into the economies of developing countries. The role of

[7] In his seminal studies of transit forecasting conducted in the late 1980s, Wachs (1990) found "nearly universal abuse" of this kind.

SOEs in African manufacturing was probably the most alarming. In the 1970s, the SOE share of manufacturing output in industrialized countries was typically only a few per cent, often zero. But in the developing world, the SOE share of manufacturing was in the 30–70 per cent range, on the order of 15 times the share in industrialized countries (Schmitz, 1996).

By the time of an explosive debt crisis in the early 1980s, most of the economies of Sub-Saharan Africa (SSA) were in a state of near collapse. The IMF, World Bank, and other MDBs considered the situation critical, requiring urgent action. In 1979, the World Bank launched its structural adjustment lending program, making available large resource injections in exchange for borrower commitments to correct economic imbalances, usually with spending reductions and efforts to reduce the public sector's role in the economy. SOE reforms were a key element of almost every adjustment operation (Nellis, 2005).

After a series of failed efforts to reform SOEs without changing the nature of public ownership, donors, DFIs, and MDBs began to plan operations that would engage the private sector in the ownership and management of SOEs. By the late 1980s, divestiture of commercial enterprises was well underway for government-owned hotels, agribusinesses, airlines, mines, oil refineries, etc. Concessions, management contracts, and leases were also being used for these enterprises, but much less frequently (Candoy-Sekse, 1988). These contracting forms, along with divestiture and joint ventures, were all brownfield solutions to SOE problems—methods for using private participation of one form or another to improve the performance of existing infrastructure assets. Greenfield projects, like IPP projects, were just underway in the 1990s to build new infrastructure, but these were more market-driven, involved MDB lending to private companies, and were therefore not the central focus of structural adjustment or other public sector reform efforts.

By the 1980s, privatization of SOEs had already started in Senegal, Niger, Kenya, Ghana, Côte d'Ivoire, and Guinea. Many other countries were under donor and MDB pressure to follow suit. Several features of the World Bank's implementation of SOE privatization during structural adjustment operations are worth noting:

- "Privatization" included very different kinds of modalities. Actual divestiture of SOEs happened almost exclusively with commercial and manufacturing enterprises that operated in competitive markets and required little or no regulation. These kinds of sales dominated the privatization landscape from the late 1980s through the early 1990s. SOEs that existed as utility monopolies in sectors where equitable and reasonably commercial tariff setting was difficult, were almost never sold, and in fact were not even focused on until the 1990s. Instead they were subjected to non-divestiture brownfield solutions, like management contracts, leases, concessions (or in some cases mixed public–private ownership). All of these brownfield solutions were routinely referred to as "privatization" and became, along with divestiture and liquidation, key elements in many of SSA's adjustment lending programs (Nellis, 2005).

- Privatization quickly became a dominant Bank policy under structural adjustment, driven by desperation to find solutions to SOE problems. Five World Bank loans per year in Africa in the 1980s explicitly called for privatization. But by the mid-1990s, the annual number of such loans in Africa alone had accelerated to 15. In the 1990s, the "non-privatization" reforms of the 1980s, were almost completely rejected by the development community, or seen only as preparation for some form of privatization (Manibog et al., 2003).
- This abrupt move into privatization was the result of deep frustration that donors, DFIs, and MDBs felt with the failed results of earlier reforms. As such, it was an approach taken without much practical experience with the results of these processes, or much empirical evidence clearly establishing the benefits of privatization. Theoretical justifications were formidable, but overall, the shift from previous reforms to widespread privatization has been characterized as "a leap of faith" (Nellis, 2005).

Infrastructure SOEs like power and water utilities became the focus of structural adjustment in the 1990s. It was already obvious that non-divestiture options were much more acceptable to government counterparts for any kind of SOE. Public protests and labor union unrest were much more common with changes in ownership than with reforms that left enterprises in government hands. Plus, there was never really any serious consideration by donors, DFIs, or MDBs of forcing the divestiture of monopoly infrastructure utilities (Nellis, 2005). So, by the mid-1990s, leases, concessions, and management contracts were being used as privatization tools far more frequently than they had been a decade earlier. But the number and variety of SOE sales and liquidations had increased even more sharply, so under structural adjustment, ownership changes still dominated most of the MDB work. A World Bank survey published just before the Asian Crisis in 1997 found that although over 200 brownfield concessions, leases, and management contracts had been concluded by that time, the total represented only about 8 per cent of total SOE privatizations, but expectations were that much more would be done with infrastructure by the end of the decade (Sarbib, 1997).

Concessions, leases, and management contracts were already well known and widely used in commercial sectors by the time donors, DFIs, and MDBs started proposing them as methods for "privatizing" infrastructure SOEs in the 1990s. Leases and management contracts had enjoyed decades of successful use in the private sector, most notably in the hotel industry (for more on management contracts, see Chapter 6). When the privatization of commercial enterprises started in developing countries in the 1980s, dozens of government-owned hotels were quickly "privatized" via management contracts. Governments of developing countries were often familiar with leases and concessions, because these kinds of contracts were widely used to develop natural resource projects in mining, petroleum, agribusiness, and forestry, from which many governments derived significant revenues. Brownfield concessions quickly became a highly recommended mechanism for "privatizing" infrastructure utilities (Guislain and Kerf, 1995).

MDB experts had advocated caution and extensive preparation in the use of the different privatization options. Cautious preparation was deemed necessary because, as a World Bank analyst noted, "the Bank has not proven to be particularly adept at advising governments on the timing or detailed mechanics of privatization ventures" (Nellis, 1989). Later evaluations showed that much of the recommended preparation was not done, probably because of the haste to find some way to reform SOEs after the failures of earlier methods in the 1980s. By the mid-1990s, approximately 15 privatization operations were being launched annually in Africa alone (Nellis, 2005). The selection of privatization options was based primarily on negotiations with government counterparts rather than analysis, and operations were initiated before lessons were learned from previous efforts. Monitoring and evaluation of privatization programs was often not done (Campbell-White and Bhatia, 1998). Performance targets were often inappropriate or too ambitious (Castalia Strategic Advisers, 2005). All of this led to a fundamental lack of data with which to evaluate ongoing privatization efforts (Estache, 2005).

The misunderstanding regarding risks associated with brownfield concessions, cited earlier as the first reason why investors became disenchanted with these contracts, was likely abetted by the speed and lack of preparation of deals that were recommended and tacitly supported by MDBs like the World Bank. But structural adjustment also brought with it additional project risks that were somewhat outside the normal analytical scope of private investors. One of these was the political risk associated with project modalities that were not very popular with government owners. Many governments resented being forced to use any of the brownfield privatization options—divestiture, joint ventures, concessions, management contracts, or leases. Most of these arrangements were opposed by labor unions and civil society groups. Most involved visible teams of highly paid expatriates and at least the appearance that governments had given up sovereign ownership or control of valuable assets. In countries with colonial histories, structural adjustment was often viewed as a type of neo-colonial prescription by the MDBs. All of this added up to a form of political risk that subjected contracts to stresses during implementation, resulting in failures by governments to raise agreed end-user prices, pay their own bills for water or electricity, renew contracts that were performing well, or even endeavor to solve problems so that contracts would not terminate prematurely.

Donors, DFIs, and MDBs eventually admitted that the benefits from privatization were smaller than expected and not as equitably distributed as desired (Gomez-Ibanez, 2007). The use of non-divestiture contracting models, like concessions, leases, and management contracts quickly lost momentum following the Asian Crisis and after that, never again achieved widespread popularity. By the late 1990s, the World Bank and other MDBs had shifted from structural adjustment to a stronger focus on more flexible reform strategies directly targeting poverty reduction. In 2002, the Bank introduced Poverty Reduction Strategy Papers as a way to plan reform efforts over which counterpart governments would have more responsibility and control. The growing controversy around structural adjustment and privatization resulted in a rapid decline in the frequency of these operations, particularly divestiture, leaving many SOEs still under government ownership by the end of the 2000s. However, brownfield concessions never completely disappeared. They continued to be used sparingly, mostly for transport projects in middle-income countries. As already noted, they achieved a brief comeback in 2012, with government-supported deals in countries like China and Brazil. But the major inducement for doing such deals in developing countries, in the form of the policy-based lending under structural adjustment, was gone.

4.7 PPP Risks and Returns in a New Light

Private investors and operators frequently amend their perceptions of project risks and returns in response to market developments, especially in cases of upheavals like the Asian crisis and the global financial crisis which took place a decade later. In contrast to the early 1990s, when recommendations and funding support from donors, DFIs, and MDBs gave investors comfort regarding brownfield concessions, these projects are now viewed as highly risky. They involve a combination of the following types of risk: financing risk associated with investments in poorly maintained government assets; demand risk associated with the questionable willingness and/or ability of end users to pay for infrastructure services; and political risk resulting from popular opposition to these structures together with fragile political and regulatory support. Projects that combine these characteristics, such as brownfield water concessions, tend to be avoided by the private sector unless governments or their development partners supply substantial amounts of funding support. This fact is confirmed by the almost total absence of projects of this kind over the last 15 years.

Projects that involve the opposite characteristics are of course now much more popular with investors and operators. They include: (i) the construction and use of new assets; ii) the provision of wholesale as opposed to retail services;

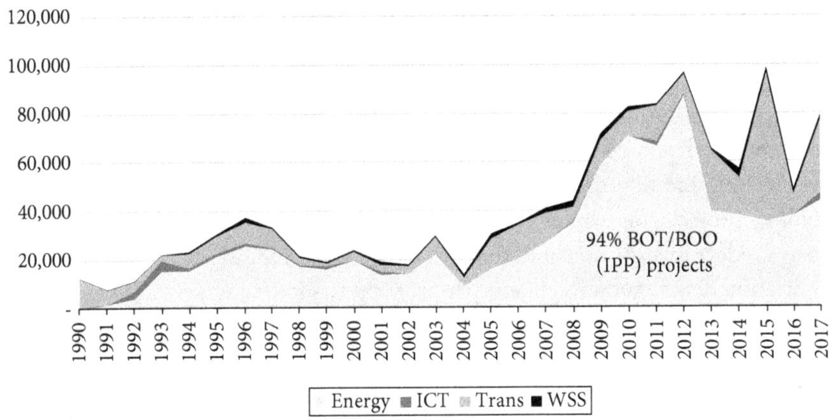

Figure 4.3 Greenfield PPPs by Sector, All Developing Countries, 1993–2015, in 2018 US$ millions

Source: World Bank, 2018.

and (iii) strong popular and political support, particularly when payments to private operators are to be made by governments, or backed by government-guaranteed off-take agreements. Thus, IPP projects, done on a greenfield basis, backed by take-or-pay off-take agreements, and done in environments where businesses and home owners are starved for affordable power, represent one of the most desirable and still growing forms of PPP in developing countries (Figure 4.3).

Cellular telephony illustrates the same kind of risk–reward calculus. Although these projects involve retail service delivery, they enjoy widespread willingness on the part of customers to pay the full costs of service (encouraged by pre-payment systems), plus the fact that required investment in associated assets is smaller than that needed in traditional infrastructure sectors. The potential rewards of investment in cellular telephony so outweigh the risks that private operators and their financial backers now usually implement these projects on a merchant basis. While these projects involve the construction of new facilities, unlike a traditional greenfield concession there is no on-going public–private risk-sharing relationship formalized in a contract. Therefore, these merchant projects are often not classified as PPPs. The private developer assumes the construction, operating, and market risk for the project, but by the same token normally does not share the project rewards—concession fees are not paid to the government. Such projects are particularly attractive to private partners in robust, liberalized markets where the government provides no revenue guarantees, but also does not regulate prices. The role of government in such projects is usually limited to licensing.

Brownfield concessions still exist and new projects of this nature are still occasionally being done in developing countries, although this is mostly limited to middle-income countries. Private investors and operators have made adjustments in their approaches to brownfield concessions in order to strengthen profits and cash flows and reduce their risk–return ratios. First, large international service providers are bidding more selectively on brownfield opportunities, particularly avoiding projects for which preparation is incomplete and information about existing assets missing. Second, the intentional underbidding of projects with the expectation of renegotiation later no longer appears to be a widely used technique for dealing with inherently risky projects. Third, several techniques are being used to supplement profits. Technical assistance fees have become more common features of brownfield concessions. Often treated as costs and charged pursuant to separate contracts, they reduce the profits of the concession company, but have the effect of transferring cash to the company shareholders and increase the project's effective overall profitability.

Similarly, when concessionaires buy new equipment, or carry out renovation, repairs, or maintenance, they often use related businesses to undertake the work or source the equipment, rather than compete out such services on a lowest-cost basis. The resulting transfer prices represent income for the larger group of companies of which the concessionaire may be a part. Like technical assistance fees, such transfers are treated as costs and therefore reduce the concessionaire's income, even though their real impact is more like that of a shareholder dividend.

Governments have also shown a willingness to take on some of the demand risk by managing the retail distribution themselves and guaranteeing a bulk service fee to the concessionaire or by paying the private partners a set fee for distribution, thus taking on more of the demand risk themselves. Governments have also demonstrated a readiness to mitigate financing risk by linking concession fees more closely to profitability of the project, and by providing some or all of the capital funding needed for a project.

This last area represents probably the biggest change in brownfield concessions since the late 1990s, and accounts for why these contracts for a brief moment in 2012, again reached the record investment levels of 1997 (in real terms). Over the last decade (since the global financial crisis) governments and their development partners have increasingly replaced scarce commercial finance with public money from government budgets (debt, equity, and subsidies) or debt from donors, DFIs, and MDBs. This is especially true for brownfield concessions. In 2015 (the first time that the World Bank distinguished public and private sources of PPP finance), private finance played a dominant role in energy sector projects, 96 per cent of which were greenfield IPP projects (Table 4.2). That same year, transport projects, about half of which are brownfield projects, received more than half of their funding from governments and DFIs.

Table 4.2 PPPs in Energy and Transport, Sources of Finance, All Developing Countries, 2015

Sectors	Private Sector	Public Sector	Donors/MDGs	Total Investment
Energy 4% brownfield	65%	16%	19%	\$31.7 b
Transport 48% brownfield	49%	41%	10%	\$20.7 b

Source: Chao and Saha, 2016; World Bank, 2018.

4.8 Conclusions

The history of brownfield concessions offers some of the answers to questions about why expectations regarding PPPs in developing countries were so high in the early 1990s and why it took so long for those expectations to change. As with other brownfield solutions to SOE problems promoted by donors, DFIs, and MDBs under structural adjustment, these contracts were never actually very popular with governments or investors in the first place. They were attractive to the international development community mostly as forms of "privatization" (like management contracts, leases, and affermage contracts) that were preferable to more extreme brownfield solutions like liquidation or divestiture in addressing what seemed like urgent problems with monopoly infrastructure utilities. They were contracting modalities borrowed by the development community from commercial sectors and heavily promoted for use in solving SOE problems, rather than contracts generated by commercial market transactions. But in the public sector these kinds of contracts faced severe challenges—they were pressed into service to reform badly mismanaged utilities, rather than serve as simple mechanisms for sharing risks and profits in lucrative commercial sectors like hotel administration and mining.

The acceptance of these contracts by reluctant governments was incentivized with policy-based lending that usually also included funding for the design and tendering of these contracts. MDB involvement encouraged potential private partners to assume that the contracts were well designed and prepared, and would be fully honored. Because of endorsements and financial support from MDBs in the early 1990s, no one paid much attention to the risks associated with these deals. However, private investors and operators learned enduring lessons regarding PPP risks and rewards when many of these contracts collapsed during the Asian crisis, as inadequate risk mitigation measures failed. In low-income countries, brownfield concessions have been avoided ever since, with private partners engaging in these deals only when governments or MDBs agree to take on considerable levels of financing risk. The fate of brownfield concessions largely explains the failure of PPPs in general to gain a foothold in the developing world.

In the meantime, greenfield projects have kept alive the PPP market in poor countries, becoming by far the most widely used PPP form, with projects concentrated in power generation and mobile telephony.

Chapter 5 presents a case study of the Nelspruit water PPP, signed in South Africa in 1999, which illustrates many of the problems that came to be associated with brownfield concessions in SSA. Other kinds of water PPPs have been developed in Africa, such as leases and management contracts, as well as affermage projects in West Africa. But Nelspruit, along with a similar project signed a few months earlier, also in South Africa, and a project in Gabon (recently cancelled by the government), are commonly recognized as the most successful classic brownfield water concessions signed in SSA. "Classic" refers to the fact the private partner was obligated to manage the retail operations of the utility, including customer billing and collections, as well as invest in the system's assets. South Africa is of course not a low-income country, but a brownfield concession of this kind has never been successful in a low-income country in SSA. In addition, although this PPP is still in operation after 20 years, no other project of this kind was ever again attempted in South Africa—both the government and the private sector learned valuable lessons from the Nelspruit experience, as Chapter 5 attempts to explain.

References

Baietti, A., W. Kingdom, M. van Ginneken. 2006. "Characteristics of Well-Performing Public Water Utilities." Water Supply & Sanitation Working Notes, No. 9. Washington, DC: World Bank.

Campbell-White, O., A. Bhatia. 1998. *Privatization in Africa*. Washington, DC: World Bank.

Candoy-Sekse, R. 1988. "Techniques of Privatization of State-Owned Enterprises, Volume III." World Bank Technical Paper No. 90. Washington, DC: World Bank.

Castalia Strategic Advisors. 2005. "Experience with Private Participation in Sub-Saharan African Infrastructure: What are the Lessons for Future Policy?" Unpublished report prepared for the African Infrastructure Department of the World Bank.

Chao, J., D. Saha. 2016. "Sources of Financing for PPP Investments 2015." Washington, DC: World Bank.

De Fraja, G., C. Stones. 2004. "Risk and Capital Structure in the Regulated Firm." *Journal of Regulatory Economics*, 26(1): 69–84.

De Lemos, T., M. Betts, D. Eaton, L. Tadeu De Almeida. 2000. "From Concessions to Project Finance and the Private Finance Initiative." *The Journal of Project Finance*, 6(3): 19–37.

Ehrhardt, D., T. Irwin. 2004. "Avoiding Customer and Taxpayer Bailouts in Private Infrastructure Projects: Policy Toward Leverage, Risk Allocation, and Bankruptcy." Policy Research Working Paper 3274. Washington, DC: World Bank.

Estache, A. 2005. "What do we know about Sub-Saharan Africa's Infrastructure and the Impact of its 1990s reforms?" *Universite Libre de Bruxelles*, Ecares Working Paper, May 25.

Estache, A., J. Strong. 2000. "The Rise, the Fall, and... the Emerging Recovery of Project Finance in Transport." Policy Research Working Paper No. 2385. Washington, DC: World Bank.

Flyvbjerg, B. 2005. "Policy and Planning for Large Infrastructure Projects: Problems, Causes, Cures," Policy Research Working Paper 3781. Washington, DC: World Bank.

Foster, V., C.M. Briceno-Garmendia. 2010. *Africa's Infrastructure: A Time for Transformation*. Washington, DC: World Bank.

Foster, V., T. Yepes. 2006. "Is Cost Recovery a Feasible Objective for Water and Electricity? The Latin America Experience." Policy Research Working Paper 3943. Washington, DC: World Bank.

Gomez-Ibanez, J. 2007. "Alternatives to Infrastructure Privatization Revisited: Public Enterprise Reform from the 1960s to the 1980s." World Bank Policy Research Working Paper No. 4391. Washington, DC: World Bank.

Guasch, J.L. 2004. *Granting and Renegotiating Infrastructure Concessions: Doing It Right*. WBI Development Studies. Washington, DC: World Bank.

Guislain, P., M. Kerf. 1995. "Concessions—The Way to Privatize Infrastructure Monopolies." World Bank Public Policy for the Private Sector Note No. 59. Washington, DC: World Bank (October).

Israel, A. 1992. "Issues for Infrastructure Management in the 1990s." World Bank Discussion Paper 171. Washington, DC: World Bank.

Kerf, M., R.D. Gray, T. Irwin, C. Levesque, R.R. Taylor. 1998. "Concessions for Infrastructure: A guide to their design and award." World Bank Technical Paper No. 399. Washington, DC: World Bank.

Lawyers' Environmental Action Team, the Legal and Human Rights Centre, the Tanzania Gender Networking Programme, the Center for International Environmental Law, and the International Institute for Sustainable Development. 2007. "Amicus Curiae Submission in Case No. ARB/05/22 before the International Centre for Settlement of Investment Disputes between Biwater Gauff Ltd. and United Republic of Tanzania." March 26.

Leigland, J. 2018. "Changing Perceptions of PPP Risk and Return: The Case of Brownfield Concessions." *The Journal of Structured Finance*, 23(4): 47–56.

Manibog, F., R. Dominguez, S. Wegner. 2003. *Power for Development: A Review of the World Bank Group's Experience with Private Participation in the Electricity Sector.* World Bank Operations Evaluation Department, IFC Operations Evaluation Group, MIGA Operations Evaluation Unit. Washington, DC: World Bank, IFC, MIGA.

Marshella, T. 2001. "Debt Financing of Projects in Emerging Economies: Lessons from Asia." *The Journal of Project Finance*,7(2): 30–4.

Martin, L. 2005. "Public–Private Partnerships in the Water Sector of the EECCA Region: Update and Recommendations for the Improvement of Service Delivery."

Paper presented at the Conference of EECCA Ministers of Economy/Finance, Environment and Water, OECD Task Force for the Implementation of the Environmental Action Programme for Central and Eastern Europe, Caucasus and Central Asia Yerevan, Armenia, November 17–18.

Nellis, J. 1989. "Public Enterprise Reform in Adjustment Lending." World Bank Policy, Planning, and Research Working Paper No. 233. Washington, DC: World Bank (August).

Nellis, J. 2005. "The Evolution of Enterprise Reform in Africa: From State-Owned Enterprises to Private Participation in Infrastructure—and Back?" World Bank ESMAP Technical Paper No. 084. Washington, DC: World Bank.

Pomerleano, M. 1998. "Corporate Finance Lessons from the East Asian Crisis." *Public Policy for the Private Sector*, Note No. 155. Washington, DC: World Bank (October).

Pozzo di Borgo, P., A. Labeau, R. Eskinazi, J. Dehornoy, A. Parte, M. Ameziane. 2006. "Sub-Saharan Africa: Review of Selected Railway Concessions." Africa Transport Sector, Report No. 36491. Washington, DC: World Bank.

Sarbib, J.L. 1997. "Privatization in Africa: Present and Future Trends." Paper presented at the African Development Bank Group Annual Meeting Symposium on "Private Sector Development in Africa," Abidjan, May 21.

Schmitz, J.A. 1996. "The Role Played by Public Enterprises: How Much Does It Differ Across Countries." *Federal Reserve Bank of Minneapolis Quarterly Review*, 20(2): 2–15.

Sirtaine, S., M. E. Pinglo, J. Guasch, V. Foster. 2004. "How Profitable Are Infrastructure Concessions in Latin America? Empirical Evidence and Regulatory Implications." PPIAF Trends and Policy Options. Washington, DC: World Bank.

Wachs, M. 1990. "Ethics and Advocacy in Forecasting for Public Policy." *Business and Professional Ethics Journal*, 9(1 & 2): 141–57.

World Bank. 2018. PPI Project Database. Accessed at: http://ppi.worldbank.org/customquery?mode=1

5

Case Study

Nelspruit—SSA's Last Water Concession

5.1 Introduction

In 1995, as donors, development finance institutions (DFIs), and multilateral development banks (MDBs) pursuing structural adjustment activities were beginning to look for ways of using private participation to help reform existing infrastructure utilities, World Bank experts explained why "Concession-type arrangement are well suited for privatizing sectors with monopolistic characteristics" (Guislain and Kerf, 1995, 1):

> In its classical (or narrow) sense, a concession is a public utility: it provides a public service to end users. Direct payment of the concessionaire by the users, who are not party to the concession contract, was seen as a defining feature of this scheme. Examples of such concessions include bridges, tunnels, toll roads, and water and power distribution systems (Guislain and Kerf, 1995, 3).

But as the discussion in Chapter 4 suggests, the popularity of this "classical" brownfield concession model, involving investment plus retail operation, was short lived. Rapidly changing investor perceptions of risks and returns during and after the Asian crisis made public–private partnerships (PPPs) of this kind far less attractive. And by then it had become clear that such projects were being aggressively promoted by MDBs, DFIs, and donors more because they were seen as reform tools than because they represented solid commercial investment opportunities for the private sector.

In developing country regions like Sub-Saharan Africa (SSA), these lessons were learned quickly and rarely forgotten, particularly in sectors like water and sanitation. In the 1990s, the reform of urban water supply was one of the highest infrastructure priorities—millions of Africans lacked access to piped water and sanitation services or received very low-quality service. It was hoped that brownfield water concessions would be a principal way of generating urgently needed investment in the sector (Marin, 2009). Since the early 1990s, several attempts have been made to structure leases and management contracts in Africa's water sector, with varying degrees of success. But these projects typically did not involve

Public–Private Partnerships in Sub-Saharan Africa: The Evidence-Based Critique. James Leigland, Oxford University Press (2020).
DOI: 10.1093/oso/9780198861829.001.0001

major capital investment. Only three "classical" brownfield water concessions, involving investment and supply to end users, have ever reached financial closure in SSA; none after 2000.

Two of these concessions were signed months apart in South Africa, by far the strongest and largest economy in Africa at the time, and already in possession of an investment grade rating from an international credit rating agency. Two decades later those two contracts are still in operation, making them among the most successful brownfield water concessions in the developing world, at least in terms of longevity.[1] But the South African government has never formally acknowledged any of the successes of these projects or tried to replicate them in other urban areas. The World Bank's global review of PPPs for urban water utilities in developing countries makes only a few passing references to these projects (Marin, 2009).

This chapter examines the largest of the South African projects, located in the town of Mbombela (called Nelspruit at the time the concession was signed) in the eastern part of Mpumalanga province. How and why was this concession developed? As one of the longest operating brownfield PPPs operating in SSA, how has the concession performed in terms of costs, profits, finance, investment, equity, efficiency, and governance? What were the lessons learned from the concession? Why has the project been officially forgotten by the government despite its apparent sustainability and other outward appearances of success? In what sense is this project the last water concession in SSA?

5.2 Project Background

On April 21, 1999, the Nelspruit Transitional Local Council (TLC) signed a 30-year concession contract with the Greater Nelspruit Utility Company (GNUC), a private company partly owned by British water operator Biwater.[2] A similar 30-year contract was signed with SAUR International of France in January the same year in a small coastal community north of Durban, called Dolphin Coast. But the Nelspruit contract involved a much larger service area, and a beneficiary population (at 240,000) roughly five times the size of Dolphin Coast.

[1] By 2018, these two South African water concessions were the only ones still in operation. The third SSA water concession was a 20-year contract signed in Gabon in 1997, and renewed for five more years in March 2017. But in early 2018, the government cancelled the contract for poor performance and seized the assets of the power and water utility, SEEG, owned by the concessionaire, Veolia. Veolia countered with charges that the government owed SEEG over 41 billion CFA francs (€62.5 million) in consumption charges and unpaid value-added tax reimbursements (Global Water Intelligence, 2018; Reuters, 2018).

[2] Some of the following sections draw (with the authors' permission) from Kotze, Ferguson, and Leigland (2000).

In a study published in 2000, the city managers of both Nelspruit and Dolphin Coast explained the reasons for the concessions (Kotze, Ferguson, and Leigland, 2000). In both towns, it was the need to provide essential services to expanded numbers of city residents that prompted consideration of a partnership with a private service provider. In the post-Apartheid era, beginning in 1994, white and black areas were amalgamated, with managers of predominately white urban areas suddenly responsible for supplying essential services to huge numbers of new, previously disadvantaged citizens. Nelspruit was an extreme case: virtually overnight, the town's official population increased from 24,000 to 240,000, and the land area under its jurisdiction increased by over eight times. Because many of the new areas had never received water and sanitation services, the town's official system of infrastructure service provision was suddenly inadequate. The extent of the inadequacy was alarming: the 1994 amalgamation increased the number of residents per length of water pipe from 110 to 601, and the number of residents per length of sewer pipe from 96 to 830. The difficulties faced by the town in overcoming this shortfall with tariff revenues, or loans based on tariff income, was apparent from the obvious inability of these new residents to help cover the costs of required investment. Although the town's population had grown by ten times, the total income of the urban area grew by only 38 per cent (Kotze, Ferguson, and Leigland, 2000). Nelspruit officials concluded that they needed to seek a radical, innovative solution if they were going to fulfill their obligation to meet national targets regarding universal water service coverage.

On 26 August 1996, the city council passed a resolution to explore the possibility of a PPP for the city's water operations. The city council also appointed the Development Bank of Southern Africa (DBSA) to lead their detailed investigation of PPP feasibility. DBSA fielded a team of 16 to carry out a series of tasks including financial modeling, liaison with provincial and national government, recommendations regarding service delivery options, levels of service, related contractual mechanisms, surveys of potential financing options, and assistance with procurement and contracting.

The investigations by DBSA appeared to confirm what Nelspruit officials originally feared. The amount of capital investment needed by the city was so great that a comparison of the costs and benefits of private vs. public sector service provision seemed to require no sophisticated calculation. Continued public sector service provision would mean that universal service coverage could not be achieved. Private service provision seemed virtually the only realistic way of raising needed levels of capital investment. DBSA estimated that the total water and sanitation investment required to serve all of Nelspruit's citizens was approximately R250 million in 1997 values (Kotze, Ferguson, and Leigland, 2000). With the entire city budget allowed to grow by no more than 6 per cent annually, and no more than roughly one-third of that budget focused on water and sanitation (about R8.5 million), the council faced a situation where none of the usual sources of finance (budget surpluses, loans, grants) would be enough (alone or in combination) to offer meaningful assistance in meeting the town's capital investment needs for water and sanitation. Every municipal employee involved in the provision of water and sanitation services could forever forego payment for work, and the city still would be unable to raise the capital needed to extend these services to all of its citizens.

By September 1996, an initial Nelspruit PPP Business Plan had been prepared according to existing national government guidelines. The plan was submitted to the national Department for Constitutional Development (DCD) for project assistance. DCD funding was made available in early 1997.

By the end of November 1996, after several months of further consideration, the council concluded that it was impossible to be able to finance and manage the supply of required services without external assistance. A request for proposals (RFP) was issued on 9 December. Proposals were returned by May 1, 1997. At this point, DBSA consultants withdrew because of the bank's possible future role as financier of the eventual deal and the desire to avoid conflicts of interest if they continued to help with the procurement. To replace DBSA, the council hired a specialist team of local and international consultants to assist with proposal adjudication. Most of the funding for these consultants was provided by the US Agency for International Development (USAID) and channeled through national government. On October 10, 1997, the city council announced a preferred bidder.

On November 24, 1997, the municipal officials temporarily suspended negotiations with the preferred bidder due to the need to consult with organized labor, as requested by provincial authorities. A series of discussions followed. Union representatives offered a model of an alternative form of service provision involving public sector delivery. Further discussions took place, but no progress was made in resolving differences. In April 1998, the council lifted the moratorium on negotiations with the preferred bidder after consultation with provincial political leadership and an assessment of likely damage to the project development process resulting from any further delays. On April 21, 1999, after long negotiations involving 11 drafts of the concession contract, agreement was reached and the contact signed, 28 months after the RFP was issued.

In 2000, the Nelspruit TLC was renamed the Mbombela Local Municipality. The new municipal boundaries more than doubled the population of the municipality, but the concession area boundaries did not change. The concessionaire continued to provide services in the concession area—the Mbombela Municipality managed the water and sanitation services in the areas outside the concession area. In the interests of clarity and consistency, this chapter will continue to refer to the water concession as the "Nelspruit contract."

5.3 Contract Requirements

Nelspruit officials signed the contract with the concessionaire, the GNUC.[3] GNUC was 26 per cent owned by Biwater Operations, a South African subsidiary of Biwater; 64 per cent owned by Biwater Capital, a Biwater subsidiary incorporated in the Netherlands; and 10 per cent owned by Sivukile Investments, a South African black empowerment company. The concessionaire was given overall responsibility for operation, maintenance, and management of the municipal water system assets, as well as for raising the capital investment necessary for the expansion of services (Nelspruit TLC, 1999). As part of this activity, GNUC was made responsible for billing and collecting customer tariff payments and was given the right to apply credit control procedures in cases where customers refused to pay. Finally, in classic brownfield concession fashion, all fixed assets remained the property of the municipality, although they were leased to the contractor for the duration of the 30-year concession contract and were required to be returned in a specified condition at the end of the concession period.

The contract required that a minimum of R190 million would be spent on capital projects by GNUC over the first five years of the concession. At least 25 per cent of capital spent was required to come from the concessionaire's equity, with rest financed from debt. Any shortfall in capital requirements would have to be financed by the concessionaire through sponsor investment in the project company. GNUC would have to take the full commercial risk for the project. Among other things, this meant that GNUC's failure to meet profit expectations could not be used as an argument for increasing tariffs.

The contract also required several kinds of financial commitments by the concession company, in addition to the capital investments called for. GNUC's performance against contract targets was backed by an R8 million guarantee. The guarantee was supposed to grow annually in line with growth in the Consumer Price Index. GNUC was required to pay a "contract implementation fee" of R200,000 to the council at the time of contract signing, as well as an annual R1.25 million concession fee. These fees were to increase annually in line with the Consumer Price Index; the concession fee could be renegotiated after five years.

GNUC was also required to lease the assets of the exiting water and sanitation systems. Lease documents were included as annexures to the concession contract. GNUC agreed to pay approximately R10.6 million annually for the use of the council's moveable and immoveable assets over the first ten years of the concession period, after which the fee would drop to R100 per year. The lease payments were geared to the debts associated with the system, which in effect GNUC

[3] The company eventually operated under the name Silulumanzi.

would repay on behalf of the council. When the debts were paid, the lease payments would end.

5.4 Evaluation

Chapter 2 attempts to summarize some of the most compelling examples of the emerging evidence-based critique of PPPs by organizing them around key themes. The following subsections address those themes from the perspective of the Nelspruit concession.

5.4.1 PPP Prevalence

As Chapter 2 attempts to explain, PPPs have not, in general, met stakeholder expectations, and this has contributed to a lack of widespread use in developing countries. Periods of government enthusiasm have been followed by periods of disappointment, with the PPP mechanism never successfully gaining a strong foothold in most African countries.

South Africa's use of PPP certainly fits this general pattern. National-level South African officials had already decided not to replicate PPPs like the Nelspruit concession, even before the Nelspruit contract was signed. The post-Apartheid government had never had a strong, consistent interest in PPPs, despite the fact that the country possessed the largest and healthiest economy in Africa, something that presumably would have made PPPs much easier to develop and more sustainable than in the continent's many low-income countries. In the fashion described by Klein (2015), South Africa has embraced PPPs from time to time when particular needs arise, but enthusiasm for this mechanism has never been deep or enduring and never strongly articulated in formal policies. The country's most noteworthy PPP success, the Maputo Toll Road Concession, resulted from a combination of the need to quickly begin rebuilding the country's infrastructure after the end of apartheid, a strong desire to revitalize a long-standing trade route between the country's manufacturing center in Gauteng province and the port of Maputo in Mozambique, and the government's lack of resources needed to finance infrastructure improvements. The toll road contract, signed in 1997, was strongly championed by Nelson Mandela, who personally encouraged private sector interest in that project at an investor conference in 1996 (see Chapter 3).

The Nelspruit concession was also on the list of Maputo corridor projects presented at that conference. The toll road concession contract was tendered and signed very quickly thanks to a hard-driving project team in South Africa's Department of Transportation, who sensed that delays would open the door to debilitating ideological debates about the morality of privatization. But the high-level political support reflected in the success of the toll road was never institutionalized in policy and never accepted by many in the ruling party's rank and file. Within a few years, Mandela and many of his like-minded senior officials were no longer in positions to drive private participation in infrastructure. New leadership of the Mpumalanga province, of which Nelspruit was the capital, slowed down development of the water concession by requiring an additional long series of consultations with labor unions, which interrupted contract negotiations by six months. That delay, plus other delays in preparation, allowed unions, civil society groups, and politicians to muster and consolidate opposition to the water concession, under the banner of anti-privatization.

National government officials expressed their lack of support for the project in another fundamental way that had a significant long-term impact on project activities. At the time the Nelspruit contract was being prepared, the regulatory framework affecting water and sanitation PPPs was a patchwork of laws and regulations. In late 1998, during the final stages of contract negotiation, project lawyers uncovered several problems with the legal framework that had potentially disastrous consequences for the concession. The most important of these was the fact that the Water Services Act of 1997 (WSA) gave broad powers to the South African minister of water affairs and forestry to affect the implementation of PPP contracts in the water sector. The WSA empowered the minister to set technical standards and tariffs, intervene in any contract that he or she felt warranted intervention, and even seize private infrastructure assets, apparently without compensation or even due process. The possibility of arbitrary and capricious exercise of such powers, by future ministers hostile to private participation in public service provision, appeared to constitute a serious risk for all parties to the Nelspruit contract.

Project lawyers quickly redrafted the concession contract in early 1999, adding an "interim arrangement" that temporarily circumvented problems with the legislation (DBSA, 1999). The interim arrangement was designed to remain in place until the existing legislation could be replaced by a new law, the Municipal Systems Act (MSA), scheduled for passage in late 1999 or early 2000. In drafting the new bill, the Department of Constitutional Development pledged to resolve the problems for PPPs caused by the existing regulatory framework.

But commercial lenders were not convinced that the interim arrangement adequately dealt with the existing risks posed by the WSA and other legislation. These lenders declined to participate in the project until the MSA had solved the regulatory problems. In order to keep the project on track, the DBSA, a parastatal development financing institution, agreed to provide initial funding to the project company. With the resolution of the various legal and regulatory problems, via passage of the MSA, the issuance of implementing regulations for the WSA, and small amendments to the contract document, etc., the commercial lenders could return to the deal by purchasing some of the lending responsibilities from DBSA.

By late 1999, this arrangement appeared to be viable, and the contract was signed with DBSA financial support.

At the end of 2000, Parliament passed the MSA. But national officials had not lived up to their promises to the project. Among other things, the new act authorized the minister of provincial and local government to issue regulations limiting municipal tariff increases for any and all municipal services. However, the Act included no indication of what kinds of tariff increases would be limited, why tariffs might be limited, or what process would be followed in determining acceptable tariff levels. As authorized by the Act, the capping of municipal tariff increases could be done solely at the personal discretion of the minister (Republic of South Africa, 2000).

This section of act was a textbook example of a threat of "material adverse government action" (MAGA), which puts at risk any PPP project that relies on tariff revenues for economic viability (Leigland, 2003). Potential private sector participants in such deals, as well as various transaction experts, warned national officials that such language introduced risks into the PPP contract negotiation process, which were not easily managed by either party to the contract. Many predicted that new PPP projects would not move forward as a result. In a letter to the Minister of Finance, the Chief Executive of DBSA said, " this type of regulatory uncertainty will be a severe setback to attracting private capital to such projects, unless accompanied by a government guarantee" (Goldin, 2001). But national officials refused to alter the legislation or provide guarantees. No commercial banks have ever lent money to the Nelspruit project. No other long-term water concessions of this type have ever been developed in South Africa. Regardless of the success or failure of the Nelspruit concession, national officials had already acted on ideological grounds to severely limit the spread of PPPs in the country.

5.4.2 Costs and Profits

The studies reviewed in Chapter 1 suggest that governments and their development partners have not done a very effective job of anticipating PPP costs and profits, so assessments of value for money (VFM) frequently have been off the mark. This was certainly true in the case of the Nelspruit concession. GNUC experienced higher than expected costs and lower profits almost immediately as the company took control of the Nelspruit water system. End users in many parts of the service area simply refused pay their water bills. A willingness-to-pay survey done during project preparation seemed to suggest that people wanted household connections in most cases and were willing to pay the expected costs. But when operations began, payment levels in the townships were considerably lower than anyone expected.

Cost recovery in the townships was 38 per cent in July 2001, falling to 27 per cent by December 2001 (Brown, 2005). Widespread non-payment caused GNUC to adopt credit control measures like service cut-offs, which were allowed by the contract, but seemed draconian to residents. During this period, which also roughly coincided with a local cholera epidemic, approximately 6,000 newly installed meters were removed from the townships pursuant to service cut-offs for non-payment. This in turn resulted in illegal connections, even lower payment levels, a campaign against the contract by a political party, as well as intimidation and threats of violence directed at GNUC workers, city managers, and councilors.

National government inadvertently contributed to Nelspruit's non-payment problem by announcing in February 2001, in the aftermath of the cholera epidemic, approval of a recommended municipal policy that would ensure 6 kl of water per month to low-income households, free of charge. Nelspruit politicians quickly implemented the government recommendation, but extended free water to all households, regardless of income, in order to reduce the administrative costs of accurately targeting the water subsidy payments and remove the stigma of applying for vouchers. Councilors also added an extra 6 kl for sanitation, an extra benefit that was not part of the national government recommendation. The free basic water measures were implemented in January 2002.

No new national government subsidy funding was provided to municipalities to pay for the free water. Municipalities were expected to use existing subsidies, taxes and levies, as well as cross-subsidization to cover the cost. The result of free basic water seems to have been even lower levels of payment, and a significant drop in GNUC's rate of return (Brown, 2005). Two renegotiations of the concession contract followed. The first was an informal consultation, during which the Council agreed to grant GNUC's request for tariff increases in two stages, 10 per cent in January 2002 and an additional 10 per cent in July 2002. The Council also agreed to provide GNUC with more help with credit control, particularly because the council could no longer tolerate the political fallout caused by service cut-offs. GNUC was worried that the free water policy would lead to more non-payment because the national government seemed to have acknowledged that water should be free to citizens who felt they could not pay. Finally, the Council agreed to finance the subsidy through a portion of its national grant funds that would be passed on to GNUC. Cross-subsidization would be used to cover any remaining shortfall in funds for the water subsidy (Bender and Gibson, 2010).

However, despite the measures agreed to by the Council, GNUC's revenue losses continued to mount. Measures agreed to by the Council in order to finance the free water subsidy were not making up for losses. In early 2003, GNUC threatened to default on their contract commitments and in effect end the contract. This triggered a second, more formal contract renegotiation involving the contractor, the municipality, and a host of national government officials.

The Council eventually agreed to a sweeping list of contract amendments: reductions in GNUC's electricity bill, monitoring fee, and the fee for rental of utility assets (from R10.6 million per year to R6.6 million), and an increase in GNUC's share of the municipality's national subsidies. The most significant change was an agreement that GNUC would stop further capital expenditure needed for the upgrading program, unless the money came from grants or surplus revenue. This meant that no additional significant capital investments were made in the utility infrastructure after 2003 at the risk of the private concessionaire (Bender and Gibson, 2010).

5.4.3 Project Preparation

Across the developing world, PPP project preparation costs have been much higher than expected, and higher than the costs of preparing projects for traditional public procurement. High preparation costs present governments and their development partners with a difficult problem—who pays for preparation costs that cannot always be recovered in some way from the project? In the 1990s, this problem was often solved by assuming that the private sector should pay these costs.

The belief that PPP project preparation could be done more quickly and less expensively by shifting much it to the private sector created its own problems for projects like the Nelspruit concession. The belief was an outgrowth of the notion that implementing a PPP meant handing over government problems with infrastructure to private companies for solution. For policy makers (as well as donors, DFIs, and MDBs) this handover often meant that there was no need to spend government (or donor) time or money preparing long-term PPP projects, doing feasibility studies, assessing contracting options, etc. In many of the contracts signed in the 1990s, much of this work was assumed to be the responsibility of potential private partners; part of their normal due diligence, because if the project ultimately failed, it would be at the sole cost of the private partners.

Chapter 2 mentions an early example of the low-cost PPP project preparation problem, the Buenos Aires water concession. Signed in December 1992, this was one of the first, large brownfield concessions. Because of a perceived need to accelerate the procurement process, very little pre-bid information on the condition of the service system was collected by the government, and officials refused to take any responsibility for the quality or accuracy of the information provided to bidders. The winning bidder used the first four pages of the bid document to describe the serious lack of information made available for bidding purposes (Alcazar, Abdala, and Shirley, 2000). The poor quality of the information made the information content of bids unreliable and may have led bidders to prepare bids under the assumption that they would be allowed to renegotiate their contract as new information came to light. The concession agreement required the operator to assume all information risks and stated that "claims based on defects of information provided will not be allowed" (Aguas Argentinas S.A. Concession Contract, 1993). In fact, the project company did eventually make such claims based on what it said was new information about the condition of the assets. A series of contract renegotiations followed before the contract was prematurely cancelled in 2006.

South African officials were well aware of the Buenos Aires approach to project preparation. The process of developing the Nelspruit concession intentionally copied the Buenos Aires approach to preparation in the interests of cost and speed (Kotze, Ferguson, and Leigland, 2000). Some information about existing system assets and operating performance was provided to bidders in the RFP and project data room. The RFP also specified levels of services that the concession was required to achieve in the different residential areas. But bidders were cautioned to base their bids exclusively on their own due diligence and not assume that the municipality's information was necessarily thorough or correct. This caution was underscored by a warning that the eventual contract would have to be entered into on a "voetstoots" basis (an Afrikaans term meaning "as it stands"). As with the Buenos Aires water concession, this meant that the municipality was taking no responsibility for "latent defects," faults in the system that could not have been discovered by a reasonably thorough inspection before the contract was signed. In other words, the municipality took no responsibility for the "nature, condition, fitness of purpose, merchantability or suitability of any existing asset" (Nelspruit TLC,1999). This was a way of incentivizing the bidders to do more than "reasonably thorough" investigations into project feasibility as part of the bid process.[4]

This approach to project preparation had several far-reaching consequences for the Nelspruit project.

- The approach meant that the town did not supply bidders with a detailed project overview that inventoried and assessed the condition of all assets, organization structures, procedures, and other aspects of the existing service provision system. Project databases and asset registers were not complete at the time of bidding. The concessionaire was supposed to prepare a full asset register only during project implementation. Even the list of assets to be transferred to the concessionaire would only be made available to the preferred bidder, so could not be used in preparing bids. As one potential bidder complained during the RFP question and answer process, "Our major concern

[4] A new South African Consumer Protection Act, passed in 2012, prohibited the use of "voetstoets" clauses in sales agreements, requiring the seller to inform the buyer of the condition of the property, including any defects (whether latent or obvious). The buyer would then be able to make an informed purchasing decision. Any excluded defects found after the purchase were to remain the responsibility of the seller.

with the RFP is the lack of technical information contained therein, which will enable us to properly price the capital works involved in this project" (Nelspruit TLC, 1997, Sect. 4).

- Although the RFP contained detailed levels of service required for the different residential areas, those levels were not based on an accurate assessment of willingness and ability to pay—the biggest failure of the contract. The service levels apparently emerged from several public workshops in the township areas, where residents indicated they would pay for service as long as it was reliable and of good quality (Nelspruit TLC, 1996, 40). A "socioeconomic study" of the service area was carried out after the RFP was issued and made available to bidders before bids were due. But it was completed in less than a month by a local urban planning firm and did not lead to any significant refinements in service levels. That study is no longer publicly available; it is unclear what kind of methodology was used to assess willingness and ability of residents to pay for the specified service levels. Whatever methodology was used, it was clearly flawed. Bidders noted that even the RFP's population figures for different residential areas seemed inconsistent with figures from the South African national statistics agency (Nelspruit TLC, 1997, Sect. 7).
- Bidders were clearly concerned about the possibility of non-payment and requested a meeting with the municipality to discuss this. But city officials and their advisers considered this to be another issue that was to be handled by bidders' due diligence. A discussion with bidders on this topic was rejected by municipal officials. The RFP indicated that the municipality would accept no liability for non-payment problems (Nelspruit TLC, 1996, Sect. 17.1.2), which the concessionaire would have to deal with using contract-based rules for service cut-offs. The use of what were fairly harsh cut-off provisions (cut-offs made 14 days after written notice of non-payment) eventually exacerbated the non-payment problems that nearly collapsed the contract in 2003. After 2003, the municipality refused to allow cut-offs.
- Advisers to the municipality reasoned that a lengthy procurement process would give potential private partners time to do their own due diligence studies and thereby save the municipality preparation costs. However, such an approach not only seriously delayed procurement decisions (almost a full year between RFP issuance and announcement of preferred bidder), but it also left negotiators without any mutually agreed starting place regarding the condition of the service system that the private partner would take control of. Contract negotiations took much longer because many risks associated with the operation of the existing system were not clear. And the extended period between RFP issuance and contract signing gave anti-privatization opponents of the project extra time to marshal opposition to it. The fact that no draft contract was included with the RFP also extended negotiations.

GNUC and municipal officials were forced to construct the contract page by page, over the negotiating table. In the process of working through 11 contract drafts, the municipality lost the negotiating advantage they might have had by beginning the process with a contract draft that represented the best possible—and most realistic—arrangement for the city.

- Finally, the municipality used a combination of local and foreign-based advisers in preparing the project and negotiating the contract. But the length of time involved in the process meant that the cost of the advisory work began to undercut the municipality's intention of keeping preparation costs low. This led to some shortcomings in preparation. For example, the municipality used a highly experienced US-based consultant to act as its team leader for negotiations. But this meant that, over the long process of negotiations, team leadership lost focus. The team leader was unable to consistently participate in the process because of costs and timing problems associated with the need for frequent trips to South Africa (Kotze, Ferguson, and Leigland, 2000). The final stages of contract negotiations were handled by city officials with virtually no experience with such agreements. Similarly, the failure to identify early on the potential legal problems for the contract resulting from existing legislation may have been the result of cost-cutting efforts to push most of the legal due diligence to the bidders and rely on local lawyers with little relevant PPP experience to advise the municipality. The identification of legal issues such as this should be a priority task of consultants engaged to assess the feasibility of such projects and this failure can only be considered a very serious shortcoming of the Nelspruit preparation process.

If one were pressed to identify a single area of the project that best accounts for its failed expectations, it would probably be project preparation. The municipality's hands-off approach to project design, which combined failure to do a comprehensive evaluation of system assets and a thorough assessment of customer willingness and ability to pay for targeted service levels, meant that the city did not start the procurement process with a realistic sense of project feasibility. By insisting that the concessionaire take sole responsibility for things like asset condition (including latent defects) as well as customer non-payment, the municipality thought it was forcing the bidders to clarify key feasibility issues that city officials did not have the resources to resolve. This aggressive approach to PPP contracting—forcing private partners to take responsibility for anything that went wrong—was a common feature in early brownfield concessions. It also led to disaster during times of contract distress, as happened repeatedly during the Asian crisis. Few private concessionaires would suffer even moderate financial losses because assets had latent defects or customers would not pay their bills. Most operators would threaten to default on the agreement to force renegotiation or let the contract collapse and exploit contract termination clauses usually allowing for various kinds of financial restitution. The Nelspruit municipality and its advisers thought they were boxing their operator into a corner. Instead they were making the contract fragile in a way that the contractor could exploit for its own interests when the contract came under stress.

5.4.4 Finance and Investment

Data compiled by the World Bank in 2016 suggests that private finance is not necessarily the predominant source of investment funding for PPP projects in developing countries (Chao, 2016). Governments, or their state-owned banks, along with donors, DFIs, and MDBs, account for more than half of this funding in many cases, even in middle-income regions like Latin America. The Nelspruit concession was an early example of this trend. Commercial banks were unwilling to lend to the project when the contract was signed due to legal-regulatory risks. DBSA provided the initial funding when national government officials promised to change the legislation to deal with concerns of the commercial banks. But the legislation was not changed as promised, and DBSA remained the only project lender.

DBSA estimated that about R194 million would be required to meet capital investment requirements of the contract over the first five years (DBSA, 1999). The concessionaire agreed to install metered or restricted house or yard connections to all formal households, with communal standpipes made available in informal areas. These levels of service, plus 24-hour supply, were supposed to be achieved in some areas within three years, but the concessionaire was obligated to reach these service levels and 24-hour service for all Nelspruit households within five years.

Different levels of sanitation service were also required for all households within five years, but the basic level of service suited to low-income areas, the "ventilated improved pit" (VIP) toilet, was clearly going to be too expensive for the concessionaire to install everywhere (because the VIPs would generate no revenues for the concession). When the contract was finalized, the concessionaire was obligated only to provide technical assistance to homeowners installing VIPs at their own expense.[5]

GNUC requested R147 million from DBSA to cover 75 per cent of the capex costs over the first five years of the contract (equity was required to cover the balance of these costs). DBSA lent about R125 million: it assumed that R79 million

[5] The VIPs also proved to be too expensive for low-income households to install. After ten years of project implementation, the share of households in the service area without at least a basic level of sanitation was still over 60 per cent (Bender and Gibson, 2010).

of that would be taken up later by commercial banks and that commercial banks would also provide the additional R19 million needed to cover the full cost of the capital investment (DBSA, 1999).

GNUC began investments immediately on taking control of the system, but payment levels did not increase for reasons outline above. By early 2003, GNUC argued that additional investment would be imprudent given widespread non-payment and opposition to the contract. In the renegotiation that followed, the five-year investment total was extended over the first ten years, with R83.4 million expected from 1999 to 2004, and R105.5 million invested from 2004 to 2009. But an evaluation of the contract in 2010 found that those totals were not reached (Bender and Gibson, 2010). Only about 50 per cent of the expected capital investment was made over the first five years, and 72 per cent was made over the ten-year period. Only about 43 per cent (R54 million) of the DBSA funding (R125 million) was used for capex (Table 5.1).

By the time of the World Bank-funded review of the concession in 2010, the goal of 24-hour service for all households had not yet been reached. All households had access to high quality water, but 68 per cent (50,000 households) did not have access to 24-hour supply. GNUC made clear its intention to continue extending 24-hour service mostly using government grants but indicated that it had no intention of using additional DBSA debt or shareholder equity for such investment (Bender and Gibson, 2010).

5.4.5 Poverty Impacts

Perhaps one of the least surprising findings about infrastructure PPPs is the fact that developmental benefits in terms of poverty reduction must be purposely designed into projects, and then monitored by regulators. Private partners do not typically pursue these benefits without substantial incentivization by governments, DFIs, MDBs, and donors.

The municipality's motivation behind the Nelspruit contract was clearly the achievement of pro-poor benefits and other social objectives, particularly for the

Table 5.1 GNUC Capital Investment by Financing Source in ZAR Millions

Funding Source	1999–2004	2004–9	Totals
DBSA loan	44	10	54
Government grants		39	39
Developer contributions		19	19
Retained earnings		24	24
Totals	44	92	136

Source: Bender and Gibson, 2010.

new city residents suddenly owed city services because of expanded municipal boundaries. The Nelspruit municipality regarded the concession contract as an integral part of its effort to meet targets of the national government's plans to reconstruct and develop the country after the end of apartheid. The contract also required a host of worker and community benefits: all municipal workers involved in the provision of water and sanitation services would be employed by the concessionaire on the same or better conditions of service. The contract included requirements for staff training, as well as progressive remuneration policies like equity schemes and support for the education of workers' children. Funding was provided for community development programs, youth and female development programs, etc. Annual contributions were to be made by the project company to a community development fund. The contract included measures for the use and development of small contractors, the enhancement of local businesses and professionals, and the development of and support for small enterprises.

Nelspruit officials fully accepted the fact that the municipality would have to continue applying grant funds to the water and sanitation service system once GNUC had taken over the utility functions. The contract included details on how much grant funding was expected and how much would be passed on in support of the concession arrangement. The Council targeted these grants at indigent families and sourced the money from the municipality's portion of a national grant, called the Equitable Share. These grant funds were to be passed from the municipality to the families in the form of vouchers purchased from GNUC by the Council, which could be used to pay for water and sanitation services. The voucher system was a targeted, means-tested subsidy meant for households below the national poverty line.

Despite the voucher system and the focus of the contract on the poorest areas of the municipality, the townships, and informal settlements, the project was increasingly plagued by non-payment, illegal connections, and organized protests. The reasons for non-payment consisted of a complicated mixture of socioeconomic factors, political and ideological factors, grievances about the quality of service, as well as confusion about things like how water meters worked and how to understand water bills (Brown, 2005). But it cannot be denied that the inability of many households to pay all of the costs associated with water provision played a large part in the non-payment problem. Before the free basic water program was introduced in 2002, residents had to pay a connection charge, a deposit, and a monthly fixed charge, in addition to their water bills. The utilities harsh use of service cut-offs, removing thousands of water meters, appears to have exacerbated illegal reconnections and additional non-payment.

Because of the means testing, the voucher system was complex and expensive, for both the Council and GNUC. Up to 50 per cent of families eligible for vouchers may have been excluded from the system because of administrative inefficiencies and unwillingness of families to apply—low-income residents claimed that participation in the voucher program carried a social stigma that kept many of them from applying (Brown, 2005).

After the introduction of free water and the restructuring of the contract, progress in a number of pro-poor contract areas stopped or reversed, including the extension of 24-hour service in informal areas. In their ten-year evaluation of the contract, Bender and Gibson (2010) found that only 2 per cent of 46,634 households in informal areas had access to 24-hour water supply. Only 2,325 families had received basic levels of sanitation. Very little progress had been made in reducing the number of illegal connections in these areas or controlling water usage. The contract had vastly increased the number of households with some daily water access, improved water quality, carried out staff capacity building, and improved regular maintenance, etc. But the failure of efforts to generate expected pro-poor benefits like 24-hour access was the primary shortcoming of the concession in the view of customers and councilors and contributed to low levels of payment, particularly in underserved areas.

5.4.6 Governance

Governments of developing countries need to play a strong role in monitoring and regulating PPP performance, but local officials are not always able to do that effectively—the justification for doing a project as a PPP in the first place is often the weakness of host government institutions and their lack of skilled staff. The Nelspruit concession contract was structured to try to deal with this problem. Pursuant to the contract, the activities and performance of GNUC were supposed to be monitored by the council in accordance with the provisions of the contract and applicable legislation. Using funding provided by GNUC, the city officials created a contracts compliance office to monitor the performance of the private partner. The council was required to approve the tariffs levied for water and sanitation services; the quality and level of service provided; as well as the levels of capital investment proposed by the GNUC to meet its performance requirements. Investments were to be consistent with the overall municipal capital investment plan called for in the city's Integrated Development Plan, which also included environmental management considerations. A key annex to the concession contract was virtually a consumers' bill of rights that regulated how service was to be provided, how complaints were to be responded to, etc. A variety of penalties could be applied by the city if the contractor failed to meet any of a long list of performance targets.

The municipality's contract management function started strongly in the early years of the contract. Several employees were assigned to a contract monitoring unit, an external auditing firm was engaged, and monthly reports were submitted to a Council subcommittee. The manager of the unit reported to the deputy municipal manager who (as the former municipal manager) had led the municipality's team in the final days of the contract negotiations. This group assisted in the contract renegotiations in 2002 and 2003, but soon after that the deputy municipal manager and the unit manager both left the Council during a period of political upheaval in the municipality. From then until about the time of the World Bank-funded performance review in 2009, little monitoring took place and few reports were sent to the Council. The World Bank review found that no one in the municipality was performing any kind of financial monitoring of the concession (Bender and Gibson, 2010). The contract compliance monitoring unit still existed, but lacked the operational and financial skills to monitor and manage the concession: "It appears the concessionaire takes the lead to initiate the contract monitoring meetings with the Municipality" (Bender and Gibson, 2010).

With a contract of this kind, especially one that has been completely restructured as the Nelspruit one was in 2003, the absence of a monitoring function means that no one in the municipality knows what rate of return the project is generating, whether or not that rate of return is in any way consistent with the original agreements regarding concessionaire returns, or even if the concessionaire's financial representations are accurate. Even more importantly, the municipality has no way to know if the concessionaire's performance is acceptable in areas like 24-hour service access, water demand management, water loss prevention, customer care, customer non-payment, etc.

5.5 Conclusions

The World Bank-funded ten-year review of the Nelspruit concession concluded that "water and sanitation services in the concession area are in much better condition than if the Municipality had continued to operate them directly out of one its own departments" (Bender and Gibson, 2010, 45). But as documented by this review and explained in the preceding sections of this chapter, in many key respects the concession failed to meet expectations. It failed to use substantial amounts of private investment to improve the infrastructure and it failed to meet service delivery objectives like 24-hour service for all households. Some of these objectives may still be achieved over the remaining years of the contract, but without much stronger monitoring and management by municipal officials, this seems unlikely.

In terms of lessons of the contract, unfortunately its performance seems to confirm allegations made by anti-privatization critics that brownfield concessions of this kind rarely result in actual investment. Some of the more outlandish anti-privatization attacks on this contract in its early days have long since been proven false.[6] But the shortcomings of this concession experience have found their way into more measured ideological critiques of PPPs (Hall and Lobina, 2006).

Lessons about the nature and extent of the various kinds of preparation "costs" involved in Nelspruit (and its sister project developed at the same time in the South African town of Dolphin Coast) were not lost on other South African local officials. In spite of efforts to make bidders mostly responsible for project preparation, Nelspruit officials spent a good deal of time and money to move the contract to financial closure. In addition, intellectual and emotional commitments on the part of city councilors and managers sometimes bordered on the heroic, particular during disputes with and demonstrations by organized labor. The project was constantly plagued by misinformation campaigns alleging that the project was not "bankable," that conventional financing in support of the deal was not available because of underlying economic and institutional weaknesses, that municipal officials had been bribed to sign the contracts, etc. Because of the delay in reaching financial closure due to the need to solve legal and regulatory problems, the deal became a particular target of grossly uninformed criticism in government and the marketplace. By the time the concession contract started implementation, national government officials were noticeably absent in any efforts to defend the project. Clearly, the key lesson learned by other local officials was that, everything considered, the costs of undertaking such projects in South Africa far outweigh the potential benefits. The first two brownfield water concessions in South Africa, in Nelspruit and Dolphin Coast, unfortunately are the only two ever attempted in the country. No other classic brownfield water concessions of this kind have been completed in SSA (although other kinds of water PPPs have been financed—see Chapter 11). It does not seem like an exaggeration to say that the Nelspruit project is SSA's last real water concession.

Chapter 6 turns to another type of brownfield PPP introduced in the 1990s to deal with problems facing water and electricity utilities. These are management contracts, involving private management of government-owned service systems, usually without private capital investment. These were expected to be simple projects to develop, and attractive to private operators because without investment they were less risky than PPPs like concessions. But the experience has not been positive—these projects have been difficult to structure and negotiate, and they rarely meet stakeholder expectations. Chapter 6 attempts to explain how and why this has happened, and what is now emerging as hybrid versions of management contracts, designed to correct contracting flaws and improve performance.

[6] In a November 2001 national news story, it was reported that the contract had already led to 400 per cent tariff increases, R1000 a month water bills for indigent families, and only one water tap for every ten households (Weekes, 2001). In a largely ineffective effort to counter misinformation like this, the municipality's monitoring unit reported accurately that GNUC had actually invested over R35 million in the system to that point.

References

Aguas Argentinas S.A. Concession Contract. 1993. Concession Agreement entered into between the Argentine State and Aguas Argentinas S.A., April 28.

Alcazar, L., M.A. Abdala, M.M. Shirley. 2000. "The Buenos Aires Water Concession," Policy Research Working Paper No. 2311, Washington, DC: World Bank.

Bender, P., S. Gibson. 2010. *Case Study for the 10 years of the Mbombela (Nelspruit) Water and Sanitation Concession South Africa.* Study prepared for the PPP Unit, National Treasury, Republic of South Africa, Washington, DC: World Bank, January.

Brown, J. 2005. "Water Service Subsidies and the Poor: A case study of Greater Nelspruit Utility Company, Mbombela Municipality, South Africa." Centre on Regulation and Competition, Working Paper No. 112. Institute for Development Policy and Management, University of Manchester. Accessed at: https://assets.publishing.service.gov.uk/media/57a08c98e5274a27b20012d7/CRCwp112.pdf

Chao, J. 2016. *How are PPPs Really Financed?* Washington, DC: World Bank. Accessed at: http://blogs.worldbank.org/ppps/how-are-ppps-really-financed.

Development Bank of Southern Africa. 1999. "Appraisal Report—Board Summary: Nelspruit Water and Sanitation Concession." Project Number: 13384. DBSA, Midrand, South Africa, October 8.

Global Water Intelligence. 2018. "Gabon Seeks a New International Water PPP." GWI (March).

Goldin, I. 2001. Letter to Trevor Manual, Minister of Finance, Republic of South Africa, from the CEO of the Development Bank of Southern Africa.

Guislain, P., M. Kerf. 1995. "Concessions—The Way to Privatize Infrastructure Sector Monopolies." Public Policy for the Private Sector, Note No. 59, Washington, DC: World Bank, October.

Hall, D., E. Lobina. 2006. *Pipe dreams: The failure of the private sector to invest in water services in developing countries.* Public Services International Research Unit, London, March.

Klein, M. 2015. *"Public-Private Partnerships: Promise and Hype."* Policy Research Working Paper No. 7340, Washington, DC: World Bank.

Kotze, R., A. Ferguson, J. Leigland. 2000. "Government Facilitation of Public–Private Infrastructure Projects: Lessons from South Africa." *Journal of Project Finance* 6(1): 47–64.

Leigland, J. 2003. "Managing the Threat of MAGA in Emerging PPP Markets: A Case Study from South Africa." *The Journal of Structured and Project Finance* 8(4):49–54.

Marin, P. 2009. "Public–Private Partnerships for Urban Water Utilities: A Review of experiences in developing countries." PPIAF Trends and Policy Options Series No. 8, Washington, DC: World Bank. Accessed at: www.ppiaf.org.

Nelspruit Transitional Local Council (TLC). 1996. *Nelspruit concession for Water Supply and Sanitation services: Request for Proposals (RFP).* December 9.

Nelspruit Transitional Local Council (TLC). 1997. "Nelspruit Responses to Bidder RFP Questions." Unpublished City Council Report, March 6.

Nelspruit Transitional Local Council (TLC). 1999. *Concession Agreement Entered into Between Nelspruit TLC and the Greater Nelspruit Utility Company (Proprietary) Limited.* April 21.

Republic of South Africa. 2000. *Local Government: Municipal Systems Act, Act No. 32, 2000.* Government Printing Office, Pretoria.

Reuters. 2018. "Gabon Accuses France's Violia of Polluting Amid Concession Dispute." Reuters, February 27. Accessed at: https://www.reuters.com/article/us-gabon-veolia-environ/gabon-accuses-frances-veolia-of-polluting-amid-concession-dispute-idUSKCN1GB2OO

Weekes, A. 2001. "Water Privatisation Test Case 'A Total Debacle.'" *Mail & Guardian, Africa News,* November 16.

6
Management Contracts
Poor Performance or Misunderstood Objectives?

6.1 Introduction

For a relatively brief period in the early 1990s, long-term concession contracts involving both private investment and management gained popularity in the development community as potential solutions for problems with existing infrastructure utilities in developing countries. But the Asian financial crisis in 1997 precipitously ended the popularly of these "brownfield" contracts as private sponsors and operators quickly readjusted their views on the risk–return character of such projects. However, in situations where private operators were unwilling to take on any of the investment-related risk required under a brownfield concession or full privatization, donors, development finance institutions (DFIs), and multilateral development banks (MDBs) implementing structural adjustment reform programs sometimes recommended another contracting tool as a way of using private participation to strengthen the financial position and operations of a struggling utility.

These were management contracts, used mostly for water, transport, and electricity utilities with existing, or brownfield, assets that urgently needed better management to facilitate improved service delivery, sustainable commercial-like operations, and more capital investment. Such contracts involved hiring professional private-sector managers for relatively short periods of time, paying them a fee for services (often supplemented with success fees based on performance), and relieving them of responsibility for investing equity or raising debt for related infrastructure investment. In the wider family of public–private partnerships (PPPs) for infrastructure services, management contracts appeared to be simpler and less risky for private partners than any other type of PPP, and therefore seemed likely to be relatively easy for governments to structure, negotiate, and oversee.

But the reality has been quite different. Management contracts have been used much less frequently than most other kinds of PPP since private participation in infrastructure started to become popular in the 1990s. Part of the problem is that many management contracts have been controversial with domestic stakeholders, including labor unions, civil society groups, consumers, news media, as well as

Public–Private Partnerships in Sub-Saharan Africa: The Evidence-Based Critique. James Leigland, Oxford University Press (2020).
DOI: 10.1093/oso/9780198861829.001.0001

politicians and government officials. Many contracts have been terminated early, or not renewed. Supporters of these contracts blame much of this criticism on ill-informed stakeholder expectations about what the contracts were meant to achieve. But critics point out that even when contract performance is measured against the output targets specifically associated with the contracts, it usually has not been fully satisfactory.

After 2010, use of the conventional management contract model, which for infrastructure dates back to the late 1980s, sharply diminished. Bilateral donors, DFIs, and MDBs continue to promote, and sometimes pay for, what are still referred to as management contracts. But the conventional model seems to be losing popularity. Increasingly, hybrid contracting models are emerging, often resembling construction or service contracts as much as PPPs. These hybrid approaches are currently being tested in several developing countries, like Sierra Leone and Liberia. But their performance has yet to be subjected to rigorous evaluations.

There are no comprehensive, cross-country studies of management contracts to help clarify the reasons for the emergence of these hybrid forms. The lack of such studies is probably due to the absence of comparative data on contract structures and performance. In order to better understand these hybrid forms, this chapter begins by reviewing the origins of these brownfield infrastructure solutions. The circumstances under which these kinds of agreements began to be used for infrastructure services provides insights into the successes and failures of management contracts, particularly in the water and electricity sectors of SSA countries. Second, a sample of high-profile contracts is examined to identify key lessons that inform this kind of contracting today. Third, these lessons are used to demonstrate how and why hybrid contracting alternatives to the conventional model have emerged. A fourth and concluding section of this study discusses the policy implications of these emerging hybrid forms.

6.2 Water and Electricity Management Contracts

This chapter and the case study collection in Chapter 7 cover both water management contracts and electricity management contracts. Both sectors seem to have the kinds of problems that management contracts can address. In the power sector, private sector investment has emerged as a powerful tool for use in closing the electricity access gap, particularly in generation, where independent power producer (IPP) projects are proving to be effective mechanisms for improving efficiency and lowering costs. However, a critical ingredient in a successful IPP project is missing in many developing countries—a credible buyer, or off-taker, of the electricity. In Sub-Saharan Africa (SSA) most of these off-takers are utilities that are not financially viable, and most must rely on a constant stream of government subsidies to remain operational. A recent study by the World Bank found that only two of 39 power utilities in SSA cover the total cost of service with collected cash (Trimble et al., 2016). A further 18 countries cover operating costs, but do not collect sufficient revenues to cover capital costs. The study concludes that policy and regulatory issues, like underpricing, account for about 40 per cent of the hidden costs that officials should be able to reduce. However, the rest of these costs are mostly the result of management shortcomings like under collection of bills, system losses, and overstaffing. Among other things, the poor performance of these utilities raises significant doubts about the ability of these entities to make good on contractual commitments to regularly purchase power from private providers willing to invest in generation. Effective management contracts could help government utilities acting as off-takers of electricity improve their creditworthiness and become more credible partners for IPP projects.

The potential role for management contracts in the water sector is similar. Huge amounts of investment will be needed to meet the water-related targets for the Sustainable Development Goals (SDGs) agreed to in 2015. The SDGs are much more ambitious than the Millennium Development Goals (MDGs) in that they call for universal access to safe water, sanitation, and hygiene by 2030. But as with electricity, the problem with water is not just about finance. When the authors of the Africa Infrastructure Country Diagnostic (AICD) study surveyed progress toward achieving the water MDGs in 2009 (about halfway to the 2015 MDG targets), they concluded that Africa's financing needs could be massively reduced if African governments took steps to close an "efficiency gap" that was costing the water sector US$2.7 billion a year (Foster and Briceno-Garmendia, 2010). Improving water utility cost recovery could reduce the financing gap by US$1.8 billion a year; addressing operating inefficiencies would harvest a further US$0.9 billion saving a year. Improving the quality and timeliness of budget execution would yield an additional reduction of US$0.2 billion a year. Again, management contracts should be able to help with these kinds of management improvements, and help make the water sector more receptive to needed private investment.

The actual use of management contracts in the water and power sectors has been closely related, especially because this contracting form was pressed into use as a generic reform tool meant to be applicable to a wide range of state-owned enterprises (SOEs) pursuant to structural adjustment activities in the 1990s. So, management contracts have never been the exclusive province of either water or power. Successes and failures in one sector have influenced efforts to use contracts in the other sector. Figure 6.1 indicates that there is considerably more experience with management contracts for water and transport than with those in the electricity sector.

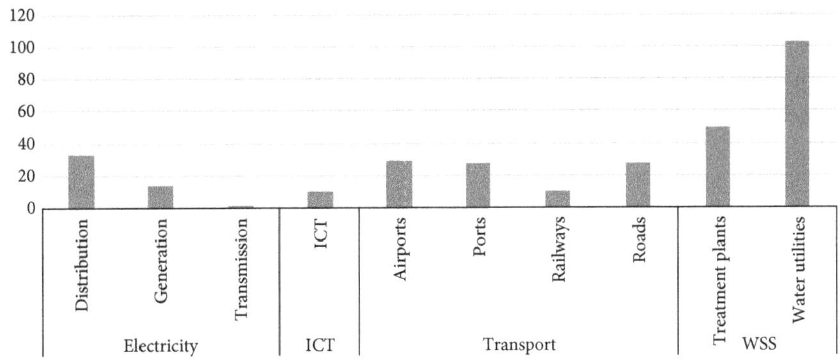

Figure 6.1 Numbers of Management and Lease Contracts by Subsector, All Developing Countries, 1990–2017

Source: World Bank, 2018.

6.3 The Origins of Infrastructure Management Contracts

Chapter 5 described the crisis with SOEs that dates back to the 1970s. Although some of these SOEs were well managed, most experienced problems attributable to a conflicting mix of sociopolitical and commercial objectives. The mix resulted in a range of problems: managers without the autonomy to take necessary commercial decisions; overspending enabled by overborrowing; below-cost pricing (justified as socially necessary); failures to collect customer charges; supervision by boards of directors who protected the interests of parent ministries rather than their SOEs; and generally poor monitoring, reporting, and follow-up. Much of this resulted from the incompetence of untrained managers, many of whom obtained their jobs through political connections. Very few SOEs generated revenue sufficient to cover operating costs, depreciation, and capital investment. Most consistently experienced net losses and many existed in a persistent state of negative net worth. Many were kept functioning with the proceeds of excessive government borrowing.

By the end of the 1970s, the World Bank and other MDBs initiated what is sometimes described as a first phase of SOE reforms to begin dealing with the bewildering number and variety of SOEs owned by governments of developing countries, and the associated expansion of government debt (Gomez-Ibanez, 2007). The SOE reforms were central elements of most of the structural adjustment lending done by MDBs during this period. But this initial phase of SOE reforms did not emphasize the use of solutions involving private participation, like divestiture, concessions, or management contracts. Most of the focus during this period was on efforts to improve enterprise performance without involving the private sector to change the nature of public ownership or control. This phase identified key SOE problems and established a blueprint for reform that was later used to structure management contracts.

The objective of this first phase was to help SOEs operate in a "business-like" fashion by pursuing more commercial-like objectives such as cost recovery. Efforts to build managerial capacity and strengthen managerial incentives were combined in adjustment operations focusing on arrangements that came to be known as "performance agreements," the principal adjustment tool during this first phase of SOE reforms (Gomez-Ibanez, 2007). Unlike the management contracts used in the next phase of SOE reform, performance agreements were non-legal arrangements that preserved government ownership and control of the SOEs. They were negotiated between governments and SOEs, and usually included quantifiable performance targets that were specified for a given period. These agreements were supposed to represent a way for government officials and SOE managers to agree on key elements of commercialization that the SOE would then attempt to achieve. Salary increases, promotions, and other rewards for managers were used to incentivize performance against the targets. The agreements also created obligations for government officials who typically promised not to intervene in the day-to-day management of the enterprise. A variety of different names were used for these agreements, including contract plans, memoranda of understanding, statements of corporate intent, and performance contracts. By 1989, over 100 performance agreements were in operation in developing countries, and an additional 100 were in preparation (Nellis, 1989a).

However, by the end of the 1980s, donors, DFIs, and MDBs were already concluding that performance agreements had not dramatically improved SOE financial performance. These agreements clearly worked best with commercial enterprises operating in competitive markets. Financial targets for such enterprises were simpler, more easily agreed on and monitored, and managerial autonomy was more readily accepted by government officials. For infrastructure SOEs operating in non-competitive markets, all of this was more difficult. Across SSA, governments consistently failed to meet most of their performance agreement obligations regarding equity injections, managerial autonomy (price increases were frequently rejected), work force reductions (also rejected), and settlement of payment obligations by government agencies (perhaps the most common problem). The fundamental problem, widely recognized by the end of the 1980s, was that these were not legally enforceable contracts.

Such agreements continued to be used, especially in West Africa, until the mid-1990s, but then largely disappeared. The World Bank's final judgment on these mechanisms came in a series of evaluations prepared in the late 1990s by the Bank's Public Sector Management Division. Much of this work culminated in an econometric evaluation of 500 performance agreements in China, a country with hundreds of thousands of SOEs, 88 per cent of which were under performance agreements by 1989. The China study found that, on average, the agreements did not improve SOE performance and may have made it worse (Shirley and Xu, 2001). By 1994, Chinese officials had already anticipated these kinds of conclusions and had almost completely stopped using performance agreements in any significant way.

Disappointment with the results of the first phase of public enterprise reform led to a second, starting in the early 1980s and peaking in the late 1990s, which emphasized private sector ownership and management of SOEs—all of which was generally referred to as "privatization." The SOE privatization push began to focus on infrastructure services in the mid-1990s, after non-privatization SOE reform efforts, like performance agreements, had completely stalled by the end of the 1980s (Leigland, 2018). Non-divestiture privatization was expected to create situations in which either governments or private owners and operators could appeal to courts of law to enforce compliance with contractual obligations—thus solving the fundamental problem with performance agreements, the frequency with which governments reneged on commitments made in such agreements. With management contracts, government promises regarding managerial autonomy, equity injections, tariff increases, work force reductions, and the settlement of government's utility debts, were all supposed to become legally binding.

The use of these non-divestiture privatization options for commercial enterprises represented a modest share of privatization transactions in the early days of structural adjustment. By the end of the 1980s, the sale and liquidation of government-owned commercial enterprises was well underway. Management contracts and leases were also being used to privatize commercial enterprises, but less frequently. And SOEs providing monopoly infrastructure services were not yet being targeted for any form of privatization. A survey in 1988 found that management contracts (59 in total) accounted for 18 per cent of the total number of "privatizations" underway at the time, but none of these were planned or underway for infrastructure services (Candoy-Sekse, 1988). The role of management contracts for infrastructure SOEs gradually expanded until the Asian crisis in 1997, when the use of all kinds of brownfield infrastructure PPPs started a rapid decline (Leigland, 2018).

A large part of the reason why management contracts were mostly unsuccessful for infrastructure services can be explained by understanding how these kinds of contracts came to the attention of donors, DFIs, and MDBs in the first place—why these contracts were successful in other sectors. Leases and management contracts were already routinely used in commercial sectors by the time that structural adjustment started in the late 1980s. Research on the advantages of using management contracts to limit business risks faced by international companies in developing countries had been published in the late 1960s (Gabriel, 1967). Twenty years later, Michael Brooke (1985) was acknowledged by the World Bank as the leading authority on management contracts in commercial sectors. Brooke's research demonstrated that although the use of management contracts had grown considerably since the 1960s, it was still an elusive topic, mainly because so many variations on the basic model were being used, under such a large variety of names and definitions.

Perhaps above all, Brooke's work suggested that management contracts for commercial businesses were already part of a continuum that extended from consultancy contracts, through service and management contracts, and on to leases, affermage contracts, and concessions, with fluid boundaries separating contract types. Strict, conventional boundaries between types of contracts on this continuum were frequently breaking down in practice, based on the demands of specific situations: management contractors often took equity positions in projects or rebated payments back to owners; management contracts sometimes included performance incentives, sometimes did not; management contractors or lease holders were sometimes given control over investment decisions without having to accept investment risk.

In no commercial sector were management contracts better developed and more widely used than in international hotel administration. Hotel leasing dated back to the early 1900s, and management contracts were introduced in the 1950s as global hotel expansion generated a need for major operators to protect valuable brands (e.g., Hilton, Sheraton, Hyatt, etc.) from potential risks associated with owning hotels in foreign countries, especially developing countries. For owners, the management contract model provided professional but routine management of these businesses, plus it made possible a valuable association for their hotels with famous hotel brand names. By almost any measure, hotel management contracts have become a highly successful form of real estate transaction. By 2009, 800 management companies were operating 12,000 properties worldwide pursuant to some form of management contract (De Roos, 2010).

A World Bank study in the late 1980s, assessed the performance of management contracts, as they were being rolled out mostly for commercial enterprises pursuant to structural adjustment operations (Hegstad and Newport, 1987). The authors attempted to identify the comparative advantages of different types of management contracts by identifying the problems best addressed by each contracting type. A central focus of the study is on what the authors call the "pure" form of management contract—contracts that engage an operator to carry out management functions, on a short-term basis, without requiring the operator to take an equity position in the enterprise or supply supporting services like capacity building or technical assistance (which if required, would typically be contracted via separate agreements). These contracts in commercial sectors like hotel administration involved straightforward management tasks, rather than fundamental business rehabilitation. The first task of the contractor was to prepare a simple business plan and budget. The budgets and plans usually emphasized basic administration, recruitment and training of staff, and marketing. Relatively straightforward and easily measured metrics, mostly focused on profit or cash flows, served effectively as performance measures. Success fees and penalties, usually involving a share of profits or losses, were used to incentivize that performance. In addition to hotel administration, the authors found these kinds of contracts well established in sectors like agribusiness (particularly for plantation management), mining, domestic airports, petroleum refineries, as well as other kinds of business enterprises (tanneries, ceramics, cement, food processing, etc.). The authors concluded that this "pure" form of management contract was usually successful in meeting owner expectations as long as basic business preconditions were in place, including realistic contract objectives, a neutral or supportive operating environment, an owner who was convinced of the contract's potential value, and a contract that delegated the authority needed to meet contract objectives.

6.4 The Lack of Management Contract Performance Evaluations

Since the early 1990s, the most concentrated and successful use of management contracts and leases has been in middle-income regions like East Asia (for water and sanitation) and Latin America (for transport). As of 2018, SSA ranked third in terms of total use of these contracts by a region, but many of these contracts had been terminated early or not renewed (Table 6.1).

By the mid-2000s, with the end of the privatization push under structural adjustment and the introduction of Poverty Reduction Strategy Plans and the MDGs in 2005, management and lease contracts in International Development Association (IDA) countries began to lose momentum (Figure 6.2).

However, despite the passage of more than a decade since the slowdown in contract formation, there are no studies of management contracts that match the spread and sophistication of the econometric evaluation of 500 performance agreements in China by Shirley and Xu (2001). Most evaluations have been

Table 6.1 Numbers of Management and Lease Contracts by Region and Sector, 1990–2017

Region	Electricity	Transport	ICT	WSS	Totals
East Asia & Pacific	3	9	0	48	60
Europe & Central Asia	19	11	0	28	58
Latin America & Caribbean	5	42	0	34	81
Middle East & North Africa	0	8	6	12	26
South Asia	6	7	0	6	19
Sub-Saharan Africa	15	16	4	25	60
Totals	48	93	10	153	304

Source: World Bank, 2018.

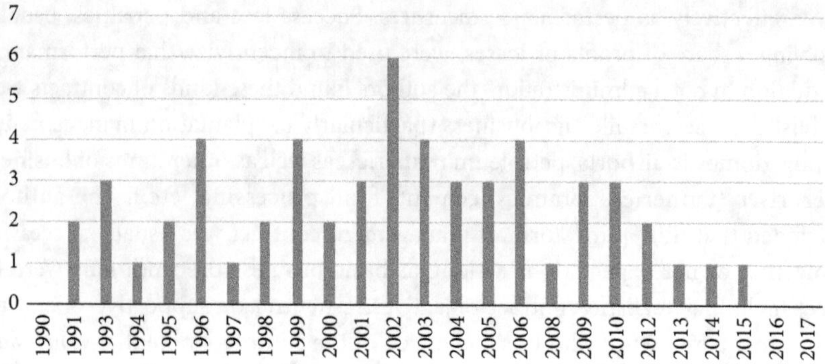

Figure 6.2 Numbers of Management and Lease Contracts in IDA Countries by Year, 1990–2017

Source: World Bank, 2018.

anecdotal. They often do not agree on how many management contracts have actually been concluded in SSA. These studies do tend to agree that when management contracts were moved beyond commercial sectors and used as tools to reform SOEs, the results were disappointing, especially in low-income countries. A World Bank internal evaluation of its power sector work in the 1990s (Manibog et al., 2003) noted that the Bank's pursuit of power sector reforms in SSA relied heavily on management contracts, "most of which did not work well." A 2005 Harvard case study noted that roughly half the countries in SSA had attempted to "involve the private sector in the management of their electricity distribution companies," but in half of these cases the contracts were aborted during development or cancelled after only a few years (Gomez-Ibanez, 2005).

Eberhard et al. (2011), identified 17 management contracts for electricity in 15 countries, but noted that only three of these contracts remained in operation because of cancellation and decisions not to renew after scheduled termination. The authors found that contracts often improved utility collection rates and revenues and reduced system losses, but rarely did so in a way that facilitated funding for investments. In addition, many contracts failed to leave behind improved commercial operations, capacitated staff, or better customer care. The report concluded that the use of management contracts in SSA "has proved complex and contentious" (Eberhard et al., 2011). A more recent survey concluded that the research literature generally recognizes "the failure of management contractors to achieve sustained performance improvements" (ECA, 2015), but acknowledged that the literature was still quite limited.

The performance of management contracts in the African water sector has been even less well researched than the performance of electricity management contracts. An internal World Bank evaluation of its work in the water sector, covering 1997–2007, found that management contracts were used in association with 28 World Bank projects (IEG, 2010). Six of these were in SSA, but only two were found to be moderately successful for water and sanitation services. Marin (2009) concluded that management contracts helped to improve revenue collection and service continuity, but had little effect on the most challenging service delivery issues like unaccounted-for-water and access. The AICD study confirmed Marin's findings (Foster and Briceno-Garmendia, 2010). Like electricity management contracts, water contracts had problems with distress, disputes, and the failure of government to renew the agreements. Nor is there any compelling evidence that water management contracts helped to leverage significant infrastructure investment.

A fundamental reason why there has been so little empirical evaluation of these contracts relates to the general lack of data collection and analysis of the various kinds of "privatization" modalities implemented during the structural adjustment period. Campbell-White and Bhatia (1998) confirmed that privatization programs were often inadequately monitored and evaluated, leading to situations where privatization could not be justified based on empirical evidence of benefits. Buchs (2003) found that from 1991 to 2002 no monitoring was put in place to assess fiscal impact of privatization, resulting in an inability to anticipate the outcomes of privatization activities. The World Bank's internal evaluation of its power sector work in the 1990s found that project monitoring and evaluation systems had not been well established, making it difficult to understand the country factors behind privatization performance (Manibog et al., 2003). Antonio Estache (2005) concluded that a fundamental lack of data made the evaluation of privatization efforts extremely difficult. And Nellis expressed frustration after leaving the World Bank: "Detailed data on what took place in the 1990s must exist in the World Bank project and African country records; but no summations, similar to those cited for the earlier period, are readily available" (Nellis, 2005). The frustrations of Nellis, Buchs, Estache, and others, with the lack of privatization data by the mid-2000s, continue to plague researchers trying to evaluate management contacts today: "There is a clear absence of cross-country studies that examine the performance of management contracts in SSA" (ECA, 2015).

Aside from making retrospective evaluations difficult, this lack of monitoring and evaluation probably accounted for some of the shortcomings exhibited by these contracts during the 1990s and 2000s. According to International Finance Corporation (IFC) economist Thierry Buchs, the privatization process from 1991 to 2002 exhibited "the tendency to focus on privatization transactions rather than on sector reorganization" (Buchs, 2003, 1). The same thing was noted in a 2003 internal evaluation of World Bank Group work in the electricity sector in the 1990s. The evaluation noted that reform efforts went well beyond the existing policy that called for commercialization and corporatization before privatization (Manibog et al., 2003). This was because Bank staff members were finding it too difficult to achieve commercialization first, as was supposed to have happened in countries that pioneered successful electricity sector reforms. As a consequence, brownfield privatization solutions, including management contracts principally in SSA, quickly became proxies for the achievement of commercial viability, even when underlying performance had not significantly changed. The WBG evaluation found that Bank staff never received operational guidance on how to implement these solutions. The evaluation found that the lack of guidance, combined with the lack of preparation, resulted in overall sector outcomes that were disappointing, especially with regard to the use of management contracts.

As structural adjustment began to focus on the privatization of infrastructure in the mid- 1990s, analysists like Nellis (1989b) were warning that all kinds of privatization needed to be carefully prepared, and that regulation and competition needed to be improved before private participation could proceed in a productive manner. But much of that kind of preparation was not done. Recommendations regarding privatization options were typically justified on theoretical grounds and negotiations with governments rather than empirical evidence of performance or lessons learned from previous efforts. In the haste to make some kind of tangible progress with SOE reforms, after the failures of commercialization and performance agreements in the 1980s, the number of privatization operations funded each year in the 1990s quickly accelerated. MDBs were constantly struggling to speed up actual implementation of these operations. As a result of this, project monitoring suffered, along with efforts to respond quickly to project shortcomings in the design of new projects.

6.5 Understanding Contract Shortcomings

Because of the work by Brooke (1985), Hegstad and Newport (1987), and others, by the time management contracts were beginning to be more frequently used for infrastructure services in the 1990s, information was available on the inherent limits on what these kinds of contracts were capable of doing. A substantial body of literature on utility performance measurement also already existed, thanks to an intensive decade of work on performance agreements (e.g., Jones, 1991).

The following subsections summarize utility management contract performance problems by using the simple evaluation framework developed by Hegstad and Newport (1987). On the basis of their survey of 40 management contacts, the authors identified interrelated factors that serve as essential "preconditions" for the effective use of these contracts. Hegstad and Newport's work is now over 30 years old, and their focus was heavily weighted toward commercial enterprises. But their preconditions represent World Bank common sense thinking about management contracts just as structural adjustment programs were beginning to turn their focus toward brownfield solutions to problems with water and power utilities and other infrastructure SOEs.

6.5.1 The Problem Must be Limited to Management

Hegstad and Newport (1987) note that management contracts may help to solve "temporary management-related problems," but not inherent business deficiencies. In this respect, enterprise owners need to conduct an analysis of problems to make sure that they are not the result of either fundamental market conditions that will persist however strong management might become, or extreme business shortcomings (like staff capacity issues, or widespread non-payment for services) that would be beyond the reach of a normal management contract.

In fact, most utility management contracts were not preceded by studies justifying the use of this arrangement. The contracts were often justified—and sometimes oversold—on the basis of theoretical arguments, as was the case with many other privatization measures (Nellis, 2005). As with conventional contracts for hotels, utility management contractors typically were required to prepare a methodology and workplan after they were selected to manage the utility. But because the utility problems extended well beyond simple management issues, the planning process tended to take longer and be more resource intensive than expected. This resulted in impatient owners and unrealistic workplans requiring large financial resources that often were unavailable (Antmann, 2017).

6.5.2 The External Operating Environment Must be Supportive

The authors noted that if the enterprise operates in a hostile business environment the benefits of management contracts are unlikely to be realized. Environmental problems include things like restrictions on pricing, owner interference in commercial decision making, the precedence of social and political objectives over business objectives, and disputes with owners over success fees and penalties.

Interference by government-appointed boards of directors was common with utility management contracts largely because boards were typically made up of representatives of different ministries and agencies, with little or no business experience. Directors usually had loyalties to their immediate ministerial employers rather than to the power or water utility they were supposed to be overseeing. Mistrust between boards and utility managers was common, as were disputes about the size of performance fees. Also, government failure to raise tariffs to cover at least operating costs was a common problem, even when tariff adjustments were required by the contracts. As with non-legal performance agreements in the 1980s, a persistent kind of government interference in management contracts was the refusal of governments to require SOEs and other agencies and departments to pay their electricity and water bills.

6.5.3 The Owner Must be Fully Supportive

Hegstad and Newport (1987) noted that the enterprise owner must be convinced that a management contract is the optimal solution to enterprise problems and be fully supportive of it. They found that this often was not the case when these contracts were agreed to by owners because the agreements had been made a condition of financing, or because they had been presented as the only solution to enterprise problems.

Governments were pressured into most of their utility management contracts by donors, DFIs, and MDBs, who also often paid for some or all of the contract costs for limited periods. In many cases, the contracts were considered by development partners to be transitions to more substantial kinds of privatization like concessions or joint public-private ownership. But governments often saw these contracts as "costly reform measures needed to secure donor finance and had no intention of taking the process any further" (Foster and Briceno-Garmendia, 2010). When funding support ended, usually after an initial phase of the contract, governments typically became liable for costs going forward, and consequently lost interest in continuing the arrangement. Unlike concessions or leases, management contracts involve no payments to government and represented costs that must be paid on a regular basis, regardless of whether or not utility revenues are increasing. The potential costs to government seemed especially onerous in cases where contracts involved what seemed to locals like expensive salaries for expatriate staff.

6.5.4 Contract Objectives Must be Achievable by the Manager

Hegstad and Newport (1987) also noted that the contract must provide enough authority and control for the manager to effectively achieve contract objectives. During planning and pre-negotiation stages of contract preparation, owners need to explicitly define objectives and address the issue of how much authority and managerial discretion is needed by management contractors to achieve those objectives. For contract objectives that go beyond basic financial performance, contracts would have to clearly define linkages between objectives and measurable performance targets.

The delegation of authority to power and water utility contractors was often incomplete because objectives were not always clearly specified. Specific performance targets were sometimes left out of the early contacts, making measurement of achievement impossible. As objectives and targets began to be included, the targets were usually limited in number and kept relatively simple in order to avoid confusing government counterparts and complicating the process of determining success fees, which counterparts had to manage. But most contracts struggled to find a small number of targets, linked to performance fees and penalties, which adequately captured all of the key contract objectives. Problems finding accurate data to establish baselines and measure contractor performance also plagued many of these contracts, and in fact, the improvement of management information systems was often supposed to be a high-priority objective of these contracts (so the information was usually unavailable when the contracts were designed). Finally, as might have been expected, private contractors often proved adept at maximizing success fees by selectively achieving targets, while failing to achieve higher-level objectives that were government priorities, but often difficult to measure.

Tables 6.1 and 6.2 use the framework of "preconditions" developed by Hegstad and Newport (1987) to summarize the successes and failures associated with a selection of the highest profile water and electricity management contracts in SSA for which there have been case studies or collected performance data. These cases are discussed in more detail in Chapter 7. As noted at the outset, "success" is defined here as the term is used by Gokgur and Jones (2007) to mean arrangements involving the private sector participation, which substantially improve performance and distribute benefits equitably enough that the arrangement can be sustained. The tables illustrate how difficult it has been for management contracts to meet expectations in SSA.

6.6 Emerging Hybrid Contracts: Examples from the Electricity Sector

The phase of SOE reform that emphasized privatization, was generally considered to have been more successful than earlier efforts to use measures like performance agreements. But the benefits of privatization were not enough to maintain the development community's enthusiasm for structural adjustment's harshly prescriptive approach. By the end of the 1990s, donors, DFIs, and MDBs like the World Bank had begun to adopt more collaborative reform strategies (Leigland, 2018). Privatization of SOEs, particularly divestiture, began to sharply decline. By the end of the 2000s, many infrastructure enterprises, including most water and power utilities in SSA, remained under government ownership and control. This suggests a role for arrangements like management contracts, if their shortcomings can be addressed and performance improved.

To address these shortcomings, some donors, DFIs, and MDBs have started experimenting with hybrid alternatives to conventional management contracts, particularly in the electricity sector. There is not yet any single, widely accepted contracting format, but the approach seems to incorporate several basic lessons learned from the history of conventional management contacts:

Table 6.2 Performance Review of Selected Electricity Management Contracts in Sub-Saharan Africa

Contract/Year	Majority Stakeholder Assessment	Interrelated Preconditions for Success (Hegstad and Newport, 1987)			
		1. Objective: Must be limited to management issues	**2. External Environment: Noninterference by govt officials**	**3. The Owner: Convinced the contract is the optimal solution**	**4. The Contract: Objectives clear, measurable, achievable**
Ghana (ECG) 4 years 1994	Unsuccessful: Contract not self-financing as expected; no improvement in utility financial performance; contract not renewed	Unexpected hyperinflation and currency devaluation impacted revenues; supply could not meet surprise surge in power demand	Govt refused to set cost- reflective tariffs or require SOEs to pay power bills; contractor denied full control over commercial operations	Contract financed by donors and MDBs; government unwilling to consider broader sector reforms	Data not available to set performance baselines or evaluate performance; contract measurement methodology vague
Sources: Opam and Turkson, 2000; World Bank, 1999.					
Mali (EDM) 3 years 1995	Unsuccessful: Contract cancelled by govt; conflicting donor/govt views re purpose—mgmt improvement or preparation for a concession?	Drought and unexpectedly high power demand led to frequent blackouts that were blamed on the contractor; tariffs not cost-reflective	Donors blamed govt for interference & unfair criticism of contractor; govt refused to increase tariffs to cover costs as agreed or to require agencies to pay power bills	Donors pressured the government to accept the contract as a condition of financial support	Performance targets were to be set only after 2 years of implementation; mgmt not free to implement necessary commercial changes
Sources: Gomez-Ibanez, 2005; World Bank, 1998.					

Namibia (NE) 6 years 1996	Unsuccessful: Contract not renewed; considered expensive; SOE power company successfully lobbied to take over the operation	Contractor criticized for lack of investment, for which it had little responsibility; many local towns unhappy because of exclusion from service area prior to the contract	Government supportive until some towns sided with the SOE power company to criticize the contract and propose changed arrangement	Government viewed mgmt as a routine function requiring little expertise; gave the business to the SOE power company at end of contract	Little prescriptive contract detail; no performance indicators or targets; no way to document contract successes
Sources: Econ One Research, 2002; Nellis, 2005.					
Tanzania (TANESCO) 2 years 2002	Unsuccessful: Contract was renewed once; but the govt said power losses and outages had not improved, service quality was unacceptably low	Increased generating costs (as new IPPs came on line) and hydropower shortages limited revenue for investment and technical improvements	Government was generally supportive, but relations with the BOD soured as directors refused to meet with anyone other than the utility MD	The contractor's fixed fees were paid by a donor; when full privatization later rejected, govt was reluctant to pay full costs of any extension	Limited number of performance targets did not match ambitious contract objectives; some key targets met, but not all key objectives
Source: Ghanadan and Eberhard, 2007.					
Kenya (KPLC) 2 years 2006	Unsuccessful: Contract was not renewed; govt officials unhappy with high expat salaries, performance disputes, labour problems, media criticism	Investment needed and promised by WB; but contract term too short and investments not made soon enough for contract to avoid blame for sector problems	Government generally did not interfere in contract operations; power pricing reforms allowed tariffs to rise in line with escalating costs during contract	Contract was a condition for WB investment, WB paid for first two years; but govt not convinced of need for contract to improve KPLC performance	Vague data requirements for performance targets led to a long, public dispute over 1st-year success fees
Sources: Mwangi, 2008; Eberhard, et al. 2011; Word Bank, 2014; ECA, 2015.					

Table 6.3 Performance Review of Selected Water Utility Management Contracts in Sub-Saharan Africa

Contract/Year	Majority Stakeholder Assessment	Interrelated Preconditions for Success (Hegstad and Newport, 1987)			
		1. Objective: Must be limited to management issues	**2. External Environment: Noninterference by govt officials**	**3. The Owner: Convinced the contract is the optimal solution**	**4. The Contract: Objectives clear, measurable, achievable**
Guinea 10-yr lease; 2-yr mgmt contract 1989	Unsuccessful: Lease not renewed; water prices increased, collections & connections contract increased slowly; utility did not become commercially viable as planned	Price of water was high due to widespread non-pay of water bills; plus a weak judicial system that made collection from end-users difficult	Immediate conflict between contractor & govt; no independent authority created to enforce contractual agreements; govt agencies not required to pay water bills	Govt pressured into contract by donors & WB—$103m "adjustment" loan contingent on contract	No performance targets specified; complex, volatile contracting arrangements; no independent regulator to assess performance
Sources: Brook, 1999; Menard and Clarke, 2000b.					
Mozambique 15-yr lease; 5-yr mgmt contracts (4) 1999	Unsuccessful: Foreign contractor withdrew after 2 years; contracts restructured with local partner, but performance was poor, water prices increased; profits were negative; lease not renewed	Floods disrupted water treatment; subsequent cholera epidemic blamed on contractor; needed investments by the government were delayed	Govt insisted on pricing water below costs and limited retrenchments; contractor argued that govt inflexible re legitimate need to adjust contract & increase fees	Govt reportedly "owned" the reforms, but the contract was a condition for receiving $130m from donors and qualifying for IMF debt relief; WB dominated contractor selection	Rewards/penalties not included as incentives to reach contract targets; performance baselines never established so targets meaningless anyway
Sources: PPIAF, 2009; Gokgur and Jones, 2006.					

South Africa (Johannesburg) 6 years 2000	Unsuccessful: Contract produced a well-functioning ring-fenced utility, but was not renewed and did not lead to a concession as planned when contract tendered	Operational objectives were achieved: to consolidate separate utility departments, extend services, & corporatize/commercialize the utility	Govt generally supportive; utility managers had reasonable levels of independence & discretion; strong corporate culture	Originally, govt viewed contract as preparation for a concession, but later gave in to unions and others and returned utility to public management	Performance benchmarks and targets were realistic, but contractor waived success fees in order to win bid and position for follow-on concession
Sources: Marin, 2009; Baietti, Kingdom, and van Ginneken, 2006.					
Tanzania (Dar es Salaam) 10-yr lease 2002	Unsuccessful: Govt terminated contract after 21 months, citing poor quality service, operating losses, breach of contract; expat executives deported	Contractor responsible for billing, tariff collection, O&M, but dependent on rehab & investment that govt was slow to implement	Critics speculated that the govt used the contract to obtain sector loans from donors, then terminated the deal before dispute resolution finished; govt agencies not required to pay water bills	Contract was a condition for a \$144m sector loan from the World Bank & donors, and IMF debt relief	Performance targets included, but absence of independent regulator meant that the govt evaluated performance; quality of govt data was suspect
Source: ICSID, 2008; WaterAid Tanzania, 2008.					
Ghana (Accra) 5 years 2005	Unsuccessful: Contract did not transition into a concession as planned (nor was it renewed); govt said contract failed to reduce water losses or achieve other expected improvements	Contractor performance was mixed, but contract vague re targets & responsibilities; contractor blamed for water shortages & tariff increases mostly beyond its control	Initially, the govt did not interfere, but elections in 2008 brought to power an opposition party that had campaigned against the contract; resulted in more interference	Contract was a condition for a \$120m WB and donor investment program; as pressure increased from antiprivatization groups govt lost enthusiasm for the contract	Contract performance targets vague; as late as 2010, agreements still not reached re final details of indicators, baselines, penalties, and incentives
Sources: GWCL, 2013; Ghana Management Contract, 2005.					

First, it is widely accepted now that attempts to reform or improve the operation of infrastructure utilities need to begin with a diagnosis of enterprise problems. Among other things, the diagnosis needs to differentiate problems that are internal to the enterprise from external problems with policies, regulation, etc. And the experts who carry out the diagnostic work should not be the same ones who implement solutions. This helps ensure that reform action plans are prepared in the interests of the enterprise and its owner rather than done in a way that accommodates the skill set of those assigned to implement the changes. Owners and development partners should oversee the preparation of these action plans and agree on objectives, before the plans are implemented.

Second, enterprise problems can of course be very different for different utilities, but in almost all cases they revolve around themes that have now been well researched in developing countries. They typically include the need to start with water or electricity loss reduction, particularly the reduction of non-technical (or commercial) losses that represent avoidable financial losses for the utility. And in dealing with losses, there is now a wealth of information from Latin America and Asia regarding revenue protection programs involving smart metering, customer data bases, and other cost-effective technology-driven solutions that were not available in the 1990s. Action plans can now incorporate a largely standard collection of management improvement components like organizational restructuring, management information systems (MIS), revenue protection programs, local staff training, and customer service improvement strategies. This kind of action planning has proved successful in India, El Salvador, Chile, Colombia, and other developing countries (Antmann, 2009). Some bilateral donors are experimenting with similar kinds of "corporate development" techniques in efforts to reform water utilities without necessarily involving private management (SECO, 2015; Rebel Group, 2016).

Third, it is no longer assumed that private participation in the management of a utility is essential for improved operations in most countries. In his review of utility loss-reduction approaches, Antmann (2009) concluded that "private sector participation is not a necessary or sufficient condition for success in sustainable reduction of losses by electricity distribution companies." Recent World Bank policy research publications that focus on performance improvements in electricity distribution utilities cite the need for private investment in the sector, but rarely even mention private involvement in utility management (Kojima and Trimble, 2016; Trimble et al., 2016). As one World Bank report notes, as long as institutional frameworks, appropriate norms, and solid policies are in place, "the structure and ownership of the utility appears not to be an important driver of performance" (World Bank, 2016). In the water sector, soon after the end of structural adjustment it was recognized that fundamental reforms "cannot be substituted by private sector participation" (Baietti, Kingdom, and van Ginneken, 2006). More recently, other avenues to water utility improvements, not necessarily involving private participation, are also now being explored (World Bank, 2017).

Fourth, it now seems clear that there are situations in which it helps to have a private management contractor in place to implement management improvement action plans (Antmann, 2017). But as noted, these action plans should be developed and agreed to by government owners and development partners *before* the contracts are signed with private managers. The job of the contractor is to implement the action plan in order to stabilize basic functions of the utility. Once stabilization is achieved, the contractor has accomplished its mission—the purpose of the contract is not necessarily to serve as a transition to other more substantial kinds of private participation like concessions or divestiture. This new approach tends to emphasize the temporary, exceptional nature of management contracts and tries to ensure strong government ownership of utility action plans with the recognition that using expensive, expatriate managers can work only for a very limited period of time, after which local staff must assume a significant share of management responsibilities.

Management contracts reflecting these kinds of lessons have been signed in Sierra Leone and Liberia and are planned in Benin and several other countries. The Sierra Leone contract is so far perhaps the purest example of a hybrid that deeply contrasts with conventional kinds of management contracts traditionally promoted by donors, DFIs, and MDBs (Box 6.1). The Sierra Leone bid documents (Republic of Sierra Leone, 2015) illustrate how such an agreement satisfies key preconditions for contract success, like those identified by Hegstad and Newport (1987):

- **The problem must be limited to management.** Whether or not utility problems are narrowly limited to management issues, an action plan is prepared for the utility, which focuses on a largely standard collection of management improvement components mentioned above. If there are wider sector problems, the intention is to address them with technical assistance and investment via other donor- and MDB-funded programs, and to treat the management contract strictly as a management tool to stabilize basic functions of the utility. The contractor is viewed as a manager who implements pre-designed improvements, rather than a consultant who analyzes problems, identifies solutions, and carries out implementation. To underscore this distinction, the World Bank procurement procedures used for the Sierra Leone management contract were those reserved for non-consulting services, instead of the quality- and cost-based selection procedures used for consultancy services.
- **The external operating environment must be supportive.** There are limits to what can be done to keep governments from interfering in these contracts or refusing to meet their contractual obligations. Monitoring and evaluation

Box 6.1 A Hybrid Electricity Management Contact in Sierra Leone

In 2013, a World Bank Project Appraisal Document announced the Bank's intention to support the Government of Sierra Leone in concluding a "Performance Based Contract for Utility Operation and Management" (PBCUOM). Under this contract, a private operator would be given full management control of the GoSL's Electricity Distribution and Supply Authority (EDSA) and authorized to manage a range of activities for a short time period (two to five years), in return for a fee that was performance based.

- The main deliverable under the PBCUOM would be the implementation of a comprehensive business plan for the utility, which the GoSL and the Bank would work on together "well ahead of procuring the PBCUOM." The Bank would mobilize its own internal expertise across several departments to help select objectives, detailed activities, and related results for the plan. The design work would also be assisted by consultants paid for by another project.
- When a Request for Proposal was issued in August 2015, contract was referred to simply as a "management contract," but the hybrid character of the arrangement remained evident:
- The key elements of the business plan provided to all bidders were (i) the establishment of a new organizational structure centered on customer satisfaction; (ii) the implementation of "state of the art" MIS; and (iii) a comprehensive staff training plan. Hundreds of systems and procedures were identified in the bid documents as required elements of the plan.
- The contract performance targets involved simply full implementation of "all plans, programs, activities, tasks, and milestones" described in the EDSA's business plan, along with indicated timelines and deadlines.
- Performance penalties were based on delays in implementation: a penalty of 0.03 per cent of the total amount of the contract would be applied for each day of delay in compliance with the time schedule of any of the activities in the business plan for reasons under the responsibility of the contractor.
- The annual base fee was set at one-third of the total fixed fee over the three-year period of the contract.
- The contact would involve no incentive remuneration.
- The contract exit strategy was to ensure that a team of well-trained local utility staff was in place and running the utility at least six months before the termination of the contract, with the contractor's own staff playing a supporting advisory role during that period.

The management contract was signed on October 14, 2016, and the selected contractor assumed duty on November 1, 2016.

Sources: World Bank, 2013; Republic of Sierra Leone, 2015.

efforts are being strengthened with these new contracts, as are efforts to find capable independent advisors to work with government oversight boards. But these new contracts also remove some of the areas of frequent disagreement between boards and managers. The contract work plan is developed and agreed to by governments and development partners before the contract is signed, so is not something to argue about with contractors. These contracts also aim to remove the most contentious area of implementation: the use of incentive remuneration. The Sierra Leone contract is referred to as performance-based, but success fees are not paid and penalties are levied only for delays in implementation.

- **The owner must be fully supportive.** Several measures are taken to generate—and maintain—strong government ownership of and support for these contracts. The pre-contractual government agreement on the contract action plan has been mentioned. Action plans produced under these conditions also tend to reflect the view that these utilities need to prioritize commercial objectives, the early achievement of which is necessary to begin showing immediate results and allay concerns of government officials regarding progress and costs. Priorities attractive to owners, which need early support, include well-managed billing and collections (based on early MIS achievements), as well as the need to recruit and build the capacity of local staff as quickly as possible, to foreshorten the controversial use of expensive expatriate staff.
- **Contract objectives must be capable of achievement by the manager.** These contracts tend to have simpler structures than conventional versions, and again reduce the opportunities for dispute between government owners (represented by supervisory bodies) and managers. Key performance indicators (KPIs) that measure progress toward desirable outcomes, always difficult to design, can sometimes be replaced with discrete outputs. The request for proposal (RFP) for the Sierra Leone management contract describes the contract's performance targets as "basically, the full implementation of all plans, programmes, activities, task and milestones" detailed in the utility action plan (Republic of Sierra Leone, 2015). In effect, these new contracts shift risk-sharing more toward the owner and its development partners and further away from the private operator. This makes the contract less of a classic PPP and more like a service contract or an engineering, procurement, and construction (EPC) contract. By the same token, success fees can be reduced or eliminated as in the case of the Sierra Leone contract, with the operator paid only on the basis of output achievement and penalized only in terms of implementation delays (as with EPC contracts). Arguments about operator remuneration, which have irreparably damaged owner–operator relations on so many conventional management contracts,

are expected to be less frequent and less severe as the roles of KPIs and success fees are diminished.

6.7 Conclusions

The infrastructure management contracts traditionally used for water and electricity in SSA are all part of a long tradition of conventional contracts. For 50 years these kinds of contracts had been used successfully in commercial sectors to engage experienced operators to carry out routine management functions for businesses like hotels. When structural adjustment operations of the 1980s began to privatize SOEs, these kinds of management contracts were obvious options for the "privatization" of government-owned agribusinesses, mining facilities, local airports, and hotels, which governments did not want to sell. When structural adjustment operations turned to public utilities in the 1990s, management contracts were seen as logical solutions for "privatizing" monopoly service systems that realistically could not be sold.

But few of the conventional management contracts used for utility services in developing countries have met stakeholder expectations; some have been spectacular disappointments. In most cases, these management contracts were not the result of market transactions between willing buyers and sellers, focused on addressing the kinds of routine management issues that had been handled so successfully in commercial sectors. Instead, most were donor-driven reform measures expected to solve severe problems that resulted from policy shortcomings and fundamental business deficiencies. This meant that expatriate utility operators were sometimes asked to do more than they were capable of, which was particularly challenging in inhospitable policy, legal, and regulatory environments.

Some donors, DFIs, and MDBs have now concluded that if basic preconditions for management contract success are absent when a contract is being considered, either action needs to be taken to realize the preconditions in some way or the contract needs to be modified accordingly. By 2013, some MDBs, DFIs, and donors were actively experimenting with hybrid kinds of contracts that combine features of conventional management contracts with features of non-PPP arrangements like service contracts or EPC contracts. In other words, these hybrid forms represent a retreat from some of the PPP features of conventional management contracts that were eventually recognized as overly ambitious. Hybrid contracts currently have been signed in Sierra Leone, Liberia, and a few other countries, and are planned for use several more.

Whether or not these hybrid arrangements will meet the expectations of stakeholders in a way that conventional management contracts have failed to do, will not be fully resolved until these new contracting models have a chance to generate results and are subject to cross-country evaluations. But governments and their development partners need to come to terms with an inescapable conclusion of almost 40 years of experience with traditional kinds of management contracts in infrastructure sectors—the chances are very small that conventional models will meet expectations of most stakeholders in developing countries.

Chapter 7 presents a series of short case studies of the water and electricity management contracts included in Tables 6.1 and 6.2. The chapter attempts to identify contracts that are viewed by stakeholders as successful in the sense of substantially improving performance and distributing utility benefits equitably enough that governments are comfortable sustaining the contracts—either by renewing them or securing new ones. The case studies illustrate how difficult it has been for water and electricity management contracts to successfully meet stakeholder expectations in SSA.

References

Antmann, P. 2009. *Reducing Technical and Non-Technical Losses in the Power Sector.* Background Paper for the World Bank Group Energy Sector Strategy. Washington, DC: World Bank (July).

Antmann, P. 2017. "Management Contract: A transitory arrangement to improve operational performance of distressed electricity utilities." Presentation to the Office of the Vice President, Federal Republic of Nigeria, by the World Bank Power Sector Recovery Program (November).

Baietti, A., W. Kingdom, M. van Ginneken. 2006. "Characteristics of Well-Performing Public Water Utilities." Water Supply & Sanitation Working Notes, No. 9. Washington, DC: World Bank (May).

Brooke, M.Z. 1985. "International Management contracts: Servicing foreign markets and selling expertise abroad." *Journal of General Management* (11)1: 4–15.

Buchs, T.D. 2003. "Privatization in sub-Saharan Africa: Some Lessons from Experiences to Date." International Finance Corporation. Unpublished Working Paper (December).

Campbell-White, O., A. Bhatia. 1998. *Privatization in Africa.* World Bank Directions in Development. Washington, DC: World Bank.

Candoy-Sekse, R. 1988. *Techniques of Privatization of State-Owned Enterprises, Volume III.* World Bank Technical Paper No. 90. Washington, DC: World Bank.

De Roos, J.A. 2010. "Hotel Management Contracts – Past and Present." *Cornell Hospitality Quarterly*, 51(1): 68–80.

Eberhard, A., O. Rosnes, M. Shkaratan, H. Vennemo. 2011. *Africa's Power Infrastructure: Investment, Integration, Efficiency.* Washington, DC: World Bank.

Economic Consulting Associates (ECA). 2015. *Evidence and Gaps in Evidence in Use of Management Contracts for Electricity Distribution and Supply.* Report prepared for Evidence on Demand, UK Department for International Development (DFID), by Climate, Environment, Infrastructure and Livelihoods Professional Evidence and Applied Knowledge Services (CEIL PEAKS).

Estache, A. 2005. "What Do We Know About Sub-Saharan Africa's Infrastructure and the Impact of its 1990s Reforms?" Working Paper, Ecares, *Universite Libre de Bruxelles* (May 25).

Foster, V., C.M. Briceno-Garmendia. 2010. *Africa's Infrastructure: A Time for Transformation.* AICD Flagship Report. Washington, DC: World Bank.

Gabriel, P.P. 1967. *The International Transfer of Corporate Skills: Management Contracts in Less Developed Countries.* Cambridge, Mass: Harvard University Press.

Gokgur, N., L. Jones. 2007. "Privatization of Mozambique Water Sector." Report prepared for the Africa Private Sector and Infrastructure Department, World Bank (October).

Gomez-Ibanez, J. 2005. "EDM (Energie du Mali)." Case Study CR14-05-1811.0, Kennedy School of Government Case Program. Cambridge, MA: Harvard University.

Gomez-Ibanez, J. 2007. *Alternatives to Infrastructure Privatization Revisited: Public Enterprise Reform from the 1960s to the 1980s.* Policy Research Working Paper No. 4391. Washington, DC: World Bank (November).

Hegstad, S.O., I. Newport. 1987. *Management Contracts: Main Features and Design Issues.* World Bank Technical Paper No. 65. Washington, DC: World Bank.

Independent Evaluation Group (IEG). 2010. *Water and Development: An Evaluation of World Bank Support, 1997–2007.* Volume 2: Appendixes. Washington, DC: World Bank.

Jones, L. 1991. "Performance Evaluation for State-Owned Enterprises," in *Privatization and Control of State-Owned Enterprises*, edited by R. Ramamurti and R. Vernon, EDI Development Studies. Washington, DC: World Bank.

Kojima, M., C. Trimble. 2016. *Making Power Affordable for Africa and Viable for its Utilities.* Washington, DC: World Bank.

Leigland, J. 2018. "Changing Perceptions of PPP Risk and Return: The Case of Brownfield Concessions." *The Journal of Structured Finance* 23(4): 47–56.

Manibog, F., R. Dominguez, S. Wegner. 2003. *Power for Development: A Review of the World Bank Group's Experience with Private Participation in the Electricity Sector.* Operations Evaluation Department. Washington, DC: World Bank.

Marin, P. 2009. Public-Private Partnerships for Urban Water Utilities: A Review of Experience in Developing Countries. PPIAF Trends and Policy Options No. 8. Washington, DC: World Bank.

Nellis, J. 1989a. "Contract Plans and Public Enterprise Performance." World Bank Discussion Paper No. 48. Washington, DC: World Bank (February).

Nellis, J. 1989b. "Public Enterprise Reform in Adjustment Lending." Policy, Planning, and Research Working Paper No. 233. Washington, DC: World Bank (August).

Nellis, J. 2005. *The Evolution of Enterprise Reform in Africa: From State-Owned Enterprises to Private Participation in Infrastructure—and Back?* ESMAP Technical Paper No. 084. Washington, DC: World Bank (November).

Rebel Group International. 2016. "Review of Success Stories I urban Water Utility Reform: Final Report." Report prepared for the Swiss State Secretariat for Economic Affairs (SECO), Bern (March).

Republic of Sierra Leone. 2015. *Bidding Documents for a Management Contractor for Electricity Distribution and Supply Authority.* Freetown: Ministry of Energy.

Shirley, M.M., L.C. Xu. 2001. "Empirical Effects of Performance Contracts: Evidence from China." *Journal of Law, Economics and Organization*, 17(1): 168–200.

Swiss State Secretariat for Economic Affairs (SECO). 2015. *Independent Evaluation: SECO's Corporate Development of Public Utilities.* SECO Quality and Resources Unit, Bern (February).

Trimble, T., M. Kojima, I.P. Arroyo, F. Mohammadzadeh. 2016. *Financial Viability of Electricity Sectors in Sub-Saharan Africa: Quasi-Fiscal Deficits and Hidden Costs.* Policy Research Working Paper No. 7788. Washington, DC: World Bank (August).

World Bank. 2013. "International Development Association Project Appraisal Document on a Proposed Credit in the Amount of SDR 26.1 Million (US$40 Million Equivalent) to the Republic of Sierra Leone for Energy Sector Utility Reform Project." Report No: 82634-SL. Washington, DC: World Bank (November 21).

World Bank. 2016. *Improving the Performance of Electricity and Water and Sanitation Utilities in Sub-Saharan Africa*. Energy and Extractives Global Practice, Conference Edition. Washington, DC: World Bank (October).

World Bank. 2017. *Joining Forces for Better Services? When Why, and How Water and Sanitation Utilities Can Benefit from Working Together*. Water Global Practice. Washington, DC: World Bank (August).

World Bank. 2018. PPI Project Database. Accessed at: http://ppi.worldbank.org/customquery?mode=1

7
Case Studies
Searching for Successful Management Contracts in SSA

7.1 Introduction

Leases and management contracts for infrastructure services have not been evaluated with the same rigor or sophistication used for arrangements like non-legal performance contracts, which dominated state-owned enterprise (SOE) reform efforts in the 1980s and early 1990s (see Shirley and Xu, 2001). Largely because of that, there is no widespread agreement about the value of management contracts for infrastructure service delivery. The International Finance Corporation (IFC) Transaction Advisory Services Department, which sells advisory services to governments wishing to make use of public–private partnerships (PPPs), claims that its work helping to set up management contracts has been successful, and justifies that claim with a variety of "impact stories" available on the IFC website (IFC, 2017). But the research literature on these contracts—although still limited—generally recognizes "the failure of management contractors to achieve sustained performance improvements" (ECA, 2015, iii).

Despite the controversies, management contracts continue to be used for water and electricity services in developing country regions like Sub-Saharan Africa (SSA). Donors, DFIs, and MDBs continue to promote, and often pay for, these kinds of contracts. The proliferation of these deals has slowed considerably over the last 20 years, but has not completely stopped.

Why have governments, particularly in Africa, been so willing to sign these kinds of contracts, despite their consistently poor performance? Why has that performance not appreciably improved after almost three decades of experimentation? Why do donors, DFIs, and MDBs continue to promote these mechanisms? What lessons have been learned about the pre-conditions necessary for the conventional management contract model to meet expectations? The case studies in this chapter explore these questions. The studies attempt to identify the factors that make such contracts successful. "Success" here is defined in the same way the term is used by Gokgur and Jones in their many

Public–Private Partnerships in Sub-Saharan Africa: The Evidence-Based Critique. James Leigland, Oxford University Press (2020). © James Leigland.
DOI: 10.1093/oso/9780198861829.001.0001

evaluations of infrastructure "privatization," which for them included PPPs of all forms as well as divestiture:

> In sum, a successful privatization is not just one where the deed gets done, but where performance improves substantially and the results of that change are distributed equitably enough to sustain the process (Gokur and Jones, 2007, 1).

7.2 Project Profiles

7.2.1 The First Success Story: Côte d'Ivoire (1959–90)

One of the reasons why management contracts began to spread in SSA in the 1990s was the fact that in a few countries such contracts had been successful. This was the case with PPP contracts in Côte d'Ivoire's electricity and water sectors. These arrangements became models for other SSA countries, but models that proved difficult to replicate because their application in Côte d'Ivoire had been unique in several respects.

By the 1990s, Côte d'Ivoire already had substantial experience with private sector involvement in its water sector. In 1959, a private French water company, SAUR, won a 30-year concession contract for water supply to Abidjan. But the private operator of the system was required to be subject to Ivoirian law and be majority-owned by Ivoirian shareholders, so SAUR set up a new enterprise, Société de Distribution d'Eau de Côte d'Ivoire (SODECI). SAUR was the largest SODECI shareholder with 46 per cent of the shares, individual Ivoirian investors owned 45 per cent of the company, 5 per cent was held by the Ivoirian government, and 4 per cent by individual French investors. Over the next few years, SODECI signed five lease contracts and three management contracts for water services in other municipalities, and eventually signed management contracts and service contracts for some of the urban sewerage systems. In 1967, SODECI's role in Abidjan was reduced somewhat when the concession was converted into a management contract, but the government remained generally satisfied with SODECI's performance. In 1974, SODECI was awarded a 15-year contract for the operation and maintenance of urban water systems in all other Ivoirian cities.

By the 1980s, the Ivoirian economy was collapsing due to macroeconomic problems. In response, the country's first structural adjustment program was adopted in 1983. SODECI's performance remained satisfactory, but the World Bank recommended movement back to a full concession contract so that the private company could take responsibility for all aspects of water sector investment and be responsible for all sector debt service payments (previous investments by the government were judged to have been poorly targeted). SODECI and the government considered the concession arrangement to be too risky for the operator, and social tensions were building in response to the adjustment prescriptions, so all parties compromised on a lease contract, but one that did give the operator significant control over investment planning and managing, with the actual water sector investment finance coming from the government.

The 20-year Côte d'Ivoire lease, which became effective in July 1988, was considered reasonably successful. A major factor in the project's success was the fact that the country had already used a variety of leases, management contracts, and concessions in the country's water sector, and the same private operator had been involved in the country over the previous three decades. Government officials were familiar and comfortable enough with private participation in the water sector, and with this particular private operator, that they were willing to agree to a lease that gave the private operator a degree of control over investment that was extraordinary, considering that the operator took on no investment-related risks. The lease was unusual because of that arrangement—it combined the features of a traditional lease with those of a concession to produce something close to what would later be called an *affermage* contact (Menard and Clarke, 2000a).[1]

The success of the water sector reforms triggered an interest among Côte d'Ivoire officials and their MDB counterparts in using private sector management to help with the country's deteriorating electricity sector. By 1990, financial mismanagement at Energie Electrique de Côte d'Ivoire (EECI) had nearly bankrupted the utility. It struggled to service its debts and pay employees, and paralyzing power blackouts had become frequent. Government officials refused to wait for the completion of the country's World Bank-funded privatization strategy, and rejected the use of international competitive bidding to select a private partner. Because of their long-term relationship with SAUR, government officials approached the head of France's Societe Internationale des Services Publics (of which SAUR owned 65 per cent and Electricitie de France the balance). The SODECI joint venture model was used to form Compagnie Ivoirienne d'Electricite (CIE), with SAUR owning 51 per cent of the company, the government holding 20 per cent, other Ivorians, 24 per cent, and employees, 5 per cent.

On October 20, 1990, a 15-year contract was signed and CIE began operation. At the time, the contract was referred to as a lease or management contract, but the World Bank later called it the first affermage contract signed in Africa

[1] Under an affermage contract, the operator is responsible for operations and maintenance. The operator collects the tariff directly from consumers on behalf of the government contracting authority. The contracting authority is usually responsible for major rehabilitation and new capital works. The operator earns its remuneration in the form of an agreed-upon proportion of the water tariff for water produced and sold. The difference between total revenue and operator remuneration is paid to the contracting authority who uses these funds to pay its expenses, including debt service on capital investments.

(World Bank, 2005). Pursuant to the contract, CIE managed the production and distribution of electricity for a fee. CIE collected all electricity revenues directly from consumers and handled these funds in the following manner:

(i) they retained a payment for all CIE's costs related to power generation and distribution (including electricity purchases from independent power producers (IPPs) and a retention account for the financing of major repair and maintenance works), operation and management of services provided under the CIE concession, and a profit margin;
(ii) they retained a payment equal to the sum of all taxes, duties, and fees applied to the services provided under the CIE concession; and
(iii) they made a transfer of the net balance of revenues to the national fund for the electricity sector, to repay the debt of the sector and finance new investments.

CIE was not obligated to invest capital, but could propose to undertake major maintenance or renewal of equipment after signing periodic subsidiary agreements (minimum term of one year), which outlined the sharing of costs for these improvements with the government.

The arrangement quickly established itself as a modest success. Blackouts immediately became less frequent. Residential electricity prices were cut by 10 per cent. After a decade of annual losses by the previous SOE system manager, CIE recorded a net profit over its first year of operation. These gains were actually quite limited initially (the net profit was largely due to changes in accounting procedures), but improvements became more substantial after several years. The CIE contract helped lay the foundations for a successful IPP program, beginning in 1994 with CIPREL, SSA's first IPP. The improved efficiency of electricity system operations and related revenue increases meant that IPPs could be confident that they would be paid for their power.

By the mid-1990s, benefits of electricity system "privatization" in Côte d'Ivoire seemed clear to everyone. Customers were satisfied, government revenues increased sharply, CIE workers received higher pay and more benefits—SAUR reduced the overstaffing problem with attrition-based staffing cuts rather than lay-offs. Several evaluations have concluded that CIE was a privatization success story. One success factor identified was the fact that "the contractor's experience in Francophone Africa may have had much to do with the avoidance of unresolvable disputes that wounded—sometimes fatally—other African privatizations" (Jammal and Jones, 2006). Another success factor was the government's long experience with a large variety of privatization options, including leases, affermage, concessions, management contracts, and service contracts. The government began working with the private sector decades before other African countries and the remarkable long-term stability and credibility of political institutions over that period ensured an institutional memory of the advantages and disadvantages of the various privatization options. Development of the electricity sector continued until the time of the first civil war (2002–7), after which political and economic conditions rapidly deteriorated. Nevertheless, underscoring the perceived successes of the affermage contract, a second 15-year contract was signed during the civil war, on October 12, 2005.

Although the use of management contracts, leases, and affermage contracts began to expand rapidly under structural adjustment operations during the 1990s, very few were able to repeat the successes of the contracts in Côte d'Ivoire. The Ivoirian contracts for water and electricity were later referred to as the "original privatization model" that was applied to other public utilities across Africa (De Luca, 1998, 22). But other African countries were much less comfortable with any form of privatization, so most of these other contracts involved much longer and more complex negotiations, which reflected the absence of the kind of trust between operator and contracting authority that made the Côte d'Ivoire contracts sustainable and largely successful.

7.2.2 The Guinea Water Lease (1989)

The difficulty in replicating the Côte d'Ivoire successes is illustrated by Guinea's experience with a water lease, signed in 1989. This was one of the projects most heavily influenced by Côte d'Ivoire experience with private participation. The private partner in Guinea was SAUR, who won the contact relying on its experience in Côte d'Ivoire and even using some of its employees who had gained experience working on SAUR's water contracts in Côte d'Ivoire. But the operator–government relationship in Guinea ended up being very different than it was in Côte d'Ivoire.

At the insistence of the World Bank, SAUR, and its French partner, Compagnie Generale des Eaux, were selected via competitive bidding, unlike the direct negotiation process used in Côte d'Ivoire, based on the familiarity of government officials with SAUR executives. A joint venture company was created, which was 49 per cent state owned and 51 per cent owned by the French partners. The joint venture entered into a 10-year lease of the water supply facilities serving the capital city, Conakry, and 16 other cities and towns. The two French companies signed a separate two-year management contract (officially referred to at the time as a "technical assistance contract") with the joint venture to effectively carry out the joint venture's responsibility for operating and maintaining the urban water facilities, as well as customer billing and collections.[2] The French companies

[2] This combination of a lease and management contract had been used successfully in earlier African SOE privatizations, mostly in industrial sectors. One combination, signed in October 1984,

supplied expatriate staff, including the general manager of the operation, plus home office support for day-to-day management issues, and 51 per cent of the joint venture's initial capitalization of US$3 million. A state-owned water authority (operating under a performance agreement with the government) maintained ownership of the assets, set policy and tariffs, and managed investments (only the government and its SOEs could borrow to finance investment). The World Bank assisted with a US$100 million adjustment loan that helped with tariff setting and provided investment capital to expand the network. But of all of these agreements, only the performance agreement between the government and its water authority specified performance targets (Menard and Clarke, 2000b).

Although the Guinea arrangement was successful in some ways, the actual improvements in service were much less than hoped for—water became very expensive, connections increased very slowly, and a series of conflicts developed between the joint venture and the state-owned water authority. The public–private relationship suffered from several shortcomings: the lack of concrete performance targets in the lease or management contract, the overly-complex nature of the different contractual agreements interacting in unpredictable ways, and the lack of any kind of independent authority capable of enforcing the contractual commitments.

The government's minority shareholding in the joint venture was taken on because government wanted to ensure some social benefits of commercialization in addition to increased revenue (Brook, 1999). But the state-owned water authority overseeing the lease, with an 11-member board appointed by ten different ministries, responded to internal ministerial political incentives rather than economic ones. As a result, the government sometimes acted arbitrarily in its relations with the contractor, and failed to ensure that government agencies consistently paid their water bills. The private consortium hoped that government involvement in the joint venture would help forge a closer working relationship, as it had in Côte d'Ivoire; but they also wanted the management contract to protect its equity participation in the joint venture. But the consortium had no incentives to pursue social goals and generally used their information advantage to misapply price adjustment formulas and conduct informal price negotiations with government to realize far greater compensation than originally anticipated (Brook, 1999).

Evaluators recommended that future contracts better align performance incentives for public service provision. This could be done in either one of two ways. Concessions agreements (or some of the features of concessions as in the

rescued a state-owned steel mill in Togo from a liquidation that had been strongly advocated by the World Bank. The success of the contracts, involving saved jobs, modest operational profits, and the avoidance of an embarrassing SOE asset write-off, motivated Togo to sign a series of additional lease agreements with foreign private sector companies (Bergeron, 1991).

Côte d'Ivoire lease) could give private partners more responsibility and risk for capital investment. But if the private partner was unwilling to take on any substantial commercial risk, a lease or concession should be abandoned in favor of a simple management contract "with a few, largely indisputable, performance targets" (Brook, 1999).

When the ten-year lease expired, the government asked the private operator to take on investment responsibilities while maintaining limits on tariff increases. The contractor and government disagreed about the details of the agreement and negotiations failed. In December 2000 the private operator withdrew. After another management contract, the sector returned to public management in 2003.

7.2.3 Mali Electricity Management Contract (1995)

Energie du Mali (EDM) was established in 1960. For over 30 years it remained a small, mismanaged power utility operating a handful of diesel-fired plants and hydro facilities that produced expensive, intermittent power. Customer records were inaccurate. Many consumers did not receive bills. Those that did (including government agencies) often did not pay. Service cut-offs for non-payment were rare and when they happened EDM employees could be bribed to restore service (Gomez-Ibanez, 2005). In a donor meeting in Paris in 1993, private management of EDM (along with other sector reforms) was made a pre-condition of further aid to Mali's power sector.

In 1995, a French–Canadian consortium led by SAUR won the competitive tender to operate EDM for four years. Some of the donors viewed this arrangement as preparation of EDM for a long-term concession contract, but others saw it simply as a way to make urgently needed improvements in EDM's operations. The contract was structured so that over the first two years the consortium would be compensated on a fixed-fee basis. At the end of that period, a technical review would assess performance and set targets for the last two years of the contract. Compensation over the final two years would include the fixed fee, plus an incentive payment or deduction depending on changes in bill collections, technical losses, and other performance measures.

The arrangement worked well over the first two years. The private consortium improved EDM performance in areas like customer relations, training, and investment targeting. But the consortium performed poorly in areas like improving the reliability of generators or strengthening the accounting system of the utility. Performance problems were highlighted in 1996 when months of power blackouts resulted from a drought combined with sharply growing consumer demand. The blackouts precipitated arguments about management priorities with the Malian board of directors and within the consortium. During the third year of the contract, the board, which was required to approve the EDM budget, sharply criticized the consortium's management for not addressing key problems. In March 1998, the board cancelled the contract, with nearly a year remaining.

The cancellation of the management contract led donors to seek a contracting mechanism that would not leave private operators at the mercy of a Malian board of directors. A month after the cancellation, donors met again in Paris and agreed to pressure the government to move immediately to a full concession that would allow a private operator to control the board as well as day-to-day management of the utility. In 1999, the performance of EDM continued to deteriorate and the government eventually agreed to the concession. Donor-funded consultants helped the Malian government design a 20-year concession agreement that initiated operation in 2000, under the supervision of a new sector regulator. But a series of problems plagued the new arrangement almost immediately: the tariff adjustment formula led to dramatic price increases for consumers; investments seemed too small; EDM was also criticized for the size of its expatriate staff and large management fees. The relationship between EDM and the regulator became contentious. By 2005, negotiations were initiated to transform the concession into an affermage contract, in which the contractor would be responsible only for operations and maintenance and the government would take over all responsibility for new investment.

7.2.4 Namibia Electricity Distribution Contract (1996)

Under a six-year, competitively tendered contract, signed with the Namibian government in 1996, a newly formed private company, Northern Electricity, agreed to operate the distribution infrastructure in a rural, underserved region in the north of the country—200 rural villages and three towns spread across an area of 120,000 km^2. Pursuant to the contract (originally referred to as a "lease," but later most frequently referred to as a "management contract"), the government retained asset ownership, but the contractor accepted overall responsibility for all operating expenses and revenues related to the distribution system.

Three agreements made up the contractual relationship between the government and Northern Electricity; (i) an electricity distribution trading license gave the contactor the sole right to distribute electricity in the designated region, with prices set by the government ministry for local government; (ii) a franchise agreement that maintained the ministry's formal responsibility for electricity service, but transferred operating responsibility to the private operator, who also accepted responsibility for small investments in electrification; and (iii) a lease agreement allowing the operator to operate the ministry's network assets, in exchange for a nominal monthly payment.

The contractor's technical and financial gains were later judged to be "impressive" (Econ One Research, 2002). Improvements were made in power system reliability, resulting in fewer power outages. With help from the government, the contractor funded major network upgrades and prepared a five-year network development plan. A preventative maintenance program was also implemented, which helped improve the reliability of the system. Collections increased from less than 50 per cent to 99 per cent because of improvements in customer registration, billing and collection procedures, and anti-theft measures. When it was unable to borrow money to finance its obligations with regard to electrification, the company developed a system to finance new connections by imposing a levy, equal to N$0.015/kWh, which supplemented company revenues.

Unfortunately, the three agreements formalizing Northern Electricity's responsibilities contained very little prescriptive detail and among other things did not outline methods for evaluating performance relative to indicators or targets. So, despite the operator's impressive performance in many areas, those achievements were not documented in any kind of compelling fashion. There was little basis for the operator to argue against the government's decision in February 2002 that it would not extend the contract. The national SOE energy provider, NamPower, had originally declined to manage the distribution system in the north, but by 2001 it had become interested in expanding its distribution business, particularly in the north where distribution had become profitable under Northern Electricity. NamPower formed a joint venture, Northern Regional Electricity Distributor, with several northern local authorities who were unhappy with some of the terms of the original contracts (including lack of electrification investment and what were perceived to be the operator's generous financial terms). NamPower convinced the government to hand over Northern Electricity's business in March 2002. John Nellis later wrote that Namibian stakeholders valued the improved service provided by Northern Electricity, but attributed it to "just management," meaning that they assumed anyone could replicate the private operator's success (Nellis, 2005, 44).

7.2.5 Mozambique Delegated Water Management Contract (1999)

In 1999, the Mozambican water asset management company signed a 15-year lease contract with a private company for water supply in the capital city, Maputo, and five-year management contracts for water supply in four provincial capitals in the central and northern parts of the country. The private partner was a consortium of foreign water operators and local investors led by the French private operator, SAUR. The contractor received a fee for water services in Maputo, management fees for services in the provincial capitals, rates charged for delegated works and management of the investment program, preparation of tenders, and supervision of capital works. The contract was a condition for receiving US$130m in sector loans from the World Bank and donors, plus it helped the country become eligible for International Monetary Fund (IMF) debt relief. But within months of contract signing the operator had encountered serious difficulties:

- Massive floods destroyed some of the infrastructure and disrupted operations.
- The utility ran out of water-treatment chemicals and discontinued service for several days.
- Subsequent outbreaks of cholera and other diseases were blamed on the utility.
- The managing director and technical director of the contractor-provided utility team were fired.
- Investments for which the contractor was responsible moved slowly, but the major investments for which the government was responsible (financed by donors) quickly fell even further behind schedule and negatively affected operations.
- In Maputo alone, the contractor had operational losses of over US$6.5 million at the end of the first year.

The contractor requested an increase in its fees to cover the costs of these problems, and also argued that the bid documents describing the condition of the system assets were incomplete and overly optimistic. The government refused to comply. In December 2001 SAUR terminated its involvement. After two years of discussions the government and the remaining consortium partners led by *Águas de Portugal* renegotiated the lease and management contracts to include higher fees and better specification of service obligations and procedures. The revised lease contract became effective in April 2004 for the ten years remaining in the original contract. A revised three-year management contract (2004–7) consolidated the four original management contracts and required the operator to dedicate more resources, including six full-time resident team members, to the management of services in the four provincial capitals. The government was unhappy with the performance of the operator: the quality of service improved marginally, but water losses were not reduced, water prices increased, new connections and production works fell behind schedule, the expatriate staff did not work well with local employees and turned over frequently (PPIAF, 2009). The contract was unprofitable for the private partner. The contracts included no rewards or penalties as incentives to achieve contractually specified targets and standards and in any case, reliable performance baselines were never established. This management contract was subsequently extended for an additional year and terminated in March 2008.

7.2.6 Johannesburg Water Management Contract (2000)

In 2000, Johannesburg signed a management contract with Johannesburg Water Management (Jowam), a joint venture between international water operator, Suez Group of France, and its subsidiaries in the United Kingdom and South Africa. The stated purpose of the 2000–6 contract was to consolidate six separate water services departments, each with fragmented management and operations, into a commercially viable, corporatized, city-owned utility known as Johannesburg Water. The contract is now considered to have been "successful" (Marin, 2009) and some of that success has been attributed to realistic performance targets and a flexible approach to setting performance baselines. Because reliable baselines could not be established with any confidence at the time of contract signing, a framework for doing so was developed by the contractor over the first year of the contract and specific baselines were then agreed to, with the process under the control of an independent technical auditor. But the contract also involved powerful performance incentives beyond KPIs. The city's long-term intention in 2000, clearly if informally communicated to bidders, was that the management contract would help prepare the utility for a long-term concession. The prospect of such a contract caused aggressive bidding for the management contract among international water companies that had long campaigned for work in Southern Africa. The competition was so intense that some bidders were willing to forego things like success fees in order to win the award. The overall performance of the operator was judged to be good, with targets met. But when the contract came to an end in June 2006, the city bowed to pressure from unions and civil society groups and not only did not renew the management contract, but abandoned plans for a long-term concession. Since that time, the city has managed the utility without private involvement. However, in 2016, the city cited corruption and poor service delivery as reasons for reintegrating corporatized utilities like Johannesburg Water back into the general municipal structure as regular government departments.

7.2.7 TANESCO Electricity Management Contact (2002)

The Government of Tanzania signed a two-year management contract with NETGroup Solutions of South Africa in 2002 to oversee strategy and operations of the national electricity utility, Tanzania Electricity Supply Company Ltd. (TANESCO). The contract was extended for two and a half years in 2004. NETGroup staffed the top four TANESCO management positions (later increased to five), plus carried out specific consulting assignments with personnel from its home office. The contract cost US$18–20 million. Contractor remuneration consisted of a fixed fee and variable fee supplements based on performance against pre-agreed targets. About 45 per cent of the costs were covered by utility revenues, with the balance (55 per cent) paid for by a grant from the Swedish International Development Cooperation Agency (Sida). Sida's total contribution, about US$10 million, paid for the contractor's fixed fees.

The first two years of the project focused on preparing the utility for full privatization at the end of that period, so involved no new investment in assets. Although the contract involved an ambitious list of objectives, the initial set of performance targets included only (i) revenue increases, (ii) power loss reductions, and (iii) improved quality of service. Achievement of these targets was expected to make the enterprise more attractive to private sector investors. However, by the time of the extension, the government was losing enthusiasm for full privatization, so the contract refocused on general improvements in sector performance. Increasing utility revenues was supposed to facilitate asset investment, and things like system reliability and electrification were added to the list of performance targets, while targets for power loss reductions and quality of service were dropped.

The contractor was successful in improving TANESCO's revenues—more than 99 per cent of all success fees paid out under the contract were for revenue performance. Revenues increased from US$10–12 million per month in 2001 to US$22–4 million per month in 2005–6. Increases over this period resulted from (i) a 37 per cent growth in electricity sales; (ii) a 28 per cent tariff increase; (iii) a 69 per cent increase in collections (reaching 95 per cent of customers billed in 2006), as well as (iv) a decision to carry out high-profile service cut-offs of public institutions, who were the largest debtors.

The contractor was also successful in winning the support of the utility workers despite their initial reservations and the fact that 21 per cent of the workforce was eventually retrenched. The contract benefited from consistent government support, but relations between the contractor and the TANESCO board eventually deteriorated.

Although revenues increased dramatically, poor contractor performance in other areas like power loss reductions and improved quality of service were blamed for the government's decision not to renew the contract in 2006. Technical power losses in 2006 were higher than losses a decade earlier. Non-technical losses remained high, possibly because they were not governed by a performance target—the contractor had no incentive to spend resources upgrading the system to reduce these losses. Power shortages (omitted from the performance targets for the contract extension in 2004) were high because of poor maintenance—load shedding of 12–16 hours a day was common throughout much of 2006. The contractor also failed several times to achieve the performance targets for quality of supply. An evaluation later pointed out that from a customer point of view, contracts like this are judged in terms of whether or not services are more cost-effective and reliable as a result. "In that respect, the management contract in Tanzania cannot be regarded as an unqualified success" (Ghanadan and Eberhard, 2007, 48).

7.2.8 Dar es Salaam Water Lease (2002)

Perhaps the most notable failure of a water lease in Africa was the collapse of the Dar water PPP in Tanzania. Touted originally as a breakthrough comeback of private participation in the continent's water sector, the lease contract was signed in 2002 by DAWASA, the Dar es Salaam water authority, and City Water Services (CWS), a consortium led by private British water operator, Biwater. City Water was required to invest a modest US$8.5 million, mainly in "removable assets" such as computers to run the billing and management systems during the ten-year contract. On condition that the lease was signed with a private company, the World Bank made available a US$143.5 million loan package for upgrading the city's water infrastructure.

Problems with the contract began immediately. CWS stopped paying its monthly lease fee to DAWASA only five months after the contract started implementation. CWS invested only about half the agreed US$8.5 million. The company's revenue declined by a third by March 2005. The efficiency of the billing system dropped dramatically. Connections slowed and new construction was delayed. The government also claimed that the contractor did not submit financial reports during the contract period. CWS requested two tariff increases but these were rejected due to poor technical performance. CWS staff were poorly trained and remunerated, and inadequately supervised, leading to high levels of mismanagement and poor customer care.

The contract lasted only 21 months before the government terminated it for non-performance, and had Biwater executives summarily escorted to the airport, branded as "undesirable immigrants" (Rice, 2007). Years of acrimonious legal disputes followed. An arbitral tribunal operating under the auspices of the International Centre for Settlement of Investment Disputes (ICSID) ruled on whether the company had been expropriated by the government. City Water blamed its poor performance on assets that had been poorly maintained by the government and largely incapable of generating operating revenue, and customers (including government agencies) who did not pay their water bills. The tribunal concluded that the water company had indeed been illegally expropriated by the government, but had no value. The financial estimates produced by City Water and DAWASA projected significant operating losses in every remaining year of the lease contract. The tribunal found that City Water not only had no projected profits for those four years, but had annual cash shortfalls amounting to US$30 million. There would have been no prospective purchaser for the company. In effect, the tribunal found that the government had done City Water a favor by terminating the contract and expropriating the company (ICSID, 2008).

Although CWS clearly performed poorly, the government must share some of the responsibility for problems. Some critics have argued that the actual evaluation of contractor performance was compromised in several ways. The contract included performance targets, but the contract began operation before the government had set up an independent regulator, planned as an entity to handle monitoring and evaluation. As a result, CWS evaluation was led by DAWASA, even though it was a party to the contract. Government data on utility performance had long been suspect—CWS claimed that the government had not accurately reported on water sector performance before the contract was initiated. There are also indications that once the government had secured the water sector loans from donors, official enthusiasm for the contract waned. As the relationship between CWS and DAWASA deteriorated, an independent facilitator was appointed as part of a formal dispute resolution exercise and began identifying priority issues to be resolved. But the government announced termination of the contract before the dispute resolution process could be finalized. Critics have argued that the failure of CWS was politically convenient for the government. A presidential election was a few months away. The dramatic contract termination helped shift the blame for the city's water problems to a private company and show voters that decisive government action was being taken to remedy the situation (WaterAid Tanzania, 2008).

7.2.9 Ghana Water Services Management Contract (2005)

A management contract involving operations and maintenance of water services in Accra was signed in 2005 by the Ghanaian government and Aqua Vitens Rand Ltd. (AVRL), a joint venture of the Dutch government-owned water company Vitens and the South African parastatal water company Rand Water. The "public" nature of the operator was considered important because five years earlier the government had awarded a 30-year water concession to a private US company Azurix (an Enron subsidiary). But that contract never began operations because of accusations of corruption and a groundswell of opposition to what was considered to be "privatization." The AVRL contract was considered a "public–public" arrangement. The contract objectives included the following:

- improved water pressure and flow rate;
- improved quality of potable water;
- financial sustainability of the utility;
- improved customer service;

- increased access to affordable potable water for low-income customers; and
- reduction in non-revenue water.

A major shortcoming of the contract was the failure of the parties to agree on monitoring and evaluation criteria. Most of this was supposed to be agreed on during implementation. But as late as 2010, agreements still had not been reached regarding final details of indicators, baselines, penalties, and incentives. So, for most of the contract's lifespan, its operation suffered from an unclear allocation of responsibilities between contractor and government, incomplete and unrealistic targets, performance incentives that were insufficient to motivate management and staff, a complete absence of penalties for under-performance, and vague terminology constantly subject to argument and misinterpretation.

The contract was paralleled by a US$120 million capital investment program provided by the World Bank and other development partners. The contractor was required to submit a series of "Suggested Capital Investment Reports," which the government was expected to use as guidance for capital investments. Sometime before the expiry of the five-year management contract, the government intended to competitively bid out a long-term affermage contract, to manage rollout of the larger investments and operate the expanded system (Ghana Management Contract, 2005). But when the contract expired in June 2011, it was neither renewed nor transitioned into an affermage contract. The service was brought back fully under government control. The government claimed that the private company had "failed to bring about the expected positive improvement in urban water supply" (GWCL, 2013). In fact, the company had extended service, improved water quality, and increased collection efficiency, but failed to reduce water losses and was criticized by employees for its "private sector management style." Water shortages and tariff increases, arguably beyond the contractor's control, also helped turn public opinion against the contract. Despite the fact that the operators technically were not private companies, the contract had long been a target of intense lobbying by a large collection of foreign and domestic anti-privatization civil society groups.

7.2.10 KPLC Electricity Management Contract (2006)

In 1997, Kenya's power sector SOE, Kenya Power and Lighting Company (KPLC), was unbundled to create two new enterprises, Kenya Power Company (KenGen) for power generation and KPLC to handle transmission and distribution. In July 2006, KPLC entered into a management contract, which the World Bank encouraged and supported with a US$152 million financial assistance package for the upgrading of the country's power distribution network. Canadian company,

Manitoba Hydro International (MHI), was awarded the contract in bidding against the Irish company, ESBI, and the Spanish company, Union Fenosa. The contract was to run from July 2006 to June 2008, with a possible one-year extension.

The contract included seven key performance targets that the expatriate managers were expected to achieve, including: (i) an improved operating ratio, (ii) new customer connections, as well as reductions in (iii) system losses, (iv) customer outages, (v) voltage fluctuations, (vi) the number of days the company was owed money (receivable days), and (vii) the response time to breakdowns. But from July 2007 to March 2008, the government and the three expatriate managers argued over the pay package, and in particular a Ksh30 million bonus pegged on the achievement of performance targets. According to KPLC board documents, different sources of data were used by each side in calculating some aspects of performance, plus there was disagreement regarding the role of factors like a decision to write off Ksh1.5 billion in consumer debt in calculating reductions in receivable days. A compromise was finally reached when the KPLC board agreed that five of the seven targets had been met, for an overall performance score of 74 per cent (as opposed to the 85 per cent score claimed by the contractor). That translated into a success fee of US$412,015 (Mwangi, 2008).

But a month after the success fee compromise was achieved, the Kenyan government notified the expatriate managers that it would not sanction a contract extension beyond one month, during which the managers were required to hand over the assets. Local newspapers reported that the government was skeptical about whether the performance targets set at the beginning of the contract had been achieved and whether they had been achieved with the help of the expatriates (Kimani, 2008). Government skepticism was said to center on the fact that KPLC had in any case been on an upward growth path even before the signing of the management contract, having reported a 40 per cent growth in profits by mid-2006 due to a 20 per cent increase in sales.

But the actual situation of the contract was more complicated. The contract was never intended as a transition to a longer-term PPP arrangement, and in fact only made allowance for a maximum extension of one year. There were indeed disagreements about achievement of performance targets, but board documents describe a detailed process that everyone agreed to. However, the overall compensation paid to the expatriate management team was much higher than that ever received by previous Kenyan managers, and the contractor also had to weather several labor disputes. Any contract extensions were supposed to be paid for by the Kenyan government (the first two years of the contract's operator costs were paid for by the World Bank), and that would have been difficult given other critical spending priorities that had arisen in the wake of the country's post-election civil unrest at the time. MHI and KPLC continued their association after the end of the management contract, dispelling any notion that their collaboration had broken down in Nairobi. They teamed up successfully to bid on the Liberia management contract in 2010.

7.3 In-Depth Analysis: The Liberia Electricity Management Contract (2010)

7.3.1 Overview

Many of the problems with the conventional model of management contracts are exemplified in the case of the contract to manage Liberia's national power utility signed in 2010. In December 2016, that contract reached its scheduled termination date after being extended for 18 months—a rare achievement for management contracts in Africa. But six months later the contract was being subjected to the same kinds of public attacks that have plagued these agreements since the 1990s. In March 2017, Liberia's House of Representatives announced that it was investigating accusations that the contract's objectives were contrary to the government's energy sector policy, that contract performance was "dismal," and that management of the contract may have involved "financial malpractices" amounting to as much as US$42 million (*Front Page Africa*, 2017).

The contract was originally conceived as a partial response to the fact that after nearly 14 years of civil war, Liberia's electricity infrastructure was all but destroyed and the state-owned electricity utility, the Liberia Electricity Corporation (LEC), left in ruins. In 2007–8, in keeping with the government's long experience with natural resource-based "concessions," the IFC Transaction Advisory Services Department proposed a seven-year contract referred to as a "concession," which focused on private investment in generation. But extensive market soundings could not confirm the willingness of the private sector to take on broad commercial risks associated with major investment, given Liberia's uncertain operating and policy environment.

By late 2008, IFC proposed to structure a management contract around the rehabilitation of Mt. Coffee, a hydropower power plant that had stopped functioning during the civil war. At about the same time, Norway took the leadership among the donors, DFIs, and MDBs focused on Liberia's power sector and proposed a management contract for LEC. IFC was asked to handle the structuring and tendering of such a contract and used some of its previous technical and legal due diligence to do so. Norway agreed to pay IFC fees since a completed management contract, involving no private sector investment, would be unable to generate payment of normal IFC success fees. A five-year management contract between LEC and Canadian firm MHI was signed in April 2010, with the hope of transforming LEC into a sustainable utility.

7.3.2 Contract Objectives and Performance

There was a clear intention that the contract would lead to training and capacity building necessary to help ensure the sustainability of the system improvements. The operator was given an unusual amount of control over financial, procurement, and personnel matters (including decisions regarding hiring and firing), but was subject to supervision and final decisions on some matters, including customer tariffs, by a board of directors appointed by the government. The contract called for a fixed fee of US$8.2 million over the five years, which was to be paid by development partners. Development partners also committed about US$50 million for investments in the country's electricity infrastructure, of which US$10 million was expected to come in the form of a grant for output-based aid (OBA) aimed at connecting 16,000 mostly low-income customers.[3]

In addition to the fixed fee, the contract included a performance incentive system, involving Key Performance Indicators (KPIs), success fees to be paid to the contractor for performance achievements (to be paid by donors for the first two years, and thereafter from utility revenues), as well as penalties for performance shortfalls. The KPIs included:

- new connections made;
- improvements in collection efficiency;
- reduction in losses; and
- improvements in the operational efficiency of the system (operating cost per kWh consumed).

In January 2013, the contract (due to terminate in July 2015) was extended by 18 months so that the private operator could assist with the rehabilitation of the Mt. Coffee hydropower plant, which was eventually commissioned in December 2016.

The KPI performance was mixed, but clearly suffered from some factors beyond the contractor's control. The operator significantly exceeded contract targets for new connections. Operating efficiency did not improve as anticipated in the contract, but a large part of this under-performance was due to the failure of donors to invest in power generating capacity as called for in the contract. This was confirmed in the ruling in late 2015 by an Independent Expert engaged to settle a Year 3 success fee dispute between MHI and LEC. The operator moderately missed its target for collections, in large part because of the failure of Government of Liberia (GoL) agencies to pay their electricity bills in a timely

[3] OBA grants are paid after outputs have been achieved and independently certified. In a PPP, the private partner must pre-finance outputs, such as household electricity connections, then be reimbursed for that work after certified achievement of the agreed-on targets.

fashion. The operator substantially missed its target for loss reductions, partly because GoL and donor priorities required most new connections to be in low-income neighborhoods, where power theft (from connected customers) was prevalent. In terms of overall performance as measured by success fees and penalties, MHI's cumulative success fee for the entire contract period exceeded penalties, although the incentive fee process was discontinued after the country's Ebola outbreak, which occurred mid-way through the fourth year of the contract.

However, because of the contractor's failure to stem operating loss or significantly build the commercial capacity of LEC by the end of the contract, key stakeholders like the GoL, the World Bank, and some donors concluded that contract performance had not been satisfactory and the contract should not be extended again. In 2015, a USAID-commissioned study of private sector partnership options for Liberia's power sector was prepared by McKinsey & Company, after discussions with the other stakeholders. The report made dozens of recommendations regarding reform of the Liberian power sector, many of which focused on the need for an improved LEC management contract (McKinsey & Company, 2015). As noted earlier, several months after the contract terminated, the Liberian House of Representatives initiated an investigation into possible fraud and mismanagement of the contract.

7.3.3 Pre-Conditions for the Effectiveness of the LEC Management Contact.[4]

Chapter 6 summarizes a World Bank study by Hegstad and Newport (1987), which identified factors that serve as essential, interrelated "pre-conditions" for the effective use of management contracts—factors that determine when conventional management contracts have the best chances for successful implementation. The following subsections assess whether or not these pre-conditions necessary for an effective management contract existed in Liberia.

The problem must be limited to management

The authors note that management contracts may help to solve "temporary management-related problems," but not inherent business deficiencies. Everyone knew that LEC had serious problems by the time the contract was signed in 2010, but the nature and extent of these problems were not fully understood by the government or the contractor. The initial efforts to structure this arrangement as

[4] Unless otherwise indicated, this summary of contract pre-conditions is based on (i) a review of the Quarterly Technical Consultant Reports, LEC Annual Reports, LEC Quarterly Progress Reports and (ii) discussions with various stakeholders.

a "concession," involving capital investment, reflected an awareness that LEC's problems clearly went well beyond management. And that fact was confirmed time after time during implementation of the management contract as the operator's work plan was disrupted because funding (which was only available from donors) was delayed for things like equipment purchases, training programs, and most importantly, generation investment. As with the conventional management contract model, solutions for most of the utility's problems were not detailed in the contract, although preliminary due diligence did identify some of the problems. It was the operator's responsibility to develop a comprehensive business plan over the contract's first six months. But MHI later admitted that they did not have enough time or money for due diligence and were surprised by the nearly bankrupt condition of LEC and the extreme nature of the utility's human resource problems. MHI admitted that the HR plan and a comprehensive business plan ideally could have been developed and agreed before the management contract started implementation (MHI, 2014). MHI felt that the due diligence done prior to contract signing could have been much stronger.

One problem that was literally beyond the scope of the management contract, but for which the contractor received criticism, was the fact that by design, the contract was limited to a very small, geographical area of Monrovia. But LEC, as the national Utility, had the mandate to deliver services nationwide. So even though the contract increased the number of customers to 30,000 from almost zero, this was less than 2 per cent of Liberia's population and less than 7 per cent of the population in Monrovia. With one of the lowest electricity access rates in the world, the geographic restriction on the contract's service area increasingly seemed inappropriate to stakeholders. When donors started to fund expansion of access beyond the small area of MHI operation, these new service areas lacked utility management, creating more dissatisfaction with MHI. Negotiations to expand MHI's service area were not successful because by that point board–operator relations had broken down and the GoL refused to engage with MHI, plus MHI insisted on linking such a discussion with what they considered to be overdue success fees payments.

The external policy environment must be supportive

A second problem identified by Hegstad and Newport (1987), related to the one above, is that if the enterprise operates in a hostile business environment—involving things like price controls, excessive tariffs, import restrictions, poor foreign exchange access, or direct government interference—the benefits of management contracts are unlikely to be realized. The LEC board of directors could hardly have been any more hostile to the management contract. Board members seemed unaware of, and sometimes even repudiated, board decisions in which they had participated. The board saw no reason not to interfere in routine management decision making, even contravening management decisions. Several cases of board–management conflict stand out: In 2015, the loss of the fuel duty waiver increased LEC costs by $900,000 over a four-month period. The waiver was reinstated, but the board refused to allow LEC to recover the lost costs in its quarterly tariff calculations (LEC, 2015). The board's logic in assigning a penalty to MHI for Year 3 performance and the board's failure to accept MHI's common-sense argument to the contrary (which was later accepted by a mediator), suggested a significant level of board antipathy toward the operator and the contract. Finally, discussions on the Year 3 Business Plan were dramatically disrupted due to disagreements between the operator and the government regarding LEC funding for an 18 MW HFO project. The government insisted that MHI send US$5 million to Switzerland for equipment payment, but without normal documentation. MHI refused, and as a result of the ensuing arguments, MHI's team leader was asked to leave the project and the LEC chief executive offer and financial director were also sent home by the board.

In parallel with the contract, the donors had also funded an independent "technical consultant" to help the LEC board with contract implementation and ensure that the board would understand its obligations and generally take ownership of the contract. But in this case, the technical consultant seems to have had little effect in building board capacity, board ownership of the project, or in mediating disputes between the board and the operator.

The government also consistently reneged on contract commitments to make timely payment of its own electricity bills. Over the history of management contracts, the refusal of governments to require their agencies to pay utility bills was the most frequent and dramatic kind of interference by governments in such contracts. For example, from December 2015 to June 2016, the Ministry of Finance and Economic Planning refused to pay the GoL's electricity bills because they considered the tariffs to be too high. But the Minister of Finance was an LEC board member and therefore party to the tariff setting process (LEC, 2016). In 2016, the GoL began paying overdue bills at a lower exchange rate than the published daily selling rate of the Central Bank, forcing LEC to experience exchange rate losses.

The owner must be fully supportive

For these contracts to be effective, the owner–manager relationship that underlies it must be sound. Both owner and manager must be "willing to understand and accommodate the often-conflicting interests, motives and objectives which they possess" (Hegstad and Newport, 1987, 14). Among other things, this means that the owner must be convinced that the management contract is the optimal solution to enterprise problems, and be fully supportive of it. Analysts have long recognized that government commitment to management contracts is often less in cases where the contracts result from donor or MDB pressure or offers to pay for contract costs (World Bank, 1995). Government commitment is also often less where this kind of contracting option is chosen because it seems like the least politically unacceptable form of "privatization" or it is the only option acceptable to potential private partners.

The GoL was of course desperate to improve electricity services in the country, but not all government stakeholders fully understood the contract, the performance targets, or the success fee structure. It is difficult to conclude that the Liberian government ever "owned" the LEC management contract and was convinced that it was the best possible option. The government had extensive experience with concessions in natural resource sectors, which generated substantial government revenues. The LEC board seemed acutely aware that its management contract was something different, an arrangement that involved increased costs rather than revenues, in the sense that fees had be paid to the contractor on a regular basis, whether or not enterprise revenues increased (and LEC's revenues did not substantially increase because of the contract). In the LEC case, the direct impact on government of the contract costs was minimal because the preparation and implementation of the contract was almost completely paid for by donors (even the prefunding required for OBA-funded grid connection activities was financed by NORAD). But that just made the contract seem like an inefficient donor-owned mechanism—this kind of involvement by donors has long been associated with a lack of government commitment to reform measures of this kind (World Bank, 1995).

The contract: objectives must clear, measurable and achievable

Conventional wisdom says that management contracts often struggle to improve enterprise performance if they do not include rewards and penalties that persuade management and government to work toward clearly specified performance goals. But rewards and penalties are only as good as the contract's system for measuring performance, and the long history of research on utility performance measurement suggests that measurement systems in most management contracts have not been well designed (Jones, 1991; Tallapragada et al., 2009). Performance targets must be realistic, unambiguous, discrete, and understandable to key stakeholders. The manager must also have sufficient authority and management control to achieve the performance targets specified in the contract.

The performance indicators chosen for the LEC contract were traditional technical and commercial measures used on a long succession of conventional management contracts, but by the same token reflected the weakness of such indicators in capturing the overall financial and managerial sustainability of the enterprise, particularly for a utility that was very small and largely dysfunctional at the time of contract signing:

- The indicators violated the "fundamental principle of performance evaluation" (Jones, 1991) because they weighted benefits and various costs components asymmetrically—for example, if the operator increased operating costs in the process of installing prepaid meters in poor neighborhoods, an increase in output could be credited three times (it increased collections and connections, and decreased losses caused by faulty meters), while the increase in costs was debited only once (operating efficiency fell, if generation did not increase).

- Many of the things measured by the KPIs were beyond the operator's control, especially anything having to do with the timing or availability of funding, all of which had to come from donors and be used pursuant to donor procurement rules. For example, planned progress could be made in making new connections if committed funding was actually available when it was needed, procurement processes could be navigated in reasonable amounts of time, and suppliers actually made timely delivery of the equipment. In Liberia, the links in this delivery chain frequently broke down, for reasons having nothing to do with the management contact. Donors were to blame for some of these problems, and that underscored the fact that much of what the KPIs measured was beyond the operator's control.
- By their nature, KPIs encourage operators to devote a disproportionate share of resources to the achievement of objectives that are associated with financial rewards. But as noted in the USAID-commissioned study by McKinsey & Company (2015), the KPIs in the LEC contract did not cover some important project outcomes like staff capacity building or customer care. Output metrics for both kinds of outcomes have long been used by donors on development projects, so the reasons for the failure to include something similar in the LEC contract are not clear.
- The inclusion of a "fixed-fee retention mechanism" was meant to allow the LEC Board to withhold some or all of the quarterly fixed fee payments to MHI pending fulfillment of all scheduled contract objectives, including those not associated with KPIs, like good quality reporting and effective general management. In reality however, retention amounts were only withheld pending delivery of specific outstanding deliverables, mostly reports of various kinds. Presumably, this was because, without clear benchmarks and metrics for non-KPI objectives, it was difficult to determine whether the operator had made sufficient progress toward these objectives in a particular quarter.
- As with many contracts of this kind, the cap on penalties was disproportionate to the cap on success fees. Penalties and success fees were calculated in the same way, but success fees were capped at US$2 million per year, and penalties were capped at 15 per cent of the annual base fee. So even if the contractor incurred the maximum penalties every year, the five-year penalty total was US$1,228,770 compared with a potential maximum total success fee of US$9 million over the same period. This meant, for example, that the sizeable success fee for rapid turnaround in operating efficiency in Year 1

more than compensated for penalties in most other areas in subsequent years. World Bank staff noted that the low penalty caps, along with the relatively large size of the base payments, meant that the operator's remuneration was largely acceptable to the operator without the addition of success fees—the success fees did not seem to provide much additional motivation for the operator.

7.4 Conclusions

Clearly, the 11 management contracts for water or electricity reviewed in this chapter have been remarkably unsuccessful. Many of these contracts generated some benefits and have been defended by some stakeholders. However, all but two of these contracts were terminated early or not renewed. The renewals were one-time only extensions of contracts that were heavily criticized by government owners. None of these contracts were widely endorsed by a majority of influential stakeholders as having met expectations.

The reasons for these failures are also fairly clear, particularly when viewed from the perspective of the Hegstad and Newport (1987) framework of success "pre-conditions." Almost all of these contracts were driven by the prospect of sector investment by donors, DFIs, or MDBs. These contracts were generally viewed as expensive and largely unnecessary by host governments. Many were paid for by donors for initial periods, but discontinued when governments became liable for costs. So, in virtually all of these cases, the government owners remained unconvinced that the contracts represented the best solution to sector problems. Owners were not motivated to require government agencies to pay their water or electricity bills, nor were they willing to structure boards of directors to constructively support the contracts.

The underlying problems with these contracts echoed issues that Nellis (2005) and others identified in the broader SOE privatization programs launched as part of structural adjustment lending—the contracts were not selected and designed as the result of analysis, but via negotiation to find the brownfield infrastructure solution least unpalatable to governments. As a result, there was confusion about the objectives of these arrangements, and how the progress toward those objectives could be measured. There was nothing to keep a check on expectations of stakeholders, and contracts were frequently blamed for failing to solve sector problems for which they were not responsible.

These case studies confirm some basic lessons about the use of management contracts for water or electricity, cited in Chapter 6:

- Any effort to improve the management of water or electricity utilities should be preceded by a careful diagnosis of basic reasons for management deficiencies. And the diagnosis should be carried out by someone other than those expected to implement solutions.

- Improved utility management should start with efforts to reduce non-technical losses, and this represents a well-researched area of utility management involving cost-effective technology-based solutions tested in Latin America and Asia. Such solutions were not available in the 1990s, but are now applicable even in low-income countries with donor and MDB support.
- Private participation via management contracts (or any other kind of brownfield infrastructure solution) is not essential for implementing the cost reduction strategies mentioned earlier. Reform efforts should not begin with the assumption that private participation represents a long-term solution in every case.
- When private participation can help in implementing cost-reduction strategies, it needs to be seen as a temporary measure to stabilize utility operations and prepare local management and staff to take over operations as soon as possible.

Chapter 8 turns to IPP projects, the polar opposite of management contracts. IPPs are greenfield projects usually designed, owned, and operated by private companies. Unlike management contracts and other brownfield solutions, IPPs generally have nothing to do with the operation of government-owned utilities, except selling them power. Even though IPPs require huge capital investment, they are more successful and more popular with both public and private actors than any other kind of PPP—more successful than all other kinds of PPPs combined. But benefits of IPPs may not always outweigh the economic development costs. Chapter 8 explains some of the tradeoffs involved in the widespread promotion of IPPs in developing countries.

References

Bergeron, I. 1991. "Privatization Through Leasing: The Togo Steel Case," in R. Ramamurti and R. Vernon (eds.), *Privatization and Control of State-Owned Enterprises*. EDI Development Studies. Washington, DC: World Bank.

Brook, P.J. 1999. "Lessons from the Guinea Water Lease." Public Policy for the Private Sector, Note No. 78. Washington, DC: World Bank (April).

De Luca, L. 1998. *Labour and social dimensions of privatization and restructuring (public utilities: water, gas, electricity)*. Geneva: International Labour Office.

Econ One Research. 2002. "Northern Electricity Distribution Service in Northern Namibia: A Case Study in the Private Provision of Rural Infrastructure." Report prepared for PPIAF (July 31).

Economic Consulting Associates. 2015. *Evidence and Gaps in Evidence in Use of Management Contracts for Electricity Distribution and Supply.* Report prepared for Evidence on Demand, UK Department for International Development (DFID), by Climate, Environment, Infrastructure and Livelihoods Professional Evidence and Applied Knowledge Services (CEIL PEAKS).

Front Page Africa. 2017. "Legislature Halts Liberia Electricity Corporation Contract Negotiations." June 8.

Ghana Management Contract. 2005. *Management Contract for Ghana Urban Water between Ghana Water Company Ltd. and Vitens Rand Water Services BV and Aqua Vitra Ltd.* (October).

Ghana Water Company Ltd. (GWCL). 2013. "Notice of Dissolution of Ghana Urban Water Ltd." Public Notice (July 29).

Ghanadan, R., A. Eberhard. 2007. *Electricity Utility Management Contracts in Africa: Lessons and Experience from the TANESCO-NETGroup Solutions Management Contract in Tanzania, 2002–2006.* MIR Working Paper, University of Cape Town (March).

Gokgur, N., L. Jones. 2007. "Privatization of Mozambique Water Sector." Report prepared for the Africa Private Sector and Infrastructure Department, World Bank (October).

Gomez-Ibanez, J. 2005. "EDM (Energie du Mali)." Case Study CR14-05–1811.0, Kennedy School of Government Case Program. Cambridge, MA: Harvard University.

Hegstad, S.O., I. Newport. 1987. *Management Contracts: Main Features and Design Issues.* World Bank Technical Paper No. 65. Washington, DC: World Bank.

International Centre for Settlement of Investment Disputes (ICSID). 2008. *Award Rendered in ICSID Case No. ARB/05/22, Biwater Gauff (Tanzania) Ltd., Claimant v. United Republic of Tanzania, Respondent.* Washington, DC: ICSID.

International Finance Corporation (IFC). 2017. "Electricity Powers Growth for Liberia's Small Businesses." Stories of Impact. Washington, DC: IFC.

Jammal, Y., L. Jones. 2006. "Impact of Privatization in Africa: Cote D'Ivoire Electricity." Unpublished paper sponsored by the Norwegian Trust Fund, managed by the Investment Climate Department and Africa Private Sector and Infrastructure Department of the World Bank (October).

Jones, L. 1991. "Performance Evaluation for State-Owned Enterprises," in R. Ramamurti and R. Vernon (eds.), *Privatization and Control of State-Owned Enterprises*. EDI Development Studies. Washington, DC: World Bank.

Kimani, D. 2008. "Kenya Power Won't Renew Manitoba Expats' Contract." *The East African* (Nairobi) (April 15).

Liberia Electricity Corporation (LEC). 2015. Annual Report for the fiscal year ended June 30, 2015. Monrovia: LEC.

Liberia Electricity Corporation (LEC). 2016. Annual Report for the fiscal year ended June 30, 2016. Monrovia: LEC.

Manitoba Hydro International (MHI). 2014. "MHI Comments on September 2014 Draft of Electricity Utility Management Contracts in Africa – Lessons and Experience from the LEC-MHI Management Contract in Liberia, 2010 – 2014, Raciborski and Eberhard." Unpublished memorandum (September 14).

Marin, P. 2009. Public-Private Partnerships for Urban Water Utilities: A Review of Experience in Developing Countries. PPIAF Trends and Policy Options No. 8. Washington, DC: World Bank.

McKinsey & Company. 2015. "Liberia utility private sector partnership options: Key initiatives for implementation." PowerPoint prepared for Power Africa, USAID (October).

Menard, C., G. Clarke. 2000a. *Reforming Water Supply in Abidjan, Cote d'Ivoire: A Mild Reform in a Turbulent Environment.* Policy Research Working Paper No. 2377. Washington, DC: World Bank (June).

Menard, C., G. Clarke. 2000b. *A Transitory Regine: Water Supply in Conakry, Guinea.* Policy Research Working Paper No. 2362. Washington, DC: World Bank (June).

Mwangi, D.M. 2008. "The Kenya Power and Lighting Company Ltd., Paper to the Audit Committee of the Board: Recommendations for Finalising the 2006/7 Success Fee Calculation for Manitoba Hydro International." Unpublished memorandum (March 4).

Nellis, J. 2005. *The Evolution of Enterprise Reform in Africa: From State-Owned Enterprises to Private Participation in Infrastructure—and Back?* ESMAP Technical Paper No. 084. Washington, DC: World Bank (November).

Public–Private Infrastructure Advisory Facility (PPIAF). 2009. *Delegated Management of Urban Water Supply Services in Mozambique: Case Study of FIPAG and CRA.* PPIAF and World Bank Study. Washington, DC: World Bank.

Rice, X. 2007. "The Water Margin." *The Guardian* (August 16).

Shirley, M.M., L.C. Xu. 2001. "Empirical Effects of Performance Contracts: Evidence from China. *Journal of Law, Economics and Organization*, 17(1): 168–200.

Tallapragada, P., M. Shkaratan, A.K Izaguirre, J. Helleranta, S. Rahman, S. Bergman. 2009. *Monitoring Performance of Electric Utilities: Indicators and Benchmarking in Sub-Saharan Africa.* Washington, DC: World Bank.

WaterAid Tanzania. 2008. "Why Did City Water Fail? The Rise and Fall of Private Sector Participation in Dar es Salaam's Water Supply." Dar es Salaam: WaterAid. Accessed at: file:///C:/Users/JL/Downloads/Why%20did%20City%20Water%20fail%20-%20The%20rise%20and%20fall%20of%20private%20sector%20participation%20in%20Dar%20es%20Salaam%E2%80%99s%20water%20supply%20(2).pdf

World Bank. 1995. *Bureaucrats in Business: The Economics and Politics of Government Ownership.* Policy Research Report No. 15037. Washington, DC: World Bank (October 8).

World Bank. 2005. "Implementation Completion Report on a Credit in the Amount of US$79.66 Million to the Republic of Cote D'Ivoire for a Private Sector Energy Project." Report No. 32564. Washington, DC: World Bank (June 27).

8
SSA's IPP Policy Dilemma

8.1 Introduction

Chapter 4 attempted to explain that in low-income countries greenfield project structures are less likely to experience problems with cash flows and profitability and are more attractive to sponsors and operators than projects like brownfield concessions. This is particularly true for project structures that involve: (i) the construction and use of new assets, as opposed to taking over poorly maintained existing assets; and (ii) the provision of wholesale as opposed to retail services, with payments made by governments, backed by government-guaranteed off-take agreements denominated in hard currency. Thus, greenfield independent power producer (IPP) projects, backed by take-or-pay off-take agreements denominated in US dollars, represent lower risks to cash flows and profitability than, for example, retail water distribution concessions involving end-user tariff payments in local currency.

IPP projects are non-utility electricity generators, privately financed, owned, and managed, which sell power to off-takers pursuant to long-term power purchase agreements (PPAs). Because of their attraction for the private sector, and their general effectiveness in adding generating capacity, IPP projects are the most widely used form of public–private partnership (PPP) in the developing world. This is especially true in low-income countries where they make up almost three-quarters of all PPPs. However, compared with middle-income countries, low-income countries make very little use of any kind of private participation in infrastructure so the use of IPP projects has made only a marginal impact in these countries. Just over half of all countries in Sub-Saharan Africa (SSA) have introduced IPP projects and these facilities play a dominant role in only a few of these countries.

One might expect to see a more enthusiastic embrace of IPP projects in low-income countries, defined here as countries eligible for support from the International Development Association (countries whose gross net income per capita is below US$1,215, most of whom are in SSA). These countries are starved for electricity generating capacity. All of SSA, population 1.1 billion, has about

Public–Private Partnerships in Sub-Saharan Africa: The Evidence-Based Critique. James Leigland,
Oxford University Press (2020). © James Leigland.
DOI: 10.1093/oso/9780198861829.001.0001

97,000 MW of installed generating capacity (and South Africa accounts for around half of that). In contrast, South Korea, population approximately 51 million, has over 100,000 MW of installed capacity.

Although the need for more electricity-generating capacity in developing countries is urgent, especially for SSA countries, and IPP projects have been popular with the private sector and effective in adding generating capacity in the power sectors of many developing countries, the development community seems somewhat ambivalent about whether or not to recommend a massive scale-up in the use of IPP projects in these countries. Are IPP projects in low-income countries really beneficial or not? Should they be encouraged and facilitated? If so, under what conditions? Some segments of the development community, such as DFIs and MDBs that specialize in lending mostly to private companies, aggressively promote the widespread use of IPP projects. Other segments, including many researchers and policy experts, seem much more conservative in their advocacy of IPP projects.

This chapter argues that this ambivalence regarding the value of IPP projects reflects a policy dilemma that many experts are aware of but unsure of how to resolve effectively. By promoting IPP projects as partial solutions to power sector problems in developing countries, experts run the risk of making other sector problems harder to solve. This dilemma seems to be particularly apparent in power sectors of low-income countries, especially in SSA, which are largely unreformed in most key respects. In these cases, when donors, DFIs, or MDBs promote IPP projects as elements of sector reform programs, not only are the benefits of IPP projects likely to be much less than they could be, but other sector reforms may be less likely to reach successful completion. In this sense, and to borrow from Robert P. Bork's famous criticism of inconsistencies at the heart of US antitrust policy (Bork, 1978), the promotion of IPP projects in most low-income countries is a "policy at war with itself." This dilemma raises concerns about the motivations behind the many IPP projects that are facilitated in these countries and what can be done to deal with this dilemma.

The discussion in the following pages attempts to explain this dilemma by covering the following issues:

- The popularity of IPP projects in the developing world, particularly middle-income countries, along with data showing that low-income countries desperately need more generating capacity.
- The development community's ambivalence regarding IPP projects in low-income countries, despite the success of these projects in middle-income countries.
- The origins of this ambivalence in the IPP project track record since 1990, and the ways in which it reflects a policy dilemma.

8.2 IPP Project Prevalence

The prevalence of IPP projects in the developing world is testimony to the comparative advantages these projects have in terms of attracting private finance. From 1990 to 2017, PPP investment in power in developing countries was over ten times larger than PPP investment in water and sanitation (World Bank, 2018). Power generation is the only sector in which global investment numbers do not appear to have been affected by the 2007–8 global financial crisis. In fact, PPP-related investment in energy reached an all-time record level in 2009, accounting for over 45 per cent of all such private investment across the developing world, more than investment in telecommunications (and all other sectors) for the first time since 1997. From 1990 to 2017, IPP projects accounted for 40 per cent of all PPP-related investment in non-International Development Association (IDA) countries (countries that are not eligible for support from the IDA) (Figure 8.1).

In low-income countries, IPP projects account for a substantially larger share of total PPP-related investment. In "IDA countries", IPP projects accounted for 70 per cent of all PPP-related investment from 1990 to 2017 (Figure 8.1). But on average, the private sector still plays a negligible role in infrastructure service delivery in these countries, including power sectors.

As of 2014, 19 SSA countries had vertically integrated utilities acting as "single buyers" of electricity from IPP projects. Six countries had achieved some vertical separation of generation, transmission, and/or distribution, but still used

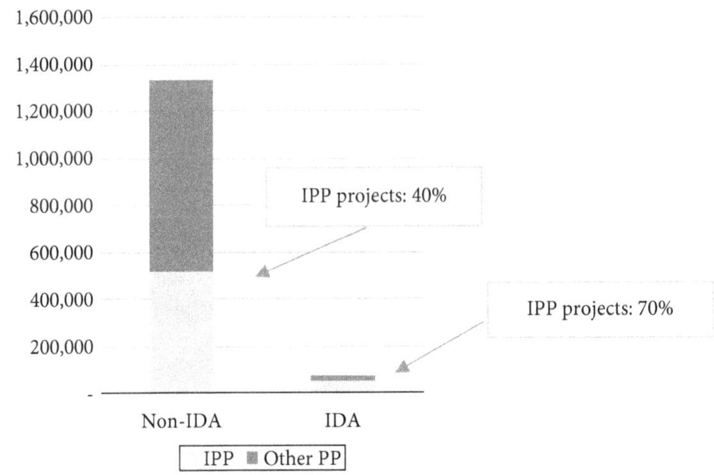

Figure 8.1 IPP Projects as a Percentage of all PPP Investment, IDA vs. Non-IDA Countries, 1990–2017, US$ billions (nominal values)

Source: World Bank, 2018.

government-owned utilities as single buyers of IPP power and restricted wholesale competition in their markets. The remaining 23 SSA countries had not yet introduced IPP projects (Eberhard et al., 2017, 396). In most cases, other than the creation of sector regulators, there has been little or no momentum to move forward with what donors, DFIs, and MDBs identify as the standard list of recommended "sector reforms."

Although half of SSA countries have introduced IPP projects, more than two-thirds of the electricity distributed in SSA is still generated by state-owned and operated utilities. Approximately 18 per cent of distributed power is purchased from captive power plants at mines and factories, and from PPPs like IPP projects, emergency power rentals, and concessions on state-owned generation assets. About 11 per cent of power distributed in SSA comes from imports (Trimble et al., 2016, 24–5).

It is not as if low-income countries do not desperately need more investment in power generation. A region like SSA, home to most of the world's low-income countries, has failed to keep pace with other developing country regions in building installed generating capacity. SSA's capacity has developed at only about 3 per cent annually over the last three decades, falling far behind as the region's annual GDP growth rate has accelerated to about 5 per cent in recent years (Eberhard et al., 2017). As of 2015, the total installed capacity of the 47 countries in SSA, excluding South Africa (population about 944 million without SA), is about equal to that of Taiwan (population 24 million) (Figure 8.2).

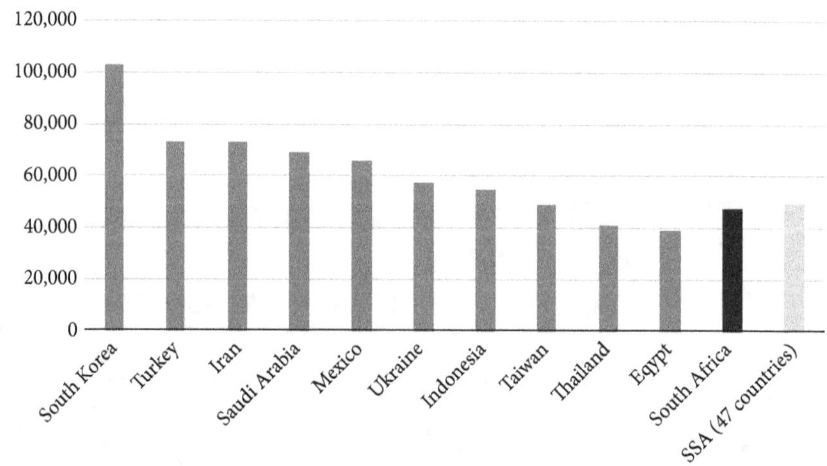

Figure 8.2 Total Electricity Installed Capacity in Africa and Selected Countries, 2015, Megawatts

Source: USCIA, The World Factbook, 2018.

8.3 Ambivalence About IPP Projects in Low-Income Countries

Despite the popularity of IPP projects in developing countries, and the need for more generating capacity in most of these countries, the development community displays a degree of ambivalence when it comes to recommending a dramatic scale-up of IPP projects in these countries. The ambivalence results from a clash of two different perspectives on IPP projects and their development value.

On the one hand, the proliferation of IPP projects is strongly endorsed by government officials in many developing countries, the private sector, and DFIs and MDBs like the International Finance Corporation (IFC), Netherlands Development Finance Company (FMO), Group Agence Française de Développement (PROPARCO), and Deutsche Investitions und Entwicklungsgesellschaft (DEG), which specialize in lending mostly to private companies on near-commercial terms. Writing about the need for more IPP projects in Sub-Saharan Africa (SSA), the manager of IFC infrastructure operations in SSA, Bertrand Heysch de la Borde, called IPP projects the "low hanging fruit of public-private partnerships in infrastructure" and cited the "transformational impact of private investment in power generation" (de la Borde and Charafi, 2013, 10, 12). In an interview with law firm Baker McKenzie, IFC investment officer David Tinel was quoted in 2014 as claiming that the IFC had helped finance over 80 per cent of all IPP projects in Africa in the previous five or six years (Baker McKenzie, 2014). Recent research has confirmed that a variety of development banks, including the IFC, play critical roles in supporting most IPP project transactions in SSA by providing advice, financing, and risk mitigation products (Eberhard et al., 2016).

This positive view of IPP projects manifests itself in the aggressive competition among these development banks to finance IPP projects, but also in occasional efforts to collaborate on projects. In 2015, Norfund (a private equity company owned by the Norwegian Ministry of Foreign Affairs) and Commonwealth Development Corporation (CDC—the UK's development finance institution) jointly acquired 100 per cent ownership of Gobeleq Africa, which was claimed to be the leading private power producer in SSA. Both Norfund and CDC have long and impressive IPP project track records in SSA, but the direct ownership and control of Gobeleq is designed to allow them to develop projects at a much faster pace over the next decade (Odendaal, 2015).

Evaluations of IPP projects also tend to be quite positive, in the sense that these projects are often found to be effective in adding to a country's power generating capacity. A pioneering set of studies conducted by a Stanford University program in the mid-2000s, found that most of the projects in the 12 countries studied met reasonable government expectations (Woodhouse, 2005). A recent review of IPP projects in SSA concludes that "Independent power projects make a significant contribution to meeting Africa's power needs. There is no doubt that IPPs are worth the effort." (Eberhard et al., 2016, xxxvii).

However, at the same time as they seem to be recommending the use of IPP projects, these same observers argue that a number of significant reforms—or at least plans for reforms—are needed before attempting such projects. De la Borde and Charafi, in the 2013 report cited earlier, warned that "good governance is a key precondition if IPP projects are to thrive" (de la Borde and Charafi, 2013, 10). Similarly, Eberhard and his co-authors cautioned that "Like any other private investment, IPP projects will not materialize in the absence of a suitable enabling environment" (Eberhard et al., 2016, xxiii).

These comments suggest an ambivalence about the value of IPP projects, because as these observers well know, the reforms they identify as necessary preconditions for IPP projects have not been introduced in most African countries, including those implementing IPP projects. Researchers have found little or no association between IPP projects in SSA and the existence of reforms such as independent regulation, least-cost generation planning, competitive bidding, cost-reflective tariffs, sector unbundling, improvements to transmission and distribution infrastructure, or efforts to ensure the financial health of off-taker utilities: "There seems to be no clear relation among reforms, degree of competition and the success of countries to attract IPP projects" (Eberhard et al., 2016, xxxviii). Nor is there any clear association between the existence of IPP projects and financial viability or efficiency of power sector operations in SSA, in terms of things like pricing of services, collection of bills, staffing, and control of power losses (Trimble et al., 2016, 34–5). If the IFC and other development banks have facilitated most of SSA's IPP projects, then they have done this in the absence of reforms they have acknowledged are required to establish "a suitable enabling environment" for these projects.

As already noted, this chapter argues that this ambivalence regarding the value of IPP projects in low-income countries reflects a policy dilemma. By promoting IPP projects in the unreformed power sectors of low-income countries, donors, DFIs, MDBs, and the private sector are creating situations in which not only are the benefits of IPP projects much less than they could be, but other sector reforms may be less likely to happen. This is the essence of the IPP policy dilemma, a policy "at war with itself."

8.4 A Short History of Power Sector Reforms

Understanding the history of IPP projects is important for making sense of this policy dilemma, but key facts about the history are sometimes missing in published accounts of power sector reforms. According to the conventional view, these reforms started in the mid-1990s, and began by following a widely recognized sequence of best-practice steps, but ended in stagnation after a decade or so. With the exception of a few Latin American countries, the reform sequence has almost never been fully completed, with some steps (like regulatory agencies and IPP projects) more widely adopted than others.

A recent World Bank working paper is the latest in a long series of Bank efforts to document the diffusion of power sector reforms across the developing world (Foster et al., 2017).[1] The paper repeats the conventional narrative of IPP project origins, noting that the "earliest power sector reforms" began in the 1990s, and followed "a package of power sector reform measures known as the Washington Consensus" (Foster et al., 2017, 3). The paper argues that this dissemination slowed significantly by the early 2000s, as reforms began to be applied selectively, based on "ease of implementation," and due to limiting conditions involving system size, income levels, strength of the rule of law, etc. (Foster et al., 2017, 4). Thus, for many developing countries, power sector reform programs were announced but were never carried through.

But this conventional view of IPP project origins omits or obscures several important details about the history of power sector reforms in developing countries, which help explain the nature and extent of the policy dilemma described here. Power sector reforms failed to run their recommended course of measures not because of the aforementioned limiting conditions but simply because governments did not want to carry through with all of the recommended reforms. And this fact was already becoming apparent in the 1980s. Previous chapters describe how problems with state-owned enterprises (SOEs) (weak management, overstaffing, dependency on subsidies and excessive public borrowing) helped to trigger aggressive reforms driven by policy-based lending by the World Bank and other MDBs, and supported by the International Monetary Fund (IMF), which became known as "structural adjustment." The first phase of structural adjustment reforms targeting SOEs involved efforts to build managerial capacity and strengthen managerial incentives by using "performance agreements." These non-legal agreements preserved government ownership and control of the SOEs, but tried to enhance SOE performance by establishing performance targets for SOE managers as well as obligations of government owners to ensure support for the SOEs as needed. By the end of the 1980s, hundreds of such agreements were in place or under development, and in SSA, these agreements were "most commonly applied to electricity producers and suppliers" (Nellis, 1989a, 73).

However, by the early 1980s, it was becoming clear that these agreements were not successful in improving SOE financial performance. The fundamental issue was reluctance by government officials to fully support the terms of the agreements.

[1] Earlier World Bank surveys of this kind include ESMAP (1999) and Besant-Jones (2006). Recent World Bank studies of a similar nature include Huenteler et al. (2017), Rudnick and Velasquez (2018), Bacon (2018), and Pardina and Schiro (2018).

Government officials and SOE managers negotiated performance agreements, but they made little effort to see that the agreements worked (Nellis, 1989a, 1989b). And performance agreements for electricity utilities were no more successful than any other kind (Shirley and Xu, 1997, 40). Across SSA, governments consistently failed to meet most of their performance targets regarding equity injections, managerial autonomy, cost-reflective tariffs, work force reductions, and settlement of payment obligations by government agencies. In SSA, this pattern of government resistance regarding reforms was a recurrent feature of structural adjustment programs in the 1980s:

> Particularly with regard to infrastructure SOEs one saw in the 1980s persistent repetition in a sequence of both adjustment and investment loans of the same set of policy and structural conditions, indicating that the changes had not been enacted the first, or even the second or the third time called for (Nellis, 2005, 35).

A World Bank study of performance agreements later asked "why would governments introduce the contract process and then not try to make it work?" (Shirley and Xu, 1997, 33). The answer was that these agreements were typically viewed by the signatories as donor-driven arrangements, and not as credible obligations. Politicians and senior officials were not really convinced that such measures were necessary for good governance and efficiency of operations, hence the absence of meaningful support. Officials were willing to enter into the agreements, no matter how unnecessary or unrealistic they seemed, "because the contracts allowed them to earn foreign assistance" (Shirley and Xu, 1997, 33). So, already by the end of the 1980s, a pattern of passive-aggressive government resistance to SOE reforms was established, which would repeat itself in the 1990s as more reforms were proposed.

Chapters 4 and 6 explained how the widespread failure of performance agreements quickly gave way to more extreme measures insisted on by the development community, involving private sector ownership and management of SOEs. All of these solutions whether involving actual change of ownership or just private management, were routinely referred to as "privatization" and became key elements in many of SSA's adjustment lending programs (Nellis, 2005). For SOEs like water or power utilities MDBs like the World Bank never suggested that any kind of privatization was an end in itself. In its 1993 power sector policy statement, the World Bank outlined a basic approach to reform, promoting IPP projects, concessions, and management contracts within a wider context of structural sector reforms (World Bank, 1993). There was no elaborate exposition of the sequence of reforms prescribed in the 1993 policy, but rather a simple prioritization of basic reforms considered necessary, with a recommendation that commercialization and corporatization precede any actual attempts at privatization, as ways of introducing competition and innovation.

But the World Bank's own internal evaluations found that the 1993 statement failed to provide any strategic or operational guidance on how to achieve an overall reform package (Manibog et al., 2003). At the time, the Bank anticipated that staff would "learn by doing." "However, this technocratic view did not give adequate weight to the political economy of reform and proved too optimistic" (Manibog et al., 2003, xvii). At the same time, many of the Bank's government clients had no interest in achieving commercialization and corporatization for their utilities if that meant reforming governance and state ownership. Governments, especially in Africa, agreed to various forms of privatization, with little or no intention of tackling more significant sector reforms. Evaluations subsequently concluded that many African governments felt pressured to accept privatization proposals from donors, DFIs, and MDBs, with which they fundamentally did not agree:

> most African leaders were not persuaded that the emphasis on private initiative was applicable and appropriate in their settings. But the dire financial circumstances in which they found themselves had increased their reliance on donors in general and the IFIs in particular. African governments felt they had little choice but to go along with policies requested and required by their financiers. They could marginally amend the content and scale and slow the pace of the implementation of policies, and they could employ passive non-compliance to dilute their impact—but only in the rarest of cases could they and did they explicitly reject them (Nellis, 2005, 37).

This combination of a lack of guidance from the Bank for its staff's interventions and prescriptions, plus the reluctance of governments to pursue broader sector reforms beyond an occasional IPP project or management contract, meant that these PPPs eventually were accepted as proxies for the achievement of commercialization rather than arrangements that might result and benefit from commercialization (Manibog et al., 2003). For World Bank staff, concluding a PPP contract became a convenient indicator that sector reform was advancing. For government counterparts, IPPs could be valuable in adding power-generating capacity as long as the dominant government-owned sector institutions continued their control over sector rents and patronage jobs. Other kinds of PPPs, like management contracts, often were necessary to access sector finance from donors and MDBs, but could be allowed to expire from a lack of support after a few years, just as performance agreements had been abandoned in the 1980s (see Chapters 6 and 7).

By the end of the 1990s, it was clear that the recommendation to precede privatization measures with fundamental sector reforms, as advocated in the 1993 paper, was not being followed by governments in SSA, or by MDB staff. Instead, prompted by prevailing electricity supply crises, PPPs like IPP projects and management contracts were being introduced into countries that usually demonstrated no real commitment to other reforms. In Africa these IPP projects were brought on line next to government-owned and operated generation facilities, and required to sell their power to government utilities acting as "single buyers" of power, pursuant to long-term PPAs. The single buyers would then handle transmission and distribution to end users. In most of these cases, other than IPPs, a few management contracts, and the creation of sector regulators, little or no action was taken to achieve what donors, DFIs, and MDBs identified as the total package of recommended "sector reforms."

By the mid-2000s, donors, DFIs, and MDBs stopped using terminology like "structural adjustment" and "privatization" because it had become politically unpalatable in client countries. More collaborative, less prescriptive approaches to development planning were introduced, like the World Bank's "poverty reduction strategy plans" and the Millennium Development Goals (MDGs), agreed to in 2000. For power and water utilities, an effort was made to carve out and retain the PPP elements of the privatization reform strategy, which the development community refused to relinquish. But this meant sharply distinguishing "PPPs" from "privatization," denying that these concepts are even related, even though the original association is quite clear in MDB project documents from the 1990s. The effort to distinguish these terms continues today and is widely supported by DFIs and MDBs (World Bank et al., 2014). But Michael Klein admits, as many others have recognized, that the differences between PPPs and privatization are largely cosmetic. Compared with "privatization," "'PPP' is a politically benign term, at least for now" (Klein, 2015, 3).

8.5 The Use of IPP Projects to "Capture and Stall" Further Reforms

The first major effort from World Bank Group (WBG) to implement the prescriptions of the Bank's 1993 power sector lending policy (World Bank, 1993) was the Private Sector Energy Development Project (PSEDP I and II) in Pakistan from 1988 to 1999. The project focused on a number of power sector reforms needed to complement the completion of a collection of IPP subprojects, the largest of which was the 1,292 MW Hub Power Project.

For Pakistan, Hub was the first private infrastructure project and the first limited recourse financing. Hub was also the World Bank's first private infrastructure project, the first use of a Bank-financed infrastructure fund to support private projects, and the first use of the Bank's Partial Risk Guarantee (PRG). PSEDP also marked the first major involvement in IPP project support by other WBG members as well: the IFC provided debt and equity to five of the IPP subprojects and the Multilateral Investment Guarantee Agency (MIGA) extended guarantee coverage to three subprojects. At the time, no other low-income country had made private investment the core principal of its energy policy (Fraser, 2005).

Even though the project facilitated closure of 19 IPP subprojects, the overall outcome of the project was a disappointment. The economic, financial, institutional, and technical aspects of the project fell far short of expectations. The Bank's Implementation Completion Report (World Bank, 2001a) and an independent review by the Bank's Operations Evaluation Department (World Bank, 2001b) agreed on a number of major shortcomings of project implementation. The most glaring of these involved the fact that loan covenants requiring the achievement of the project's sector reform objectives were simply not complied with by the government, and insufficient attention was paid to this failure by Bank project staff. The original project design included measures for sector restructuring and policy reform, but the government failed to implement them. By creating new institutions to implement the 1994 IPP project policy, and encouraging the use of guarantees and other generous incentives, PSEDP unintentionally enabled the power utility—Water and Power Development Authority (WAPDA—and the sector ministry to "capture and stall" the implementation of structural changes:

> The single buyer model has risks in terms of preserving the role of the sector ministry in investment decisions, possibly shielding financiers of generation projects from market risks and government interference in electricity wholesale trading (World Bank, 2001a, 24).

The government simply ignored the recommendations of its own least-cost expansion program in terms of generating capacity, fuel selection, and technology. Competitive bidding of IPP projects was abandoned and the government contracted too many projects, using inappropriate technology and producing power that was too expensive. The financial incentives used to attract private investors and operators were later deemed to be "excessive" (World Bank, 2001a, 18). WAPDA was ultimately unable to absorb the PPA costs, with tariffs indexed to the US dollar. WAPDA's problems were exacerbated by the fact that power demand in Pakistan increased more slowly than anticipated, leading to excess generating capacity for several years. WAPDA also suffered from low collection rates and widening tariff cross-subsidies. The lack of procurement transparency and the large number of projects with inflated costs led eventually to claims that the program was plagued with corruption. In 1998, the government issued notices of intent to terminate 11 IPP projects developed with support from the program, representing two-thirds of the private power capacity contracted. Most of these contracts were later renegotiated. Why did World Bank project staff not pay more attention to lagging institutional reforms?

> the exceptional success of the IPP program in mobilizing private finance created a diversion for management, both in the design and the supervision stages, lessening their attention on the reform of the sector itself (World Bank, 2001a, 19).

Bank staff seem to have made the mistake of thinking that private investment was a substitute for reform, and ignoring the consensus view in the Bank that "private investment in generation should not take place in front of reforms which *at a minimum* address distribution efficiency and tariff policies" (World Bank, 2001a, 24). In its independent review of PSEDP, the Bank's Operations Evaluation Department noted that "Private investment does not substitute for reform, and should not be attempted without at least the basic reform elements in place" (World Bank, 2001b, 3).

In spite of PSDEDP's problems, the Bank's internal review found that the project was a "pioneering" use of a limited recourse build–own–operate (BOO) project structure for a large-scale infrastructure project in a developing country: "The Hub subproject paved the way for private power projects internationally, and the complex documentation that it generated has become a reference for similar projects" (World Bank, 2001b, 2). In 1999, Hub was selected as the "Deal of the Decade" by *Euromoney Institutional Investor* (Fraser, 2005).

8.6 The Development Community's Trojan Horse Strategy

Although convincing governments to precede IPP projects with more basic sector reforms was seldom achieved in practice, MDB policy advisers were reluctant to recognize the proliferation of IPP projects in unreformed markets as counterproductive. In what now seems like wishful thinking, some experts concluded that "countries that have admitted independent power producers have been more ready to take other reform steps" (Bacon, 1999, 7). Others were so confident in the value of IPP projects that it did not seem to matter if governments wanted no further reforms—if IPP projects could be implemented, they would generate their own reform momentum:

> At first sight, IPP projects seem innocuous and desirable in reasonable doses. Properly done, they generally are. But during their development they raise nagging questions about the efficiency and competitiveness of the integrated, government-owned utility and the means by which it is regulated. Once IPP projects are introduced into the mix, these questions tend to ferment, leading the more progressive forces within and outside the country to seek answers, explore alternatives, and set about to change the existing industry's structure
>
> (Roseman and Malhotra, 1996, 1).

The idea of "encouraging IPP projects as a route to more extensive reform" has been characterized by the Energy Sector Management Assistance Program (ESMAP) as a widespread "trojan horse strategy" (ESMAP, 1999, 3). MDBs, led by the WBG, facilitated the proliferation of IPP projects in the absence of crucial reforms, with the expectation that such reforms would follow. MDBs other than the World Bank were of course involved in promoting private participation in the electricity sectors of developing countries during the 1990s. But an internal evaluation by the Bank concluded that the level of such support from other development institutions was "small compared to the WBG" (Manibog et al., 2003, 9). Williams and Ghanadan (2006) underscored the importance of the World Bank Group in leading the power sector reform agenda among members of the development community.

Within the WBG, this focus on IPP projects during the 1990s suited the ambitions of the IFC and MIGA, as they grew to become dominant players in the infrastructure development landscape. During that decade the Bank (IDA and IBRD) shifted away from power generation, as a kind of division of labor began to take shape within the Group, which was eventually formalized in the private sector development strategy issued in April 2002 (World Bank, 2002). The Bank focused on reforms, such as investment climate improvements and related institution building, governance, financial sector policies, and public finance. (The Bank did preserve some involvement in power sector transactions through its administration of Partial Risk Guarantees.) The IFC and MIGA remained focused on implementing privatization transactions in support of which, the Bank presumably would be creating the appropriate enabling environment.

The IFC's overall commitment levels increased precipitously by the middle of the decade, and beginning in the early 2000s, IPP projects became the single most successful IFC product, accounting for the single largest subcategory of infrastructure investments (Kenny et al., 2018). In other words, the IFC pursued a long series of IPP project transactions in countries, many of which had not yet reformed important elements of their power sectors. Beginning in FY90 with US$45 million in cumulative gross approvals for power projects, investments grew to US$4.4 billion over the next ten years, with 82 per cent of this directed at greenfield power generation (Manibog et al., 2003, xviii). Between 2005 and 2015, the IFC financed more than 2.5 GW of generation capacity in SSA alone. From 2013 to 2015, IFC averaged US$850 million in annual commitments to SSA's power sectors. About 90 per cent of that investment was in generation (IFC, 2015).

In contrast to the IFC and MIGA during the 1990s, the World Bank's reform-intensive portfolio performed poorly and quickly fell far behind the IPP project transactions being concluded by its sister institutions. A Bank self-evaluation in 1999 singled out the power lending portfolio as one of the Bank's worst performers (Manibog et al., 2003, xxi). For example, the Bank's internal evaluations found few successful examples of work on power sector regulatory improvements during the decade. Such work was deemed to be essential for sustainable sector reform and occupied a good deal of Bank resources. But these activities proved to be slow and focused on lengthy capacity-building exercises that became ends in themselves (Manibog et al., 2003, 51). Improvements in sector planning, procurement, regulation, and management lagged far behind the emergence of IPP projects in many of the WBG's client countries, contributing to expensive and inflexible PPAs, inappropriate technology choices, unnecessary increases in generating capacity, and other problems.

8.7 "Washington Consensus" or "Structural Adjustment"?

The characterization of power sector reforms in the 1990s as having something to do with "the Washington Consensus" (Foster et al., 2017) only adds to the confusion about the origins and purposes of IPP projects. The "Washington Consensus," in any of its many different incarnations, is not usually thought of as offering guidance on power sector reform and has never actually involved much consensus (Birdsall et al., 2010).[2] Therefore, referring to it as a "package" of power sector reform steps that can be "sequenced" according to "the original logic" (Foster et al., 2017) confuses what actually happened in the field with the elaborate theoretical reform structures and sequences described and prescribed by a host of different researchers—the power sector research literature quickly became overpopulated in the 2000s with studies purporting to identify the optimal descriptive or prescriptive structures and sequences of power sector reforms, using terminology like "reform scorecard" (Bacon, 1999), "standard prescription" (Hunt, 2002), "standard model" (Littlechild, 2006), "standard menu" (Williams and Ghanadan, 2006), "textbook architecture" (Joskow, 2006), "standard textbook model" (Victor and Heller, 2007), and "hybrid model" (Gratwick and Eberhard, 2008).[3]

And as noted earlier, these reform sequences had little to do with actual MDB sector policy or practice.[4] Nor did these reform sequences reflect the interests of government counterparts who principally viewed IPP projects as ways of dealing with power supply problems and maintaining the flow of funding into the sector from development partners, rather than reform steps. Contrary to the expectations

[2] Lee and Usman (2018) suggest that "Washington Consensus" is not a very accurate way to characterize power sector reform recommendations in the 1990s. Consensus was absent from the beginning. John Williamson, the originator of the term, included among his ten recommended policies a call for more public expenditure on infrastructure—something omitted from virtually all conventional lists of recommended power sector reforms in the 1990s.

[3] Recent research on power sector financial viability and hidden costs (Trimble et al., 2016) has the potential of offering a much more precise way to measure sector performance improvements resulting from successful problem solving, than simply adding up measures deemed to be reforms and noting whether or not the "optimum order" of reforms was followed, regardless of the actual impact of these steps on sector performance.

[4] By 2004, the World Bank's emphasis on structural adjustment lending and SOE privatization had largely come to an end. In early 2004 the World Bank published an operational guidance note for WBG staff entitled "Public and Private Sector Roles in the Supply of Electricity Services" (World Bank, 2004). This was meant to rectify the deficiencies in operation guidance observed in the Bank's 2003 review, led by Manibog. The note cautioned against prescriptive, one-size-fits-all recommendations for privatization across countries, and advised staff to consider the full range of reform options.

of hopeful MDB researchers like Roseman and Malhotra (1996), these governments did not move much beyond a view that IPP projects were indeed "innocuous and desirable in reasonable doses."

The role of structural adjustment lending in driving power sector "reform" in the 1990s was critical. But very few of the often-cited accounts of this period mention policy-based lending, much less its role in pressuring governments to accept reforms proposed by donors, DFIs, or MDBs even when officials had little or no intention of carrying through with reforms. Much of the core literature fails to even mention the role of structural adjustment or MDB pressure for power sector reform during the 1990s (Bacon, 1999; Bacon and Besant-Jones, 2002; Besant-Jones, 2006; Joskow, 2008; Kessides, 2012; Barnett, 2014; Eberhard et al., 2016). Several authors describe structural adjustment as among the "push–pull" factors motivating reform (Zhang et al., 2008; Nepal and Jamasb, 2011; Sen, 2014; Jamasb et al., 2015). Gratwick and Eberhard suggest that MDBs did not impose reform, but only promoted it: "IFIs were at the forefront of reform, but they were not alone. Domestic actors and international policy consultants had a role to play as well in shaping and ultimately carrying out reform policy" (Gratwick and Eberhard, 2008, 3952). However, the World Bank certainly intended to impose reforms when necessary. Its 1993 power sector policy document made clear that "commitment lending" would characterize its involvement in power sectors going forward: "The Bank will give such assistance only when satisfied with the government's institutional and structural reform policies for the power sector" (World Bank, 1993, 18).

A number of researchers convincingly show that the World Bank and other MDBs appear to have carried through on these intentions, by demonstrating strong associations between foreign financial aid and reforms in the 1990s (Henisz et al., 2005; Zelner et al., 2009; Erdogdu, 2014; Gore et al., 2018). Newbery (2002) suggests that MDB support for IPP projects in unreformed power markets may help delay serious consideration of further sector reform. Williams and Ghanadan are among the few mainstream researchers to suggest that governments often acceded to structural adjustment demands even when the demands had detrimental effects on public utility finances (Williams and Ghanadan, 2006, 838). In one of the few World Bank studies to highlight structural adjustment pressures for power sector reforms in the 1990s, Lee and Usman (2018) acknowledge the tremendous influence of the World Bank during this period, as well as risks that "institutional rationality" can overwhelm assessments of what really makes sense in terms of the specific needs of individual countries.

In his evaluation of structural adjustment efforts to reform SOEs in Africa during the 1990s, Nellis says that government intentions should have been obvious: "It was clear, or should have been, that many African governments were not committed to the reform, and were doing the minimum necessary to placate the IFIs and maintain the dialogue—and the resource flow" (Nellis, 2005, 3).

Why would power sector reforms have proliferated between 1995 and 2005, and then stagnate after that (Foster et al., 2017)? The answer appears to be that this decade roughly coincided with the period during which SOE reforms under structural adjustment focused on water and electricity utilities. By 2005, the structural adjustment lending programs had ended, at least in name, and with that, much of the pressure applied on countries to adopt MDB-sanctioned reform measures in order to receive sector loans.

Nothing better underscores the fact that IPP projects were largely to do with problem solving and maintaining financial support from donors, DFIs, and MDBs than the surging popularity of Chinese-funded generation projects in SSA since 2009. As of 2014, Chinese-funded generation projects existed in 19 countries and were rapidly growing in numbers, investment, and megawatts installed. Project structures typically involve an engineering, procurement, construction (EPC) contract, plus financing from the China Exim Bank or one of the other Chinese state-owned banks. By 2014, Chinese-financed power projects had already exceeded IPP projects in terms of total investment (by about 17 per cent) and were on a trajectory to overtake IPP projects in terms of megawatts of installed capacity (Eberhard et al., 2016, 18, 25–6).

SSA governments increasingly see Chinese projects as alternatives to IPP projects, at least in terms of the issues that really matter to them—quickly rolling out generating capacity in ways that seem to involve favorable financial conditions. But Chinese projects have little or nothing to do with sector reforms associated with private participation. Rather, these are "turnkey" projects financed by loans from Chinese policy banks made directly to the relevant governments who pay contractors, usually Chinese construction companies. These kinds of projects do not appear in any of the aforementioned standard packages of reform steps, because in many cases these projects represent a full-scale retreat from traditional reform agendas—the resulting facilities are owned and operated by government utilities, thus strengthening the sector role of existing government ministries and agencies. Channeling the investment funding through these government entities, without the usual MDB auditing and performance monitoring requirements, would also be popular with corrupt governments because of the substantial opportunities for financial mismanagement.

8.8 The Mis-Characterization of IPP Projects as Reforms

The conventional view of power sector reform characterizes countries that failed to make the transition beyond single buyers and IPP projects to more competitive wholesale markets as having "partially" reformed their markets (Foster et al., 2017). According to this view, further reforms were "delayed" for a variety of reasons. But the evidence suggests a different reason for stalled reforms—government officials in these countries viewed IPP projects as practical ways of adding generating capacity, with the added benefit in some cases of doing so in a manner that retarded any further reform. But exactly what were these officials trying to protect, and how did "partial" reform elements, like IPP projects, help with that?

Sector ministries and state-owned single-buyer utilities clearly have strong interests in avoiding the creation of competitive wholesale markets, particularly in countries with weak governments or corrupt officials.[5] The ministries lose the lucrative benefits associated with decisions about investments in generation capacity. The utilities lose control over the sector's day-to-day financial affairs, and the various associated opportunities for rents, patronage appointments, and corruption (Kessides, 2004). The energy sector in low-income countries—especially in SSA, with its complex mix of public and private actors, entrenched centers of monopoly power, substantial cash transactions, low levels of transparency, etc.—has long been recognized as notoriously prone to corruption (Lovei and McKechnie, 2000). IPP projects can be introduced without changing the status quo in most of these areas, plus "the privatization process itself can create corruption incentives," leading to increases in the cost of projects by 30–50 per cent (Rose-Ackerman, 1996, 2).

The single-buyer/IPP project model preserves those key roles and does so in way that resists more changes because of rigid PPA contract structures that create risks and increase costs for longer-term reform efforts. For example, the eventual integration of IPP projects into competitive markets is one of the goals of sector reform, but achieving this outcome is a challenge that few countries have successfully managed. PPAs act as barriers to such integration because of their long duration, their take-or-pay or fixed capacity charges—designed to create stable and certain IPP project revenues, their protection of the IPP project against market risk, as well as their use of service requirements that are typically less demanding than market rules that promote competition. Options exist for integrating IPP projects into competitive markets, but some of these (e.g., forced contract renegotiation) are extremely risky and potentially costly, so much so that gains for consumers that are expected to result from such an integration, are "likely to be delayed over a relatively lengthy transition period or may never be realized" (Woolf and Halpern, 2001, 8).

It is possible to structure PPAs to facilitate eventual integration, for example by reducing the period of time during which the IPP project is insulated from market risks (Woolf and Halpern, 2001, 25). But the combination of the various risks

[5] Wholesale and retail competition are often thought to be impractical in countries with small power systems, where sector unbundling is unlikely to be cost-effective. But, IPP projects and single-buyer contracts could still be introduced in these systems to enhance competition "for the market" rather than "in the market" (Jamasb, 2002, 43). However, a reason for not doing this is that in a small system the high visibility of IPP projects quickly begins to erode the power and influence of existing sector ministries and utilities, especially if the IPP projects are efficiently managed.

associated with IPP projects in low-income countries, and the fact that most IPP projects in these countries result from unsolicited bids and direct negotiation, mean that private sponsors usually take the dominant role in PPA negotiations. Sponsors are of course reluctant to relinquish PPA benefits, especially if the result is integration into a more competitive market that puts at risk their guaranteed revenues.

A collection of the problems and risks associated with IPP projects and single-buyer markets, like those prevalent across SSA, were identified early on during the roll-out of SOE reform efforts under structural adjustment (Gray and Schuster, 1998; Lovei, 2000; Lovei and McKechnie, 2000; Kessides, 2004; Fraser, 2005). These problems include the following:

- The model in place across Africa involves a state-owned utility (the single buyer) that has no stronger incentives to operate honestly or efficiently, or to reject political influence, than any other government institution. Decisions about investments in generating capacity or the dispatch of power generated by public versus private facilities are made by civil servants who are not judged by the financial consequences of their actions, and who are often unable to resist pressure from powerful interest groups who lobby for government-guaranteed capacity increases. Single buyers can use their position to restrict market entry by new IPP projects; they can also restrict the development of potentially productive cross-border electricity trade with neighboring countries that have adopted less restrictive market models.
- A key impact of the single-buyer/IPP project model comes from protecting private investors from market risk and retail-level regulatory risk, by using PPAs denominated in US dollars and including fixed capacity charges or take-or-pay commitments. In effect, taxpayers bear most of the risk associated with IPP projects rather than investors or customers. The single buyer is obligated to make payments to IPP projects pursuant to PPAs, but if it fails to do so, the government must step in. This support represents a substantial contingent liability formalized in government guarantees, something not ignored by credit rating agencies.
- The model also does not involve direct contracts between generators and distributors and this means that distributors have weak incentives to effectively carry out tariff collection, demand forecasting, or procurement. This is because the single buyer remains state owned, and therefore often faces political disincentives when it comes to punishing distributors that are delinquent with regard to payments for power received. When there is no punishment for non-payment to the single buyer, the distributors lose their incentives to take actions that are politically costly for them, including managing costs and disconnecting non-paying customers.

- Because the single-buyer model typically involves inflexible, long-term PPA contracts incorporating fixed capacity payments or take-or-pay requirements, the model does not easily or quickly adjust when electricity demand falls below expectations. Ideally, in such a situation electricity prices would drop, stimulating demand. But under the single-buyer model, the effective wholesale price of power increases because the fixed capacity charges must be spread over a reduced volume of electricity purchases. When these high prices cannot be passed on to final consumers, as was the case during the Asian crisis, IPP projects must be forced to renegotiate their PPAs or taxpayers must bear the losses.
- As has already been mentioned, the single-buyer model represents a partial market liberalization measure that hampers the further progress toward wholesale electricity markets that fully harness competition to lower costs for consumers. Again, this is because of the long-term nature of the PPAs used to attract private investment, which also typically involve take-or-pay requirements or fixed capacity charges. These are measures that protect the IPP project from market risk and mean that the projects also have few competitive incentives to improve the efficiency of their generation. But these measures also mean that IPP projects have little incentive to voluntarily participate in a competitive market.

Since the 1990s, recommendations have been made to precede IPP projects with broader sector reforms, or such reforms have been expected to following the introduction of IPP projects. But as this discussion indicates, researchers have found little or no association between IPP projects in SSA and the existence of sector reforms like independent regulation, least-cost generation planning, competitive bidding, cost-reflective tariffs, sector unbundling, improvements to transmission and distribution infrastructure, or even efforts to ensure the financial health of off-taker utilities. Small sample sizes make statistical analysis of these associations difficult, but this lack of association seems supported by at least the appearance of a lack of association between IPP projects and financial viability or efficiency of power sector operations (Table 8.1), and a lack of association between IPP projects and private sector perceptions of power sector performance (Table 8.2).

8.9 Conclusions

The story of IPP projects in low-income countries is as much about the development community, as it is about the attitudes of the governments involved. During the years (1995–2005) when the SOE reform efforts under structural adjustment

Table 8.1 IPP Projects and Power Sector Performance in SSA

Country	Private generation as percent of installed capacity***	Power Sector Performance**			
		Operating costs per kWh billed	Utility operating costs vs. cash collected per kWh billed	Total utility costs vs. cash collected per kWh billed	Quasi-fiscal deficit as a percent of GDP
	Rank	Rank*	Rank*	Rank*	Rank*
Côte d'Ivoire	100.0%	20	29	26	26
Senegal	100.0%	28	24	16	29
Cameroon	99.2%	13	14	11	12
Mozambique	86.6%	5	4	14	14
Uganda	63.0%	18	5	1	1
Nigeria	47.7%	17	32	32	10
Sierra Leone	37.5%	32	15	18	15
Togo	34.7%	29	22	6	24
Kenya	31.3%	14	7	12	13
Madagascar	23.3%	25	33	33	28
Ghana	22.4%	12	11	5	7
Rwanda	22.4%	30	25	23	18
Tanzania	21.3%	15	9	4	3
Zambia	9.8%	3	17	17	19
Angola	9.0%	NA	NA	NA	NA

*The higher the ranking the lower the cost

***Source*: Trimble, et al., 2016.

****Source*: Foster, et al., 2017.

focused on water and power utilities, government officials in these countries were incentivized to comply with privatization reform packages in order to continue receiving development aid. Government officials acquiesced when they realized that their development partners interpreted the implementation of "privatization transactions" like IPP projects as positive indications that more extensive reforms were underway. IPP projects helped solve specific problems. For governments, IPP projects met an immediate need for more generating capacity, but they also helped to maintain the sector "status quo" in terms of power and patronage configurations. For private-sector-oriented DFIs and MDBs, IPP projects represented popular products that helped to grow loan portfolios as these institutions competed for market share with their institutional peers. Inherently, IPP projects were not really elements of reform programs, at least not from the perspective of most host governments.

Fifteen years ago, the WBG facilitated this situation by formalizing among its agencies a power sector division of labor that enabled the IFC and MIGA to pursue transactions like IPP projects, largely unfettered by any need for supporting

Table 8.2 IPP Projects and Private Sector Perceptions of the Power Sector, SSA

Country	Private generation as percent of installed capacity***	Private Sector Perceptions of the Power Sector**				
		Number of electrical outages in a typical month	Average duration of typical outage	Average losses due to outages (% of annual sales)	Percent of firms owning or sharing a generator	Percent of firms identifying electricity as a major constraint
	Rank	Rank*	Rank*	Rank*	Rank*	Rank*
Côte d'Ivoire	100.0%	10	19	17	33	35
Senegal	100.0%	22	41	10	13	21
Cameroon	99.2%	27	9	31	30	24
Mozambique	86.6%	5	30	6	41	10
Uganda	63.0%	24	6	32	22	12
Nigeria	47.7%	41	4	38	7	22
Sierra Leone	37.5%	33	5	23	2	27
Togo	34.7%	21	39	14	21	23
Kenya	31.3%	23	17	25	18	7
Madagascar	23.3%	25	40	35	38	11
Ghana	22.4%	29	11	39	23	34
Rwanda	22.4%	11	29	8	26	4
Tanzania	21.3%	30	14	37	27	18
Zambia	9.8%	17	3	34	4	17
Angola	9.0%	19	34	27	36	13

*The higher the ranking the more problems reported

***Source*: World Bank, Enterprise Surveys, 2016.

****Source*: Foster, et al., 2017.

reforms, while the World Bank (IBRD/IDA) pursued reforms to planning, regulation, governance, and management. But the reform efforts did not keep pace with the IPP project transactions. As a result, the promotion of IPP projects as solutions to sector problems, in sectors where further reforms are not underway or planned, helps to ensure that the benefits of IPP projects are far less than they should be. This creates a kind of policy dilemma, forcing a choice between two unsatisfactory alternatives: should DFIs and MDBs press ahead with IPP projects, the full benefits of which are limited by inaction on sector reforms, or should sector reforms be allowed to "catch up" by slowing the pace of IPP project development and risk an even larger gap between generating capacity supply and demand? Most policy experts now seem to accept the existence of this dilemma, although the private sector, their financiers, and many governments of developing countries still do not. But some policy experts suspect the existence of a larger, more paradoxical, problem—in cases where IPP projects are promoted as "reform" measures in otherwise unreformed power sectors of low-income countries, the projects may help to retard further reforms. More research is required to make a compelling case for the existence of this paradox, but clearly the lack of synchronization between the roll-out of IPP projects and sector reforms in many developing countries is creating problems.

In theory, the resolution of this IPP policy dilemma is straightforward: ways need to be found to strengthen the association between IPP projects and broader sector reforms and improved sector performance, an association that we now know is far from automatic. Sector reforms or plans for sector reform need to be in place before IPP projects are developed. However, actually doing this is not so simple. It cannot be denied that IPP projects are effective tools for expanding generating capacity, and many developing countries desperately need more capacity. The private sector recognizes IPP projects as potentially profitable and relatively low risk. MDBs and DFIs seeking private sector clients and increased market share recognize that IPP projects represent opportunities for significantly expanding their lending portfolios. Perhaps most importantly, the experiences under structural reform, beginning with "performance agreements" in the 1980s, suggest that governments in many developing countries want more generating capacity without disturbing the status quo power and patronage configurations of their power sectors. Asking that IPP project transaction work decelerate and wait for reforms to "catch up" is not a practical resolution of this IPP policy dilemma.

The only reasonable option then is to speed up reforms. Donors, DFIs, and MDBs like the World Bank have been trying to do this, with limited success, since the 1990s. But the development players with real leverage to deal with this issue are the DFIs and MDBs that specialize in lending to private companies and play principal roles in making most of these IPP project transactions happen. If institutions like IFC, FMO, PROPARCO, DEG, Norfund, CDC, and others can be persuaded to take a more developmental approach to their transactions, the development community might begin to make more headway in resolving this IPP policy dilemma.

Chapter 9 focuses on a new approach to the development of IPP projects in SSA, renewable energy IPP tender programs. Using competitive tenders to lower IPP project costs, combined with the rapid reductions in the equipment costs associated with wind and solar projects, may mean that renewable energy IPP projects will become the power sector PPPs of the future in Africa. Development partners have always played key roles in IPP projects in low-income countries—what has been the role of donors, DFIs, and MDBs in designing and implementing these renewable energy IPP tender programs? What lessons can be learned from the different implementation approaches used? What impact do these kinds of programs have on the "IPP policy dilemma" described in this chapter? In other words, do these renewable energy IPP projects facilitate broader sector reforms, or inhibit the progress of such reform?

References

Bacon, R. 1999. "A Scorecard for Energy Reform in Developing Countries." Public Policy for the Private Sector Note No. 175. Washington, DC: World Bank (April).

Bacon, R. 2018. *Taking Stock of the Impact of Power Utility Reform in Developing Countries: A Literature Review.* Policy Research Working Paper No. 8460. Washington, DC: World Bank (May).

Bacon, R., J.E. Besant-Jones. 2002. "Global Electric Power Reform, Privatisation and Liberalisation of the Electric Power Industry in Developing Countries." World Bank Energy and Mining Sector Board Discussion Paper 2. Washington, DC: World Bank.

Baker McKenzie. 2014. "The rise of export credit and development finance in major projects." EE Publishers (November 25). Accessed at: http://www.ee.co.za/article/rise-export-credit-development-finance-major-projects.html

Barnett, A. 2014. "Political Considerations Relevant to Energy and Economic Growth." London: UK Department for International Development.

Besant-Jones, J.E. 2006. *Reforming Power Markets in Developing Countries: What Have We Learned?* Energy and Mining Sector Board Discussion Paper No. 19. Washington, DC: World Bank (September).

Birdsall, N.A., A. de la Torre, F.V. Caicedo. 2010. *The Washington Consensus: Assessing a Damaged Brand.* CGD Policy Paper 211. Washington, DC: Center for Global Development (May).

Bork, R.H. 1978. *The Antitrust Paradox: A Policy at War with Itself.* New York: Basic Books.

de la Borde, B.H., Y. Charafi. 2013. "An Inconvenient Truth." *Private Sector & Development: Independent Power Producers: A Solution for Africa?* 9–12. Paris: PROPARCO (December 16).

Eberhard, A., K.N. Gratwick, E. Morella, P. Antman. 2016. *Independent Power Projects in Sub-Saharan Africa: Lessons from Five Key Countries.* World Bank Directions in Development. Washington, DC: World Bank.

Eberhard, A., K.N. Gratwick, E. Morella, P. Antman. 2017. "Independent Power Projects in Sub-Saharan Africa: Investment trends and policy lessons." Energy Policy 108: 390–424.

Energy Sector Management Assistance Programme (ESMAP). 1999. *Global Energy Sector Reform in Developing Countries: A Scorecard.* Washington, DC: World Bank (July).

Erdogdu, E. 2014. "The Political Economy of Electricity Market Liberalization: A Cross-Country Approach." *Energy Journal* 35(3): 91–128.

Foster, V., S. Witte, S.G. Banerjee, A. Moreno. 2017. *Charting the Diffusion of power Sector Reforms across the Developing World.* Policy Research Working Paper No. 8235. Washington, DC: World Bank (November).

Fraser, J.M. 2005. *Lessons from the Independent Private Power Experience in Pakistan.* Energy and Mining Sector Board Discussion Paper No. 14. Washington, DC: World Bank (May).

Gomez-Ibanez, J.A. 2007. *Alternatives to Infrastructure Privatization Revisited: Public Enterprise Reform from the 1960s to the 1980s.* Policy Research Working Paper No. 4391. Washington, DC: World Bank (November).

Gore, C.D., J.N. Brass, E. Baldwin, L.M. Maclean. 2018. "Political autonomy and resistance in electricity sector liberalization in Africa." *World Development.* doi.org/10.1016/j.worlddev.2018.03.003

Gratwick, K.N., A. Eberhard. 2008. "Demise of the standard model for power sector reform and the emergence of hybrid power markets." *Energy Policy* 36: 3948–60.

Gray, R.D., J. Schuster. 1998. "The East Asian Financial Crisis—Fallout for Private Power Projects." Public Policy for the Private Sector Note No. 146. Washington, DC: World Bank (August).

Henisz, W.J., B.A. Zelner, M.F. Guillen. 2005. "The worldwide diffusion of market-oriented infrastructure reform, 1977–1999." *American Sociological Review* 70(6): 871–97.

Huenteler, J., I. Dobozi, A. Balabanyan, S.G. Banerjee. 2017. *Cost Recovery and Financial Viability of the Power Sector in Developing Countries: A Literature Review.* Policy Research Working Paper No. 8287. Washington, DC: World Bank (December).

Hunt, S. 2002. *Making Competition Work in Electricity.* New York, NY: Wiley.

International Finance Corporation (IFC). 2015. "IFC: A Major financier and Developer of African Power." Washington, DC: IFC (December 31). Accessed at https://www.ifc.org/wps/wcm/connect/4f85b058-ff86-41a5-879c-fca4a6e2e7fe/africa-power-05-print.pdf?MOD=AJPERES

Jamasb, T., 2002. "Reform and regulation of the electricity sectors in developing countries." Working Paper CMI EP 08/DAE 0226. Department of Applied Economics, University of Cambridge (August).

Jamasb, T., R. Nepal, G. Timilsina. 2015. "A Quarter Century Effort Yet to Come of Age: A Survey of Power Sector Reforms in Developing Countries." Policy Research Working Paper No. 7330. Washington, DC: World Bank.

Joskow, P.L. 2006. "Introduction to Electricity Sector Liberalization: Lessons Learned from Cross-Country Studies. In *Electricity Market Reform: An International Perspective*," edited by F.P. Sishansi and W. Pfaffenberger: 1–32. Oxford: Elsevier Limited.

Joskow, P.L. 2008. "Lessons learned from the electricity market liberalization." *The Energy Journal, Special Issue (The future of electricity: Papers in honor of David Newbery)*: 9–42.

Kenny, C., J. Kalow, V. Ramachandran. 2018. *Inside the Portfolio of the International Finance Corporation: Does IFC Do Enough in Low-Income Countries?* CGD Policy Paper 115. Washington, DC: Center for Global Development. Accessed at https://www.cgdev.org/publication/insideportfolio-international-finance-corporation-does-ifc-do-enough-low-income

Kessides, I.N. 2004. *Reforming Infrastructure: Privatization, Regulation, and Competition*. Washington, DC: World Bank and Oxford University Press.

Kessides, I.N. 2012. "The Impacts of Electricity Sector Reforms in Developing Countries." *The Electricity Journal* 25(6): 79–88.

Klein, M. 2015. *Public–Private Partnerships: Promise and Hype*. Policy Research Working Paper No. 7340. Washington DC: World Bank.

Lee, A.D., Z. Usman. 2018. *Taking Stock of the Political Economy of Power sector Reforms in Developing Countries: A Literature Review*. Policy Research Working Paper No. 8518. Washington, DC: World Bank (July).

Littlechild, S. 2006. "Foreword: The Market versus Regulation." In *Electricity Market Reform: An International Perspective*, edited by F.P. Sishansi and W. Pfaffenberger: xvii—xxix. Oxford: Elsevier Limited.

Lovei, L. 2000. "The Single-Buyer Model: A Dangerous Path toward Competitive Electricity Markets." Public Policy for the Private Sector Note No. 225. Washington, DC: World Bank (December).

Lovei, L., A. McKechnie. 2000. "The Costs of Corruption for the Poor—The Energy Sector." Public Policy for the Private Sector Note No. 207. Washington, DC: World Bank (April).

Manibog, F., R. Dominguez, S. Wegner. 2003. *Power for Development: A Review of the World Bank Group's Experience with Private Participation in the Electricity Sector*. World Bank Operations Evaluation Department, IFC Operations Evaluation Group, MIGA Operations Evaluation Unit. Washington, DC: World Bank, IFC, MIGA.

Nellis, J. 1989a. "Contract Plans and Public Enterprise Performance." World Bank Discussion Paper No. 48. Washington, DC: World Bank (February).

Nellis, J. 1989b. *Public Enterprise Reform in Adjustment Lending*. Policy, Planning, and Research Working Paper No. 233. Washington, DC: World Bank (August).

Nellis, J. 2005. *The Evolution of Enterprise Reform in Africa: From State-Owned Enterprises to Private Participation in Infrastructure—and Back?* ESMAP Technical Paper No. 084. Washington, DC: World Bank (November).

Nepal, R., T. Jamasb. 2011. "Reforming the Power Sector in Transition: Do Institutions Matter?" Cambridge Working Papers in Economics (CWPE) 1125 & Electricity Policy Research Group Working Paper (EPRG) 1109. Electricity Policy Research Group, Faculty of Economics, University of Cambridge, February.

Newbery, D.M. 2002. "Issues and Options for Restructuring Electricity Supply Industries," Working Paper CMI EP No. 01/DAE No. 0210, Department of Applied Economics, University of Cambridge, Cambridge.

Odendaal, N. 2015. "UK, Norway conclude Globeleq Africa acquisition." *Engineering News*, September 14.

Pardina, M.R., J. Schiro. 2018. *Taking Stock of Economic Regulation of Power Utilities in the Developing World: A Literature Review.* Policy Research Working Paper No. 8461. Washington, DC: World Bank (May).

Rose-Ackerman, S. 1996. "The Political Economy of Corruption—Causes and Consequences." Public Policy for the Private Sector Note No. 74. Washington, DC: World Bank (April).

Roseman, E., A. Malhotra. 1996. "The Dynamics of Independent Power: IPP projects seed top-to-bottom reform." Public Policy for the Private Sector Note No. 83. Washington, DC: World Bank (June).

Rudnick, H., C. Velasquez. 2018. *Taking Stock of Wholesale Power Markets in Developing Countries: A Literature Review.* Policy Research Working Paper No. 8519. Washington, DC: World Bank (July).

Sen, A. 2014. "Divergent Paths to a Common Goal? An Overview of Challenges to Electricity Sector Reform in Developing versus Developed Countries." University of Oxford Institute for Energy Studies Working Paper 10. Oxford: University of Oxford.

Shirley, M.M., L.C. Xu. 1997. *Information, Incentives, and Commitment: An Empirical Analysis of Contracts between Government and State Enterprises.* Policy Research Working Paper No. 1769. Washington, DC: World Bank (May).

Trimble, T., M. Kojima, I.P. Arroyo, F. Mohammadzadeh. 2016. *Financial Viability of Electricity Sectors in Sub-Saharan Africa: Quasi-Fiscal Deficits and Hidden Costs.* Policy Research Working Paper No. 7788. Washington, DC: World Bank (August).

United States Central Intelligence Agency. *The World Fact Book*. Accessed in 2018 at: https://www.cia.gov/library/publications/the-world-factbook/fields/2236.html

Victor, D.,T.C. Heller (eds.). 2007. *The Political Economy of Power Sector Reform: The Experiences of Five Major Developing Countries*. Cambridge: Cambridge University Press.

Williams, J.H., R. Ghanadan. 2006. "Electricity Reform in Developing and Transition Countries: A reappraisal." *Energy* 31: 815–44.

Woodhouse, E.J. 2005. "The Experience with Independent Power Projects in Developing Countries: Interim Report," Program on Energy and Sustainable Development Working Paper No. 39. Center for Environmental Science and Policy, Stanford University, February.

Woolf, F., J. Halpern. 2001. *Integrating Independent Power Producers into Emerging Wholesale Power Markets.* Policy Research Working Paper No. 2703. Washington, DC: World Bank (November).

World Bank. 1993. *The World Bank's Role in the Electric Power Sector.* A World Bank Policy Paper. Washington, DC: World Bank (January).

World Bank. 2001a. "Implementation Completion Report on a Loan in the Amount of US$150.0 Million to the Islamic Republic of Pakistan for a Private Sector Energy Development Project." Report No: 22157. Washington, DC: World Bank (May 11).

World Bank. 2001b. "ICR Review: Private Sector energy Development Project." Operations Evaluation Department Report No. ICRR 10953. Washington, DC: World Bank (July 9).

World Bank. 2002. *Private Sector Development Strategy: Directions for the World Bank Group.* Washington, DC: World Bank (April 9).

World Bank. 2004. *Operational Guidance for World bank Group Staff: Public and private sector roles in the supply of electricity services.* Washington, DC: World Bank (February).

World Bank. 2016. Enterprise Surveys. Washington, DC: World Bank. Accessed at: https://www.enterprisesurveys.org/

World Bank. 2018. PPI Project Database. Accessed at: http://ppi.worldbank.org/customquery?mode=1

World Bank, Asian Development Bank, and Inter-American Development Bank. 2014. *Public-Private Partnerships Reference Guide, Version 2.0.* Washington, DC: World Bank.

Zelner, B.A., W.J. Henisz, G.L. Holburn. 2009. "Contentious Implementation and Retrenchment in Neoliberal Policy Reform: The Global Electric Power Industry, 1989–2001." *Administrative Science Quarterly* 54(3): 379–412.

Zhang, Y., C. Kirkpatrick, D. Parker. 2008. "Electricity Sector Reform in Developing Countries: An Econometric Assessment of the Effects of Privatisation, Competition, and Regulation." CRC Working Paper 31/2002, Institute for Development Policy and Management, University of Manchester.

9
Case Studies
IPP Tender Programs in SSA—Disruptive Moments or Business as Usual?

9.1 Introduction

Globally, electric power utilities and the systems they manage are beginning to experience radical changes, largely because of the intersection of a number of different trends. These trends, documented in a recent MIT study, include the decentralization of systems due to the rapid growth in distributed generation; the emergence of proactive, price-conscious consumers of electricity; the proliferation of information and communications technology (ICT) in all aspects of energy production and consumption; the rapidly reducing costs, and increasing use, of variable renewable power sources like wind and solar energy; accelerating efforts to mitigate climate change by decarbonizing energy systems; and an intensification of the interconnections between electricity and other kinds of infrastructure services like communications and transport (MIT, 2016).

These changes are taking place most dramatically in the United States and Europe, where they are already beginning to have disruptive effects on the centralized, top–down manner in which utilities have traditionally provided energy services. But developing countries are also experiencing the effects of some of these changes, and efforts to capture the benefits of these changes have led in a few cases to new kinds of independent power producer (IPP) projects and new ways of selecting IPPs. One unintended consequence of these new kinds of IPP projects, mostly involving renewable energy, has been their contribution to what African energy expert Anton Eberhard calls a "disruptive moment" (*Engineering News*, 2017). The disruption potentially upsets the status quo of vertically integrated, state-owned monopoly single-buyer utilities in regions like Sub-Saharan Africa (SSA).

Chapter 8 theorized that traditional IPP projects in low-income countries (LICs) with unreformed power sectors, like most SSA countries, can help solve immediate problems with lack of generation capacity, but often do not produce all the benefits expected of them, and may inhibit further reforms. However, renewable energy IPP tender programs, like those implemented recently in South Africa, Uganda, and Zambia, may be different. This chapter explores whether or not such programs may

Public–Private Partnerships in Sub-Saharan Africa: The Evidence-Based Critique. James Leigland, Oxford University Press (2020).
DOI: 10.1093/oso/9780198861829.001.0001

have more profound effects on reform than traditional IPP projects, because of their careful structuring and document preparation, competitive tendering, and procurement and contracting overseen by government agencies other than the traditional government-owned single-buyers of power.

The suggestion is not that reform consequences of these tender programs are completely intentional. Such consequences may result because these IPP programs unintentionally highlight the poor performance of dominant power utilities intent on stifling competition and maintaining their control over the resources of their sectors. The IPP tender programs in South Africa, Uganda, and Zambia have resulted from a mix of influences, prioritized somewhat differently depending on the stakeholders involved (donors, development finance institutions (DFIs), multilateral development banks (MDBs), sector regulators, other government officials, the private sector, etc.). The influences reflect the aforementioned intersecting power sector development trends, especially the rapidly reducing costs of renewable energy, the need to decarbonize power sectors to help with climate change mitigation, and an understanding and acceptance of distributed (decentralized) generation.

Have "disruptive moments" been precipitated in these countries by the unexpected degree of success achieved by their renewable energy IPP tender programs? If so, will the windows of opportunity for reform stay open long enough for sustainable change to the status quo? Or are these projects simply business as usual, with the IPP projects unlikely to generate all the benefits expected of them and in some cases helping to retard further reforms?

This chapter reviews these programs, by addressing the origins of renewable energy IPP projects, assessing why such projects were targeted in these countries, identifying the success factors that propelled the achievements of these particular programs, and evaluating the likelihood of further sector reforms. The results have been mixed. All three countries seemed to have experienced disruptive moments to some degree, but those "moments" may not lead to sustainable changes in the power sector status quo in each case.

9.2 Overview: From Carbon Markets to IPP Projects

9.2.1 Climate Change: The Original Driving Force

An initial driving force behind renewable energy IPP projects in developing countries was the concern of donors, DFIs, and MDBs about climate change. Beginning in the early 2000s climate change began to emerge as an issue that seemed to require urgent action. Estimates of the costs of climate change mitigation and adaptation in developing countries varied widely, ranging from US$170 to US$475 billion per year. National and international institutions responded to the climate change challenge by earmarking billions of dollars in funding for carbon emission mitigation, and dozens of international funds and financing vehicles were established. These included the Clean Technology Fund (CTF), Global Environment Facility (GEF), and the Clean Development Mechanism (CDM) established by the Kyoto Protocol. CDM was expected to be one of the most powerful of the climate change financing mechanisms. It channeled funding from greenhouse gas (GHG) emitting entities in developed countries to carbon-reducing activities in less developed countries. Each eligible project earned certified emission reductions (CERs), payable at a market price for each ton of carbon it reduced.

Developing countries were at the center of initiatives like CDM even though most of these countries played a relatively small role in carbon emissions compared with industrialized economies like the United States, China, or EU countries. This was because emission cuts were thought to be less expensive in developing countries than developed countries, so it seemed that developing countries had greater potential for reducing emissions than developed countries. And because emissions by developing countries were expected to sharply increase as their economies grew and matured, it seemed that decisions made about infrastructure projects in these countries could play a large positive role in long-term efforts to control climate change. In any case, LICs were expected to suffer the most from climate-related problems. The adverse effects of climate change threatened sustainable economic growth and poverty reduction in these countries, so it seemed appropriate that initiatives like CDM be designed to incentivize developing countries to make the right decisions about low-carbon infrastructure, with industrialized countries paying for implementation.

9.2.2 The Emergence of Renewable Energy IPP Projects

CDM had several well-known limitations, including the extreme volatility of carbon markets which became a significant deterrent to widespread CDM use. The World Bank, in collaboration with several donors, eventually articulated a new strategy for accelerating investments in low-emission technologies, which by the mid-2000s was already moving the development community in the direction of renewable energy IPP projects supported by donors, DFIs, and MDBs. The strategy involved several basic concepts (Baietti, 2013):

- First, the principal objective of these efforts was to accelerate investment in low-carbon projects and enterprises, with carbon reduction as a highly desirable, but indirect, outcome of successful implementation. In other words, the "reducing carbon" objective of traditional carbon finance programs like CDM was not leading to enough of the right kinds of investments and in some cases seemed to be distorting markets. On the other hand, the "accelerating investment" objective arguably had a better chance of helping to transform markets in a way that could lead to an accelerated, sustainable flow of large, upfront capital investments needed for low-carbon purposes.

- Second, the similarity of green technology projects to other infrastructure projects was appreciated, along with the fact that green technology projects could rely on proven project financing approaches to source investment. This was a recognition that much of the needed low-carbon investments should come through the same kinds of commercial financing channels that already provided private debt and equity to public infrastructure projects, especially via PPPs. The use of such funding for climate change-related objectives would therefore depend ultimately on the willingness of governments to enter into PPPs for these purposes, rather than "green" targeting decisions made unilaterally by donors, DFIs, MDBs, or private investors.
- The role of development partners was recognized as important because, in the 2000s, the major difference between traditional infrastructure PPPs and low-carbon projects was that low-carbon investments required financial support to mitigate externalities that private investors could not pay for and users could not afford. Low-carbon projects could be evaluated, structured, and financed using the same fundamental principles as other kinds of infrastructure projects. But resources for supplemental subsidies had to be available for these projects, and in developing countries that meant support was needed from development partners like donors, DFIs, and MDBs.

9.2.3 The Evolving Project Motivation

Climate change concerns continue to play a role in driving renewable energy IPP projects, especially because these concerns continue to be promoted by development partners who also supply the subsidy support for projects in LICs. Climate change-related arguments have been increasingly taken up by African actors like regional economic communities (RECs) and other regional bodies. But concerns about climate change have been supplemented with other issues driving the renewable energy agenda among governments in SSA. A combination of several related issues began to motivate more serious government consideration of the use of renewable energy IPP projects, including rising fossil-fuel prices and more reliable, and less expensive, renewable energy technology. All of this added up to lower risks for private investors who began to see renewable energy as a feasible, long-term alternative to conventional power technologies. After 2011, renewable energy's share of power projects in developing countries began to exceed conventional energy sources for the first time, and since 2011 has ranged from 72 to 95 per cent of all projects (World Bank, 2018a).

Another important issue motivating the use of these IPP projects was the well-documented need for more electricity generation in Africa. That need was already massive and growing rapidly—traditional, large-scale projects owned and developed by governments or private companies were not being done quickly enough to close the supply–demand gap. At the same time, some renewable resources that could help close this gap, especially hydropower, solar, and wind, were available and increasingly less expensive, but generally far from being fully exploited. By 2010, Africa accounted for 10 per cent of the world's economically feasible hydropower potential, but only about 7 per cent of this potential was being exploited (Foster and Briceno-Garmendia, 2010).

Renewable energy IPP projects were particularly helpful in expanding generation capacity in Africa because of their potential to have significant impacts quickly. Although these projects tend to be small to medium-sized (often less than 100 MW), they nevertheless can make large contributions to national power generating capacity in a region like SSA, where 17 countries have power systems less than 500 MW and 14 less than 100 MW (Eberhard et al., 2016). As South Africa eventually demonstrated, relatively large amounts of solar or wind-generating capacity can be added quickly to national grids (with construction periods of around 12 months), compared with the time it takes to construct facilities needed for hydro or coal-fired generation.

The World Bank's Private Participation in Infrastructure (PPI) Project Database provides an overview of the kinds of renewable energy PPPs that reached financial close in Africa in 2012, the peak year for renewable energy PPPs, when they accounted for 95 per cent of all power projects. These were all greenfield IPP projects (build–operate–transfer—BOT or build–own–operate-—BOO), mostly using solar, wind, or small hydro (Table 9.1). Renewable energy IPP projects continue to be the most frequently used kind of power project in SSA Africa and are growing steadily in numbers.

9.2.4 From FiTs to Competitive Bidding

Along with financing and encouragement, development partners also strongly advised developing countries to use feed-in tariffs (FiTs) to acquire renewable energy generation capacity. FiTs had long been the default option recommended by donors, DFIs, and MDBs because of the widespread use of these tariff mechanisms in Organisation for Economic Co-operation and Development (OECD) countries. The philosophy behind FiTs is simple: because existing electricity tariffs are thought to be insufficient to fully compensate investors who design, build, and operate renewable energy facilities, governments agree to higher than normal tariffs for these producers as a way to accelerate these investments. A FiT is a guaranteed minimum price per unit of power (normally kWh or mWh), over a stated fixed-term period. The power is sold into the grid, normally with priority or guaranteed access and dispatch. Feed-in premiums (FiPs) are similar to FiTs. Energy producers sell electricity at market prices, but a premium is added to the market price to compensate producers for the higher costs of production, thus mitigating financial risks.

Table 9.1 Renewable Energy PPPs in SSA, 2012

Country	Number of deals	Types of PPP	Total Investment (US$ m)	Total Capacity (MW)	Technology								
					Hydro, small (<50MW)	Hyrdo, large (>50MW)	Wind, onshore	Geothermal	Biomass	Waste	Solar PV	Solar CSP	Wave
Angola	2	BOT, BOO	165	42	2								
Burkina Faso	1	BOO	6	12	1								
Cameroon	2	BOT	1 750	1 550		2							
Cape Verde	1	BOO	80	28			1						
Congo, Rep.	1	BOO	325	240				1					
Ethiopia	1	BOO	120	60			1						
Gabon	2	BOT	358	78	2								
Ghana	3	BOT, BOO	677	297		1			1		1		
Kenya	7	BOO	1 245	642			2	3		1			1
Liberia	1	BOO	170	36						1			
Madagascar	1	BOT	18	15	1								
Mauritius	6	BOO	88	151			2			4			
Mozambique	1	BOT	2 900	1 500		1							
Namibia	3	BOO	360	118	1		2						
Nigeria	1	BOT	26	39	1								
Rwanda	1	BOO	12	4	1								
São Tomé & P.	1	BROT	50	–	1								
Senegal	1	BOO	288	154			1						
Sierra Leone	1	BOO	30	15					1				
South Africa	39	BOO	5 681	2 078	1		10				24	4	
Tanzania	3	BOT, B(OO (2)	441	203			2			1			
Uganda	13	BOT (6), BOO (6), RLT	1 262	750	6	2			1	4			
Zambia	4	BOT, BOO, Full	1 853	798	2	2							
Zimbabwe	3	BOT, BOO	63	143	2							1	
Totals	**99**		**6 356**	**3 382**	**21**	**8**	**21**	**4**	**3**	**11**	**25**	**5**	**1**

Source: World Bank, 2018b.

Globally, FiTs are still the most widely-used mechanism for securing renewable energy, but competitive bidding (also referred to as auctions or tendering) is a procurement mechanism that governments are increasingly using as an alternative. Usually the selection of bidders is principally based on price, but non-price factors can also be included in the evaluation (e.g., job creation or industrial development). Bidders offer the lowest prices that they would be willing to accept in exchange for the design, financing, construction, and operation of power-generating facilities. In the past, bid prices for renewable energy projects have usually been higher than standard market rates, but as technology becomes less expensive, power prices are also coming down. Governments may cap prices at the maximum amount that they are willing to pay.

Tendering is increasingly seen as an alternative to FiTs, because in many cases it seems to ensure the lowest possible cost of electricity. FiTs are set by governments at levels that they think are fair and attractive to private suppliers. But FiTs are sometimes set too high and need to be reduced over time to avoid windfall profits for developers at the public's expense. Tendering lets the market decide what level of pricing is fair; but tendering is also an expensive process for everyone concerned, and sponsors sometimes underbid in order to win contracts with the hope of renegotiating higher prices later (a practice known as "lowballing").

Tendering is now the fastest growing form of private-generating selection. Globally, the number of countries that have adopted renewable energy tendering has increased from six in 2005 to at least 67 by mid-2016 (IRENA, 2017). Tendering, combined with technological improvements and manufacturing advances, as well as overcapacities in the global market, have precipitously lowered renewable energy prices. Solar photovoltaics (PV) module prices decreased by about 89 per cent between 2009 and 2015.

Competitive tenders have made possible three noteworthy African programs designed to procure renewable energy IPP projects. These three programs, in South Africa, Uganda, and Zambia, are examined as case studies in sections 9.3, 9.4, and 9.5.

9.3 South Africa: Renewable Energy IPP Procurement Program (REIPPPP)[1]

9.3.1 Introduction

South Africa is one of SSA's few upper middle-income countries (MICs). Although Nigeria's economy is now officially ranked as the largest in Africa,

[1] This section relies heavily on Leigland, 2016; Eberhard, Kolker, and Leigland, 2014; and Republic of South Africa, 2011–13.

South Africa's has long been the most sophisticated and robust, with the deepest financial markets and one of the highest investment grade credit ratings. The country currently has a population of about 56 million, and a GDP per capita of US$13,400. But over the last several years, the country's real GDP growth rate has slowed to less than 1 per cent and unemployment has risen to 27 per cent. About 20 per cent of South Africa's population lives below the poverty line.

South Africa's electricity-generating capacity is more than half of the total installed capacity in SSA. But that huge capacity was built mostly without private participation and even today, IPP projects account for less than 5 per cent of the total. South Africa's electricity sector is dominated by Eskom, the state-owned, vertically-integrated utility. Eskom is responsible for transmission, direct distribution to about 50 per cent of customers, and 95 per cent of generation—it acts as the single buyer of the remaining 5 per cent. The other half of customers are supplied by Eskom indirectly through 179 municipal and provincial distributors. The National Energy Regulator of South Africa (NERSA) is responsible for approving tariffs and licensing generators, transmitters, distributors, and traders.

In the 1970s and 1980s, Eskom overestimated demand growth and initiated a massive investment program. As a consequence, in the 1990s the utility had significant overcapacity and stopped building new power stations. However, by 2004, it was clear that demand for power was rapidly approaching available capacity. Demand was rapidly catching up with supply—reserve margins were dropping sharply. By the end of 2007, the country was experiencing widespread load shedding, something that came as a shock to South Africans, who considered blackouts normal in the rest of Africa, but not in their country.

While the South African government recognized the need for IPP projects to be allowed to help supply more generating capacity, procurement programs run by Eskom for IPP projects were mostly unsuccessful. Critics speculated that as the country's sole power generator at the time, Eskom may not have wanted to introduce competition that could cast the efficiency of its own operations in an unfavorable light. No IPP project contracts were signed by Eskom except for a handful of short-term power purchase agreements (PPAs) with industrial generators.

The country had renewable energy targets set by the government as early as 2003. But there was never any significant international pressure for South Africa to reduce GHGs—the country was not forced into commitments under the Kyoto Protocol. But policy makers had been mindful of the country's heavy reliance on coal for power generation and the resulting risks that the country's relatively high levels of carbon emission might pose to the economy's future international competitiveness.

The 2003 targets were not met, but continuing government research work appears to have provided the basis for the country's president to make a surprising pledge at the 2009 COP15 meeting in Copenhagen that South Africa would significantly reduce its CO_2 emissions by 2025. South Africa subsequently hosted the 2011 COP17 in Durban, where the government signed a high-profile agreement with business and other stakeholders regarding renewable energy policy and related job creation. The NERSA backed the government's commitment with a renewable energy feed-in tariff (REFiT) policy. Initial published FiTs were generally regarded as generous by developers, but the legality of FiTs within South Africa's public procurement framework was unclear, as was Eskom's commitment to a program that would facilitate IPP projects.

9.3.2 REIPPPP

Eventually, legal advice confirmed that FiTs were inconsistent with existing public finance and procurement laws. The Department of Energy (DOE) announced that the REFiT regime would be replaced with a competitive bidding process for renewable energy, known as the Renewable Energy IPP Procurement Program (REIPPPP). REIPPPP marked a significant change of strategy by the South African government. Because of Eskom's earlier failures to make progress with IPP projects, DOE took direct control of the new program. They also sought the assistance of the National Treasury's PPP Unit to manage the process. A small team of mostly mid-level technical staff from DOE and the PPP Unit established a project office that functioned effectively outside of the formal departmental structure of national government to act as a facilitator for the REIPPPP process.

Relatively small amounts of funding for program start-up were provided by donors, the Development Bank of Southern Africa, and Jobs Fund managed by National Treasury. After the first round of bidding, the program became largely self-sufficient by relying for funding on bidder registration fees and fees paid by successful IPP project companies. The program remained completely off the formal government budget through the first four bidding rounds.

The tenders for different technologies were held simultaneously, beginning with a first round in 2011. Bidders could bid for more than one project and more than one technology. Caps were set on the total capacity to be procured for individual technologies in order to limit the supply to be bid out and therefore increase the level of competition among the different technologies and potential bidders.

The request for proposal (RFP) package included standardized, non-negotiable, PPAs and implementation agreements (IAs). PPAs required that the transactions be denominated in South Africa Rand and that contracts have 20-year tenors. IAs were to be signed by the IPPs and DOE and effectively provided a sovereign guarantee of payment to the IPPs, by requiring DOE to make good on these payments in the event of an Eskom default.

The tender program included a strong reliance on non-price factors in bid evaluation. Bidders were required to meet certain minimum thresholds with regard to things like jobs for South Africa citizens, local black ownership and management of project companies, financial contributions to local communities, and spending on local manufacturing content. Because these localization measures accounted for 30 per cent of bid value, they played an important role in the REIPPPP procurement process—much more important than the 10 per cent maximum bid value that non-price factors were required to play in other South African government procurement programs.

The vast majority of program stakeholders, from both the public and private sectors, judged REIPPPP to be highly successful over its first four rounds. Over this period, South Africa ranked among the top ten countries globally in terms of renewable energy IPP investments, ahead of Canada, Brazil, Spain, and France. Between 2012 and 2015, the program attracted US$19 billion in private investment in 92 IPP projects, totaling 6,327 MW, with wind and solar PV prices among the lowest in the world. To put REIPPPP's achievement in perspective, the total installed generating capacity of a country like Nigeria (with a population of 190 million vs. 50 million in South Africa) is usually listed at about 6,000 MW, with only about 3,500 MW actually available on any given day.

9.3.3 Assessment

REIPPPP is a unique story of IPP project development in SSA. This was a domestically designed, managed, and financed program, not designed and driven by donors, DFIs, or MDBs, although small amounts of donor funding were used by REIPPPP early on, and MDBs like the International Finance Corporation (IFC) eventually provided some of the financing for the individual IPP projects. The program was initially catalyzed by South African policy positions on climate change mitigation, and the desire to achieve local economic and community benefits—an emphasis that has been generally lacking in IPP project development programs designed by development partners. But REIPPPP's momentum was maintained after it became clear that the program was bringing down the costs of renewable power (like solar) to levels below that of coal-fired power, and could be used as a way of building new generation capacity far more quickly than was possible with thermal or large hydro projects.

Nor was the program a haphazard and undisciplined effort to add generation capacity in a fashion that bore no relationship to formal sector planning efforts, as has been the case with so many IPP projects in SSA. The amounts and types of power targeted by REIPPPP were determined via a well-established, formal government planning process that involved ministerial determinations based on the government's Integrated Resource Plan, which specified how much generation capacity was needed, from which sources, and whether from Eskom or IPP projects.

But how did all this come about? Chapter 8 describes how single-buyer utilities in Africa, which also generate power, have worked effectively to maintain their dominant positions in these powers sectors, in order to continue benefiting from patronage appointments and rent-seeking opportunities. One way they do this is by resisting the introduction of IPP projects or by controlling their entry and operations to ensure against potentially embarrassing competition. When REIPPPP started, Eskom and the rest of the South African power sector were already long overdue for major reforms involving or enabling private participation. Eskom, as a vertically integrated single-buyer and principal generator of power (and the largest power utility in Africa) had already spent years protecting its monopoly status by, among other things, almost completely blocking the introduction of IPP projects.

What changed by 2011 to allow South Africa to sign more investment, for more IPP projects, than had been achieved across the entire African continent over the previous 20 years? REIPPPP exploited a window of opportunity created by the confluence of two factors: (i) a brief (and somewhat inexplicable) period of high-level political support for renewable energy, which coincided with a period during which Eskom's control over the power sector weakened; and (ii) intense private sector interest in and support for the IPP procurement program.

High-Level Political Support

When REIPPPP began its tender program in 2011, it benefited from a relatively long history of policy statements supporting the use of renewable energy for climate change mitigation and economic development, especially job creation. But this was not too different from other African countries. However, what was different was the degree of high-level political support that was signaled by South African President Zuma's surprise commitments to green energy during the COP15 and COP17 meetings. The support from the president is not easily explained—South Africa voluntarily committed to reduce carbon emissions although it faced no binding obligations under the United Nations Framework Convention on Climate Change or the Kyoto protocol. Moreover, the government proceeded with this commitment even though its Copenhagen offer was subject to the receipt of financial assistance that never materialized. For a country so dependent on coal for its energy, and facing extraordinary poverty and development challenges, this was a striking break from the past.

This political support for renewable energy occurred at a time when Eskom's dominance over the country's power sector was diminishing. Ever since a 1998 government White Paper recommended power sector reforms in South Africa, including the unbundling and partial divestiture of Eskom, the utility lobbied vigorously to block reforms and limit the use of IPPs. Over the years, it was supported in these efforts by powerful political interests like labor unions, economic interests like energy user groups, as well as senior politicians and sector officials who benefited from patronage appointments and rent-seeking opportunities

(Eberhard and Godinho, 2017). Eskom had historically been a strong and creditworthy utility, but that situation changed because of debt incurred to finance a very large investment program and NERSA's unwillingness to approve tariff increases that would cover all of Eskom's costs, some of which it judged to be imprudent. So, revenues began falling short of operating or total costs. Eskom's financial and managerial performance began to deteriorate and highlighted the need for performance improvements and strengthened creditworthiness. The emergence of load shedding in 2008 and Eskom's failure (or unwillingness) to add new capacity through IPP projects using the 2009 REFiT, put the utility in a vulnerable position and allowed DOE to wrest away control of the renewable energy program in 2011. DOE effectively ended the REFiTS and started REIPPPP.

In retrospect, REIPPPP did a remarkable job of maintaining political support for as long as it did. Some the characteristics that maintained this support, included the following:

- **Rapid-response problem solving.** The largely ad hoc institutional status of the DOE IPP unit, acting at arm's length from DOE as a kind of dedicated project office, allowed an operating approach that emphasized rapid-response problem solving to help the program show early progress and pre-empt criticism.
- **An effective program champion.** The DOE IPP unit had a team leader who could interact convincingly with senior government officials, effectively explain and defend the program in meetings with stakeholders, deal with development partners, select and manage consultants, communicate with the private sector, and manage a complicated procurement and contracting process.
- **A compelling case for renewable energy.** The DOE IPP unit repeatedly made the case for the program at every opportunity, in informal government meetings, conferences, cabinet meetings, and presentations before Parliament—no one was allowed to forget that the program had strong justifications.
- **Off-budget program funding.** The transaction costs for the REIPPPP program were high, but REIPPPP established a mechanism to capture fees from closed projects. This self-sustaining status kept the program off budget and helped pre-empt criticism that it was too expensive.
- **High quality transaction advice.** The DOE IPP unit selected experienced local and international transaction advisers to guide program implementation. By maintaining the high quality of transaction advice, the DOE unit avoided criticism from the private sector and independent industry experts.
- **Accelerated rollout of generating capacity.** Despite the high initial cost of renewable energy, at least when the program started, REIPPPP offered South Africans something they thought they urgently needed in 2011, a relatively fast way to roll out new power-generating capacity.
- **Sharp cost reductions because of competitive tendering.** The shift to competitive tendering helped tariffs come down precipitously after Round 1, and

this reduction was a major factor in the government's willingness to continue its support for REIPPPP as a "successful" program.

- **Non-negotiable program characteristics.** The REIPPPP team used non-negotiable bid documents and contracts to control bidder behavior and restrict opportunities for gamesmanship or time-consuming negotiations. All of this resonated with government officials who wanted to make sure that REIPPPP was managed by, and in the interests of, South Africans, rather than private businesses.
- **Economic development benefits.** REIPPPP's economic development requirements have been controversial, confusing, and expensive for bidders to respond to, but helped to generate support for these programs from politicians and the general public (Leigland and Eberhard, 2018).

Private Sector Attraction: The Economy

Along with political support, the program needed private-sector interest to be successful. And to some extent, private-sector support helped maintain political support because private companies, local financiers, donors, DFIs, MDBs, and local media gave the program extremely positive reviews, almost without exception. Private-sector support was generated in two ways: (i) through basic program characteristics that were a function of the size and health of the South African economy; and (ii) intentional features of the program design that were of particular interest to the private sector.

- **Strong economy.** Much of the program's attraction for investors can summed up by the fact that in 2011, South African ranked at or near the top of all African countries in terms of things like government effectiveness, regulatory quality, political stability, control of corruption, rule of law, market size, economic freedom, and ease of doing business.
- **Program size.** REIPPPP was the largest national IPP program ever attempted in Africa. The program immediately caught the attention of the global renewable energy industry, particularly because the European renewable energy markets had been in decline.
- **The South African banking sector.** The country's banking sector was the largest, deepest, and most sophisticated in Africa. While perceived to be conservative and expensive, it was essential in helping REIPPPP achieve so many closed transactions in a relatively short period of time.
- **Other advisory resources.** South Africa also had a relatively wide array of other kinds of sophisticated advisory services needed for REIPPPP projects, including legal firms and technical consultants to help with the design of competitive bids and project implementation.
- **Investment grade rating.** South Africa's investment grade rating (matched by Eskom's rating) meant that banks and investors would accept sovereign

guarantees without requiring an additional layer of political risk insurance, as would be the case in virtually every other African country.

Private Sector Attraction: Program Design Features

In addition to basic attractions like the size of the program and health of the economy, REIPPPP included a number of design features that also helped attract private sector interest:

- **Potential project profitability.** REIPPPP began by offering developers opportunities to make reasonable profits. Round 1 tariff caps were set at or near previous REFiT levels, meaning that the projects could potentially make equity returns close to 17 per cent. This helped initiate investor interest in the program, which carried over into subsequent bid rounds.
- **Multiple bidding rounds.** A key design alteration made before August 2011 was to change REIPPPP from a once-off tender to a rolling series of bid rounds. This helped build confidence in the program among operators and investors and generated increasing levels of competition as more and more of these players begin to participate in subsequent tender rounds.
- **Exemption from PPP regulations.** Exempting IPP projects from national PPP regulations allowed REIPPPP to avoid time-consuming PPP rules that would have dramatically slowed the program.
- **Sovereign guarantees.** The program benefited from sovereign guarantees written into the IAs to back Eskom's purchase of power from the renewable energy projects. These sovereign guarantees were required despite Eskom's investment-grade credit rating because of concerns regarding Eskom's rapidly weakening financial standing.
- **Business-friendly approach.** The DOE IPP unit had extensive experience working with the private sector, and exhibited none of the mistrust of private business that sometimes characterized other government agencies in South Africa. Dialogue with private sector counterparts on key REIPPPP issues was maintained during all of the bid rounds.
- **Bankable documentation and efficient tendering.** REIPPPP implemented an efficient, professional procurement process that issued timely RFPs, employed clear qualification and evaluation criteria, used bankable contract documents, as well as appropriate credit enhancements.

9.3.4 The Disruption of Eskom's Status Quo

As the success of REIPPPP grew, from an untested program using an approach (tendering vs. REFiTS) that was not recommended by donors, DFIs, or MDBs, Eskom began to pay attention to it and take steps to slow down the program. It quickly became apparent that Eskom's transmission planning was lagging behind, or had not been adequately synchronized with, the REIPPPP award of new generation projects.[2] The risk was growing that some completed renewable energy IPP projects would not be able to connect to the grid in a timely fashion because of Eskom transmission delays.

Simultaneously with REIPPPP's growing success and Eskom's increasing concerns, high-level political support for REIPPPP began to wane as the president and his cabinet began to focus on nuclear power as a solution to the country's power needs. By the end of 2014, the South African president had apparently decided to promote an arrangement with Russian state nuclear firm, Rosatom, to build 9.6 GW of nuclear power generating capacity in South Africa by 2030. At that point, any existing high-level support for REIPPPP, from the presidency or his cabinet, sharply diminished, and cabinet ministers remained silent as Eskom began to reassert its control over the power sector.

Eskom declared in mid-2016 that it would not sign additional PPAs for renewable projects because of what it considered to be the high costs of these long-term commitments. This left a number of procured projects in limbo, along with the entire sequence of new bid rounds. Over two dozen IPP projects procured in 2015 remained unsigned until April 2018. By then, President Zuma had resigned (in early 2018), his nuclear ambitions for the country had largely been discredited, and his cabinet had been mostly replaced. Plans were initiated to restart REIPPPP, possibly with a fifth bid round to be announced in early 2019. But REIPPPP had suffered at least some long-term reputational damage. The tender requirements that had incentivized bidders to source equipment locally had the intended effect of facilitating local business start-ups after 2011. But with Eskom's refusal to sign PPAs, the local industrial development component of REIPPPP came to a halt and many of these local businesses closed.

By 2018, it was clear that Eskom was experiencing major conflicts of interest in its role as the single-buyer of power. Despite the success of REIPPPP, the utility had been effective in protecting the sector status quo—from 2000 to September 2018, the IPP project share of power generation had increased from 5 per cent to only 8.8 per cent (Laing, 2018). And the sector status quo had facilitated Eskom overstaffing, mismanagement, and unprecedented levels of internal looting during the last years of Zuma's presidency. By the end of 2017, Eskom had lost all three of its investment grade credit ratings. In July 2018, Eskom audits disclosed

[2] The problem was generally not the transmission connections to the nearest substations that most developers were funding or constructing themselves, but rather the deep connection investments that Eskom needed to make to strengthen the transmission backbone in order to evacuate all the new energy that was generated in these remote areas. Eskom claimed that these investments were unaffordable, and pointed out that as the off-taker it would eventually be liable for deemed energy payments—payments for energy that could be produced, but is not produced because it cannot be fed into the grid. So, Eskom's inability or unwillingness to make these deep connection investments became a perverse rationale for slowing down REIPPPP.

R19.6 billion (US$1.5 billion) in irregular expenditure since 2012, including from "criminal conduct." At that point, Eskom's outstanding debt totaled R387 billion, almost 60 per cent of which had been sovereign guaranteed—almost three-quarters of all sovereign-guaranteed borrowing by the country's state-owned enterprises (SOEs) (Hofstatter, 2018). Declining power sales, increasing costs, and repeated unsuccessful requests to the regulator to allow double-digit tariff increases led African energy expert, Anton Eberhard, to characterize Eskom's situation as the "classic utility death spiral" (Businesstech, 2017). By the end of 2018 the utility was close to financial collapse, as new rounds of massive power cuts began to disrupt the economy. In February 2019, the newly elected president accepted the recommendations of an expert panel and announced that Eskom would be unbundled into three separate government-owned companies handling generation, transmission, and distribution.

The process of reforming Eskom will be long, expensive, and contentious. South Africa's labor unions see unbundling as a prelude to privatization and have vowed to resist the process, with violence, if necessary. Other vested sector interests that have benefited from the status quo will likewise resist change. The process may or may not be successful. But it is clear that the country has experienced the kind of disruptive moment described in the introduction. And that moment was precipitated by the success of REIPPPP.

9.4 Uganda: Global Energy Transfer Feed-in Tariff (GET FiT) Program[3]

9.4.1 Introduction

With a population of just over 39 million and a GDP per capita of US$2,350, Uganda is categorized as a "least-developed country" by OECD. The country has achieved some development successes. The proportion of the population living in poverty more than halved from 1993 to 2013. The incidence of extreme poverty measured by the international poverty line of US$1.25 a day, declined from 72 per cent of the population in 1993 to 31 per cent in 2013. But efforts to continue this pro-poor momentum have slowed recently as economic growth has slowed. Average annual GDP growth was 4.5 per cent in the five years to FY17, compared to 7 per cent achieved during the 1990s and early 2000s. This slowdown in growth reflects a number of problems faced by the economy, including adverse weather, the civil unrest in neighboring South Sudan, global economic uncertainties, and private sector credit constraints.

[3] This section relies heavily on Republic of Uganda, 2014; World Bank, 2014; and DFID, 2018.

Uganda was one of the few Africa countries that completely unbundled its power sector beginning in 1999, in response to the World Bank's structural adjustment lending programs focused on the reform of SOEs. The power sector was separated into separate companies responsible for generation, transmission, and distribution. The government also introduced private participation into the sector via concessions for generation and the main distribution grid. A regulator (ERA) was created to promote a least-cost approach to resource development and stimulate investment and competition in the sector.

The transmission company Uganda Electricity Transmission Company Ltd. (UETCL) functions as the system operator, dispatcher of almost all power generated in the country, and the sector's single buyer of bulk power (and signatory to all PPAs). But UETCL, like the other unbundled companies, remains state owned despite long-standing plans to privatize it so it is not completely independent of government influence. Legislation requires that IPP projects be developed under the direction of the regulator, ERA, while UETCL shares responsibility for public engineering, procurement, and construction (EPC) projects and traditional PPPs with the generation company. However, in several cases over the last ten years, the Ministry of Energy and Mineral Development (MEMD) has taken the lead on large power procurements despite the apparent absence of legislation authorizing it to do so. In 2005, Umeme Ltd. became the major privately owned electricity distributor in Uganda after winning a 20-year concession contract.

Uganda has one of the lowest electricity access rates for households in the world with just over 20 per cent of households with grid access. In rural areas, only about 7 per cent of homes are connected to the grid. The government has criticized Umeme for high prices and poor-quality electricity services, and claims it has not done enough to improve access. The country ranks 32nd out of 45 SSA countries in terms of business claims of losses due to power outages. In 2018, Ugandan President Museveni indicated his unhappiness with Umeme and by the end of the year said the concession contract might not be renewed.

9.4.2 REFiT Supplemented with GET FiT

By the time Uganda's long-delayed Bujagali hydropower project began limited operation in 2011 the government realized that it needed more generating capacity to avoid power shortages and reliance on expensive rented thermal power plants.[4] The government was already planning several mega-project power solutions like the Chinese-built 600 MW Karuma hydro power plant. But more

[4] Bujagali is a 250 MW IPP project that is among the first and largest privately financed hydropower projects in SSA.

generating capacity was needed in the interim so government officials decided to accept donor offers of funding and technical assistance to initiate a program to exploit renewable energy resources by contracting with small-scale IPP projects.[5] For reasons having to do with climate change, renewable energy schemes were highly attractive to development partners who had worked with Uganda on earlier energy sector activities. These development partners were more than willing to offer financial and technical support, so the government's responsibilities for managing and financing the program were minimal.

The government had already created a REFiT program in 2007 with a two-year life-span. FiTs were set at levels expected to encourage private developers to build and operate renewable energy-generating facilities. After slow acceptance by project developers, the program was extended from 2011 to 2014. But REFiT's initial tariff levels were not high enough to attract developers. Uganda's sector regulator was also reluctant to raise the FiTs because of affordability impacts on government and rate payers who had long benefited from tariffs well below cost recovery levels.

The German development bank KfW and other donors and MDBs suggested a solution that was attractive to the government. The development partners offered to provide extra financial assistance to these small renewable energy IPP projects. The scheme, known as Global Energy Transfer Feed-in Tariff (GET FiT), was formally launched by ERA in May 2013, with support from the KfW and DFIs and donors representing Norway, Germany, the United Kingdom, and the European Union. Four competitive tenders were run from 2013 to 2015 to select privately financed, small-scale renewable energy projects for support. Initially, the projects involved small hydro, biomass, and bagasse. In January 2014, a special EU-supported tender was launched focusing on solar PV, which evaluated bids in terms of price as well as quality (earlier bid rounds had looked only at quality). GET FiT provided three kinds of "market enhancements":

- The first was an output-based top-up payment to the IPPs to allow a reasonable return on investment, while minimizing the need to increase REFiTs and the electricity retail tariff. This top-up payment, referred to as a "premium" payment (or FiP, i.e., "feed-in premium"), was made available to small renewable energy projects on a competitive, first-come-first-serve application basis (as long as the funding lasted). The premium payment was designed to increase the cash flow of the projects during their initial operating years, thus significantly increasing the projects' internal rates of return.

[5] The European Union, through the EU Africa Infrastructure Trust Fund, indicated that it would be willing to provide €15 million in grants to support a special competitive bidding program for solar SPPs.

The total GET FiT payment for a specific project was determined relative to estimates of the total energy (GWh) the power plant was expected to generate during its contracted period (20 years). Half of the GET FiT premium was paid to the project after it began commercial operation. The remaining half was paid over the first five years of plant operation. The premium was adjusted during this period for any deviation between the power plant's projected plant output and actual operation. Decisions regarding which projects benefited from these payments were made by an independent "investment committee" recruited from academia, non-government organizations (NGOs), and the private sector. Determinations were based on criteria such as technical and economic viability, and international environmental and social standards.

- A second kind of GET FiT "market enhancement" was offered by the government in coordination with several development partners. It came out of an assessment that identified priority risk mitigation instruments for attracting private sector participation in small renewable energy projects. The World Bank agreed to provide partial risk guarantees (PRGs) to support the development of these IPP projects. The PRGs were required to mitigate against PPA and IA payment risks, by backstopping letters of credit issued by commercial banks, which developers could draw down in the event that the transmission company (as the single buyer) interrupted its payments. In effect, the PRG's were expected to securely allocate those risks to the public sector, which the private sector could not manage, thus reducing the private sector's risk exposure under these investments.
- The third market enhancement was a private financing mechanism that offered debt and equity at competitive rates. Working with selected local Ugandan commercial banks, Deutsche Bank offered long-term project financing needed to help projects close financing gaps. The terms and conditions of this financing reflected the improved risk profiles of projects supported by the two previously mentioned GET FiT market enhancements. This financing was designed as an additional facility—it was not a dedicated fund focusing exclusively on GET FiT projects, and private developers were thus free to obtain financing from any available source.

In addition to financing, the expert support provided by development partners helped with the overall design and management of the REFiT program. For example, KfW worked with the Ugandan regulator to streamline and standardize the program's PPAs and IAs. The standardized agreements were eventually used for all of the REFiT projects. The documents reduced project transaction costs by accelerating the signing processes and contributing to the bankability of projects with clear terms and conditions.

9.4.3 Assessment

A number of facts that need to be kept in mind when considering the performance of GET FiT are outlined in the following subsections.

Program Targets

When the program began in April 2013, GET FiT's goal was to help REFiT reach a target of 15 approved projects and 125 MW of total installed capacity. This target was revised upwards in 2014 to 170 MW. By early 2018, after the bid rounds had ended, it seemed clear that 17 projects would be added to the grid by the program, for an installed capacity of 158 MW. Two of these were solar IPP projects (a total of 20 MW); the rest were a mixture of small hydro, biomass, and bagasse.

Stakeholder Assessments

Stakeholder assessments have been positive. As PPAs were being signed for the first four GET FiT projects in early 2015, the World Bank's Public–Private Infrastructure Advisory Facility (PPIAF) conducted an international "PPP Short Story Competition." The winning entry was an account of the "tangible positive outcomes" of GET FiT:

> The Get FiT approach leverages private investments in the energy sector and thereby secures energy supply at affordable cost, which generates direct economic benefits for Ugandan citizens (Rieger, 2015).

By early 2018, most of the 17 projects had reach financial close and were under construction if not already commissioned. All of the donor money allocated to support the program had been committed. There was no indication that tendering would continue, but UK Department for International Development (DFID—GET FiT's largest donor) had extended its involvement in the program from March 2020 to the end of 2024 to accommodate delayed projects that would need premium payments.

In GET FiT's 2017 Annual Report, ERA declared that the program had helped the country's electricity supply industry "shine as a perfect example of how best to leverage support from development partners to attract and harness private sector capital for infrastructure development" (GET FiT, 2018). In a project review published in early 2018, DFID claimed that "The program is creating a transformational shift in the investment climate for renewable energy in Uganda" (DFID, 2018, 10). The DFID review also noted that despite the transaction orientation and small scale of the program, it was "playing an important role in strengthening the Government systems that it works through" (13).

Donor Design and Ownership

GET FiT was a program designed, financed, and implemented almost exclusively by Uganda's development partners rather than by government actors or agencies. REFiT was a Ugandan government program, but GET FiT was primarily a donor program, and the donors were of course pursuing their own objectives in supporting the program. In the case of the United Kingdom, which provided over half of the total program costs (£51 million of £92 million), the main objective was climate change mitigation. The United Kingdom's financing came from its International Climate Fund, and its objective was to "assist Republic of Uganda in pursuing a climate resilient low-carbon development path resulting in growth, poverty reduction and climate change mitigation" (DFID, 2013, 2). KfW supplied some of the financing needed by the program and also managed GET FiT pursuant to a contract with DFID. KfW set up and chaired the investment committee, which determined which projects received premium payments, and also recruited and managed the implementation consultant and evaluation consultant, who handled program implementation, monitoring, and evaluation. KfW played the central program role in making sure that various international environmental social standards were observed by the projects, that the government was moving quickly enough to connect projects to the national grid, and monitored and managed all other program risks. Apparently out of concern about management of the donor money, DFID noted that "no money goes through GOU systems" and the DFID–KfW contract had "low proximity to GOU in terms of delivery" (DFID, 2018).

Program Requirements

As managed by development partners, the qualification requirements for GET FiT solar program bidders were quite onerous, especially considering that the amount of power auctioned was quite small. Requirements for reputational due diligence, technology design, site selection, etc., were as stringent—or more so—than those of REIPPPP, a much larger program. Equipment specifications in the RFP were very detailed, and included things like requirements for cabling to be used in the plants (Kruger and Eberhard, 2016). In terms of project size, the solar bids were strictly limited to 5 MW, and could not be more than 3 km away from the grid. Bidders had to conduct their own feasibility and grid stability studies, despite a lack of information provided by the government. Cost of grid extensions were to be covered by the developers. All bids were required to comply with IFC environmental and social performance standards. Bid bonds, higher than those required by REIPPPP, were also required. Later evaluations concluded that "possibly unnecessarily detailed and stringent requirements" led to high costs and risks for project developers and resulted in relatively high power costs for the government (Kruger and Eberhard, 2016).

Government Involvement

The need for FiPs was driven in the first place by ERA's unwillingness to set FiTs at appropriate levels and understand that the tariffs would need to be escalated over time. ERA finally made some changes in a limited way during 2013. A fundamental review of REFiT levels was carried out at the end of 2014 and recommended further increases in base FiTs, which eventually happened in 2016. But it was not just tariff setting that was problematic, the government was also extremely slow to connect IPP projects to the grid, and very slow to extend customer grid connections in under-served areas. The 2017 GET FiT Annual Report noted that 80 per cent of Ugandans still lacked access to electricity, despite the increases in generation. Another UK concern was the sustainability of social and environmental standards without someone like KfW enforcing them:

> This level of scrutiny and enforcement may not continue for projects outside of GET FiT, and it is unlikely that ERA would have as strong support from the other GOU organizations to deliver this enhanced approach (DFID, 2018).

Government Capacity Issues

One of the reasons why Uganda's development partners took on almost all responsibility for designing and implementing GET FiT was the lack of government capacity to do so. In 2018, DFID admitted that the amount of technical assistance, legal services, and implementation management required to successfully implement GET FiT was "more extensive than originally planned." DFID noted that in working with ERA they "continuously struggled to ensure that off-taker planning and investing is aligned with the need to connect each power producer with a PPA to the grid" (DFID, 2018). In other words, connection infrastructure was not being planned or built in a timely fashion. The regulator also needed help to prepare a new grid connection code and a framework for regulating the wheeling of power (transmission through a third-party network). Improvements were needed to the framework for compliance monitoring of transmission and distribution licenses. Basic capacity building was also needed to accelerate the regulator's processing of project license approvals, to keep pace with the results of the GET FiT auctions. Above all, the sector lacked coordination and comprehensive least-cost planning. DFID recognized the need for technical assistance and capacity building as part of GET FiT, but the final project budget breakdown shows only 2 per cent of the GET FiT program total (less than £2 million) allocated for technical assistance, all of it to the regulator (DFID, 2018).

Private Investment

Very little private investment was actually leveraged by the program. DFID admits that only one of the IPPs (Kakira Bagasse) accessed commercial bank debt for all of the financing needed for its GET FiT project. Of the 17 final GET FiT projects, 12 of them were completely debt financed by DFIs. Only four had commercial loans—two of these were backed by the developers' corporate balance sheets, and only two involved project finance, the conventional financing mechanism for IPP projects. Because only the project-financed IPP projects were eligible for PRG support, and these developers found risk coverage elsewhere, no PRGs were used as part of GET FiT. DFID explains the absence of commercial finance in terms of a lack of technical competence and energy sector experience among local banks. But in DFID's words, "the project will create a sustainable and growing private sector-led market for electricity generation in Uganda" (DFID, 2018). The "market enhancements" described earlier were intended to deal with the main obstacles to private finance. None of this happened. The only kind of financing successfully leveraged by GET FiT came from DFIs.

9.4.4 Disruptive Moment or Business as Usual?

Most stakeholders have judged GET FiT to have been a successful program, confirming that renewable energy IPPs can be rolled out relatively quickly at reasonably low cost. But GET FiT seems not to have triggered a "disruptive moment" for the government, as described in section 9.1. GET FiT is officially acknowledged as a success, but there seem to be no plans to continue the IPP program. Instead, the government is currently moving decisively away from private participation by putting its faith in the ability of two new, large hydropower projects to produced power less expensively than IPPs. These are power plants financed and built by China, the 183 MW Isimba plant and the 600 MW Karuma plant. Both projects will be owned by the government.

The Ugandan government has long had a love–hate relationship with power sector reform and private participation in the sector. On the one hand, Uganda was the first African country to follow the power sector reform recommendations of the World Bank during the late 1990s, when structural adjustment lending was being used to reform SOEs. By 2005, Uganda had unbundled its power sector into separate companies and begun the process of structuring private concessions for power generation and distribution (Eberhard et al., 2016). Uganda's Bujagali project, strongly supported by the World Bank, was the first and is still among the largest hydropower IPP projects in SSA.

But like other countries that unenthusiastically acceded to MDB reform demands during the structural adjustment years in order to continue receiving funding, Uganda never fully embraced private participation in its power sector. Those reforms remain highly controversial in the country. All of the unbundled sector entities are still government owned and the transmission company acts as a traditional single buyer of electricity. The long and painful process of developing the Bujagali project apparently confirmed for many Ugandan officials that IPP projects are costlier and take much longer to develop than conventional projects procured and managed by governments (Meyer et al., 2018). This attitude became apparent in 2015 when the Ugandan parliament approved government participation in the two Chinese-built hydropower projects mentioned earlier. The process leading up to approval was highly politicized, marked by allegations of corruption and an almost complete lack of competition and transparency. The two projects also seem to reflect exceptionally poor power sector planning. Since Isimba and Karuma came on line in 2019 the country's power supply is expected to exceed demand by as much a 100 per cent (Meyer et al., 2018). Because most of this new power involves capacity payments or take-or-pay arrangements, the government will be forced to pay for much more power than it can sell to end users.

Finally, the development partners behind GET FiT probably ensured a lack of sector disruption by avoiding a head-on confrontation over the issues of sector reform. In order to ensure smooth implementation of the program and avoid the opposition of entrenched sector interests, neither the generation company (UEGCL), nor the single buyer of power from IPPs, the transmission company (UETCL), were directly involved in the program. The government counterpart for GET FiT was the regulator, ERA, because it was nominally authorized to develop IPP projects. But this meant that the program did nothing to build the capacity of the sector's single buyer of electricity to run future auctions, much less challenge the monopoly, top-down, structure of the sector. The ability of a program like this to achieve sustainable sector change was questioned by program evaluators (Castalia, 2016).

9.5 Zambia: Scaling Solar[6]

9.5.1 Introduction

Zambia is classified by the OECD as a least-developed country. It has a population of just over 14 million and a GDP per capita of US$3,997. Over 60 per cent of the population lives below the national poverty line. Life expectancy is just 49 years (ten years below the average for LICs) and indicators like under-five child mortality and maternal mortality are very high even judged by LIC standards.

But Zambia has had a period of sustained economic success. The economy grew at 5.7 per cent annually over the last decade and Zambia was among the ten fastest growing economies of SSA in 2012. This fast growth enabled it to attain the equivalent of lower MIC status on the basis of its nominal per capita income

[6] This section relies heavily on Fergusson et al., 2015; Kruger and Eberhard, 2016; and DFID, 2017.

(although OECD still classifies Zambia as a least-developed country because of other problems). The government's development plans now aim to reduce poverty, create jobs, and make Zambia a prosperous MIC by 2030.

Starting in 2015 the Zambian economy, which depends heavily on copper exports, began to experience economic shocks related to the drop in worldwide commodity prices and a severe drought that reduced hydropower generation in the country and triggered an electricity shortages.[7] The government is now requesting support from the International Monetary Fund (IMF), who will likely stress measures meant to reduce government expenditure and increase revenue, stabilize the kwacha exchange rate, reduce inflation and interest rates, practice better debt public debt management, and restore market confidence.

One priority area targeted for infrastructure improvement in Zambia electricity supply. Zambia's power sector is dominated by ZESCO Ltd., a vertically integrated, state-owned utility that acts as the sector's single buyer of power. There is no longer a legal requirement for ZESCO to act as the single buyer, but it continues to play this role by default, as the owner of the transmission system and the licensed system operator (Chimbaka, 2017). The government has talked for a decade about ending ZESCO's monopoly status in the sector and introducing an independent system operator, but such reforms have not yet materialized.

ZESCO supplies power to everyone in the country except a large proportion of the country's copper mining companies who are supplied by Copperbelt Energy Corporation (CEC), a private company that purchases power from ZESCO and uses its own transmission network to supply the mines, the largest category of electricity consumer. But ZESCO cannot cover operating costs largely because tariffs are 30–40 per cent underpriced. Part of the problem with tariffs is the fact that rates were negotiated with mining companies years ago, and have not increased to reflect changing costs. Other areas of potential hidden costs, like bill collection and transmission and distribution (T&D) losses, are largely under control, but overstaffing is high. Electricity access in rural areas is only about 4 per cent.

The sector also lacks long-term planning capability. That led to a gradual overreliance on hydropower and subsequent power shortages when drought affected water levels in 2015. The sector currently lacks least-cost planning as well as a comprehensive strategy for generation procurement. The sector has an independent regulatory agency, the Energy Regulation Board (ERB), which is responsible for licensing, tariff setting, and service standards. But ERB lacks the willingness or ability to maintain cost-reflective tariffs.

The government has signed several different kinds of IPP projects, including the Sinohydro Kafue Gorge Lower hydro IPP, the TATA Itezhi-Tezhi hydro IPP, and the Maamba Coal-Fired Power IPP. Other IPP projects have been completed or are in advanced stages of preparation. Beginning with its 2006 national

[7] At the time, hydropower accounted for 90 per cent of the electricity generation in Zambia.

development strategy document, "Vision 2030," the government announced intentions to add more renewable energy to the country's power mix, but a focus specifically on renewable energy IPP projects began to germinate only after the experiences with renewable energy programs in South Africa and Uganda. The government also hoped to involve the private sector in the power sector improvement process in rural areas, but has been slow to develop an enabling environment to facilitate off-grid power projects financed by private entities.

In 2014, the government incorporated the Industrial Development Corporation (IDC) to take over government ownership of 33 SOEs, including ZESCO. IDC is mandated to take an independent commercial approach to overseeing government's interest in these companies. This includes helping the companies improve their internal operations, raise commercial finance, develop supporting infrastructure, and co-finance investments with the private sector. The government has also given IDC responsibility for directly taking on new greenfield infrastructure projects with private sector participation. Thus, IDC became the chief counterpart for the Scaling Solar program.

9.5.2 Scaling Solar

In 2015, IFC Transaction Advisory Services Department proposed a plan to the government, which involved development and financing of several large-scale solar PV IPP projects to be procured through an IFC-designed program that became known as Scaling Solar. The program represented millions of dollars in assistance and very low risks to the government because virtually every important aspect of the program would be handled by IFC, from project site location, document preparation, procurement management, to project financing. The government agreed, IDC became the IFC counterpart for program implementation, and in July 2015 a request for pre-qualification was issued for two projects. Forty-eight solar developers responded and 11 were prequalified, all well known in the international market place. In February 2016 a RFP was issued to the prequalified firms, and after proposals were submitted and evaluated, the winning bids were announced in June 2016. The tenders resulted in winning bids of 6c/kWh for a 52 MW project (won by a consortium consisting of NEOEN and First Solar) and 7.8c/kWh for a 34 MW project (won by ENEL Green Power). These bids were lower than the best prices achieved by the South African REIPPPP Program and comparable to prices achieved in the most advanced of frontier solar markets. A second round of Scaling Solar tendering was eventually implemented in Zambia, targeting 500 MW.[8]

Scaling Solar represented a change in IFC's thinking about investment in renewable power IPP projects, which was heavily influenced by a survey of

[8] A second Scaling Solar program was announced in Senegal in February 2016. A third was announced in Madagascar in May 2016. And a fourth was kicked off in Ethiopia in January 2017.

potential solar markets in Africa as well as the successes of South Africa's REIPPPP. REIPPPP demonstrated how to attract large developers by directly addressing their perceptions of risks and uncertainties. Investors had not been attracted to solar IPP projects in SSA because FiTs, promoted by donors, DFIs, and MDBs, had not targeted the right amount of solar power in the right locations. Moreover, directly negotiated contracts were too slow and expensive to conclude because they did not involve competitive pricing, entailed high transaction costs, were hampered by limited government capacity to negotiate deals, and plagued by high perceived risk. REIPPPP attracted large investors with scale, repetition, transparency, bankable project documentation, deep financial markets, and highly capacitated, private sector-friendly program management. Most of this could not be replicated in other African countries, at least not without outside help.

The intention behind Scaling Solar was to offer the following: (i) delivery speed and efficiency through bankable template documents, "stapled" financing (automatically available to winning bidders) to help avoid drawn-out negotiations, and low-cost tender preparations; (ii) optimization and risk management through site selection to minimize uncertainty, ensuring each project is optimized for the grid, with stapled political risk insurance and off-taker credit enhancement to lower risks; and (iii) economies of scale by encouraging multiple auction rounds (and eventually involving multiple countries to create a regional market).

In some respects, the IDC provided some of the same kinds of responsiveness and flexibility that characterized the effective management of REIPPPP by the South African DOE IPP unit. But the key to Scaling Solar was the role of the IFC in arranging, coordinating, and providing virtually everything needed for the program to reach financially closed deals, with a considerable amount of assistance from other MDBs, DFIs, and donors. The IFC offered a "one-stop-shop" for coordinating several WBG instruments and guiding IDC counterparts through the entire bid process. Figure 9.1 illustrates the process, which was designed to be completed in 24 months.

IFC functions included the following:

- Preparation of key project documentation, including PPAs and government support agreements. This process reportedly lasted 12 months, involved law firms like Linklaters and Norton Rose, and was paid for by DFID, the Dutch Ministry of Foreign Trade and Development Cooperation, the Danish royal Ministry of Foreign Affairs, and the Private Infrastructure Development Group. The documents were made available to both the government as well as bidders on a non-negotiable basis.[9]

[9] IFC insists that country clients of the Scaling Solar programs accept without changes the standard templates used for project documents like PPAs. Nigeria reportedly wanted to use their own PPA, but IFC refused, and a Scaling Solar program did not move forward in that country (DFID, 2017).

Project Preparation	Bid Preparation	Tender Process & Award	Financial Close	Construction & Operation
- Technical & economic analysis for optimal size & location of PV plants - Site investigations - Legal & regulatory analysis	- "Localization" of template tender documents - "Localization" of template project documents - Attachment of "stapled" financing, insurance, & credit enhancement	- Request for qualification - Bidder consultation - Request for proposals - Proposal review & award - Signing of project documents	- Contracting for equipment, construction & operation - Final project approvals - Finalization of loan agreements, insurance & risk management	- Construction - Commissioning - Operation
6 months			6 months	12 months

Figure 9.1 Scaling Solar Processes and Milestones
Source: Adapted from Fergusson et al., 2015.

- Engagement and management of consultants to carry out feasibility studies, site selection, project size determination, grid stability, interconnection, stability and integration studies, and other due diligence (technical, legal, tax and accounting, insurance, social, and environmental) on behalf of the government. Donors like DFID and US Agency for International Development (USAID) paid for these studies.
- Management of the tender process on behalf of the government, including preparation of the request for quotation (RFQ) and RFP, as well as bid evaluation (each bidder was provided access to the due diligence conducted by the IFC so they would not need to incur these costs).
- Coordination of the development of credit-approved term sheets with in-principle IFC credit committee approval. The term sheets included indicative terms for limited recourse financing from IFC investment (developers would not have to arrange their own financing or guarantees). Of the three tranches of financing deemed necessary for the project, IFC offered one for debt on commercial terms, and one for debt on concessional terms determined by available grant funding. Sourcing the third tranche was left to the sponsors. The two tranches of IFC financing, based on IFC's project due diligence prior to the tender exercise, was the core of the "stapled financing" package made available to winning bidders.
- Coordination of the development of term sheets, political risk insurance from Multilateral Investment Guarantee Agency (MIGA), and PRGs from the World Bank (IDA). Arrange a payment guarantee letter of credit for the developers backed by the IDC. All of this was also part of the stapled financing package.

9.5.3 Assessment

The success of Scaling Solar is tempered by the following key facts about the program.

Project Size

GET FiT successfully used tendering for two small solar IPP projects and became the first SSA country other than South Africa to do so. But Scaling Solar successfully tendered larger projects than GET FiT, by allowing the IFC to select project sites with adequate grid integration where power could be adequately evacuated. All of this permitted IFC to restrict participation in Scaling Solar to only large international developers with the financial resources to implement large projects. Because these kinds of large international firms can tolerate low equity returns on pioneering projects in new markets, the resulting bid prices reached record low levels.

Small Developers

Because of its focus on size and speed, Scaling Solar's pre-qualification criteria effectively excluded smaller developers. The process was rigorous and transparent. Some small bidders did prequalify, but the IFC decided to limit bidding to firms they considered to be the most serious and credible developers with the lowest costs of capital, enabling them to offer the lowest tariffs, and the least risk of failing to reach financial closure.

Local Economic Development

REIPPPP used preferential procurement to incentivize local community development and domestic manufacturing of components used in the IPP projects. And this approach was judged to be successful, at least until Eskom stopped signing PPAs. Scaling Solar took a different approach, focusing on speed of rollout and achieving the lowest possible developer prices. Forcing bidders to spend time and money to ensure local economic benefits, must have seemed counterproductive given these objectives. Scaling Solar did incorporate a mechanism to allow eventual public offerings of project shares on the Lusaka Stock Exchange, with Zambian citizens allowed to buy up to 20 per cent to total project equity. But the average Zambian citizen would not be financially able to purchase such shares.

Tariffs

The record low power prices achieved by Scaling Solar were not fully reflective of normal costs or risks of projects in Zambia because highly concessionary funding was used to prepare and eventually finance the projects. IFC and Zambian officials argue that this is better than subsidizing projects with FiTs or capital grants because the program is better designed and managed, individual projects are better sited, project documentation is more bankable, the process is faster, demonstration effects are more pronounced (facilitating possible replication in other countries), transaction costs for developers are lower, etc. But it is unrealistic for other governments in Africa to assume that 6c/kWh can be routinely achieved, whether or not these governments have access to the full range of supporting services that IFC provided in Zambia on a highly concessional basis. Ultimately the final tariff for any project will always reflect country-specific and project-specific features and, of course, market appetite. There already seem to be cases in other SSA countries where governments are insisting on unrealistically low tariffs because of the Zambia Scaling Solar experience—without the benefit of IFC's preparation and financing. In this way, Scaling Solar has the potential to do serious harm to the renewable power market in Africa.

Benefits of Project De-Risking

In the words of a DFID case study of Scaling Solar, the program "effectively removes material risk from the project" (DFID, 2017). The program structure shifts most of the significant project risks and project development costs away from private developers to the IFC or the government. Bidders do not have to select project sites, obtain access to the land, carry out feasibility studies, select equipment, arrange financing and financial risk mitigation, or prepare and negotiate contracts.[10] IFC not only offered most of the financing, it provided a significant share of it on concessional grounds—something that may have been unnecessary given the interest of commercial banks in these projects (Kruger and Eberhard, 2016). DFID notes that all of this de-risking leaves only a few areas left for differentiation in a competitive bidding exercise, including equity returns, pricing of EPC contracts, and owner's overheads (DFID, 2017). And the ability to compete on the basis of these factors can mostly be reduced to the amount of technical and financial resources available to competing developers (so small developers were effectively excluded from the competition). The kind of message that a tender process of this nature sends to the public and private partners in these projects (or other African governments) is unclear. The low prices resulting from this kind of structured tender process do not accurately reflect the risks of private investment in Zambia. What in a process like this is going to lead to improvements in Zambia's power sector or its ability to provide services to its citizens? What does the process communicate to the private sector about how to do these kinds of projects in countries like Zambia? IFC claims it is creating a market

[10] IDC leased the land for the two sites selected by IFC. After the tender process, the land was subleased to the two project special purpose vehicles for the duration of the PPAs. The two sites already had substation and transmission infrastructure in place. Sponsors needed only to fund and build grid interconnection works, which were specified in the non-negotiable PPAs included with the RFPs (Kruger and Eberhard, 2016).

for solar IPP projects in Zambia, rather than distorting the market, but that claim seems questionable.

Capacity Building

IFC argues that the most effective form of capacity building associated with a Scaling Solar-type program is host country involvement in preparing these projects and managing the procurement process. But the low levels of skills and experience in IDC and ZESCO, combined with a very limited exposure to a single tender exercise almost completely managed by IFC, mean that very little sustainable capacity development has actually taken place. And as DFID's case study points out, Scaling Solar involves almost no focus on the long-term sustainability of the program itself. Things like market structure (grid code amendments), legislation, regulation (IPP project licensing), master planning, and customer pricing, all need to be revised and updated if a program like Scaling Solar is going to be more than a once-off tender exercise. But perhaps more importantly, these kinds of revisions and updates arguably were needed *before* a program like Scaling Solar was implemented. The addition of less than 100 MW is not much of a benefit to a 2,743 MW power sector that has much more fundamental problems than lack of generating capacity. Zambia's sector is plagued by weak planning, faulty regulation and customer pricing, and dominated by a poorly managed, vertically integrated, state-owned utility.

Conflicts of Interest

DFID's case study of Scaling Solar notes that the program poses an "optical challenge" due to the simultaneous involvement of IFC Transaction Advisory and IFC Investments (DFID, 2017). IFC has long noted the possibility of a conflict of interest (COI) in such situations and has responded to critics by maintaining that potential conflicts are managed by a "Chinese wall" that prohibits its advisory services from sharing information with its lending arm (Dawson, 2013). In practice, this is handled mostly by sequencing: IFC normally does not take advisory and investment roles at the same time on a PPP (IEG, 2013). And information is not normally shared between the two kinds of teams because of policies that restrict staff access to internal information outside their business line (IFC, 2009). But Scaling Solar represents a departure from this kind of COI management, presumably in the interests of rolling out much needed generating capacity, while keeping tariffs as low as possible.

Institutional interests were also clearly in play here. By focusing on the rapid development of large projects, involving technology that is relatively straightforward and not site specific (like wind or hydro), and using a standardized template approach to documentation, all of which tailors each project for IFC financing, IFC created an attractive product for clients with poorly managed power sectors and a popular product line for its own business. Speed, size, and replicability clearly are the Scaling Sola priorities. Sector reforms needed to make the best use of this additional capacity, like least-cost planning, pro-poor service extensions, loss reductions, optimized pricing, and capacity building, are not addressed, possibly because they might slow down the project development process or raise questions about the size of the projects or the technology used. Scaling Solar certainly will not lead to an IFC monopoly over solar projects in Africa, as some critics have charged. Other DFIs and MDBs will no doubt attempt to undercut IFC when it comes to financing the projects that IFC has so carefully prepared. But there may be some truth to the claim that commercial finance, as well as other MDBs, are being crowded out of these kinds of deals. With the huge supporting resources supplied by development partners, Scaling Solar has the appearance of a brilliant marketing strategy for IFC to use in its ongoing competition with other financiers, both public and private.[11]

9.5.4 A Disruptive Moment Postponed?

It is not yet clear whether or not Scaling Solar made any contribution to the kind of power sector "disruptive moment" described in the introduction to this chapter. Scaling Solar has been recognized as a successful program in Zambia if only because of its notoriety in SSA: the winning price of 6c/kWh on the NEOEN/First Solar project was lower than the best prices achieved in South Africa and far lower than the average winning price achieved by GET FiT (16.37c/kWh). Even though the Scaling Solar price was the result of heavy subsidization, it established a new benchmark for the kind of pricing that was possible with solar IPP projects. The example was not lost on countries like Uganda and Nigeria, where government officials began to insist on prices of no more than 7–8c/kWh for new projects.

Scaling Solar also peaked government interest in trying to access more renewable power. In late 2017, the Zambian government agreed to initiate a GET FiT program along the lines of the Ugandan predecessor. In line with the government's REFiT strategy, GET FiT Zambia aims to procure 200 MW of renewable energy projects within three years, by signing PPAs with small- to medium-scale IPP projects up to 20 MW. A first phase has involved a tender for up to 100 MW of solar PV capacity, launched in late 2018.

[11] Scaling Solar happened at a time when IFC was aggressively expanding its lending for renewable energy power generation projects. From 2005 to 2008, IFC's lending to IPPs (for both renewable energy and thermal plants) surged into a dominant position in IFC's infrastructure lending portfolio, expanding its share of all commitment from 29 percent in 2001–4, to just over 40 percent of all commitments. But from 2009 to 2012, lending to thermal projects fell off by 32 percent, and lending to renewable energy IPPs (including hydropower projects) remained flat. To maintain power generation's share of the portfolio in the face of sharply increasing lending for transportation projects, IFC ramped up lending for renewable projects by 32 percent over the 2013–16 period (Kenny et al., 2018). Scaling Solar issued its first RFPQ in July 2015.

The extent to which all of this will disrupt the existing top–down monopoly structure of Zambia's power sector is not yet clear. The need to restructure ZESCO and end its sector monopoly has been seriously discussed in Zambia since the mid-1990s (Chimbaka, 2017). ZESCO's performance is clearly below average as compared other utilities in the region. Overstaffing is a serious problem. Development partners have recommended the unbundling of ZESCO, the introduction of transparent competitive procedures for appointment of staff, as well as the implementation of basic utility performance improvement measures like revenue protection programs and advanced metering infrastructure.

In 2017, the Zambian cabinet commissioned a diagnostic study that made recommendations for dealing with ZESCO's "serious operational challenges," which the cabinet approved for implementation by a "Zesco Reforms Implementation Team" headed by the Cabinet Secretary (African Energy, 2018). Details of the recommendations were not immediately released, but some news sources have suggested that recommendations included the unbundling of ZESCO as well as sharp reductions in ZESCO's wage bill (African Energy, 2018). Civil society groups and in Zambia and local media outlets have expressed concern over the lack of details about the reforms, worry that Chinese companies may somehow be involved in the restructuring, and speculate that substantial reform actions are not likely to take place until after the presidential and general elections in 2021 (Lusakatimes, 2018).

The "disruptive moment" probably has been postponed in Zambia. It is possible that Scaling Solar may contribute unintentionally and indirectly to reform, but the fact that the program was designed, financed, and managed exclusively by development partners and only facilitated a handful of IPPs, may blunt the "disruptive" potential of the program's impacts. The fact that, in the interests of smooth program rollout, IFC's implementing counterpart was the IDC, rather than the sector's vertically integrated, single-buyer utility, probably also helped the sector avoid attention to needed reforms.

9.6 Conclusions

Competitively tendered, renewable energy IPP projects clearly offer a number of important potential benefits to host countries. The programs in South Africa, Uganda, and Zambia suggest that tendered IPP projects can reach closure more quickly than traditional kinds of directly-negotiated IPP projects, can be less complicated (because they use standard documents and contracts), with lower development costs, and are more transparent with lower risks of rent seeking or corruption. These tender programs also seem to have helped bring down the costs of renewable energy to levels that are competitive with thermal and hydro power.

However only the South African program has clearly played a role in disrupting the status quo of the country's vertically integrated, state-owned monopoly single-buyer utility. That role was largely a result of the accomplishments of REIPPPP in terms of the number of IPP projects, the size of private investment, and the resulting increase in generating capacity—all of which dwarfed the accomplishments of GET FiT and Scaling Solar. The fact that REIPPPP was a South African achievement, designed, financed, and implemented with almost no assistance from development partners, gave South Africans an acute sense of what is possible in their power sector. And as a MIC, South Africa also has a critical mass of educated, reform-sensitive citizens who try to hold government to account. But these characteristics may not have been enough to truly disrupt anything without the ominous specter of the country's potential economic collapse triggered by a thoroughly looted and bankrupt Eskom, once the largest and most powerful electricity utility in Africa. Without Eskom's implosion, the country's new renewable energy IPPs might simply have helped the utility avoid load shedding and maintain most of its sector dominance.

Ultimately, these programs may have some involvement in driving sector reforms, but they have not resulted from reform intentions and are unlikely to be primary reform drivers. They have done relatively little to disrupt the power sector status quo in these countries. Power sector reforms seem unlikely to happen soon in Zambia and Uganda partly because the renewable energy IPP tender programs have been promoted as "successes" in each country, by donors, DFIs, MDBs, as well as local politicians and government officials. Celebration of these successes may reduce the pressures on governments for further sector reforms. As Chapter 8 argued, this may signal the existence of a policy dilemma—the promotion of IPP projects as reform elements in unreformed power sectors of developing countries is a policy "at war with itself." The resulting IPP projects do not achieve all the benefits they are capable of and may retard further reforms. Finding a way to deal effectively with this dilemma involves finding ways of strengthening the association between IPP projects and broader sector reforms. This is as much a challenge for these renewable energy IPP programs as it is for traditional, directly negotiated IPP projects. DFIs and MDBs who make possible most of the IPP projects in LICs, including projects developed through these tender programs, need to better synchronize IPP project development with sector reforms.

Chapter 10 turns to the issue of blended finance, the use of concessional funding to catalyze private sector investment—exactly what the IFC and bilateral donors were trying to achieve with the heavily subsidized renewable energy tender programs in Zambia and Uganda. This kind of subsidy support for PPPs appears to represent the future of PPPs in low-income regions like SSA, even though large amounts of concessional funding represents a retreat from the classic private investment PPP model as it was developed and promoted in the 1990s.

But is it possible for a program like Scaling Solar to provide too much subsidy for a PPP project? How should blended finance be evaluated? Where are the boundaries beyond which subsidy support becomes "too much"?

References

African Energy. 2018. "Zambia: Zesco Restructuring." *African Energy Newsletter*, Issue 382, December 6. Accessed at: https://www.africa-energy.com/article/zambia-zesco-restructuring

Baietti, A. 2013. *Green Infrastructure Finance: A Public–Private Partnership Approach to Climate Finance*. Washington, DC: World Bank and AusAid.

Businesstech. 2017. "Eskom's 20% Price Increase Points to the "Beginning of a Death Spiral": Analysts." Businesstech, September 24. Accessed at: https://businesstech.co.za/news/energy/199662/eskoms-20-price-increase-points-to-the-beginning-of-a-death-spiral-analysts/

Castalia Strategic Advisors. 2016. "First Performance Review and Baseline report for GET FiT Uganda." Report to Government of Uganda represented by KfW, May.

Chimbaka, B. 2017. "Establishment of the Independent System Operator for Enhanced Competition: Zambia's Case." Presentation by the Zambian Energy Regulation Board at the Third Annual Competition and Economic Regulation (ACER) Conference, Dar Es Salaam, Tanzania, July 15. Accessed at: https://static1.squarespace.com/static/52246331e4b0a46e5f1b8ce5/t/5982fa2abebafb73ffda229b/1501755952860/Parallel+3B_Besa+Chimbaka_ERB+Zambia.pdf

Dawson, S. 2013. "Activists Urge World Bank to Disinvest from Private Water Companies." Thompson Reuters Foundation, October 3. Accessed at: http://news.trust.org//item/20131003125451-xompv/

Department for International Development (DFID). 2013. "DFID–KfW Contract: DFID 6202 GET FiT East Africa Programme—Uganda, Roll-Out Phase 1." London: DFID. Accessed at: https://devtracker.dfid.gov.uk/projects/GB-1–203624/documents

Department for International Development (DFID). 2017. "Case Study: IFC's Scaling Solar Programme, Zambia." Infrastructure and Cities for Economic Development (ICED) Evidence Library. Unpublished paper. Accessed at: http://icedfacility.org/wp-content/uploads/2017/12/ICED_Case_Zambia-Scaling-Solar.pdf

Department for International Development (DFID). 2018. "Annual Review: On and off grid small scale renewable energy in Uganda (GET FiT)," March 24. London: DFID. Accessed at: https://devtracker.dfid.gov.uk/projects/GB-1–203624/documents

Eberhard, A., C. Godinho. 2017. "A Review and Exploration of the Status, Context and Political Economy of Power Sector Reforms in Sub-Saharan Africa, South Asia and Latin America." MIR Working Paper, Management Programme in Infrastructure Reform & Regulation, Graduate School of Business, University of Cape Town.

Eberhard, A., K.N. Gratwick, E. Morella, P. Antman. 2016. *Independent Power Projects in Sub-Saharan Africa: Lessons from five key countries.* World Bank Directions in Development. Washington, DC: World Bank.

Eberhard, A., J. Kolker, J. Leigland. 2014. *South Africa's Renewable Energy IPP Program: Success factors and lessons.* The World Bank Institute and the Public Private Infrastructure Advisory Facility (PPIAF). Washington, DC: World Bank.

Engineering News. 2017. "Big opportunity for change amid renewables-led disruption." *Creamer Media's Engineering News*, September 22. Accessed at: http://www.engineeringnews.co.za/print-version/energy-sector-has-opportunity-to-change-amid-disruptive-moment-caused-by-renewables-2017-09-22

Foster, V., C. M. Briceno-Garmendia. 2010. *Africa's Infrastructure: A Time for Transformation*, AICD Flagship Report. Washington, DC: World Bank.

Fergusson, J., D. Croft, Y. Charafi. 2015. "Scaling Solar: Making the Sun Work for Africa." *2015 Africa Energy Yearbook*. London: EnergyNet Ltd.

GET FiT Uganda. 2018. Annual Report 2017. KfW and Multiconsult. Accessed at: file:///C:/Users/JL/Downloads/GET-FiT%20Annual%20Report%202017%20(1).pdf

Hofstatter, S. 2018. "Counting the Cost of State Capture." *Financial Mail*, September 6.

Independent Evaluation Group. 2013. *Assessing the monitoring and Evaluation Systems of IFC and MIGA: Biennial Report on Operations Evaluation.* Washington, DC: World Bank.

International Finance Corporation (IFC). 2009. *IFC Support to Infrastructure: Transactions in Power, Transport and Water.* Washington, DC: IFC.

International Renewable Energy Agency (IRENA). 2017. *Renewable Energy Auctions: Analysing 2016.* Abu Dhabi: IRENA.

Kenny, C., J. Kalow, V. Ramachandran. 2018. *Inside the Portfolio of the International Finance Corporation: Does IFC Do Enough in Low-Income Countries?* CGD Policy Paper 115. Washington, DC: Center for Global Development. Accessed at: https://www.cgdev.org/publication/insideportfolio-international-finance-corporation-does-ifc-do-enough-low-income

Kruger, W., A. Eberhard. 2016. "Renewable Energy Auctions in Sub-Saharan Africa: Review, Lessons Learned and Recommendations." MIR Working Paper, Management Programme in Infrastructure Reform & Regulation, Graduate School of Business, University of Cape Town.

Laing, R. 2018. "Eskom Retains its Power Over SA." *Business Day*, November 1.

Leigland, J. 2016. *Enhancing Domestic Private Sector Development in Africa: A focus on renewable energy.* Addis Ababa: United Nations Economic Commission for Africa, April.

Leigland, J., A. Eberhard. 2018. "Localisation Barriers to Trade: The case of South Africa's renewable energy independent power program." *Development Southern Africa*, 35(4): 569–88.

Lusakatimes. 2018. “China to Take Over Zesco—Africa Confidential.” *Lusakatimes*, September 4. Accessed at: https://www.lusakatimes.com/2018/09/04/china-to-take-over-zesco-africa-confidential/

Meyer, R., A. Eberhard, K. Gratwick. 2018. “Uganda's Power Sector Reform: There and back again?” *Energy for Sustainable Development* 43: 75–89.

MIT. 2016. *Utility of the Future: An MIT energy initiative response to an industry in transition*. Boston, MA: MIT. Accessed at: http://energy.mit.edu/research/utility-future-study/

Republic of South Africa. 2011–13. “REIPPPP Tender Notices and Briefing Notes.” Department of Energy. Accessed at: http://www.ipp-renewables.co.za.

Republic of Uganda. 2014. “GET FiT Program Uganda, Overview Brief.” Accessed at: file:///C:/Users/Jim/Downloads/GET%20FiT%20Info%20Brief%20(1).pdf

Rieger, S. 2015. *GET FiT Uganda*. PPIAF PPP Short Story Competition, Essay Winner. Washington, DC: Public–Private Infrastructure Advisory Facility.

World Bank. 2014. “Project Appraisal Document on a Proposed Series of IDA Partial Risk Guarantees in the Amount of US$160 Million Equivalent in Support of Projects Under the Renewable Energy Development Program in the Republic of Uganda.” Washington, DC: World Bank, February 20.

World Bank. 2018a. *Low-Carbon Infrastructure: Private participation in infrastructure (PPI) 2002 to H1 2017*. Washington, DC: World Bank.

World Bank. 2018b. PPI Project Database. Accessed at: http://ppi.worldbank.org/customquery?mode=1

10

The Future of PPPs in Low-Income Countries

Blended Finance

10.1 Introduction

If PPPs continue to account for between 20 and 25 per cent of infrastructure investment in middle-income developing countries (although much less in low-income countries), this suggests that governments and their development partners may be finding some situations in which private–public partnerships (PPPs) can achieve sustainable operations. The evidence-based critique of PPPs suggests some of the required circumstances for doing these transactions, but these are not the same as what was envisioned in the 1990s. For example, it is no longer assumed that self-sustaining PPPs that fully cover all operating and capital costs, are workable and desirable in a large variety of infrastructure service delivery situations in poor countries. Sustainable PPPs in the poorest countries are mainly hybrids, combining some elements of classic PPPs with those of consulting or engineering, procurement, construction (EPC) contracts. These hybrids involve less of a role, and lower risks, for private sector operators and financiers, and more responsibility (and higher risks) for governments and their development partners.

In other words, it is now clear that for PPPs to be sustainable, compromises need to be made regarding many features of these projects that were considered definitive in the 1990s. The key compromise involves a much stronger role that "blended" or subsidized finance now must play in ensuring private sector profits from PPPs. Blended finance impacts PPPs in several ways. First, project preparation is no longer left solely to private partners, but is increasingly paid for and managed by governments and donors. This is meant to increase the likelihood that the preparation will be done thoroughly, in a way that benefits the government owner of the project rather than the private partners, and also increases the ability of the PPP to generate at least some development benefits, especially for poor people. Second, it is now recognized that significant amounts of private finance are available only if governments and development partners share the financing burden using public or concessional money. Development partners are

Public–Private Partnerships in Sub-Saharan Africa: The Evidence-Based Critique. James Leigland, Oxford University Press (2020). © James Leigland.
DOI: 10.1093/oso/9780198861829.001.0001

also now routinely expected to provide guarantees and other risk-mitigation mechanisms to help ensure that public partners meet their PPP contractual commitments. Third, because governments must play a stronger role in PPP project development and oversight, improving PPP-related governance in poor countries typically requires more funding and pressure from development partners than seemed necessary in the past.

"Blended finance" is an increasingly popular concept among members of the international development community who support private infrastructure investment. No precise, single definition of the term is universally accepted as authoritative, but it is usually used to refer to the complementary use of both concessional and private finance to make below-market-rate investment funding available to commercially sustainable infrastructure projects. The intention behind this blending is to use the concessional element to catalyze additional commercial investments to help make economically beneficial projects commercially viable. Blended finance of this kind can be deployed via guarantees, loans, equity, or grants. In theory, blending is supposed to reduce its subsidy element to only what is needed to attract the commercial financing necessary for the project, so as not to cause unnecessary market distortion. But determining what is the optimal blend has been difficult in practice.

The OECD attributes a recent rise in the popularity of blended finance to the realization that much more private investment is needed to help developing countries meet the 17 Sustainable Development Goals (SDGs) and 169 targets covering various sectors, which make up the key elements of the 2030 Agenda for Sustainable Development. Blended finance is seen as a tool for leveraging private finance in support of the SDGs, largely through PPPs. Private finance is the key to growing the billions of dollars currently deployed as development finance into the trillions of dollars needed to achieve the SDGs (World Bank, 2015). The participants in the 2016 World Water Week in Stockholm heard that the single largest SDG financing gap (over US$1 trillion) exists for the eight targets associated with the SDG focused on water and sanitation: "Blending different types of available private, public and philanthropic resources will allow the water sector to leverage and mobilize additional private capital" (Cortes, 2016, 2). The Organisation for Economic Co-operation and Development (OECD) has concluded that most of the major donor countries make use of blended finance for development purposes. More than 189 funds were channeling blended finance to projects by 2016, and over US$80 billion in private sector finance had been mobilized since 2015 (OECD, 2017).

Blended finance is clearly being used to help facilitate private investment in infrastructure, and in fact seems to be a necessity for sustainable infrastructure PPPs in poor countries. But this new focus on using blended finance in support of PPPs raises several questions. Will the use of blended finance make a major contribution in leveraging more private investment into infrastructure in low-income countries, or will it simply make up for some of the PPP shortcomings and help maintain relatively low levels of PPP-related private investment in these countries? Is it possible that PPPs supported by blended finance will make a significant contribution to the achievement of SDGs? What does the performance track record of these kinds of projects say about their ability to generate socioeconomic benefits that outweigh project costs? What kind of authoritative guidance is available to help ensure the prudent, productive use of blended finance in support of PPPs? What kind of compelling argument can be made for the use of blended finance in these cases?

This chapter addresses these questions by discussing, first, what we know about blended finance from the 25-year experience with subsidy use. Second, what lessons have been learned from that experience regarding justifications for blended finance. Third, what are some of the risks associated with different blended finance modalities, like grants, loans, guarantees, and equity. And fourth, how are all of these considerations brought together in the selection and structuring of PPP projects to benefit from blended finance.

10.2 Historical Background

Blended finance is a diverse, complicated, and often controversial subject that is not always clearly understood or defined in the work of development practitioners and academicians. Though the terminology is relatively new, the principles underlying the concept have been discussed and debated for decades. The key to understanding these long-standing questions about the concept is the fact that, by definition, blended finance involves a significant subsidy element. It is the use of a subsidy to catalyze private investment in infrastructure that has made blended finance somewhat difficult to use as well as controversial.

The use of subsidies has not always been viewed as complementary to private financing of infrastructure. In the early 1990s, the growing popularity of private involvement in service delivery operation and management was to a large extent a reaction against inefficient government provision of services, either directly by government enterprises or indirectly with the help of government subsidies. Traditionally, governments tended to assume that market outcomes could not be pro-poor, and opted to provide goods and services themselves. As Department for International Development's (DFID) 2008 *Private Sector Development Strategy* pointed out, the result of this intervention often was to distort markets and "crowd out" the private sector. Because government and donor resources were limited, these direct interventions often failed to meet the needs of the poor or generated temporary and unsustainable supply. In the worst cases, the supply of the goods and services became forms of patronage (DFID, 2008).

By the end of the 1980s, widespread problems with poorly conceived state-run basic services provided the impetus for an economic policy reversal that emphasized market-based provision of these services. But the development community's acceptance in the early 1990s of market-based service provision as the only appropriate mechanism, which became a central tenet of state-owned enterprise (SOE) reform strategies under structural adjustment, at times went too far. Private participation on a self-sustaining basis, with customer tariffs set at full cost-recovery levels, was too often viewed as viable solution in a large variety of infrastructure service situations (e.g., Israel, 1992). When absolutely necessary, it was assumed that costs of services provided to poor customers could be supported by cross subsidization, with wealthier customers paying more to cover shortfalls in revenue. But traditional forms of government intervention, including the use of government subsidies, were viewed by many development professionals as a thing of the past for basic services, like water, power, and transport. It was assumed that if the services were properly managed, they could recover operations and maintenance (O&M) costs as well as capital investment costs from tariffs charged to users.

By the mid-1990s, the World Bank began sharply cutting back its infrastructure lending because of the expectation that the private sector would largely fill infrastructure investment and service delivery needs in many developing countries. However, by the end of the 1990s, the experience of the Asian financial crisis demonstrated that (among other things) the private sector could not always be expected to take on the full commercial risks associated with basic service provision. And although measures like cross subsidization proved to be useful, they were often inadequate to generate sufficient revenues to fill the gap between actual costs of provision and what poor customers were willing and able to pay (Leigland, 2008). Furthermore, a growing body of research recognized that full cost recovery from user fees had rarely been achieved even in industrialized countries, much less in the developing world (Foster and Yepes, 2006).

By the early 2000s, private participation in infrastructure was still well below levels of the mid-1990s, and in fact would take a full ten years to recover to its 1997 peak. Members of the development community realized that more substantial public sector sharing of costs and risks was warranted and even essential in many cases, in order to facilitate private participation. In particular, "market failures" were often cited as obstacles preventing market and private sector development in basic infrastructure sectors. As a result, interest was rekindled in the use of government subsidies, to at least partially cover service delivery costs in poor areas (Brook and Smith, 2001).

The last two decades have seen a rapid increase in the use of grants to enable PPPs. But concerns linger about the use of these grants. While they can be useful tools for overcoming market failure, nonetheless, as "subsidies" they are often suspected of being subject to misuse. The experience of the 1970s and 1980s in sectors like agriculture convinced many observers that grants often provide undesirable subsidization of inputs and credit, especially when combined with unsolicited and opaque tendering procedures frequently used in PPP procurements (Meyer, 2011). Moreover, the design of subsidy schemes is complex and their allocation mechanisms can be expensive, which raises concerns about their cost effectiveness (Vogel and Adams, 1997; Irwin, 2003).

One reaction to this concern about grants has been the rapid spread of results-based financing (RBF) and in particular, output-based aid (OBA) approaches to subsidy provision. OBA helped to address many of the weaknesses of government subsidies that were so apparent in the 1980s. It did this by linking payments to performance, made possible by tying subsidy disbursements to the achievement of clearly specified results—or outputs—that directly support improved access to basic services. The World Bank began to document what was known about OBA in the early 2000s (Brook and Smith, 2001). After the official launch by several bilateral donors in 2002 of an OBA trust fund program in the World Bank (the Global Partnership on Output-Based Aid or GPOBA), over 200 OBA schemes were quickly identified and evaluated for lessons learned (Mumssen et al., 2010).

More recently, "blended finance" has emerged as a general term that refers to a wider spectrum of subsidies used to catalyze infrastructure investment. Performance-based grants used to attract private participation and market-based finance remain a charter member of the blended finance club. But the approach now includes non-grant blending mechanisms such as equity contributions, loans, and loan guarantees, among other instruments. According to OECD surveys, the principal actors driving the use these blended finance approaches include the most prominent institutions involved in international development:

- In 2012, the World Bank Group's private sector arm, the International Finance Corporation (IFC), began a focused effort to use blended finance instruments to reach beneficiaries of projects in countries, that were too poor to be IFC clients, given the latter's country risk restrictions. In order to avoid jeopardizing its triple-A credit rating, the IFC is doing this by mixing or blending donor grant money with its own debt and equity funding (which the IFC considers to be market-based), to reduce the cost of loans or guarantees in these countries. The IFC claims to use blended finance to make economically viable projects financially viable, so that they can attract or "crowd in" additional private participation, especially in IFC priority areas like climate change and small and medium enterprise (SME) finance (IFC, 2012).
- The EU channels grant funding through a number of regional loan and grant "blending facilities" like the EU–Africa Infrastructure Trust Fund (ITF). Although some of this funding has been used for private sector projects, most of it has been used to prepare projects for public funding by

European multilateral development banks (MDBs) like European Investment Bank (EIB) and European Bank for Reconstruction and Development (EBRD). Using blended finance to facilitate MDB funding, rather than private sector finance, is justified in these cases on the basis that the projects promote "EU conditionalities" like political, social, and environmental reforms consistent with EU policy objectives (EBRD, 2011).

- Bilateral donors, like DFID and US Agency for International Development (USAID), are especially keen to demonstrate to tax payers that they are using their development budgets wisely. This may mean mixing grant funding with commercial sources of finance or simply requiring that their money be paid back in some fashion. USAID has long provided partial credit guarantees, arguably at below market rates, in order to catalyze private investment. As in the case of the IFC, most of this blended financing is designed to leverage additional private finance so that donors do not use their scarce resources for the entire investment (UK Government, 2012).
- Finally, elements of the private investment community also qualify as providers of blended finance. These so-called "social" or "impact" investors operate like venture capital firms, raising money from philanthropic sources and investing it as "patient" debt or equity in projects that serve people in "base of the pyramid" (BOP) markets (Friedman, 2007; Novogratz, 2011). Impact investing involves blended finance in the sense that this is mostly private sector funding invested as loans or equity, but with expectations of delayed returns or lower returns than normally would be the case. However, because impact investment opportunities have proved to be much more scarce than these investors expected ten years ago, a number of impact investment firms have been engaged in a debate about whether or not to call on bilateral donors and philanthropic sources of capital to make outright grants available to kick-start projects that will only offer reasonable investment opportunities after a period of initial, heavily subsidized development (Koh et al., 2012).
- At the World Economic Forum (WEF) 2015 Annual Meeting in Davos, WEF and OECD organized a "Blended Finance Marketplace" to illustrate how the strategic use of public and philanthropic financial instruments can enable the private sector "to realize risk-adjusted returns" while "deploying capital at scale in fast-growing sectors across emerging and frontier markets" (WEF, 2015).

10.3 Justifying Blended Finance for PPPs

As blended finance becomes more popular, the OECD and other international groups have developed recommended principles for its use (OECD, 2018), and are monitoring blended finance programs and projects to flesh out more detailed recommendations regarding policies and procedures. However, lessons learned about some of the considerations to keep in mind when using blended finance are fairly clear in the economic literature that compares and contrasts different forms of subsidized finance (e.g., Irwin, 2003). Three elements of justification are discussed in the remaining paragraphs of this section. A fourth element—the identification and mitigation of risks associated with blended finance modalities—is discussed in section 10.4.

Justifying the use of subsidies is complicated and resource intensive. But it is an important exercise for several reasons. Using blended finance to support PPP projects means that these projects are being subsidized, and subsidies are generally not neutral market interventions. If they are based on incorrect analysis and assumptions their costs can easily outweigh their benefits. They can waste public money that might be better spent in other ways, and can have serious negative effects on market development. Instead of crowding in private investment, subsidized finance can easily crowd it out and seriously undermine objectives of impact, outreach, competition, cost effectiveness, and sustainability. Economists generally agree that as much as possible, subsidized finance should be designed in such a way that it is market enhancing and not market distorting (van der Meer and Noordam, 2004). The development community's painful experience in the 1980s with the various negative effects of subsidy use suggests that deploying blended finance in support of infrastructure PPP projects should be carefully justified in several ways.

10.3.1 Basic Eligibility for Blended Finance Support

The main intended benefit of using blended finance is "additionality," the facilitation of private investment that would not otherwise occur. Additionality is discussed in more detail later, but it should be obvious that the pursuit of additionality means that blended finance support ought to be provided only to projects that genuinely cannot be commercially viable without it. If a PPP project would happen anyway without subsidy support, the justification for deploying blended finance diminishes and becomes more a matter of whether or not the services provided are affordable. This in turn usually raises difficult questions about how governments regulate the pricing of services to end-users and the extent to which they have adequate pro-poor tariff policies.

Eligibility also involves a practical issue. The more subsidy support a project needs to become sustainably commercial, the less cost-effective is blended finance. This is because as blending support for a project increases, it quickly reaches a threshold beyond which it would be less expensive and more sustainable to implement it as a public project supported by concessional lending, rather than a PPP (Carter, 2015). This makes it important for subsidy providers to try to support projects that are "near commercial" in nature.

Finally, it is difficult to estimate the degree of need for blended finance on either an ex post or ex ante basis. For projects that have reached financial close, this determination is usually made by simply calculating leverage ratios—the relative amounts of concessional and commercial money that make up the total project financing package. But such ratios can disguise projects that are poorly designed and implemented, generate excessive profits, or actively do damage to the environment or disadvantage local residents.

To confirm basic eligibility for blended finance in a way that takes into account all of these issues, private partners in PPP projects need to be selected via competitive procurement, with requested subsidy amounts considered as a key selection criterion. Competitive pressure can help control subsidy requests. The procurement exercise can require the use of internationally accepted performance standards for things like environmental protection and resettlement.

10.3.2 Rationale #1: Correcting Market Failure

A PPP project may need blended finance to help it become commercially viable, but the use of that kind of support also requires a deeper rationale in order to guard against market distortion or the waste of resources on poorly designed projects. Two rationales are normally emphasized in the literature on subsidies. The most compelling is one that ensures against market distortion in project implementation by correcting what is described as "market failure." In fact, donors, DFIs, and MDBs routinely use—and sometimes require—evidence of market failure to justify interventions using any kind of below-market-rate finance for development purposes. But assessing and documenting market failures are not necessarily simple or straightforward exercises, especially considering differences of opinion among development practitioners regarding what the term actually means (Donovan, 2006).

There is a long tradition of critical economic literature suggesting that designers of subsidy schemes often misunderstand what constitutes "market failure," and which market failures are best corrected by subsidized finance (e.g., Vogel and Adams, 1997). Some World Bank evaluations of subsidized finance programs used extensively in agriculture and rural development have found that economic rationales for subsidized lending programs are generally weak, with programs justified in terms of desirable outcomes, but little evidence that planned interventions could be expected to be effective.

These kinds of programs often define market failure in terms of lack of markets, lack of working capital, lack of access to credit, etc. But although these obstacles to development are said to be caused by market failure, there is often little evidence or analysis presented to support such claims (van der Meer and Noordam, 2004; Meyer, 2011). Economists often recommend the use of rigorous analysis to clearly identify obstacles that seem to reflect market failure, determine whether subsidized finance can solve the problems, and confirm that the likely development impacts of using subsidized finance outweigh the distortion effects it can have.

It is important to understand the standard market failure rationale in order to evaluate whether or not subsidized finance is economically justified. "Market failure" does not necessarily mean that markets are not contributing to worthwhile social or economic goals. Market failure occurs when the market fails to allocate resources efficiently. Standard economic theory recognizes several types of market failure, including imperfect competition, imperfect or asymmetric information, public goods, and externalities (Arnold, 2011). The IFC notes that the main market failures relevant for blending concessional funds with commercial finance are associated with the existence of public goods and/or positive externalities. These failures exist when the social returns from an investment exceed the private returns the investor expects to capture, leading to under-investment. In such a situation, the provision of some form of subsidy may help to close this gap and promote investments expected to deliver significant socioeconomic benefits (IFC, 2012).

However, many obstacles to development may not be market failures. The fact that the private sector does not invest in certain kinds of projects is not always evidence of market failure. Commercial finance might be unavailable for many reasons other than market failure: it may be the result of government policies or regulation that limit profits; it might reflect low levels of demand; it could be a function of a lack of creditworthy borrowers (Zerbe and McCurdy, 1999).

Even if development practitioners can confirm the existence of market failure, subsidized finance might not be a solution or may not be the best solution. Governments or donors can help the private sector overcome market failure and make private investment sufficiently profitable and economic growth more equitable by providing a variety of interventions in areas like information dissemination, legislation, regulation, basic physical infrastructure, capacity building, as well as investment resources. Externalities and related market failures seem like priority areas for interventions, but economists warn that they are ubiquitous and cannot always be addressed comprehensively, much less simultaneously. In short, not all market failures can be solved efficiently by interventions, and not all pose serious problems for increased private investment.

10.3.3 Rationale #2: Equity or Distributional Objectives

Governments and their development partners also employ other kinds of reasons for providing subsidized finance in situations where socioeconomic benefits appear to outweigh possible market distortion. The IFC and some donors recognize the need to achieve equity or distributional goals with blended finance, such as promoting affordable access to basic services like clean drinking water for under-served groups (IFC, 2012). There is a good deal of literature on this topic, much of it produced during efforts over the last three decades to use grants to serve these purposes. Key considerations include ensuring that subsidies: (i) are transparent, carefully targeted at intended beneficiaries, and capped; (ii) involve appropriate incentives for service providers; and (iii) are either justified economically or can be demonstrated to be a least-cost way of achieving intended distributional or equity objectives (WTO, 2006).

10.3.4 Summarizing Costs and Benefits

The rationale for using blended finance needs to be confirmed with an assessment demonstrating that the socioeconomic benefits of the subsidized project outweigh the costs (Zerbe and McCurdy, 1999). This suggests that, despite the difficulties, development practitioners should try to assess the financial and economic costs and benefits of the subsidies as part of the process of project design.

Several categories of costs are typically associated with the use of blended finance to support PPP projects:

- **Subsidy costs:** Subsidization associated with grants is relatively straightforward, but subsidization associated with non-grant instruments like loans, guarantees, and equity can be transparent (e.g., lower interest rates) or much less transparent and more difficult to measure (e.g., exemptions from normal requirements to pay out dividends on equity investments, or where exact measures of interest rate subsidies are not disclosed for confidentiality reasons). Among other things, lack of transparency can lead to a real risk of oversubsidization because the blending activities of donors, DFIs, and MDBs are not coordinated (Ernst & Young, 2012, 56). But even for transparent subsidies, understanding the role of the subsidy element is not always straightforward. Subsidy elements may not be quantified in project designs, documented, or reported after the fact. In a review of EU Blending Facilities, ODI researchers found a "lack of specific data on…the exact contribution of the grant components of blending mechanisms" (Gavas et al., 2011, 7).
- **Transaction costs:** Transaction costs can be a substantial share of the total subsidy costs, because of the need to carefully justify how the subsidies are used. But such costs are often hidden in the actions of administrators, lenders, investors, etc., rather than explicit elements of financial contracts or other documents. For the recipients of blended finance, considerable transaction costs may be involved in preparing proposals or applications for funding. For both administrators and applicants, the preparation and review of project specific economic cost–benefit and financial viability analyses can be expensive and difficult. But some experts strongly recommend that these

studies need to be done in any case, unless well-designed rules of thumb for use in project screening are consistently used (Wiens and Guadgni, 1998; van der Meer and Noordam, 2004).

- **Market distortion costs:** Although difficult to quantify in many cases, most experts recommend that some attempt be made to identify and assess the undesirable side-effects of blended finance on markets, especially outcomes like unfair competition. In 2001, a donor working group established to review the use of subsidies in small enterprise development recommended the use of initial "market assessments" to determine if the market development impacts of such interventions outweighed any distortion effects (Committee of Donor Agencies for Small Enterprise Development, 2001). Anticipating such impacts is a critical part of the evaluation of decisions regarding whether or not to use of blended finance.
- **Opportunity costs:** The use of blended finance may divert money from aid alternatives that represent more efficient uses of money. It may also contribute to a concentration of aid money in particular sectors or countries, or reflect a lack of focus on projects that are socially desirable, but less profitable (Pereira, 2017).

Several kinds of benefits may be associated with blended finance:

- **Financial additionality:** The main expected benefit of blended finance is financial additionality. This usually refers to mobilization of additional private sector finance for the targeted projects at affordable costs. In other words, financial additionality means leveraging in more private sector finance than would have been possible without the blending. Additionality is often poorly measured or ignored, mostly because of problems with counterfactual analysis. It is difficult to know with any precision what a private sector investor or lender would have done in the absence of blended finance. In most cases, program benefits are estimated with standard metrics involving things like the total value of private sector project financing, which is usually assumed to be leveraged investment. But these indicators can easily overstate the degree to which the blending actually altered decisions by private sector lenders or investors. Reasons for this are mainly different kinds of substitution behavior by private sector lenders and investors, which take advantage of the subsidy element without actually increasing the total amount of private sector investment when net changes in the entire financial sector are considered (Vogel and Adams, 1996).
- **Development additionality:** This second kind of additionality refers to development outcomes and impacts generated by the additional finance in terms of things like social and economic benefits (Andersen et al., 2019). For example, economic benefits may come in the form of additional taxes

paid by borrowers, additional employment generated by financed projects, and fewer government subsidies paid to these projects. Blended finance may also generate substantial social and environmental benefits, such as climate change adaptations or mitigation, and provide development benefits for women, children, and other disadvantaged groups (IFC, 2012).

- **Demonstration effects:** A special kind of additionality worth singling out is the realization of demonstration effects. These can occur in situations where the market misperceives the costs and benefits of certain kinds of activities and under-invests as a result. For example, private companies often underestimate their ability to make sufficient profits from the delivery of basic services to poor populations, even with the help of subsidies. Governments often assume that it will be too difficult to maintain control over the supply and quality of basic services, or keep private companies from realizing exorbitant profits at the expense of poor customers. By using blended finance to jump-start successful PPP infrastructure projects, it is possible to demonstrate that market perceptions are incorrect, that such projects can work to the benefit of the parties involved, while also reducing levels of poverty. This kind of demonstration effect facilitates correction of a market failure by providing more accurate and complete information about how these projects can be made to work. The IFC argues that demonstration effects are particularly valuable in the case of early market entrants. Successful "early movers" can demonstrate the business case to later entrants, and this demonstration effect can constitute the public good or positive externality that can justify special subsidized financing support (IFC, 2012).

10.4 Risks of Blended Finance Modalities

Another element in the justification of blended finance involves the identification and mitigation of risks associated with blended finance modalities. Risks are important elements in deciding what kinds of blended instruments should be used on a particular PPP project. This section reviews the use of grants and non-grant instruments in the blended financing of such projects.

10.4.1 Output-Based Aid

The use of OBA approaches in subsidy provision is perhaps the first and most fully documented of the modern approaches to blended finance. OBA links payments to performance, by making the disbursement of subsidies dependent on the achievement of clearly specified results—or outputs—that directly support improved access to basic services. By specifying the outputs to be delivered, and paying subsidies to service providers only when those outputs have been achieved, OBA shifts performance risk to the service provider (the private partner in a PPP), while better targeting funds to intended beneficiaries.

OBA is usually justified on equity or distributional grounds. The IFC uses OBA because it can be used to efficiently support the delivery of basic services, "where policy concerns justify public funding to complement or replace user-fees" (IFC, 2012, 9). A variety of evaluations have substantiated significant benefits of OBA. But OBA involves considerable costs as well. Some observers have pointed to the high transaction costs associated with the justification and design of such activities, as well as with implementation (the achievement of outputs must be independently verified). OBA schemes can also be complex, with multiple payments contingent on the confirmed achievement of multiple outputs.

This cost and complexity, when combined with the need for service providers to pre-finance investments (for which OBA reimburses them only after output achievement) sometimes makes OBA schemes less than effective at catalyzing private investment. The basic private sector view of these subsidies is reflected in the attitude of many local commercial lenders who typically refuse to treat OBA subsidies as collateral or any other kind of security for loans (Kumar et al., 2010). These kinds of problems have been cited in the past as reasons why OBA does not seem to have scaled up as much as would be expected based on its various performance reviews (Tremolet et al., 2010).

10.4.2 Annuity Schemes

Annuity schemes involve PPPs in which the private partner receives its remuneration via periodic payments by government rather than tariff payments based on actual use of the services by end users. So, for example, a private company that designs, builds, and operates a toll road may receive annual or semi-annual annuity payments (sometimes referred to as unitary payments) from government to cover its capital and operating costs and profits and, in effect, reduce the risks that project revenues may not reach the private investor's threshold rate of return. The government may or may not charge end users for these services, but the private service provider does not depend on these user fees.

Annuity schemes are often justified on the basis that project-generated revenues are uncertain or insufficient to attract private operators and investments (Booth, 2006). In infrastructure projects, such as roads with traffic flows that are insufficient for full cost recovery via tolls, sponsors cannot achieve an investor's threshold rate of return. Such projects often require very high annuity payments to attract private participation. In these cases, governments are effectively blending grant money into the annuity payments, intentionally or sometimes unintentionally. Annuity payment levels frequently are set via competitive bidding for the project, with the proposed size of the annuity acting as the key bid criterion. However, even with competition, the size of these payments can be significantly higher than the minimum needed to make the project financially viable. The subsidy element in such payments is not always easy to determine or well documented (WBI, 2012). The opaque nature of these project justifications has raised questions about oversubsidization and off-balance sheet borrowing and have led to government accounting rule changes in countries like the UK where annuity payment PPPs have been common under the Private Finance Initiative (PFI).

10.4.3 Upfront Capital Grants

A large variety of government grants used to facilitate PPP projects are made in situations where tolls or other user fees form part of the private partner's remuneration. In other words, instead of completely replacing user fees in the remuneration of service providers (as is the case with most annuity schemes), the grant element is designed only to bridge the gap between project costs and expected project revenues from user fees, often within a fixed toll or tariff regime. This is usually considered to be an "affordability gap" for users in cases where they have limited ability to pay a toll for services, which is set at a full cost recovery level. A one-off, upfront grant can allow governments to maintain affordable tariffs while attracting private investment to reduce capital budget outlays. At the same time these grants ensure that the private sector still shares in the risks of infrastructure delivery and operation by requiring the service provider to take on at least some of the traffic or other revenue risks that, under annuity schemes, are shifted completely to government. These kinds of subsidies have been widely used in Latin America (WBI, 2012). India's Viability Gap Fund (VGF) program, established in 2005 to support PPPs, provides a unique example of this general type of scheme. It deploys VGF subsidies to projects in basic infrastructure sectors such as transport, power, water, sanitation, and solid waste, as well as infrastructure projects benefiting special economic zones and tourism. VGF directly addresses the high upfront capital costs of these PPP projects by making the grant available at the time of financial close so it can be used during construction (Harris, 2008).

Several basic risks are associated with upfront grants. First, unlike OBA grants, VGF grants are normally paid out before construction has been completed. And the grants are usually permanent in the sense that once paid they usually are not subsequently repaid even if it turns out that the grant was not fully needed or the project terminated early. In projects that include concessionaire or contractor performance guarantees, the proceeds of paid-out guarantees are unlikely to be used to reimburse grant payments. Similarly, in the event that any compensation is due to the concessionaire on termination as a result of government default, total or partial repayment of grant funding is also not automatic. When the public sector tries to ensure that the concessionaire repays the grant, it can lead to complicated inter-creditor issues and undesirable risk transfers (Farquharson and Encinas, 2010).

Second, such grants sometimes represent a significant element of the project's total funding package—under India's VGF program, these grants have totaled as much as 40 per cent of project costs (GoI, 2008). When this happens, the grant funding can distort the balance of project risks because those risks must be borne by a smaller private sector investment share. This may result in a decrease in the private sector's expected return and increased borrowing costs, which can offset some of the financial benefits of the "free" public money.

10.4.4 Loans and Interest Rate Subsidies

Governments and development partners routinely use blended lending to catalyze private sector investments in infrastructure. The idea is to meet funding shortfalls resulting from projects unable to raise sufficient debt finance on acceptable terms. Blending here means that subsidy elements make the terms of these loans more attractive than those offered by commercial sources of debt finance. Subsidy elements can include interest rate reductions, lengthened tenors, debt service grace periods, lowering of the rank or security position of the debt, etc. Sometimes the blending is balanced to some extent by lender requirements regarding additional guarantees or the assumption of fewer risks. Justifications can vary. On occasion this kind of blending is warranted as a response to long-term market failure. At times it is justified as a temporary policy response to stimulate or reshape the market. As with blended lending facilities created during the global financial crisis, occasionally the underlying principal of these programs is to sell these loans back into the market when conditions normalize (Farquharson and Encinas, 2010).

The risks associated with this kind of lending are considerable. They include the possibility of crowding out private lending. Insufficient debt finance can result from a number of things, like lack of project or sponsor creditworthiness. But that can simply mean that the credit market is functioning appropriately in denying credit to uncreditworthy borrowers. "Correcting" this situation with blended debt might actually lead to market distortion, as potential future market entrants await similar subsidized loans or remain skeptical that projects of this nature will be commercially viable without similar support (IFC, 2012).

Debt instruments are the instrument of choice for blended finance offered by much of the development community, and MDBs have arguably pioneered the development of blended finance techniques over the last decade (Mustapha et al., 2014). This includes development banks like EBRD, Kreditanstalt für Wiederaufbau (KfW), EIB, Netherlands Development Finance Company (FMO), and a number of loan and grant blending facilities established by the European Union beginning in 2007 (European Commission, 2013). But only a relatively small fraction of this funding has gone to projects that involve private sector participation.

Since 2007, the IFC has been blending donor money with its own resources to make below-market-rate loans to catalyze private investment mostly in SME finance or climate change projects. IFC policy allows this in situations involving market failure, which can be addressed with time-bound interventions. The IFC looks for lending opportunities where projects promise strong social benefits and are commercially viable but do not attract investors because the business case is not fully convincing or costs–risks seem disproportionate because the market is nascent. The IFC has used a variety of blended debt mechanisms, including interest rate deductions, longer tenors, different debt service payment ranking, and security packages for senior debt.

Export credit agencies (ECAs) represent another major source of blended loan finance. Collectively, ECAs fund more private-sector projects in the developing world than any other class of finance institution, including the World Bank Group. ECAs are public or private agencies, mostly in industrialized countries, which act on behalf of the government to provide loans, guarantees, and insurance to support national exports of capital goods and services to developing countries and emerging markets. The loans may be supplier's credits, extended to the exporter, but they also may be buyer's credits, extended to the importer, which might be a private company, a public entity (like a sub-national government or government department), or a state-owned enterprise. Most industrialized nations have at least one ECA. Information is not widely available on the industries supported by individual ECAs, or the extent to which the support is subsidized. But the targeted investments tend to be large industrial and infrastructure projects that have levels of political or credit risk that would otherwise prohibit involvement by the exporter.

The use of interest rate subsidies to make blended finance available to regional infrastructure projects in Africa has been pioneered by the EU–Africa ITF, established in 2007 as one of the European Union's first blended finance facilities. Interest rate subsidies (IRS) use below-market interest rates to reduce the cost of borrowing for clients. The subsidies are typically provided as grants to lenders to cover a percentage of interest payments. But in actual practice, lenders often simply reduce the amount of the loan provided rather than the interest rate so the finance contract remains unchanged (Mustapha et al., 2014).

The mid-term evaluation of the EU–Africa ITF found that many stakeholders considered the IRS to be a fundamental aspect of ITF's product offering, particularly in terms of managing the debt sustainability obligations of countries classified by the IMF as "heavily indebted poor countries" (HIPCs). Without such a subsidy, members of ITF's Project Financiers Group (mostly European MDBs supporting public investment projects) would not be willing or able to invest in regions like Sub-Saharan Africa (SSA) with large numbers of HIPCs. In such countries, loans must have a minimum concessional (or grant) element of 35 per cent. The IRS therefore can provide lenders with the comfort they need to makes large infrastructure-related loans in such countries. But the ITF mid-term evaluation also noted that an IRS is less transparent than a direct grant, and poses the risk of oversubsidization when the internal calculation processes and margins used by the lenders are not shared among financiers because of confidentiality concerns, as was the case with ITF (Ernst & Young, 2012).

10.4.5 Guarantees

Since the Asian crisis, investors have often demanded reassurance that a government's commitments in support of a PPP project are actually as strong as promised. These reassurances now take many forms. Among these are a large variety of third-party risk-mitigation products, such as credit and risk guarantees, which are available for use in poor countries. MDBs like the World Bank and the IFC, as well as donors like USAID, can provide partial credit guarantees to public sector borrowers, often with a sovereign counter guarantee. Credit guarantees can help governments access finance needed to support PPP projects. MDBs and DFIs sometimes provide partial risk guarantees (PRGs), also sometimes backed by sovereign counter guarantees. PRGs can cover lenders for losses on private investment projects caused by a wide variety of government political and regulatory events ranging from expropriation to government non-payment of contractual obligations. PRGs could also be targeted at specific government actions, to give lenders comfort that government support promised to projects will be forthcoming. For example, the project company may rely on government for the project revenue stream as in availability payment PPPs, or it might rely on supplemental payments by governments in order to maintain user tariffs at certain levels (Irwin, 2007).

Donors, DFIs, and MDBs often perceive guarantees to be more cost-effective than loans or grants, because guarantees can benefit more borrowers than grants or credit lines. But guarantee programs come in for a special level of criticism from economists.

First, reasons given for these programs are at times weak. If the reluctance to lend is attributable to problems with legal and administrative frameworks, regulatory requirements, high rates of return on alternative investment opportunities, among others, then guarantees targeted at specific groups of borrowers may not represent the most appropriate strategy. In such cases, market-wide approaches that potentially support all borrowers with things like training and technology transfer may make more sense. Likewise, it seems highly unlikely that development partners would understand lender reluctance in local markets better than local lenders. These development institutions may bring experience with types of borrowers from other countries, but this knowledge may or may not be transferable across country boundaries (Meyer, 2011).

Second, guarantee schemes are also sometimes criticized on cost–benefit grounds. Benefits like additionality—that loans made with guarantees would not have been made without the guarantees—are difficult to confirm because of problems with counterfactual analysis. Evaluations of guarantee schemes in sectors like agriculture and rural development have found that subsidies have not led to significant additionality (World Bank, 2003). However, other evaluations have found "sustainable changes in lender behavior" resulting from the use of guarantees. These and other benefits of guarantees are possible if other conditions for market deepening are in place and the guarantees are viewed as "accelerators, not drivers" of market reforms (Bennett et al., 2005).

Third, the costs associated with such schemes are also difficult to assess because they typically involve significant hidden subsidies, and are expensive to set up and operate (Vogel and Adams, 1997). Transaction and monitoring costs are frequently not disclosed. Most schemes moreover do not attempt to assess the possible market and fiscal damage caused by these guarantees, particularly the crowding out of the private, non-subsidized guarantees and the contingent liabilities associated with potential calls on the guarantee and then the subsequent impact on a government's budget. The choice of implementation modalities also has significant cost implications. The management of these schemes requires significant technical expertise, more so than for loan or grant programs. They are usually set up and managed by MDBs rather than in government or donor organizations.

World Bank Group's guarantees are perhaps the best known and mostly widely used guarantees for large infrastructure PPPs in poor countries. The guarantees mitigate government performance risks that the private sector is reluctant to assume. Types of guarantees offered by the World Bank Group include partial risk and credit guarantees and political risk insurance provided by the Multilateral Investment Guarantee Agency (MIGA). The IFC offers credit guarantees of private borrower performance, including "risk share facilities" that make up 80 per cent of its blended finance transactions. Although widely used, these guarantees are vulnerable to the same kinds of criticism that apply to other credit support products: their use in correcting market failures is rarely well documented; they sometimes can distort market competition by supporting particular projects and not others; and the costs of the instruments—to both the World Bank and clients—can be very high, with benefits like additionality difficult to confirm.

10.4.6 Equity

Equity products are the least widely used form of blended finance, mainly because transaction costs can be high, and other instruments, like blended debt products, can be structured to achieve many of the same effects (IFC, 2012). A variety of MDBs include equity products in their repertoire of blending options, but they tend to use these products less frequently than the debt, guarantees, or grants.

Equity can be an attractive form of finance for PPP projects because it has no specific deadline for repayment and therefore does not represent a fixed burden on cash flows like regularly scheduled debt service payments. Equity holders often have a strong interest in the success of their investments and this may also have positive impacts on the project. But equity holders are more exposed to business risks than other financiers. Among other things equity holders are last in priority in terms of repayments in the event of bankruptcy. These risks usually make equity more expensive than debt, which means that investors expect higher returns on equity (via dividends, share appreciation, etc.) than lenders receive via the interest charged on debt instruments.

Most blended equity is used in the expectation that it will facilitate: (i) much faster closure of initial, equity-funded phases of these projects; (ii) larger amounts of senior debt, sourced more quickly and on more favorable terms for subsequent geared phases of the projects; and (iii) speedier structuring and raising of debt finance, and therefore lower overall costs to the projects (UNEP, 2008).

Equity as a blended finance tool is usually characterized by (i) below-market-rate financial returns; (ii) greater than usual tolerance for risk; and (iii) longer time horizons for the return of capital. However, as equity, this form of blended finance does require some return on investment. Therefore, a certain amount of financial rigor (as well as meticulousness around expected social returns) is required in deploying this capital. These expectations are usually negotiated ex ante when the investment is made. This form of equity can be used to share the equity risk that might otherwise discourage developers from preparing projects in new and unproven markets. It can also be used in cases where sponsors do not have sufficient equity to meet the risk-sharing expectations of senior debtors. Equity investments can also be made in venture capital or private equity funds that operate in new sectors with potentially high development impacts, as with renewable energy PPPs.

"Patient equity" and "patient capital" are terms that have become associated with the use of equity as a blended finance tool. Like "social venture capital" and "impact investing," these terms have become more widely used in the financial markets with the emergence of investors who are willing to forgo immediate, maximum financial returns for combinations of social, environmental, and more modest financial benefits, sometimes referred to as "triple-bottom line" investing ("people, planet, profits") (Friedman, 2007; Novogratz, 2011). The most prominent recent example of this phenomenon is the Global Impact Investing Network (GIIN), which includes institutions like JPMorgan Chase, Deutsche Bank, and Citigroup, along with non-profit institutions.

There are of course significant risks associated with blended equity, in terms of potential lost share capital, the possible inability to exit investment positions easily, and the costs associated with the complexities in understanding the "people, planet, profit" benefits. It is also difficult, time consuming, and therefore costly to identify and select appropriate investment opportunities. Using equity for blended finance purposes can require more due diligence than other kinds of blended finance and higher project "start-up" costs. Patient or blended equity investments face the same kinds of key questions used to evaluate other forms of blended finance, but the overall demand for detailed justification is arguably greater because of these risks (Tremolet et al., 2010).

10.5 Implications for Project Selection

Frameworks for evaluating the use of blended finance in support of PPP projects are fairly easy to conceptualize. Justifications, costs and benefits, and risks are relatively simple to identify and assess. But bringing all of this together in a transparent analysis that results in a clear and compelling decision about blended financing support for a particular infrastructure PPP has proved to be extremely difficult. A number of reviews have confirmed the absence of such analysis in many of the bilateral and multilateral programs that provide blended financing for PPPs:

- A review of five EU Blending Facilities found little information available regarding how specific projects were selected for support, how the grant share in blended support was determined, or precisely what were the outputs and outcomes of these blending programs. There was no evidence of cost–benefit analysis in project selection (Gavas et al., 2011).
- Similarly, a review of subsidy schemes in agriculture finance attempted to summarize the performance of USAID's Development Credit Authority (DCA) guarantee program. The review concluded that, although DCA has an impressive track record of leveraging private sector finance, details were vague and incomplete regarding the selection of borrowers and the justifications of guarantee designs. Total cost estimates were unclear or incomplete (total costs routinely excluded the cost of managing the guarantees or program oversight). Justification of the guarantees in terms of market failure also tended to be missing. Again, there was no evidence of cost–benefit analyses (Meyer, 2011).

- World Bank policy states that, with a few exceptions, cost–benefit analysis must be carried out for all of its projects at appraisal. But an evaluation by the World Bank's Independent Evaluation Group found that the use of cost–benefit analysis dropped from 70 per cent of all projects in 1970 to 25 per cent in 2008, largely because of problems with data and the quantification of costs and benefits (IEG, 2010).
- A World Bank assessment of the use of subsidy mechanisms to facilitate PPPs in selected Latin American countries (Mexico, Colombia, and Brazil) found that although all of these programs claimed to use subsidized finance to transform economically viable projects into financially viable ones, none of these schemes routinely conducted value-for-money (VFM) or cost–benefit analysis. The reason for this, summarized in the assessment, was because such analysis was viewed as "difficult, time-consuming, and subject to manipulation" (WBI, 2012, 115).

Most of the reviews and evaluations cited here stress the need for improvements in ex ante analysis of the use of blended finance for PPPs. Training and capacity building are said to be needed, along with more consistent enforcement of policies requiring the use of analytical techniques. The basic challenge is recognized as the need to address the clear difficulties in quantifying benefits and costs associated with blended finance projects. The World Bank's Independent Evaluation Group has argued that, despite the difficulties, a high degree of rigor needs to be preserved in balancing quantitative and qualitative ex ante economic and financial evaluation methods in justifying projects (IEG, 2010).

But there has also long been a recognition among practitioners that formal analytical techniques may not be capable of fully meeting these kinds of expectations. François Bourguignon, then the chief economist of the World Bank, conjectured that when economic cost-benefit analysis was applied in the preparation of infrastructure PPP projects, the techniques may have been overwhelmed by a combination of problems. These included incomplete or inaccurate data, the complexities of mixed public–private funding options, as well as so-called "political economy" issues such as weak governance and the behavioral responses to controversial projects by beneficiaries and bureaucrats (Bourguignon, 2006). Bourguignon speculated that the inability to cope with these problems accounted for the World Bank's declining use of cost–benefit techniques in infrastructure project appraisals since the 1980s—the techniques became associated with unrealistic evaluations and failed projects and consequently were no longer widely used.

In light of these difficulties, some subsidy providers have abandoned the idea of requiring the use of formal cost–benefit analysis in the justification of blended finance support for private investment. For example, the UK's DFID has defined general conditions under which its funding may be used to subsidize private investment (Box 10.1). But the guidance is vague, with concepts and terminology open to wide interpretation. The UK's Independent Commission for Aid Effectiveness has recommended that DFID provide much clearer and more practical guidance to its staff regarding private sector development programs and projects (ICAI, 2014). But as of 2019, OECD found that DFID's approach was not unusual. Most donors had gathered very little empirical information about their support for private investment, and had produced little guidance material. This was due to a lack of monitoring activity, absence of rigorous definitions of blended finance concepts, as well as untransparent deal structures: "Thus, donor countries are today unable to draw an overall picture of their blended finance operations, let along the outcomes or impact of all their development cooperation activities, including private sector mobilisation" (Andersen et al., 2019, 11).

10.6 Conclusions

The use of blended finance to support PPP projects in developing countries is already a significant part of the project landscape, especially in low-income countries. It is highly unlikely that a major scale up in the availability of such finance will have much of an impact on the achievement of the SDGs. A number of development experts now recognize that private finance, made possible by financial blending in support of projects like PPPs, is unlikely to grow billions of dollars in development finance to the trillions needed for the SDGs (Carter, 2015; Attridge and Engen, 2019). For some time, it has been widely recognized that the primary problem to be solved is a lack of bankable projects rather than insufficient investment finance (Leigland and Roberts, 2007). Blended finance is indeed sometimes used to help structure projects to help make them more attractive to the private sector, but bankability problems in developing countries are fundamentally a matter of shortcomings in policies, institutions, politics, and the technical and legal capacities of government counterparts.

If steps are taken to justify the use of blended finance, like those described in this chapter, that will complicate and slow down the process of using blended finance to support PPPs. Documenting rationales and calculating costs and benefits will certainly not accelerate the use of blended finance. And it may be true, as some experts have argued, that elaborate, quantitative justifications of blended finance in support of private investment are often misleading and a waste of resources. It is argued that the cost of oversubsidizing private investment tends to be less than the benefits that can accrue from leveraging private investment into a country where such investment is scarce (Carter, 2015).

But the history of subsidy use suggests that the costs of badly targeted subsidies are easily incurred and often not insignificant. OECD's recent findings regarding the use of blended finance by donors, DFIs, and MDBs are sobering and suggest

Box 10.1 Conditions Under Which DFID Allows Subsidies to Profit-Oriented Companies

1. ***The subsidy must always have a clear development rationale and an economic rationale***

   Subsidising a firm should be the best possible way to achieve development goals while providing value-for-money to the taxpayer. There are two primary rationales for public subsidy; firstly, overcoming market failures, and secondly, achieving equity or distributional goals.

2. ***The subsidy should demonstrate additionality***

   All subsidies should ensure additionality—that the development outcomes would not have been achieved without DFID support or would have been delayed for a sufficiently long period of time.

3. ***The subsidy should deliver sustainable development outcomes***

   Public subsidy to the private sector is intended to support investments with high developmental impact and where long-term commercial sustainability is expected. Subsidies should be time-bound and on-going subsidies should be avoided.

4. ***The subsidy should minimise market distortions***

   DFID subsidies should seek to temporarily incentivise certain investments, to nudge markets towards more socially efficient outcomes. The subsidy should be the minimum necessary and targeted as closely to the market failure as possible. Poorly designed or poorly targeted subsidies can distort markets and create inefficiency.

5. ***The subsidy should make a credible contribution to achieving systemic market impact***

   Targeting systemic market impact is important to ensure support for the development of entire markets to achieve market transformation. They should avoid locking in inefficient market distortions by only benefitting individual firms.

1. ***The subsidy should align incentives with commercial partners***

   The alignment of incentives between commercial and development partners is critical in achieving development outcomes through subsidised commercial projects.

Source: Adapted from DFID, 2015.

that no one really knows how effectively blended finance is being used (Andersen et al., 2019). The major opportunity cost of blended finance is less aid spent in traditional ways. And traditional aid is what is needed to deal with the shortcomings in policies, institutions, and technical capacity that are the ultimate problems accounting for the lack of bankable projects. Perhaps the difficulties and expense in designing and implementing these "traditional" aid activities have helped incentivize donor enthusiasm for subsidized PPPs, especially if little donor monitoring and evaluation is involved.

Blended finance has a role to play in supporting PPPs in developing countries, especially low-income countries. But it is likely to be a relatively small role. And to play that role cost-effectively some kind of transparent project evaluation needs to be undertaken and documented to demonstrate that the beneficiary PPP project is not commercially viable without the subsidy, development benefits generally outweigh costs, risks associated with the use of blended finance instruments have been identified and mitigated, and competitive procurement will be used to select the private partner and control subsidy costs.

The next chapter presents a case study of a recent water concession in SSA, which incorporates many of the compromises and hybrid characteristics described in earlier chapters, especially the use of blended finance. These compromises may make the Kigali Bulk Water PPP a successful project in the sense that it proves to be sustainable and generates at least some of the benefits expected of a PPP. The Kigali project is not Africa's first water PPP, as it is sometimes incorrectly categorized in media accounts. And it is unlikely to be replicated frequently in the region due to the limiting structural characteristics of the water sector. Nevertheless, the project serves as a useful illustration of what is necessary for the future sustainability of PPPs in SSA. But the question is, to what extent can the massive use of blended finance needed to make this project commercially viable be justified as a cost-effective use of concessional funding?

References

Andersen, O.W., I. Basile, A. de Kemp, G. Gotz, E. Lundsgaarde, M. Orth. 2019. "Blended Finance Evaluation: Governance and Methodological Challenges." OECD Development Co-operation Working Papers, No. 51. OECD Publishing, Paris.

Arnold, R.A. 2011. *Microeconomics*, 10th Edition, Mason, Ohio: South Western.

Attridge, S., L. Engen. 2019. *Blended Finance in the Poorest Countries: The Need for a Better Approach*. ODI Report (April). Overseas Development Institute, London.

Bennett, F., A. Doran, H. Billington. 2005. "Do Credit Guarantees Lead to Improved Access to Financial Services? Recent Evidence from Chile, Egypt, India and Poland," Policy Division Working Paper, Department for International Development, London, February.

Booth, K. 2006. "New Approaches to PPP in the Roads Sector: India's Annuity Concessions," PPP Resources, Institute for Public–Private Partnerships, August. Accessed at: http://www.ip3.org/ip3_site/new-approaches-to-ppp-in-the-roads-sector-india-s-annuity-concessions.html?print=1&tmpl=component

Bourguignon, F. 2006. "Closing Remarks, Rethinking Infrastructure for Development," Annual Bank Conference on Development Economics, Tokyo, Japan, May 30.

Brook, P.J., S.M. Smith. 2001. *Contracting for Public Services: Output-based Aid and its Applications*, Washington DC: World Bank.

Carter, P. 2015. *Why Subsidise the Private Sector?* ODI Report. Overseas Development Institute, London.

Committee of Donor Agencies for Small Enterprise Development. 2001. *Business Development Services for Small Enterprises: Guiding Principles for Donor Intervention*, Washington, DC: World Bank.

Cortes, S. 2016. "Blended Finance is a Missing Piece of the Water Puzzle." Conservation Finance Network, Yale Center for Business and the Environment, the Conservation Fund, Island Press (September 28). Accessed at: https://conservationfinancenetwork.org/2016/09/28/blended-finance-is-missing-piece-of-the-water-puzzle

Department for International Development (DFID). 2008. *Private Sector Development Strategy—Prosperity for all: making markets work*, DFID, London.

Department for International Development (DFID). 2015. "DFID policy framework for the provision of grants or concessional finance to for-profit firms," December 12. Accessed at: http://www.fsdafrica.org/wp-content/uploads/2015/12/15-12-07-DFID-Subsidy-Policy.pdf

Donovan, G. 2006. "When Markets Do Not Work, Should Grants Be Used?" Agricultural and Rural Development Notes, Washington, DC: World Bank.

Ernst & Young. 2012. "Mid-Term Evaluation of the EU-African Infrastructure Trust Fund, Final Report." Accessed at: http://www.eu-africa-infrastructure-tf.net/attachments/Publications/ITF%20MTE/final-report-of-the-tif-mid-term-evaluation.pdf

European Bank for Reconstruction and Development (EBRD). 2011. The European Union and the EBRD: Investing in changing economies, EBRD factsheet. Accessed at: http://www.ebrd.com/downloads/research/factsheets/EU.pdf

European Commission. 2013. "Accountability report on financing for development: review of progress by the EU and its member states," Brussels.

Farquharson, E., J. Encinas. 2010. "The UK Treasury Infrastructure Finance Unit: Supporting PPP Financing During the Global Liquidity Crisis," PPP Solutions, Washington, DC: World Bank., March.

Foster, V., T. Yepes. 2006. "Is Cost Recovery a Feasible Objective for Water and Electricity? The Latin America Experience," Policy Research Working Paper No. 3943, Washington, DC: World Bank.

Friedman, T.L. 2007. "'Patient' Capital for an Africa That Can't Wait," *New York Times*, April 20.

Gavas, M., M. Geddes, I. Massa, D.W. te Velde. 2011. *EU Blending Facilities: Implications for Future Governance Options*, ODI European Development Cooperation Strengthening Programme, January.

Government of India (GoI). 2008. *Scheme and Guidelines for Financial Support to Public Private Partnerships in Infrastructure*, Ministry of Finance, Department of Economic Affairs, New Delhi.

Harris, C. 2008. "India Leads Developing Nations in Private Sector Investment," Gridlines Series, No. 30, PPIAF, Washington, DC: World Bank.

Independent Commission for Aid Impact (ICAI). 2014. DFID's *Private Sector Development Work*. ICAI Report 35, May. ICAI, London.

Independent Evaluation Group (IEG) (2010. "Cost-Benefit Analysis in World Bank Projects," Report of the World Bank's Independent Evaluation Group, June.

International Finance Corporation. 2012. "Blended Finance at IFC: IFC's Approach to Blending Concessional Funds," Report prepared for the IFC Board of Directors, March 15.

Irwin, T.C. 2003. "Public Money for Private infrastructure: Deciding When to Offer Guarantees, Output-Based subsidies, and Other Forms of Fiscal Support," Working Paper No. 10, Washington, DC: World Bank.

Irwin, T.C. 2007. *Government Guarantees; Allocating and Valuing risk in Privately Financed Infrastructure Projects*, Washington, DC: World Bank.

Israel, A. 1992. "Issues for Infrastructure Management in the 1990s," World Bank Discussion Paper No. 171, Washington, DC: World Bank.

Koh, H., A. Karamchandani, R. Katz. 2012. *From Blueprint to Scale: The Case for Philanthropy in Impact Investing*, Report by the Monitor Group, April.

Kumar, G., I. Lieberman, Y. Mumssen. 2010. "Access to Finance in Output-Based Aid," OBA Working paper Series, Paper No. 11, October.

Leigland, J. 2008. "The Rise and Fall of Brownfield Concessions: But Some Signs of Recovery after a Decade in Decline," PPIAF Working Paper No. 6, Washington, DC: World Bank.

Leigland, J., A. Roberts. 2007. "The African Project Preparation Gap: Africans address a critical limiting factor in infrastructure investment." Gridlines Series No. 18, Public Private Infrastructure Advisory Facility (PPIAF). Washington, DC: World Bank.

Meyer, R.L. 2011. *Subsidies as an Instrument in Agricultural Finance*, Joint Discussion Paper, The World Bank, BMZ, FAO, GIZ, IFAD, and UNCDF, Washington, DC: World Bank.

Mumssen, Y., L. Johannes, G. Kumar. 2010. *Output Based Aid: Lessons Learned and Best Practices*, Washington, DC: World Bank.

Mustapha, S., A. Prizzon, M. Gavas. 2014. *Topic Guide: Blended Finance for Infrastructure and Low-Carbon Development*, DFID Evidence on Demand, January.

Novogratz, J. 2011. "The Case for Patient Capital," *Bloomberg Businessweek*, May 24.

OECD. 2017. *Blended Finance: Mobilising resources for sustainable development and climate action in developing countries.* OECD Policy Perspectives (October). Accessed at file:///C:/Users/JL/Documents/Blended%20finance/Blended-finance-Policy-Perspectives.%20OECD.pdf

OECD. 2018. OECD DAC Blended Finance Principles. OECD. Accessed at: http://www.oecd.org/dac/financing-sustainable-development/blended-finance-principles/

Pereira, J. 2017. *Blended Finance: What is it, how it works and how it is used.* Oxfam and Eurodad, London (February).

Tremolet, S., M. Scatasta, P. Borkey. 2010. "Innovative Financing mechanisms for the Water Sector," Report of the Working Party on global and Structural Policies, Environment Policy committee, Organisation for Economic Co-operation and Development (OECD), February.

United National Environment Programme (UNEP). 2008. *Innovative financing for sustainable small and medium enterprises in Africa*, UNEP Finance Initiative, African Task Force, UNEP FI, Geneva.

UK Government. 2012. "New Story Business: UK impact investment to boost development," December 7.

Van der Meer, K., M. Noordam. 2004. "The Use of Grants to Address Market Failures: A Review of World Bank Rural Development Projects," Agriculture and Rural Development discussion Paper No. 27, Washington, DC: World Bank.

Vogel, R.C., D.W. Adams. 1997. "The Benefits and Costs of Loan guarantee Programs," *The Financier*, 4(1 & 2): 22–9.

World Economic Forum (WEF). 2015. "Blended Finance Vol. 1: A Primer for Development Finance and Philanthropic Funders," WEF and OECD-DAC (July). Accessed at: http://www3.weforum.org/docs/WEF_Blended_Finance_A_Primer_Development_Finance_Philanthropic_Funders_report_2015.pdf

Wiens, T., M. Guadagni. 1998. "Designing Rules for demand-Driven Rural Investment funds: The Latin American Experience," World Bank Technical Paper No. 407, Washington, DC: World Bank.

World Bank. 2003. "Rural financial Services: Implementing the Bank's strategy to Reach the Rural Poor," Report No. 26030, Washington, DC: World Bank.

World Bank. 2015. *From Billions to Trillions: Transforming Development Finance.* Document prepared jointly by the African Development Bank, the Asian Development Bank, the European Bank for Reconstruction and Development, the European Investment Bank, the Inter-American Development Bank, the International Monetary Fund, and the World Bank Group for the April 18, 2015 Development Committee meeting (April 2). Washington, DC: World Bank. Accessed at: https://siteresources.worldbank.org/DEVCOMMINT/Documentation/23659446/DC2015-0002(E)FinancingforDevelopment.pdf

World Bank Institute. 2012. Best Practices in Public-Private Partnerships Financing in Latin America: the role of subsidy mechanisms, Washington, DC: World Bank.

World Trade Organization (WTO). 2006. *World Trade Report 2006: Exploring the links between subsidies, trade and the WTO*, The WTO, Geneva.

Zerbe, R.O., H.E. McCurdy. 1999. "The Failure of Market Failure," *Journal of Policy Analysis and Management*, 18(4): 558–78.

11

Case Study

Kigali Bulk Water—How Much Blended Finance is Too Much?

11.1 Introduction

Over the last quarter century, Rwanda has undergone a remarkable transformation beginning with social and economic destruction, followed by the restoration of stability, security, strengthened governmental politics and procedures, and sustained economic growth. The genocide and civil war that took place from April to July 1994 inflicted death and social disruption on the country's population, but also did enormous damage to the country's infrastructure: utility staff members and institutional memory were lost, customer records and utility performance information were destroyed, asset investment and regular maintenance stopped, population resettlement placed dramatic new demands on infrastructure service provision. After 1994, the government partnered effectively with the donor community and the private sector to facilitate the country's unprecedented recovery. In 2019, after an average annual growth rate of 6 per cent since 2000 and a long series of legal and regulatory reforms, Rwanda was elevated by the World Bank to the top ranking among low-income countries for "ease of doing business," ranking higher than all other African countries, as well as developed countries like Spain, France, Switzerland, and Japan (World Bank, 2019a).

A notable milestone in Rwanda's recovery was the financial closure in 2017 of a build–own–transfer (BOT) water concession in Kigali, awarded by the government to an international water management company. The project has been referred to in various local and international publications as "Africa's first water PPP" (Rwahigi, 2015; Thomson Reuters, 2018). The private partner was Kigali Water Limited (KWL), a wholly owned subsidiary of the Dubai-based Metito Group, which specializes in water and wastewater management in emerging markets. Known as the Kigali Bulk Water Bulk Concession, the US$60.8 million project was designed to secure a new, sustainable bulk water source to provide 40 million liters of potable water per day for the city of Kigali and Bugesera, a district in the Eastern Province of Rwanda. The raw water will be extracted from a borehole constructed adjacent to the Nyabarongo River (because the turbidity of water extracted directly from the river is high). The water will supplement

Public–Private Partnerships in Sub-Saharan Africa: The Evidence-Based Critique. James Leigland, Oxford University Press (2020).
DOI: 10.1093/oso/9780198861829.001.0001

existing water supplies in a strategic move to meet the rapidly growing water demands of Kigali, and help meet the government's policy targets for expanded access to water.

It is of course an exaggeration to call this project the "first" African water PPP, and it is much too early to refer to the project as successful. The continent has seen traditional long-term water concessions in Gabon and South Africa, affermage projects in West Africa, leases and management contracts in a number of countries, plus competitively tendered build–own–transfer (BOT) water treatment and storage projects in South Africa and elsewhere. But compared with other sectors, water has been the focus of relatively few sustainable PPP projects in Africa, or in low-income countries anywhere, so Kigali Water represents a significant accomplishment for the country and its public and private partners. The project also suggests the ways in which long-term, capital-intensive PPPs are likely to be viable in the future. In this sense the Kigali Water Concession demonstrates ways of compensating for many of the shortcomings of traditional PPPs, as identified in the emerging evidence-based critique reviewed in this book. But structuring a successful PPP of this kind essentially involves moderating or eliminating some of the ambitious design characteristics of PPPs thought to be definitive in the 1990s. A major feature of this project, which sharply distinguishes it from the traditional PPP model, is the use of large amounts of "blended" or subsidized finance, supplied by donors, development finance institutions (DFIs), and multilateral development banks (MDBs), to make the project viable.

A key question raised by this project is how much subsidy used to mobilized private finance is too much? Is it possible for a project like this to reach a blended finance threshold beyond which development impacts would be higher if the subsidy were used in traditional ways to facilitate policy reforms, build government capacity, and improve the investment climate to attract private participation without (or with less) subsidy support? Is it possible for such a project to exceed a threshold that signals the point at which it begins to be more cost-effective to implement it as a public project without private participation, supported with 100 per cent concessional finance, rather than as a PPP with some measure of private finance, but all the costs and complexities that come with private participation?

This chapters draws from the evidence-based critique of PPPs to attempt to answer these questions. Section 11.2 reviews the reasons why private investment in the water sectors of developing countries is so urgently needed, but so difficult. The Kigali Concession, in section 11.3, is then described and evaluated in terms of the key themes used in earlier chapters to summarize some of the most compelling examples of the emerging critique of PPPs. The amount of subsidy support used to attract private finance is estimated, and the project's blended finance leverage ratio is compared with what is currently known about average leverage ratios in developing countries. A concluding section assesses the implications of a project like this for the future of PPPs in the poorest countries. The project may represent an approach likely to be used to facilitate future infrastructure PPPs in low-income countries, but there has been very little effort to weigh the benefits of a project like this against its costs. From the rough cost–benefit calculation attempted in this chapter, it is not clearly apparent that benefits outweigh costs in this case.

11.2 Why is Private Financing of Water So Difficult?

11.2.1 The Need for Water Sector Finance

The water sector management and investment challenges facing developing countries are enormous. The Millennium Development Goals (MDGs) helped focus the world's attention on the need for better access to improved water sources and better sanitation. And by 2015, hundreds of millions of people had gained access to such sources as a result. But although the MDG target for drinking water was already met globally in 2010, none of the 48 least-developed countries had met their individual targets by 2015. By the end of 2015, 663 million people worldwide still lacked access to improved drinking water sources.[1]

The SDGs for water (SDG6), approved in 2015, are much more ambitious than the MDGs in that they call for universal access to safe water, sanitation, and hygiene by 2030. Achievement of these targets will be a difficult and expensive undertaking, even for the middle-income countries that previously met their MDG water targets. The World Bank's Water and Sanitation Program (WSP) estimates that the present value of the additional investment required just for water and sanitation until 2030 will exceed US$1.7 trillion (Hutton and Varughese, 2016). The United Nations estimates that public finances in over 77 per cent of the affected countries will be insufficient to cover this level of investment (UN Water, 2015).

Meeting this challenge is not just about finance. Water sector policies and procedures need to be upgraded across the developing world. But lack of finance is still a formidable problem. In 2009, the World Bank's Africa Infrastructure Country Diagnostic (AICD) calculated that actual capital investment in Sub-Saharan Africa's (SSA's) water sector was only about US$4.65 billion per year, but this was less than a third of the US$14.9 billion that AICD estimated was needed to meet the MDG targets for water and sanitation by 2015. Even with institutional reforms and the elimination of specific sector inefficiencies, SSA's water sector

[1] "Improved water source" is defined as a source that has been purposely protected from outside contamination, in particular from contamination with fecal matter.

would still have faced a massive financing gap of US$9.3 billion per year (1.5 per cent of total African GDP), with the gap for fragile low-income countries at over 7 per cent of GDP—an intractable challenge (Foster and Briceno-Garmendia, 2010).

11.2.2 Little Private Sector Interest in Water

It is sometimes assumed that the water industry offers investors ideal opportunities to make money with few associated risks. The global water industry has huge capital demands, and resources devoted to meet this demand dwarf those in most other sectors (Berg and Marques, 2011). Demand for water increases steadily in predictable fashion, and signs of a growing global water resource crisis only strengthen the image of the water industry as "recession resistant" (Jin et al., 2014). Many of the investment mechanisms necessary for private finance to make its way into the water sector are available in developing countries—these include bank loans and active stock exchanges. Twenty-eight stock markets are operational in SSA and countries like South Africa, Kenya, and Nigeria have markets where subnational bonds can be issued. It seems so logical that such investments should be profitable that civil society groups periodically warn of the danger that "water barons"—that is, Wall Street banks and elitist multibillionaires—will buy up water businesses and resources all over the world and particularly in poorer nations (Yang, 2015).

But it is now very clear that the water sector in developing countries is not particularly attractive to private investors. Data being collected via the WHO and UN Water GLAAS methodology demonstrates that a water sector shortcoming that all developing country regions share to one degree or another is the lack of finance from private sources like banks, capital markets, and directly from private investors. These sources play minimal roles in the developing world and almost no role in low-income countries. The 2012 GLAAS survey estimated that, excluding households, private sector financing accounted for about 7 per cent of total spending in the developing world's water sector, but in SSA, the figure drops to below 0.5 per cent (WHO and UN Water, 2012).

This is a frustrating situation for government officials in developing countries because it is well known that, in countries like the United States and the United Kingdom, private finance has been instrumental in achieving high levels of service in the water sector (Bisaga and Norman, 2015). In 2003, shortly after the MDGs were articulated, the World Panel on Financing Water Infrastructure (referred to as the "Camdessus Panel" after its chairman) presented its report on ways of accessing new financial resources for water sector investments in developing countries (Camdessus, 2003). The report encouraged new policies, institutions, and practices, as well as a doubling of official development assistance

(ODA)—all of which would be used as part of a stronger effort by the development community to catalyze private sector investment in the sector.[2]

Although the Camdessus report was generally well received, ODA for water was not doubled and ODA flows in general (and Other Official Flows) have never been redirected by the MDBs in any significant way to facilitate more private sector lending and investment into water projects, or lending to subnational utilities. MDBs have continued to emphasize their traditional sovereign-backed lending to national governments, which is then passed down with subsidies to water providers. Developing country governments have not prioritized water sector investments in the manner that the Camdessus report recommended.

11.2.3 Water vs. Electricity: Why the Difference?

One way to highlight the difficulties in accessing private finance for water and sanitation is to contrast the sector with power.[3] The World Bank's PPI Project Database (2018) shows that in all developing countries, from 1994 to 2017, PPPs in the water sector generated only about one-tenth of the investment registered for power or transportation (Figure 11.1). The reasons for this have to do with

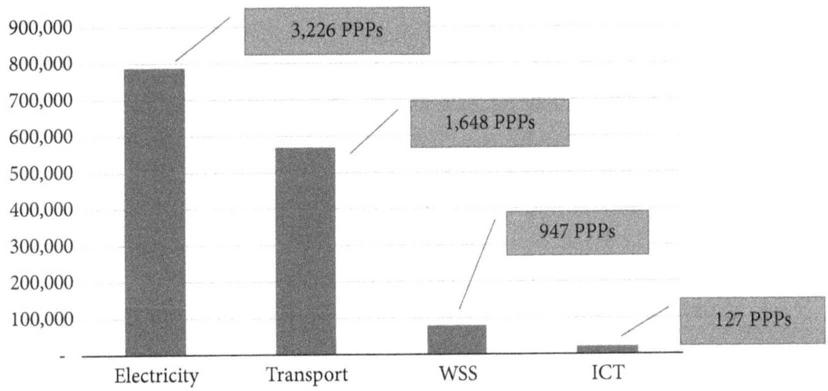

Figure 11.1 PPP Investment by Sector, All Developing Countries, 1990–2017, US$ millions (nominal values)
Source: World Bank, 2018.

[2] The Camdessus Report was followed in 2006 by the report of the Gurria Task Forces, which was issued at the 4th WWF in Mexico (Gurria, 2006). This report focused on ways of building capacity of municipalities to attract and manage finance, particularly private sector finance, for water sector investment.

[3] For more on the distinction between financing water and financing electricity, see Hanemann (2005) and OECD (2018).

how the basic characteristic of the sectors intersect with the requirements of private finance.

Electricity is relatively difficult, dangerous, and expensive to generate, easy to transport, and very hard to store. To meet demand for power in its daily and seasonal variations, electricity must be generated and distributed constantly and safely. The ease of transportation makes possible the creation of competitive markets at least for generation and distribution. This means that electricity generation is not a natural monopoly service in the same way that are some other infrastructure services, such as water supply, because multiple facilities can be built to feed power into national grids, and these can be purely private operations as long as, in most developing countries, their power is channeled through government-owned transmission and distribution facilities.

Traditional generation facilities are large, complicated, and expensive. They are often large enough to make project financing not only necessary and cost-effective, but also profitable. Generation projects typically involve completely new assets, which are clearly identifiable and separate from other assets, and have isolated, identifiable revenue streams. Tariffs and service quality are usually closely regulated, and governments often try to keep electricity tariffs affordable for households. But the benefits of power for industrial and economic development are widely recognized, as is the need for investment and expertise to generate power. So, there is somewhat less pressure on governments from customers and civil society groups to keep tariffs at below cost-reflective levels and maintain 100 per cent government ownership of power generating assets. Finally, power generation is usually a national-level activity in the sense that power, whether generated by public or private facilities, is normally channeled through national power utilities rather than directly to individual customers. (Across SSA, for example, national power utilities act as "single-buyers" of power for distribution to end users.) Power tends to be a national-level responsibility and national governments are much more likely to take responsibility for power issues, which may include sovereign guarantees to back power generating projects.

Power distribution and transmission tend to be different from power generation in many of these aspects. Distribution and transmission assets may be less expensive, not so visible or separate from other assets, and without easily identifiable revenue streams. In most cases these are not particularly new assets, but artifacts from earlier stages of infrastructure development by governments units, often at provincial or municipal levels. Many transmission and distribution assets are not well maintained. All of this is reflected in data from the World Bank's PPI Project Database. Private investment in SSA's electricity sector is heavily weighted toward construction of new assets with investment in greenfield generation, mostly in the form of independent power producer (IPP) projects, outpacing brownfield investment by eight times. In low-income countries, private investment in distribution or transmission, without any elements of generation, is virtually non-existent. AICD estimates of required infrastructure investment in Africa suggested that over 60 per cent of all needed investment was in the power sector, mostly in the form of capital investment in new generating capacity (Foster and Briceno-Garmendia, 2010).

All of these considerations make greenfield IPP projects the highest development priority private investment project in the power sector of most developing countries. These are new, privately owned and managed power plants with long-term off-take commitments, usually made by a government-owned power utility. The borrower in this case is a private company, which owns the generating facility and often possesses a substantial business track record. IPPs also represent the most potentially profitable form of private investment in power. If the host government can adequately guarantee its purchase of power, usually via iron-clad take-or-pay power purchase agreements (PPAs), and development partners are willing to contribute funding to the project (as is often the case for power, usually identified as a priority), the borrower/lender mismatches here are relatively minor, making IPP projects reasonably easy to finance. Because national-level government agencies typically sign PPAs, the agreements can be denominated in hard currency to protect investors from exchange rate risks.

In the water sector, all of the PPP project possibilities are much more like power transmission and distribution than generation. Water supply is primarily a transport problem—it is relatively expensive to transport, especially given health and safety implications, but relatively inexpensive to source, treat, and store (although climate change and pollution are steadily increasing these costs). The high cost of transport makes difficult the creation of competitive markets for water supply and makes water supply much more of a natural monopoly than power. So, for a given service area it is usually practical to have only one supplier, which is typically a government-owned entity to avoid giving one private company too much market power. And in most jurisdictions, especially in urban areas even in Africa, water transport infrastructure (underground pipes) already exists. This also makes water supply mostly a brownfield sector, with assets often old, poorly maintained, and out of sight, so difficult to evaluate. Water meters may be ineffective or non-existent, plus water charges are often blended with sanitation charges, so water and sanitation revenue streams are difficult to isolate and attribute to assets. And involving a resource that many end users view as a gift from God that should be provided without charge, water supply is a highly politicized topic in many developing countries. It is highly regulated as a result, often with water subsidized for many customers who could afford to pay more cost-reflective prices.

And because much of the most expensive transport infrastructure for water is already in place, especially in urban areas, and household connections are not essential for basic access to water supply, the investment needs in the sector are typically estimated as being much less than for power. AICD estimated that water investment accounted for about 30 per cent of the total infrastructure financing gap in Africa, with a much higher percentage of the gap attributable to maintenance and rehabilitation than in a sector like power (Foster and Briceno-Garmendia, 2010).

Due to these kinds of considerations, brownfield projects have the highest development priority in the water sectors of most developing countries. These projects involve the rehabilitation of existing assets wholly owned by governments. But many governments in these countries have become reluctant to implement such projects as PPPs, because they usually struggle to be commercially viable and, in any case, governments have been heavily criticized by civil society groups for turning essential services over to the private sector. This means that a government department or utility is more frequently the borrower for improvements in the water sector. But such entities are viewed by commercial lenders as far less creditworthy that private companies because of poor management and tariffs set at below cost-reflective levels. Development partners may be willing to help cover the capital costs of these entities, but over the long run this often does more harm than good by disincentivizing commercial behavior. Compared with power sector IPP projects, water concessions display massive borrower/lender mismatches, including huge exchange rate risks (because revenues are in local currency). These mismatches make it much less likely that private finance will be made available for water projects than for power projects.

11.2.4 Water Utilities and PPPs

In urban areas of the developing world, extending water supply coverage means working with water utilities of one kind or another. In Africa, two-thirds of the urban population depends on utility water, and piped water is still the single-largest source of water supply (although urban population growth has caused piped water coverage to decline considerably over the last 15 years). In middle-income countries, utilities typically are the only providers of water in urban areas, reaching 99 per cent of the population almost exclusively via pipe water connections. In low-income countries only about half of the urban population depends on utility water, less than half via piped connections. The rest of the urban population receives water via stand posts, boreholes, informal sharing, or water resale via vendors. However, in many urban areas in Africa, desperate residents are increasingly relying on access to surface water.

About 80 per cent of the utilities in Africa have been corporatized, often with the intention of moving them toward commercial operating principles and modern management methods. In developed municipal markets like that of the United States, the need to finance urban infrastructure has led to the proliferation of special-purpose government corporate entities (known most often as special districts and public authorities) to issue debt, and build and manage cost-recovery facilities designed to pay off the obligations. Separate corporate status has kept this debt off state and local budgets and allowed many of these entities to circumvent civil service and procurement rules to function more like business enterprises.

But in emerging economies, corporatized utilities tend to be less attractive to lenders and investors—many of these entities have been created to pursue social or political purposes or are used to keep deficit-ridden operations off the budgets of regular governments. In Africa, AICD found that corporatized utilities typically meet only about half of the good-practice criteria for enterprise governance (Foster and Briceno-Garmendia, 2010). This means that a variety of operating inefficiencies mentioned earlier persist at the utility level. These inefficiencies tend to be identified in formal credit ratings, or in credit analysis conducted by prospective lenders. Corporatized, commercialized, government-owned water utilities, such as the National Water and Sewerage Corporation of Uganda and the Athi Water Service Board in Kenya seem to be performing better than other more traditional forms of government ownership and management. But neither of these utilities has completely solved the problem of raising large amounts of finance for capital investment.

Some governments are trying to improve the internal governance of their water sectors by strengthening corporatization, improving utility management, and widening the decentralization of responsibilities to lower levels of government. AICD found that half of the countries sampled had decentralized their water utilities to bring responsibility closer to local communities (Foster and Briceno-Garmendia, 2010).

Other governments are experimenting with private participation via PPPs to improve access and efficiency, and increase capital investment. But the potential for private participation in the water sector has often been overestimated when it comes to profits and investment. Several research studies, cited in earlier chapters of this book, are worth considering in this regard (Sirtaine et al., 2004; Gassner et al., 2009; Marin, 2009; Estache and Philippe, 2012).

11.3 The Kigali Water Concession

The Kigali Bulk Water Concession involves a 27-year contract with the Metito Group, structured on a build, operate, and transfer (BOT) basis.[4] The contract

[4] The selected company, Metito, has a track record in private design and operation of water facilities in developing countries. It was the first water and wastewater company to be ISO 14001 certified. By 2017 it was managing 34 water concessions or long-term management contracts in the developing world. Metito has a shareholder base that supports its strategic expansion in the global water business. Shareholders include IFC Investments, Gulf Capital, and Mitsubishi Corporation & Heavy Industries. The Japan Bank for International Cooperation has also committed up to US$92 million via preference shares.

requires the concessionaire to design, construct, finance, and operate water production and treatment facilities that will extract groundwater from the south bank of the Nyabarongo River, treat the water to required quality standards, and deliver it to reservoirs for eventual distribution to end users. The Water and Sanitation Corporation (WASAC) is the government-owned utility responsible for urban water supply. As such, WASAC is the sole off-taker of Metito's treated water. It is responsible for the distribution and retail business of the water distribution network and is contracting with Metito to supply water on a "take or pay" basis. The Rwandan government is providing a sovereign guarantee to back all financial commitments of WASAC pursuant to this PPP arrangement.

The project's success to date is largely attributable to the fact that it is not a traditional water concession. As a greenfield project that builds and operates new infrastructure assets, which it continues to own (until the assets are turned over to the government in 27 years), the project is far more attractive to sponsors and operators than traditional brownfield projects that are more likely to experience problems with cash flows and profitability. As earlier chapters of this book have pointed out, this attraction is particularly evident in cases where projects involve: (i) the construction and use of new assets, as opposed to taking over poorly maintained existing assets; and (ii) the provision of wholesale as opposed to retail services, with payments made by governments, backed by government-guaranteed off-take agreements denominated in hard currency. Kigali water is a mirror image of a greenfield IPP project, backed by a take-or-pay power purchase agreement denominated in US dollars. Because of that similarity, Kigali water represents lower risks to cash flows and profitability than, for example, retail water or power distribution concessions involving end-user tariff payments in local currency (like the Nelspruit water concession discussed in Chapter 5).

A greenfield project of this kind was necessary in Kigali because the city's water supply problems with its brownfield system assets were already critical by the end of the 1990s. Maintenance and rehabilitation of the assets had stopped in the aftermath of the genocide and civil war, and much of the existing basic infrastructure dated to the colonial period. By the early 2000s, a World Bank study noted that urban water supply in the country was experiencing one of the highest levels of unaccounted for water in Africa, along with some of the highest water tariffs on the continent (PPIAF, 2005). A large part of this problem resulted from the increasingly poor quality of the main water source for Kigali, the Yanze River. The extremely high levels of sediment in the river, especially at times of high flow, resulted in significant filtration and treatment problems. And the volume of river water was far from adequate for the city's needs. During periods of low flow, almost the entire river flow needed to be harvested to satisfy Kigali's demand, and typically there was still a significant overall supply deficit. The five main springs on which Kigali relied for most of the balance of its water supply, especially during the dry season, were centrally located and had become enveloped by urban sprawl as the city had expanded. The springs had never been properly protected and were therefore highly vulnerable to the effects of pollution from homes and businesses. The World Bank study recommended construction of a 105 km, large-diameter pipeline running to Kigali from catchments in the north west of the country. But the cost (US$117 million in 2003) and project duration (eight to ten years of project development and construction) proved to be too much of a challenge for the government to take on at the time.

As no action was taken, the situation continued to deteriorate. According to the government's 2012 census, Kigali had a population of 1,132,686. Daily water needs were estimated at 90,000 m^3. The installed capacity of the existing treatment plans and pumping stations was over 81,000 m^3, but daily production amounted to only 64,000 m^3 because of equipment breakdowns. By 2014, Kigali was extracting water from two local rivers, including the Yanze, a nearby lake, plus the same local springs—the spring water was treated only with chorine and lime before distribution, despite the fact that only marginal protections had been added to the springs and their water quality had further degraded (UNCDF, 2018).

In 2014, the Office of the Auditor General conducted an audit of the Kigali water sector performance of WASAC's predecessor utility, the Energy, Water, and Sanitation Authority (EWSA). The audit of EWSA identified a number of severe problems (Republic of Rwanda, 2014). For example, two of the filters at the newest and largest treatment plant had not been working since 2011, resulting in a daily lost production of 14,000 m^3. The audit estimated that the percentage of non-revenue water produced by the system was 37.8 per cent, suggesting that the amount of water available for actual distribution was far less than 64,000 m^3. For a population of over one million, the utility had 55,193 customer accounts in Kigali (almost two-thirds of which represented communal standpipes), although the utility had incomplete records of meters supplied to customers (many customers were simply charged flat rates). Access to the system's water had risen from 69 per cent in 2002 to 79 per cent in 2015 (with access defined as being within 200 m of an improved water source). But the utility was also doing a very poor job of collecting revenue from customers. As of September 30, 2013, the utility's unpaid water bills totaled the local currency equivalent of about US$5.2 million.

The government performance auditors suspected that major improvements in service provision could be made by repairing pipes, pumping stations, and treatment plants. But no one knew for certain because the utility did not have an effective management information system, had virtually no records on asset condition, and could not supply auditors with any information on assets like transmission and distribution pipes in Kigali, even the location of pipes. In a response to the audit, utility managers admitted that some of the pipes in the network were more than 70 years old and had never been maintained, much less rehabilitated. In this situation, the city desperately required both brownfield and greenfield types of investment because rehabilitation needed to be combined with the construction of new infrastructure to fully address the city's water supply problems.

11.4 Evaluation

Earlier chapters have summarized some of the most compelling examples of the emerging evidence-based critique of PPPs by organizing them around key themes. The following subsections evaluates the Kigali Water Concession in terms of those themes.

11.4.1 Prevalence

As Chapter 2 attempts to explain, the failure of many PPPs to meet expectations has contributed to lack of widespread use in developing countries. In the fashion described by Klein (2015), many African countries have embraced PPPs from time to time when particular needs arise or incentives are offered by development partners, but enthusiasm for this mechanism has never been deep or enduring. PPPs have never successfully gained a foothold in the vast majority of African countries. What then accounts for the Rwandan government's decision to use a concession to address water supply problems in Kigali, and more particularly a greenfield concession?

The answer probably has more to do with what the Rwandan government did not want, than what it did want. Rwanda had been caught up in the MDB haste to make some kind of tangible progress with state-owned enterprise (SOE) reforms in the 1990s, pursuant to structural adjustment lending programs. The pace of that campaign made monitoring and evaluation difficult. Plus, war and economic disruption undermined some of these operations before anything could be learned about reasons for success or failure. Privatization efforts in Rwanda illustrate the kinds of rapid policy shifts and general confusion that resulted when both governments and their development partners were unsure of what action to take to address infrastructure service problems. Rwanda endured a long series of unsuccessful attempts by development partners to facilitate brownfield solutions to water and electricity supply problems, beginning in the 1980s. By 2015, it was clear, to the World Bank at least, that the Rwandan government had no more appetite for brownfield PPPs (Box 11.1).

Box 11.1 Private Participation in Rwanda's Water Sector: Moving Goalposts

In 1983, after unsuccessful experience with a performance contract between the government and its water and electricity utility, Electrogaz, the government used IDA funding to prepare and sign a contract with French water and electricity operator SAUR to provide Electrogaz with a five-person "management assistance team" starting in January 1984. Electrogaz had been established in 1976 to manage grid electricity and urban water supply, but by the early 1980s all of its key functions urgently needed comprehensive reform. The management team was expected to "address the issues of tariff, accounting, financial management, procurement, inventory and all other administrative operations" (although this arrangement was never classified as a management contract). By the late 1980s, after the conclusion of the SAUR contract and considerable amounts of supporting technical assistance, the financial position of Electrogaz had continued to deteriorate. By the end of 1991 the utility had accumulated losses of US$58 million. A World Bank-sponsored review of the country's power sector policy in early 1992 found excessive government interference in Electrogaz operations involving staffing and compensation, as well as a government reluctance to authorize tariff increases or even to promptly settle the electricity bills of government agencies. By 1993 the government had rejected a suggestion to split Electrogaz into separate water and electricity utilities in order to simplify management tasks, but accepted a recommendation to use a "performance-based lease contract" to bring private sector management into Electrogaz operations.

But the Rwandan civil war, culminating in the 1994 genocide, brought SOE reform efforts and other kinds of development assistance in the country to a standstill. The World Bank's efforts to help implement the lease contract were stalled for two years until activities could resume in 1995. After the war, a series of policy seminars and workshops resulted in a new government power sector strategy, announced at the end of 1997. The government now decided on a 12–18-month management contract to provide operational assistance to Electrogaz, along with a thorough study of more comprehensive privatization options. A private operator was selected, Hydro Quebec International (HQI). But contract signing was delayed because the newly appointed Electrogaz board disagreed with the results of the selection. By July 1998, negotiations with HQI were terminated when the government announced a new power sector strategy involving a split of Electrogaz into three utilities (electricity, gas, and water) and the initiation of efforts to sell each. An investment bank was

Continued

Box 11.1 Continued

recruited to help with the sale and a new law approving all of this was passed by Parliament. In May 2000, the government decided to keep Electrogaz as a single entity that would be managed by a private operator for five years, followed by privatization. In July 2000, private operators were pre-qualified, and a selected contractor was expected to be in place by December 2002. A five-year management contract with Lahmeyer International became effective in October, 2003, but by December 2004 agreement on performance targets still had not been reached between the government and the contractor. The contract was terminated early in 2006, and World Bank documents noted that the intended purpose of the contract, to improve Electrogaz operations and prepare the way for a longer-term brownfield concession, "was not achieved" (World Bank, 2015, 8).

More changes in restructuring strategy followed. In 2008, Electrogaz was split into separate utilities for water (Rwanda Water and Sewage Corporation—RWASCO), and electricity (Rwanda Electricity Corporation—RECO). In 2010, RECO and RWASCO were merged and renamed Energy, Water and Sanitation Authority (EWSA). In January 2014, EWSA was split into three commercial companies. Two companies managed energy: The Energy Utility Corporation Ltd (EUCL) and the Energy Development Corporation Ltd (EDCL). A third company was created to manage the water sector: The Water and Sanitation Corporation (WASAC). In 2015, the World Bank tried to propose another attempt at management contracts, starting with the electricity companies. The project appraisal document noted that the option was "discussed and rejected by the GoR in view of the past experience" (World Bank, 2015, 9).

Source: Various World Bank Project Appraisal Documents and Implementation Completion Reports.

11.4.2 Costs and Profits

As the Kigali water concession was reaching financial close in 2017, two years after the concession agreement was signed, the government's water sector regulator concluded that the cost of water from the project was too high and demanded a 30 per cent reduction in Metito's bulk water price. The demand, made just before the project's scheduled financial close, was partly the result of the country's suddenly deteriorating economic situation. In 2016–17 Rwanda's GDP growth rate dropped by 30 per cent because of drought, weak export prices, and a slowdown in construction following the completion of several large investment projects. Despite years of growth, GDP per capita in the country was still just over US$711 in 2016.

Against the backdrop of this deteriorating economic situation the cost of the bulk water PPP seemed too expensive. When Metito was named the preferred bidder in 2014, the official production cost of water supplied to Kigali by EWSA was about US$0.70/m^3. Metito's proposed cost to the government, which covered the various investments made as part of the project, was over US$1.1/m^3. The actual difference in costs was not quite what it seemed. All things considered, the cost to the government of producing the water used by its Kigali customers was far higher than US$0.70/m^3. At the government's production cost level and given the existing tariff structure, the utility might have made a small surplus if the system had collected revenue for all the water produced (UNCDF, 2018). But the utility's percentage of non-revenue water, at nearly 38 per cent, was among the highest in SSA. So, the government's effective pre-concession water production and supply costs were exceptionally high, well over US$1.0/m^3.

The problem faced by the government was that given the existing inefficiencies of its water management operation, the Metito contract would precipitate another tariff hike, regardless of how much additional water it made available. After the 2014 performance audit, the government was taking steps to deal with issues that had driven up its costs, like high levels of non-revenue water, water sold at below cost-reflective prices, and shortfalls in tariff revenue collection. But those measures would take time. And the concession contract was not going to help because it was structured as a greenfield PPP—it would have no impact on retail management of the system. All of these problems would remain the sole responsibility of the government. With Metito's costs at over US$1.1/m^3 it would be a struggle for the government to avoid another water price hike until they could bring retail management issues under control. By early 2017, the country's Utilities Regulatory Agency (RURA) was already being criticized in the news media for a 2016 increase in the retail price of water in Kigali of almost 17 per cent, while the cost in rural areas was dropping (Global Water Intelligence, 2017).

Metito had little room to cut costs and resisted the demand to do so. They had already pared costs and profits to minimum levels in order to win the competitive tender for the project in 2014. When the concession agreement was signed in 2015 the project-related costs seemed reasonable to Rwanda's development partners, who were providing most of the project debt. An independent technical adviser to the lenders (WSP Parsons Brinkerhoff) benchmarked the project's capital costs with other similar projects and found them to be in line with industry standards. Engineering and construction costs seemed justified. The lenders concluded that the likely profitability of the project did not appear to be excessive. An independent auditor reviewed the sponsor's project financial model and concluded that the logic, arithmetic, and assumptions of the model were consistent with the expectations about the project described in representations to lenders.

But the cost of the project still seemed too high for one of the world's least developed countries and the government continued to insist on the price reduction. In order to accommodate this demand, the parties eventually agreed to simply remove some of the key investment activities from the project and transfer them to the government for implementation. This shift in responsibilities reduced the total cost of the Metito project by about US$14 million (UNCDF, 2018). The reduction came mostly in form of eliminating the "forwarding" infrastructure that had been part of the project, in other words, transmission infrastructure needed to move the water forward into the distribution system after it was extracted and treated. This involved removing things from Metito's responsibility like a pumping station, transmission pipes, and storage reservoirs. This forwarding infrastructure was still needed for a successful project, but the government decided it would build this infrastructure, could do so at less cost than Metito, and still complete construction within the original project time frame (UNCDF, 2018). The African Development Bank (AfDB) agreed to provide concessional debt to the government for this part of the project. This arrangement allowed the total cost of the project to drop from US$75 million to just under US$62 million. The price to the government of Metito's water dropped from US$1.06/m^3 to US$0.75/m^3.

Of course, the forwarding infrastructure still needed to be paid for to make the PPP viable, but the costs and associated risks of those investments had been shifted back to the government and were no longer the responsibility of the private concessionaire. The contract had become even less of a classic PPP and more of a hybrid between a PPP and a traditional engineering, procurement, and construction (EPC) contract, the kind of contract that the government would use for the forwarding infrastructure.[5]

11.4.3 Project Preparation Costs

The preparation costs of this project were formidable, and well beyond the ability of government to pay for them, but were almost entirely covered by development partners. Serious government discussions with development partners regarding a PPP for Kigali water seem to have begun in the 2001–3 period with the preparation by World Bank staff and consultants of a "Country Framework Report" (CFR). The CFR, funded by the World Bank's Public–Private Infrastructure

[5] EPC contracts differ from PPPs in that they typically do not require the private contractor to raise finance, acquire land, manage permitting and licenses, or maintain responsibility for long-term operations and maintenance after commercial operation has been initiated.

Advisory Facility (PPIAF), a multi-donor trust fund managed by the Bank, was a comprehensive review of the country's infrastructure needs and possible ways of using the private sector to improve management and provide financing (PPIAF, 2005). The final report, issued after two years of work, underscored the urgency of improving Kigali's water supply. This was the report, referred to earlier in this chapter, which recommended a PPP to build a 105 km pipeline to bring a new supply of water to the city. The report also identified a shorter-term, less expensive, and less sustainable alternative strategy that involved extracting water from boreholes on the banks of the Nyabarongo river. This lower-cost strategy was eventually used for the water BOT that reached closure in 2017.

A follow-up PPIAF grant in 2004 helped the government organize a conference that brought together government, the donor community, and the private sector to discuss the findings and recommendations of the CFR for the energy and water sectors. The government agreed to pursue the strategy outlined in the CFR, including the water sector recommendations, and the participating development partners pledged to support the government with advice on reforms needed to make more private participation in infrastructure a reality. For the next six years, the government struggled to reform its water sector, with advice from the World Bank and other development partners. Over this period, governance of the sector went through the bewildering sequence of legal and regulatory changes described in Box 11.1.

By 2010, the government seems to have decided against a traditional brownfield water concession, opting instead for a greenfield bulk water supply project, perhaps assuming that they could reform their own management of transmission and retail distribution of water quickly and thoroughly enough to take full advantage of a dramatic increase in the supply of water. In September 2010, the government retained International Finance Corporation (IFC) as lead adviser to develop and structure such a project. For the next five years, IFC carried out a number of project preparation activities, virtually all of them funded by donors:

- **Confirmation of technical feasibility.** The team assessed the possibility of extending bulk water supply via a PPP. This involved confirming levels of demand and supply; the suitability of the sites already proposed by the government for development (and proposals for alternative sites); and supporting the government's strategic planning for Kigali water supply.
- **Structuring of the project at the selected site.** This included detailed water supply source assessments, including availability, quality, and environmental impacts; preliminary design of infrastructure facilities; selection of the PPP option; formulation of a procurement strategy; and preliminary consultation with potential investors.

- **Implementation of the transaction.** This included market consultations; preparation of all the necessary transaction documents; and implementation of a competitive procurement process.
- **Sector capacity building.** IFC realized that key sector stakeholders needed help in strengthening their ability to oversee and implement the project. PPIAF provided grant funding for a program to provide support to the project in a number of different areas:
  - Institutional support to the EWSA to strengthen its ability to oversee and implement the Kigali bulk water project. This included recommending an organizational restructuring that would allow EWSA to improve its financial, technical, operational, and commercial performance. This helped lead to the transformation of EWSA into WASAC.
  - Technical support to EWSA and later WASAC to develop a more comprehensive understanding of the distribution network and its operational performance, in order to provide strategic recommendations to improve network monitoring and reduce the levels of non-revenue water; and
  - Capacity building of government officials to improve their understanding of PPPs.

The full cost of this preparation has not been publicly disclosed. IFC Advisory is normally reimbursed for its work from a combination of fees paid by host governments and success fees paid by private partners eventually selected to implement the project. But a number of different sources of donor money are also available to IFC for work in low-income economies like Rwanda that cannot afford the full costs of preparation. A normal IFC mandate of this kind would last 12–18 months and cost US$2 million, including things like grants from PPIAF and other donors, plus the success fee. In this case however, the process took over four years to reach the selection of a preferred bidder (in October 2014), with financial close occurring nearly three years later. In this case, total preparation costs were probably in the range of US$3–5 million, almost all of which was paid for by donors.

11.4.4 Finance and Investment

Specific financing terms for the project have also not been fully disclosed, but various case studies have pieced together the funding picture (UNCDF, 2018; OECD, 2019). The total project cost was approximately US$60.8 million. The lead arranger of the financing was the Emerging Africa Infrastructure Fund (EAIF), a member of the Private Infrastructure Development Group (PIDG), a donor-capitalized group of companies that develop and finance infrastructure in the poorest countries. EAIF and the AfDB financed US$40.6 million of the capital cost of the project—US$38 million of senior debt and US$2.6 million of junior debt with all loans on 18-year terms. Donors provided US$6.2 million in capital grants. Metito provided US$11.3 million (just over US$2 million as equity and the rest as a shareholder loan). The balance was covered by a VAT refund during construction. A concessional loan of approximately US$14 million was provided by AfDB to the government to pay for the forwarding infrastructure needed by the project but removed from Metito's responsibility just before financial close.

The important point here is that, other than Metito's equity and shareholder loan, there was no other private financing in this project. Assuming US$4 million for project preparation, and including the $14 million for the forwarding infrastructure in the total project cost, the pure private sector investment in the project amounted to only about 14 per cent of the total financing. Pure private equity alone was only 2.5 per cent of the total. Recent research has estimated that blended finance leverage ratios in low-income countries are indeed low—on average, MDBs, DFIs, and donors contribute about 73 per cent of the total blended financed investment in low-income countries, to leverage about 27 per cent from private partners (Attridge and Engen, 2019). But this means that in the case of Kigali Bulk Water the private partner made about half the average contribution to the blended finance total in low-income countries.

11.4.5 Poverty Impacts

Because this project provides bulk water on a wholesale basis, it has no direct connection to end users, and plays no role in tariff setting or retail system management. Therefore, the project cannot be said to have immediate benefits for poor customers. Much depends on how the government takes advantage of the increased supply of water resulting from the project. The government has not undertaken that the project will result in reduced tariffs for poor people (the government already maintains a pro-poor "lifeline tariff" for low-income customers, and the two lowest tariff bands account for over 80 per cent of WASAC's customer base). But officials apparently expect that the project will provide other benefits:

- The government indicated that a new WASAC business plan was to be prepared, targeting new water connections for 150,000 Kigali residents classified as extremely poor by international standards.
- Metito, the project sponsor, undertook to implement a corporate social responsibility (CSR) program involving free drinking water to 670 people daily and the development of a school or medical center.

11.4.6 Governance

Private participation in Rwanda's water sector was authorized in a series of policy documents. The National Public Investment Policy (NPIP), adopted in February 2009, promoted private investment and PPPs to "accelerate delivery of strategic national infrastructure, yield long-term value for money and ensure quality public services without jeopardizing debt sustainability." The 2010 National Policy and Strategy for Water and Sanitation Services articulated similar objectives, as did Rwanda's Vision 2020. The country's Economic Development and Poverty Reduction Strategy II, 2013–18, targeted 100 per cent water coverage of urban customers by 2017/18. Strategies for achieving targets like this were to include investing in infrastructure and mainstreaming private sector development.

But the National Water Supply Policy (2016) and National Water Supply Implementation Strategy (2016) made clear that private service delivery that combined rehabilitation of existing assets, new investments, and management of commercial service delivery was permitted only in rural areas. In fact, since the early 2000s the government had encouraged rural service provision by local private companies because of its inability to effectively manage rural water operations. By 2010, 28 per cent of rural water systems were privately managed (WSP, 2010). But the government clearly viewed urban water supply as a completely different issue. As described in the 2016 documents, water supply services in urban areas were to be managed "exclusively" by WASAC, a government-owned utility operating on commercial principles (Republic of Rwanda, 2016a, 2016b).[6]

The long and circuitous history of water sector institutional reforms in Rwanda (Box 11.1) apparently convinced the government that brownfield PPPs, like concessions, leases, or management contracts, were not answers to the sector's problems in urban areas like Kigali. The government was determined to keep urban sector water operations in the hands of a state-owned utility, albeit one supposedly operated on a commercial basis. Private participation in urban areas would be limited to greenfield projects involving wholesale water supply to government-owned utilities that would handle commercial distribution.

11.5 Conclusions: How Much Blended Finance is Too Much?

The Kigali Water Concession not the first water PPP in Africa, or even the first competitively tendered water PPP. But in a market where any kind of water PPP is

[6] End users were not required to purchase water only from the WASAC, so the government did not consider it to be a monopoly in that sense. But most urban residents who did not buy water directly from WASAC did so indirectly by purchasing its water indirectly via water vendors or operators of stand pipes.

extremely rare, the project seems to have the potential to be sustainable and help reduce the magnitude of Rwanda's water supply problems. Of course, all of this can only be determined after construction is completed and commercial operations continue for a period of time. Arguably, the project's most notable distinction is that it is the first significant water PPP signed in east or southern Africa since the ill-fated Dar es Salaam water lease began operation in Tanzania in 2003. The Dar project, involving competitively tendered private operation of the urban water utility and a relatively small amount of capital investment, was expected to be sustainable because of its modest ambitions. The collapse of the project less than two years after it began operations, and the lengthy, acrimonious legal disputes that followed, effectively closed the market for traditional water PPPs in SSA for well over a decade.

The Rwanda bulk water project has been done in a way that avoids some of the problems of traditional brownfield solutions like leases, concessions, and management contracts. The project avoids those problems because it is strictly a greenfield solution, similar to an IPP project. The private partner will build and own new assets that will be used to provide water on a wholesale basis, and sold to the government's water utility pursuant to a long-term, dollar-denominated water purchase agreement (like a PPA that serves as the basis for an IPP project). As with an IPP, the Rwandan government remains responsible for the riskiest responsibilities in an urban water system: distribution of water to end users, maintaining that part of the system, connecting customers, and collecting revenue. Even the forwarding, or transmission, infrastructure, was removed from the project and handed back to the government to build and manage.

But Kigali Water is also different from traditional PPPs because it represents a more extreme form of blended finance than textbook PPP projects. Blended finance refers to the use of concessional or near-concessional finance to catalyze private sector investment. In the Kigali case, the blending was massive and took many forms: (i) substantial donor contributions paid for project preparation, virtually all of which was managed by the IFC; (ii) donor grants were used to restructure the key water sector institution to improve its management and planning capabilities; (iii) a large donor grant was supplied to bring down project capital costs; (iv) all of the debt for the project came from an MDB and a DFI, none from the private sector; and (v) when the project still seemed too expensive for the government, a substantial element of it was simply excised from the project, handed back to the government to implement, and paid for with a separate MDB loan.

Blending of this kind radically shifts the costs and risks of the project from the private partner to the government and its development partners. This of course makes the project quite different from the kinds of PPPs promoted by the development community in the 1990s, which relied almost exclusively on private finance. The challenge is to carry out blending in a way that does not use too much subsidy to mobilize necessary amounts of private finance. "Too much" can mean several things. It may mean providing more subsidy support than the minimum needed to make the project commercially viable, so that the project generates unnecessarily high equity returns. "Too much" can also mean skewing concessional money away from its core agenda of helping to eradicate poverty in the poorest countries (Attridge and Engen, 2019). This could happen, for example, when direct subsidies to private companies result in less funding for development activities that might be more transparent and effective. Such activities could include the use of grant funding to help with policy reforms, capacity building, or efforts to improve the investment climate in these countries. Finally, "too much" blending may also be used when, as some experts have conjectured, the ratio of subsidies to private finance mobilized surpasses a threshold beyond which it is more cost-effective to do the project as a traditional public project, with 100 per cent financing from donors, MDBs, and DFIs, rather than as a PPP with a limited amount of private finance, but with all the costs, risks, and complexities of a PPP (Carter, 2015).

The Kigali Bulk Water project was not subjected to a formal evaluation that assessed whether or not the total amount of blended finance used for the project was "too much." This was at least partly due to the fact that blending was carried out by different actors at different points in time, in a largely uncoordinated fashion. Because of this the project displays the kinds of shortcomings—the lack of monitoring, absence of standardized blended finance definitions, as well as untransparent deal structures—that Organisation for Economic Co-operation and Development (OECD) investigations have found at the heart of donor inability to draw a comprehensive overall picture of their blended finance operations (Andersen et al., 2019, 11).

When the blended finance from different sources used to support the Kigali project is added together, it is difficult to make a compelling argument that the financial support to the project provided by MDBs, DFIs, and donors was clearly not "too much." The amount of private investment leveraged by financial support from development partners was very low, only about 14 per cent of total project investment, if preparation costs and the cost of the forwarding infrastructure are added. This is about half the average private sector contribution to blended finance infrastructure projects in low-income countries, which is already viewed as extremely low (Attridge and Engen, 2019). The percentage seems particularly low for a country that at the time of financial close was already ranked second in SSA in terms of Ease of Doing Business by the World Bank (World Bank, 2017).

The usual argument in such a situation against using funding from donors, MDBs, and DFIs to cover 100 per cent of the project costs, and allowing the government to manage it as a traditional public project, is that speed, efficiency, and quality control would be sacrificed in design, construction, and operations and maintenance. In other words, a private company could be expected to do a better, faster job building and managing the infrastructure. But costs and preparation time would most likely be considerably less for a public project. Procurement and contracting would be simpler and take much less time. Overall costs would be less without requirements to pay a private sponsor a variety of development fees and costs, or structure the project and regulatory environment to ensure a commercial rate of return. Plus, in this case, the project participants agreed to the change in the project to move a substantial share of the work back to the government for implementation with a concessional loan. This was a tacit acceptance of the government's claim that it could build the transmission infrastructure—critically needed in a timely fashion for the success of the PPP—within substantially the same time frame and at no more cost than would be guaranteed by the private partner.

The entire project could had been implemented that way from the beginning, for example, via an EPC contract with maintenance requirements, backed by contract oversight and capacity building funded by development partners. That might have been a faster, more cost-effective solution for Rwanda's water supply problems, with the added advantage of enhancing the government's capacity to implement similar projects in the future. In this way, the Rwanda project would have anticipated the transition from PPPs to EPC contracts that is now taking place in the low-income regions of countries like India (Box 11.2). This transition

Box 11.2 From PPPs to EPCs: Back to Contracting Basics in Rajasthan

The Indian government began promoting infrastructure PPPs in the 1990s. Traditional item-rate construction contracting in India was prone to time and cost overruns, with contractors required to quote rates for individual items of work on the basis of schedules of quantities provided by the government. Once projects were built, government agencies were responsible for maintenance, but often had limited budgets and insufficient technical expertise to keep the assets functioning properly. Competitively tendered PPPs that combined design, financing, construction, operation, and maintenance, under the responsibility of a single private commercial entity, proved to be a much more cost-effective approach to the supply of critically needed infrastructure. PPPs were slow to roll out until the 2000s. The introduction of a national PPP subsidy scheme in 2004 helped ramp up private sector interest in PPPs. Known as Viability Gap Funding (VGF), this was a form of blended finance (upfront capital grants) designed to help improve the commercial viability of infrastructure PPPs that could be shown to be socially and economically beneficial. From 2005 through 2012, PPPs surged in India with over 600 projects completed, many of them supported by VGF.

Continued

Box 11.2 Continued

The surge was apparent in Rajasthan, one of India's low-income states, and one of the first states to use PPPs to finance and build highways. Approximately 5,000 km of roads have been developed in the state using PPP mechanisms (mostly BOT toll roads). And most of these projects have benefitted from VGF subsidies. However, beginning in 2012, PPPs began to lose momentum in India. The numbers of projects and amounts of investment dropped precipitously. This was particularly true in the road sector and states like Rajasthan saw their highway PPP programs go into sharp declines. There were several reasons for this. First, many of the roads with traffic volumes high enough to make toll roads commercially viable had already been taken up in projects by 2012. Second, PPPs in all sectors were failing to meet implementation milestones because of government delays in facilitating land acquisition and granting clearances and licenses of various kinds. Projects began to stall and Indian banks began to stop lending to PPPs.

The government's PPP regulatory framework permitted road projects to be done as "PPPs" with operators deriving revenue from annual or semi-annual government payments (the "BOT Annuity Model") rather than via user tolling (the "BOT Toll Model"). But annuity projects were ineligible for VGF support, because VGF rules required that 60 per cent of project revenues be generated via user fees. As the PPP market changed, VGF was also becoming less useful in other ways: the grants could not be disbursed until construction started, and then only after 100 per cent of the equity was paid in. This did not help much with contractor liquidity problems, caused by their inability to generate any project revenues until the start of commercial operation. The maximum VGF subsidy available from the national government was 20 per cent of project costs—state governments could add 20 per cent, but states like Rajasthan had limited resources for this. By 2012, VGF grants were losing their ability to catalyze private sector investment.

The government's twelfth Five Year Plan (2012–17) called for a dramatic increase in the use of an alternative to the PPP approach for difficult projects, "engineering, procurement, and construction" (EPC) contracts. EPCs are a standard type of construction contracting widely used for large or technically complicated projects, particularly in developed, competitive markets. They represent an improvement over the conventional item-rate contracts because design, procurement, construction, and commissioning are assigned to a contractor for a lump sum price. The major advantage to the government owner is that it provides a single point of responsibility and a single point of contact between the contractor and the owner. The EPC advantage to private contractors over PPPs is that contractors were relieved of the responsibility for raising finance, obtaining clearances, acquiring land, estimating traffic flows, or long-term operations and maintenance. The EPC model requires the government to pay 100 per cent of project costs, but in India this can be done by issuing bonds or securing road toll receivables after the completion of construction.

In Rajasthan, state officials have had little experience with EPC contracting or capital market finance. In 2019, the World Bank stepped in with a US$250 million loan for a highway program using EPC and EPC–PPP hybrid contracts to upgrade 766 km of Rajasthan's highways. WB funding has paid for feasibility studies that determine the commercial viability of different highway segments. Just over 60 per cent of this roadway will be built using EPC contracts. These contracts will incorporate five-year maintenance provisions and contract payments will be linked to specific staged, outputs (as compared to payments for individual items or units required in conventional item-rate contracts). The remaining 40 per cent of the roadway is judged to be somewhat more commercial and will be built using a "Hybrid Annuity Model" (HAM), which involves government financing of 50 per cent of costs during construction (with the contractor investing the other 50 per cent). The contractor would then be responsible for operations and maintenance for a ten-year period, during which the government would make semiannual "annuity" payments based on performance. Importantly, the WB will support all of this with financing and technical assistance for project preparation and market sounding, procurement training, highway management information systems, model concession documents, as well as embedded experts to help state officials oversee performance of the EPC and HAM contracts.

Sources: Government of India, 2013, 2015; World Bank, 2019b.

is likely to be facilitated by recent research that more closely examines the critical factors on which the optimal choice between PPPs and traditional procurement depends (e.g., Ross and Yan, 2015; Atmo et al., 2017).

The design of the Kigali Water Project is, in effect, an implicit endorsement of the Rwandan government's ability to solve its most pressing infrastructure problems without the help of the private sector. That, after all, is the premise behind a project that leaves the most difficult aspects of water service delivery in the hands of a state-owned company. A more substantial supply of potable water will mean very little if WASAC continues to lose substantial amounts of it in transmission and distribution, fails to collect revenues, and does not keep track of its assets or maintain them. This is of course similar to problems with IPP projects in otherwise unreformed power sectors. Wholesale supply of water and power are the least risky kinds of PPPs for private investors and operators, but retail service provision is arguably much more in need of help. Public statements by WASAC suggest that its management understands the various operational shortcomings that resulted in such a critical performance audit in 2014 (WASAC, 2016). Time will tell if they can solve these problems, but the bulk water project is a vote of confidence by the development community in the ability of the government to do so.

There do not appear to be any other particular benefits from doing the project as a PPP. Its demonstration value is low. The chances of replicating a project like this in the African water sector are relatively small for the reasons discussed earlier in this chapter. Basic water infrastructure exists in most countries, even the poorest countries. Extensions to the network and household connections are often needed, but infrastructure assets used in sourcing, treating, storing, transmitting, and distributing water are normally in place. These assets need maintenance and often rehabilitation in developing countries, but these kinds of actions mostly require brownfield-type solutions rather than complete asset replacement or major additions. Rwanda was a unique case because maintenance and rehabilitation of water system assets essentially stopped after the genocide and civil war of 1994. Two decades later, the city needed new sources of water, new treatment facilities, and new transmission assets to meet the needs of a population still largely dependent on a 70-year system serving a city population four times larger than it had been in 2004 and spread across six and one-half times the area of the 2004 city (Kigali City, 2018).

Finally, the development community's celebration of the Kigali project tends to confirm Michael Klein's assertion that the inconsistent enthusiasm for traditional PPPs in developing countries is a reflection of the realization that well-run public companies are just as efficient as private ones. If the Kigali Bulk Water project is ultimately successful, it will be because of the government-owned companies involved more than the fact that this was called a PPP.

References

Andersen, O.W., I. Basile, A. de Kemp, G. Gotz, E. Lundsgaarde, M. Orth. 2019. "Blended Finance Evaluation: Governance and Methodological Challenges." OECD Development Co-operation Working Papers No. 51. OECD Publishing, Paris.

Atmo, G., C. Duffield, L. Zhang, D. Wilson. 2017. "Comparative Performance of PPPs and Traditional Procurement Projects in Indonesia." *International Journal of Public Sector Management* 30(2): 118–36.

Attridge, S., L. Engen. 2019. *Blended Finance in the Poorest Countries: The Need for a Better Approach*. ODI Report (April). Overseas Development Institute, London.

Berg, S., R. Marques. 2011. "Quantitative Studies of Water and Sanitation Utilities: A literature survey." *Water Policy* (13)5: 591–606.

Bisaga, I., G. Norman. 2015. "Universal Water and Sanitation: How did the rich countries do it?" Finance Brief 2, Public finance for WASH. Accessed at: www.publicfinanceforwash.org

Camdessus, M. 2003. "Financing Water for All: Report of the World Panel on Financing Water Infrastructure." Report written by James Winpenny for the panel chaired by Michel Camdessus. World Water Council, March.

Carter, P. 2015. *Why Subsidise the Private Sector?* ODI Report. Overseas Development Institute, London.

Estache, A., C. Philippe. 2012. "The Impact of Private Participation in Infrastructure in Developing Countries: Taking Stock of about 20 Years of Experience." ECARES Working Paper, 2012–043, Universite Libre de Bruxelles, Brussels.

Foster, V., C.M. Briceno-Garmendia. 2010. *Africa's Infrastructure: A Time for Transformation*. AICD Flagship Report. Washington, DC: World Bank.

Gassner, K., A. Popov, N. Pushak. 2009. "Does Private Participation Improve Performance in Electricity and Water Distribution?" Trends and Policy Options No. 6. Washington, DC: World Bank. Accessed at: www.ppiaf.org.

Global Water Intelligence. 2017. "Rwanda Cuts Rural Water Price as Urban Tariff Rises." Global Water Intelligence (January 12). Accessed at https://www.globalwaterintel.com/news/2017/2/rwanda-cuts-rural-water-price-as-urban-tariff-rises

Government of India. 2015. "Report of the Committee on Revisiting and Revitalising Public Private Partnership Model of Infrastructure." New Delhi: Department of Economic Affairs, Ministry of Finance (November).

Government of India. 2013. "Scheme and Guidelines for financial Support to Public Private Partnerships in Infrastructure." New Delhi: Department of Economic Affairs, Ministry of Finance (November).

Gurria, A. 2006. "Task Force on financing Water for All, Report 1: Enhancing access to finance for local governments, financing water for agriculture." Report written by Paul Van Hofwegen, for the task force chaired by Angel Gurria. World Water Council, March.

Hanemann, W.M. 2005. "The Economic Conception of Water." Working Paper No. 1005. University of California Berkeley: Department of Agricultural and Resource Economics, UCB. Accessed at: https://escholarship.org/uc/item/08n4410n

Hutton, G., M. Varughese. 2016. "The Costs of Meeting the 2030 Sustainable Development Goal Targets on Drinking Water, Sanitation, and Hygiene." Water and Sanitation Program. Washington, DC: World Bank.

Jin, Y., B. Li, E. Roca, V. Wong. 2014. "Investment Returns in the Water Industry: A survey." *International Journal of Water* 8(2): 183–99.

Kigali City. 2018. "Kigali City Population Evolution." City of Kigali Website. Accessed at http://www.kigalicity.gov.rw/index.php?id=64&L=1

Klein, M. 2015. "Public–Private Partnerships: Promise and Hype." Policy Research Working Paper No. 7340. Washington, DC: World Bank.

Marin, P. 2009. *Public–Private Partnerships for Urban Water Utilities: A Review of Experiences in Developing Countries.* PPIAF Trends and Policy Options Series No. 8. Washington, DC: World Bank.

OECD. 2018. *Financing Water: Investing in sustainable growth.* Policy Perspectives, OECD Environment Policy Paper No. 11. OECD Publishing, Paris.

OECD. 2019. *Making Blended Finance Work for Water and Sanitation: Unblocking Commercial Finance for SDG 6.* OECD Studies on Water. OECD Publishing, Paris.

Public–Private Infrastructure Advisory Facility. 2005. *Private Solutions for Infrastructure in Rwanda: A country Framework Report.* Washington, DC: World Bank.

Republic of Rwanda. 2014. "Performance Audit Report on Water Production and Distribution in Kigali City by EWSA." Office of the Auditor General of State Finances, Rwanda (OAG), Kigali (May).

Republic of Rwanda. 2016a. *National Water Supply Policy.* Ministry of Infrastructure, Kigali (December).

Republic of Rwanda. 2016b. *National Water Supply Policy Implementation Strategy.* Ministry of Infrastructure, Kigali (December).

Ross, T.W., J. Yan. 2015. "Comparing Public-Private Partnerships and Traditional Public Procurement: Efficiency vs. flexibility." *Journal of Comparative Policy Analysis* 17(5): 1–19.

Rwahigi, M. 2015. "Rwanda Signs Water Purchase Agreement with Metito to Increase Access to Clean Safe Water." *Hope Magazine*, April 1.

Sirtaine, S., M.E. Pinglo, J.L. Guasch, V. Foster (2004), *How Profitable are Infrastructure Concessions in Latin America? Empirical Evidence and Regulatory Implications.* PPIAF Trends and Policy Options. Washington, DC: World Bank.

Thomson Reuters. 2018. "Africa's First Water PPP." *PFI Yearbook 2018.* Accessed at http://www.pfie.com/africas-first-water-ppp/21320834.fullarticle

UN Capital Development Fund (UNCDF). 2018. *Blended Finance in the Least Developed Countries: Case study 4, Kigali Bulk Water supply PPP.* UNCDF, New York.

UN Water Website. June 10, 2015. Accessed at http://www.unwater.org/sdgs/means-of-implementation/en/http://www.unwater.org/sdgs/means-of-implementation/en/

Water and Sanitation Corporation Ltd. (WASAC). 2016. "WASAC Behind Rwanda's Water and Sanitation Quick Turnaround." *Hope Magazine*, 67: 38–41 (August).

Water and Sanitation Program (WSP). 2010. "Improving Rural Water Service in Rwanda with Public–Private Partnerships." *IFC and WSP Smart Lessons.* Washington, DC: World Bank.

World Bank. 2015. "International Development Association Project Appraisal Document on a Proposed Credit in the Amount of SDR 67.70 Million (US$95

Million Equivalent) to the Republic of Rwanda for the Electricity Sector Strengthening Project." Report No: PAD1301. Washington, DC: World Bank (November 19).

World Bank. 2017. *Doing Business 2017*. Washington, DC: World Bank.

World Bank. 2018. PPI Project Database. Accessed at: http://ppi.worldbank.org/customquery?mode=1

World Bank. 2019a. *Doing Business 2019*. Washington, DC: World Bank.

World Bank. 2019b. "Project Appraisal Document on a Proposed Loan in the Amount of US$250 Million to the Republic of India for Rajasthan State Highways Development Program II Project." Report No. PAD2830. Washington, DC: World Bank.

WHO, UN Water. 2012. *The Challenge of Extending and Sustaining Services: UN-Water Global Analysis and Assessment of Sanitation and Drinking Water*. GLAAS 2012 Report. Geneva, World Health Organization.

Yang, J. 2015. "The New 'Water Barons': Wall Street Mega-Banks are Buying up the World's Water." *Market Oracle*, December 21.

12
Conclusions

Debates about the benefits of private participation in infrastructure services began as soon as public–private partnerships (PPPs) were enlisted in the desperate battle to reform state-owned enterprises in developing countries, as structural adjustment lending programs shifted toward "privatization" solutions in the 1990s. Since then, much of the discourse has taken on an ideological flavor, with representatives of organized labor and civil society groups refusing to accept that the profit motive of private companies can be harnessed in a way that protects consumers of water, electricity, and transport services against private exploitation, while providing them with services of acceptable quantity and quality. PPP advocates, represented by certain bilateral donors, development finance institutions (DFIs), multilateral development banks (MDBs), and private companies, often are just as obdurate, insisting that intelligent financial engineering of PPPs can and does achieve desirable outcomes. Each side purports to have evidence to support their position, but meaningful details tend to get lost in the midst of hyperbole. Both sides accuse the other of using data selectively to promote their position.

The discussion has now taken on an international dimension as it is becoming clear that most of the Sustainable Development Goals (SDGs) will not be met in most low-income countries without unprecedented levels of outside support. As was the case with structural adjustment in the 1990s, PPPs are once again being enlisted in a desperate attempt to solve a massive, far-reaching problem in the developing world. For several years, international bodies like the G20 have promoted the use of large regional PPPs to achieve transformational changes in low-income countries. Civil society groups have likewise ramped up their critical responses to these recommendations.

Aspects of this debate are however changing, as evidence about the performance of PPPs over the last 30 years has gradually been collected and analyzed by respected social scientists, some of whom actually promoted the use of PPPs in the 1990s. These analyses are finding their way into the civil society critique of PPPs, making these critiques more formidable and harder to ignore. In the meantime, PPP proponents continue to rely heavily on isolated success stories and the self-assured belief that a compelling case for PPPs has already been made. The proponents' focus is mostly on how to do PPPs correctly, without paying much attention to the growing body of conflicting information about what kinds of

Public–Private Partnerships in Sub-Saharan Africa: The Evidence-Based Critique. James Leigland, Oxford University Press (2020). © James Leigland.
DOI: 10.1093/oso/9780198861829.001.0001

projects really are sustainable, and in which sectors and countries. As a result, these advocates of PPPs sometimes appear more doctrinaire, and more willing to selectively use evidence, than PPP critics.

This accumulation of PPP performance data is taking the shape of an evidence-based critique, and is demonstrating that these projects in general, have not met stakeholder expectations, particularly in low-income countries. Based on some of these findings, it would be realistic to assume that PPPs could eventually account for 20–25 per cent of public sector infrastructure investment in middle-income developing countries, with a considerably lower percentage in low-income countries. These are of course not insignificant numbers, but they are nothing like what was expected of PPPs in the 1990s. Overall, the evidence shows that PPPs have never successfully gained the traction in low-income countries that they have in some middle-income countries.

The studies reviewed in this book suggest that governments and their development partners have not done a very effective job in anticipating PPP costs and profits, so assessments of "value-for-money" (VFM) using tools such as "public sector comparators" have been frequently off the mark. While this is true of all kinds of infrastructure projects in developed and developing countries, it is especially the case with PPPs. In the developing world, particularly in low-income countries, PPP project costs have been higher than expected, and profits much lower than anticipated. This outcome has not been lost on private sector investors and operators, and has contributed to the limited use of PPPs in these countries.

PPP project preparation costs have also been much higher than were assumed in the 1990s, and certainly higher than the costs of preparing projects for traditional public procurement. This is due partly to the upstream legal and regulatory preparation required in many developing countries, as well as the complexity and higher costs of PPP procurement when compared with traditional government construction contracting. Expensive VFM assessments involving public sector comparators tend to be more rigorously applied to projects involving private participation—most experts would argue that such tools should be used for both PPP procurement and traditional government contracting. High preparation costs present governments and their development partners with a difficult problem: who pays for these preparation costs if they cannot always be recovered in some way from an eventual project?

New data compiled by the World Bank in 2016 offers another important finding regarding infrastructure PPPs: in many cases, private finance is not the predominant source of investment funding for these projects (Chao and Saha, 2016). Governments, or their state-owned banks, along with donors, DFIs, and MDBs, account for more than half of this funding, even in middle-income regions like Latin America. This type of public funding appears to be essential if the aim is to attract some private finance to these projects. This reality challenges some of the traditional assumptions about the value of PPPs, especially with regard to the role of the private sector in PPP investment.

Perhaps one of the least surprising findings about infrastructure PPPs is that developmental benefits in terms of poverty reduction, are far from automatic. This has been a special focus of former World Bank economist Antonio Estache. His analytical assessments have found their way into some of the most powerful civil society critiques of PPPs. Estache and others point out that positive poverty impacts need to be deliberately designed into projects, and then monitored by regulators (Estache and Philippe, 2012). Private partners do not typically pursue these benefits without receiving substantial incentivization from governments and development partners.

Governance problems can have significant negative impacts on PPP project development and oversight. It is increasingly clear that governments need to play a strong role in PPPs, but often the ultimate justification for doing a project as a PPP is the weakness of host government institutions and their lack of skilled staff. Specialized government PPP units can help, but cannot be expected to work more effectively than other existing governmental agencies. It is not an exaggeration to say that a government that is capable of fully playing its role in designing, developing, implementing, monitoring, and regulating PPPs, may be just as successful using traditional public procurement to achieve the same objectives. This supports Michael Klein's point that well-run public companies match the performance of private firms in regulated sectors (Klein, 2015).

The larger the PPP, the greater the magnitude of all these problems. "Bigger is better" is not an adage that applies to these kinds of projects. Part of the problem is simply that the larger size of the project tends to increase project fragility—that is, the vulnerability of the project to forecasting mistakes or unforeseen changes in the project environment. Indeed, doing a project as a PPP may accentuate the problems created by size. This is the reason why transformational PPPs are so rarely undertaken successfully. Developing a project like Inga III, for example, has encountered very many problems. Even the handful of successful transformational PPPs in Sub-Saharan Africa (SSA), like the Maputo toll road concession in southern Africa—the first and only cross-border PPP road project—are mostly unique and unlikely to be replicated. The best alternative to a transformational PPP is not necessarily a project done via traditional public procurement. It may involve breaking it up into a collection of smaller projects, done as either public or private projects. Smaller projects reduce the overall investment fragility of these undertakings, making them much easier to prepare and more appealing to finance.

To understand the origins of the rise in PPP use, one needs to go back to the early tenets of structural adjustment lending by the MDBs in the 1990s. This will assist in appreciating why these mechanisms have rarely met expectations. At that time, many public sector assets like electricity and water supply utilities, desperately needed rehabilitation and more efficient management, but could not be sold to private interests or liquidated. Consequently, brownfield concessions, leases, and management contracts were developed by MDB-funded consultants as policy-driven financing initiatives, designed to "privatize" infrastructure service systems. Many governments were never particularly comfortable with brownfield concessions or management contracts, but needed the financial assistance that was often made dependent on the use of such projects.

In the post-2000 era, and after the discrediting of structural adjustment, the development community began a determined effort to sharply differentiate PPPs from "privatization." These efforts helped to obscure the origins of PPPs and the fact that governments had been pressured into many of these arrangements against what they considered to be their better judgment.

Perhaps encouraged by the endorsements of donors, DFIs, and MDBs, the private sector initially misunderstood the risks associated with brownfield concessions, accepting the textbook view that brownfield PPPs were inherently less risky than greenfield ones. But project experience, especially in low-income countries, quickly cast the risks and returns associated with these PPPs in a new light. Inadequate project preparation and due diligence failed to disclose the fact that existing assets to be taken over for rehabilitation and extension were typically in much worse condition that anyone realized. The assets had often been poorly maintained, but this fact was hidden by a parallel lack of monitoring and poor record keeping. Consequently, the service systems often required much more investment than could be recovered from system revenues, which were weaker than expected because of end-user unwillingness or inability to pay cost-reflective tariffs. The Asian financial crisis exposed the weaknesses of risk mitigation mechanisms, especially anything requiring governments to step in to rescue private partners. The resulting wave of PPP project collapses taught private investors and operators to avoid such projects unless third-party guarantees and financing were used to support them. Brownfield PPPs of all kinds have demonstrated what Klein referred to as the "waves of enthusiasm for PPPs followed by some disenchantment and consolidation" (Klein, 2015).

A project like the Nelspruit water concession clearly illustrates Klein's cycle of attraction and rejection. Structured as a classic brownfield concession, the project involved asset investment and commercial operation, and was strongly supported by South African President Mandela and his senior officials in the late 1990s. But as the concession reached financial closure in 1999, Mandela and many of his like-minded senior officials were transitioning out of government. The project was denounced by Mandela's political allies—the labor unions, the Communist Party, civil society groups, and influential elements of the local news media. The government also failed to make good on promises to amend legislation that created regulatory risks for the project's operational effectiveness and discouraged private financing. Over the course of the next 20 years, the Nelspruit concession struggled to achieve all of its key objectives. But local officials and independent evaluators continued to see net benefits in the project's operation. Meanwhile, the project's many critics discredited it to such a degree that, to date, the project has never been replicated, has been completely disowned by national government officials, and is largely ignored in international reviews of water PPPs. The average South African is unaware that one of the developing world's most long-lived urban water PPPs is still operational in their country.

While some brownfield infrastructure solutions, such as management contracts, continue to be promoted by donors, DFIs, and MDBs, over the last decade this has been happening less frequently. However, during the 1990s, development partners routinely recommended such contracts as tools for "privatizing" state-owned utilities that could not be sold and could not attract private investment. Governments were frequently persuaded with sector loans or grants to enter into these agreements, despite facing resistance from utility employees as well as customers. Management contracts are commonly used by the private sector for operating commercial enterprises, particularly in hotel management. When used for routine business-related management functions, such contracts tend to work well. But these contracts have not been suitable as tools for reforming public utilities, where private managers are required to diagnose and fix deep-rooted operational problems, train poorly capacitated staff, and recover costs from resistant end-users, including government agencies that often refuse to pay their bills. The elementary point is that host governments do not feel ownership of such contracts, and accept them only as mechanisms for accessing soft funding from donors, DFIs, or MDBs. Typically, host governments will not support management contracts financially after donor support has been phased out. This has meant that these contracts have little or no chance of meeting stakeholder expectations.

Greenfield PPPs like independent power producer (IPP) projects represent a very different dynamic. IPP projects have been remarkably successful in attracting private investment and, by far, make up the largest single category of PPPs in developing countries. In fact, without IPP project investment, the PPP track record in low-income countries would be virtually non-existent. Such projects are popular with private investors because they are far less risky than brownfield projects that must contend with existing but poorly maintained assets. In many cases, brownfield projects also involve delivery of retail services to end users, which puts these projects directly in the cross-hairs of customers who are often very unhappy with the quality of service and largely unaware that major sector problems are not the responsibility of concessionaires or management contractors to solve. By focusing on wholesale service provision, using new assets built under private supervision and with requisite quality control, IPP projects can avoid many of the risks associated with brownfield solutions. This makes IPP projects more attractive to private investors, as well as international development banks like IFC, FMO, PROPARCO, and DEG, that specialize in lending on near-market terms to private companies. These financing institutions compete with each other for market share in developing countries, based to a large extent on their ability to find suitable IPP projects to finance.

However, the accumulated evidence regarding the benefits of IPP projects suggests that from a developmental point of view, these transactions often present trade-offs. IPP projects completed in countries with otherwise unreformed power sectors are unlikely to generate the full benefits expected of such projects, and they may slow down the momentum toward achieving further reforms. This lost momentum benefits entrenched monopoly state-owned utilities that seek to control sector finances and keep charge of patronage job appointments. The inescapable conclusion is that the desperate need for more electricity generating capacity in many poor countries has combined with the motivations of the private sector and certain development banks to result in a push for IPP projects to be done regardless of lack of progress on sector reforms. This has often meant that the sector improvements, necessary to ensure that such projects generate optimal benefits, do not happen.

Competitive tender programs used to select independent power producers for renewable energy IPP projects represent a significant new alteration of the PPP landscape, particularly in SSA where very few PPP projects of any kind have been competitively tendered. Tender programs in Zambia, Uganda, and South Africa have achieved success in terms of relatively rapid rollout of renewable energy IPPs and sharp reductions in the costs of power. Some experts have expressed the view that such projects may avoid the IPP project trade-offs mentioned earlier, by helping to drive power sector reform in countries dominated by vertically integrated state-owned utilities. The reasoning is that this could happen because renewable energy is at the center of a number of intersecting power sector trends that are disrupting these sectors all over the world by highlighting the value of distributed power generation and the shortcomings of traditional, centralized, monopoly utilities.

The tender programs in Zambia and Uganda were designed and managed by development partners, heavily subsidized, and produced only a handful of IPP projects. They do not appear to have been "disruptive" in the sense of innovation in driving improvements in other aspects of sector performance. Their chances for replication, without donor subsidies, also are not promising.

The South African program, on the other hand, was designed and managed exclusively by South Africa officials and largely self-financed. It was massively successful in signing scores of IPP projects, generating huge amounts of private investment, and reducing power prices without the use of heavy subsidization. The South African program has indeed been disruptive, in the sense of demonstrating that the future of power supply will involve decentralized, private, renewable energy generation that eventually will challenge if not replace vertically integrated, state-owned monopoly single-buyer utilities. But the success of the South African program has been only one element in a constellation of sector disruptions that seem to be leading to profound sector reform, including the near-bankruptcy of the national state-owned power utility caused mostly by mismanagement and corruption. Nevertheless, the success of the South African program has helped catalyze a national debate on the need for further sector reforms. In this unique case, successful IPP projects have effectively highlighted the need for greater transformation of the sector, rather than obscured it.

PPPs are unlikely to disappear, even in low-income countries. Governments and their development partners are finding some situations in which PPPs can be sustainable if structured and supported appropriately. But the emerging evidence-based critique of PPPs suggests that these projects are quite different from those envisioned in the 1990s. For example, it is no longer assumed that PPPs can, or should try to, cover all operating and capital costs in a large variety of infrastructure service sectors in poor countries. Compared with the conventional PPP model promoted in the 1990s, successful PPPs are now mainly hybrids, combining some elements of classic PPPs with those of consulting or engineering, procurement, construction (EPC) contracts. These hybrids involve compromises regarding many of the features of these projects that were considered definitive in the 1990s.

Perhaps the most dramatic compromise is the dominating role now played in most of these projects by "blended" or subsidized finance. Governments and their development partners pay for and manage most basic project preparation work because experience shows that it cannot be left to prospective private partners. Blended finance also contributes to the capital costs of these projects, and often supports the guarantees and other risk-mitigation mechanisms insisted on by private sponsors and financiers. Various forms of concessional finance are also often necessary to strengthen the ability of host governments to responsibly participate in PPP project development and implementation monitoring.

Blended finance is most likely to be cost-effective when it is clearly justified due to need, rationale, benefits that are likely to exceed costs, and risk mitigation. But even casual analysis of these factors seems rare in the current rush to pursue SDGs and large, transformational PPPs. In some cases, like the Kigali Bulk Water Concession, so much blended finance is used to make the PPP commercially viable that such analysis seems urgently needed to confirm that the project has not yet reached the threshold beyond which it would be less expensive and more sustainable to implement it as a public project supported by grants and concessional (or near concessional) lending, rather than a PPP.

In the case of Kigali Bulk Water, it is unlikely that alternatives to traditional PPP models were considered because the original mandate given to IFC Transaction Advisory Services was to develop the project as a PPP. IFC marshaled soft loans and grant funding from a variety of different sources to make the project successful as a PPP, although with very limited amounts of private sector finance.

However, in situations where development partners are willing to use such high levels of soft loan and grant funding to finance capital investments, and government counterparts seem capable of managing EPC procurement and project oversight (with the help of consultants and capacity building programs), the possibility of non-PPP solutions needs to be considered. Kigali Bulk Water is certainly a case where alternatives could have been considered, the many Chinese-financed hydropower projects in SSA are being built as public projects with EPC contracting, and India is experimenting with EPC and EPC–PPP hybrids to fill the gap left by the declining popularity of PPPs. EPC contracts do not offer the kinds of comprehensive, long-term solutions theoretically made possible by PPPs, and private partners cannot usually achieve the rates of return possible on PPPs. But risks and uncertainty faced by private partners on PPP projects are also dramatically reduced with EPC contracting, and this can make a compelling difference in the poorest countries, where threats to project sustainability are very high.

For reasons discussed in preceding chapters, PPPs are unlikely to have major positive impacts on achievement of the SDGs or on the provision of transformational regional infrastructure, as envisioned by the G20. PPPs will continue to play modest but still important roles in the cost-effective provision of infrastructure service in many developing countries, as long as they are well structured, appropriately supported, and carefully monitored and evaluated. But sustainable PPPs will do a disservice in the developing world if they distract from the fact that the fundamental causes of poor infrastructure service delivery in developing countries have nothing to do with the availability of private investment. Those causes involve things like government policies, institutions, technical capacity, as well as the political economy realities of these countries and their relationships with development partners.

References

Chao, J., D. Saha. 2016. *Sources of Financing for PPP Investments 2015*. Washington, DC: World Bank. Accessed at: https://ppi.worldbank.org/~/media/GIAWB/PPI/Documents/Data-Notes/2015-PPP-Investments-Sources.pdf.

Estache, A., C. Philippe. 2012. "The Impact of Private Participation in Infrastructure in Developing Countries: Taking Stock of about 20 Years of Experience." ECARES Working Paper, 2012–043, Universite Libre de Bruxelles, Brussels.

Klein, M. 2015. "Public-Private Partnerships: Promise and Hype." World Bank Policy Research Working Paper, No. 7340. Washington, DC: World Bank.

APPENDIX

A Cautionary Case Study from South Asia: The Bangladesh BOT Program

A.1 Introduction

The focus of this book is on PPPs in Sub-Saharan Africa (SSA), but the evidence-based critique of these projects derives from experience in all developing countries, particularly in low-income countries (LICs). In this respect, probably the most dramatic case that best illustrates the lessons generated by this critique comes from South Asia. This is the 15-year effort to develop hundreds of PPPs for rural water schemes in Bangladesh. This program, encompassing a number of World Bank-supported projects, boldly took on a broad combination of the fundamental challenges that have doomed PPPs in developing countries since the early 1990s:

- A geographical focus on poor rural areas of one of the world's least developed countries.
- The most challenging subsector (retail distribution) of the most difficult infrastructure sector for PPPs (water supply).
- A life-threatening water quality problem that required relatively expensive new infrastructure.
- A local private sector with no PPP experience and no interest in the business of rural water supply.
- Very poor, uninformed rural end users, with convenient access to inexpensive, if unhealthy, existing sources of water.
- The perceived need to complete hundreds of build–operate–transfer (BOT) projects in a relatively short period of time in order to scale-up private provision of water in rural areas.
- A government with under-capacitated officials and agencies, and almost non-existent oversight and regulation of rural water activities.
- Existing water sector policy that favored public or community approaches to rural water management—a policy strongly supported by most civil society organizations as well as most other donors, DFIs, and multilateral development banks (MDBs) active in Bangladesh's water sector.
- A dominant role in this PPP effort by the world's most powerful MDB, willing to step into the leadership vacuum created by the government's lack of ownership of the program by taking over the design, funding, oversight, and in many cases the management of most of the key aspects of this PPP project development process.
- Perhaps not too surprisingly, the results of this effort have been very disappointing. Except for a handful of rural water BOTs, the sustainability of which is questionable,

the PPP model has not worked as expected and efforts to scale-up its use across large rural areas of the country, by concluding hundreds of BOT projects, have failed.

- This appendix examines how this program was designed and implemented, why the long-term effort has been so unsuccessful, and what lessons can be learned from the experience. What does the fate of this PPP program say about how the private sector should be involved rural water distribution in LICs?

A.2 Bangladesh's Water Crisis[1]

By the early1990s, Bangladesh had achieved remarkable success in increasing rural water supply for domestic use. Over 90 per cent of the rural population in Bangladesh was accessing the country's vast shallow water table using privately-owned hand pumps on shallow tube wells, 30-50 m deep. However, the country's apparent success with rural access to safe water ended abruptly in late 1993 with the findings by the Department of Public Health Engineering (DPHE) that vast stretches of the shallow water table were in fact heavily contaminated by naturally occurring arsenic. Since then, the nature and extent of the contamination has been mapped in various ways. A number of studies have been undertaken to determine the extent of the contamination and the population impacted. For example, a 2010 epidemiological study found that as many as 77 million people, roughly half the country's total population at the time, had been exposed to toxic levels of arsenic, and that for the population sample studied over a ten-year period, more than 20 per cent of the deaths were caused by arsenic (Argos, 2010). The World Health Organization (WHO) has notably called this arsenic contamination "the largest mass poisoning of a population in history" (WHO, 2002).

Different technologies considered for arsenic-free water focused on two fundamental approaches: (i) treatment to reduce arsenic levels, including various kinds of filtration; and (ii) technologies that facilitate access to safe water sources, such as deep tube wells, typically over 150 m deep. The former is generally seen to be effective, but expensive. The latter, deep wells connected to piped water supply networks and sometimes combined with treatment facilities, offered a relatively safe and convenient option, although still at higher costs than shallow wells. One reason for the popularity of the piped schemes was that they could mimic the service standards of the shallow tube wells, with which rural populations had become familiar and comfortable.

Since the 1980s, the default model for water delivery in rural areas of developing countries had been community management, which emerged with the help of donors largely in reaction to the inefficiencies of centralized government provision of water services in rural areas. This model was also widely used in Bangladesh. By the early 2000s, about 90 such piped water schemes had been established in rural areas of Bangladesh. Most of these schemes were operated by community water and sanitation committees.

After the discovery of arsenic contamination, the major question in Bangladesh was whether or not community management could handle the challenges associated with piped water schemes needed to deal with arsenic problems. Compared to the small,

[1] The remaining sections of this chapter are adapted from the author's contribution to an original work by The World Bank (Leigland et al., 2015). Responsibility for the views and opinions expressed in the adaption rests solely with the author and are not endorsed by The World Bank.

shallow tube wells already widely used in Bangladesh, the deep wells and piped water systems were more complicated and expensive. They required more investment, reasonably good quality construction, operations and maintenance (O&M), as well as general planning and management expertise. None of these characteristics were prevalent in the existing system of rural water provision in the country because of the widespread focus on individual household hand pump schemes. Additionally, from the global experience, it was already clear that community management schemes had shortcomings, some of which might cause serious problems if the Government of Bangladesh (GoB) were to rely too heavily on this model for rolling out a major response to the arsenic problem (WSP, 2010).

A.3 The Rationale for PPPs in Bangladesh

Given the growing realization of the severity of the arsenic issue by the late 1990s, and the challenges of public sector delivery at scale, the option of private sector participation appeared to be one approach worth considering for the delivery of safe water to large numbers of rural communities. At the time, MDBs were using structural adjustment lending to incentivize developing countries to consider various forms of privatization to improve the performance of state-owned enterprises (SOEs). PPPs were emerging as default mechanisms for engaging the private sector in the financing and operations of utilities that could not be sold or liquidated.

In Bangladesh there were never any illusions about the ability of private sponsors to recover all the costs of rural water distribution. The PPPs could not be completely commercial, but it seemed that partial commercialization might be achieved with the limited use of project subsidies. It was expected that the provision of partial subsidies to cover PPP capital costs would be able to leverage some equity contributions by private sponsors as well as by users, with ongoing O&M costs covered by user fees. Subsidies would also be paid out over time, as construction and service delivery outputs were achieved, rather than all upfront as in the case of many government subsidy programs that shifted PPP project non-performance risk to the government and away from sponsors. By the early 2000s, performance-based approaches to subsidies were already being piloted by the newly established Global Partnership on Output-Based Aid (GPOBA) from the World Bank Group (WBG).

World Bank staff convinced GoB counterparts that a PPP approach was worth testing, specifically the BOT model that the World Bank had been promoting widely in other developing country regions since the early 1990s (Augenblick and Custer, 1990). The expected advantages of a partially subsidized BOT model were summarized in textbook fashion in the last of the World Bank project design documents advocating the continued use of the model for rural water provision in Bangladesh (World Bank, 2012):

- BOTs can bring some measure of private investment to the schemes, thereby easing financial pressures on governments.
- They can make possible commercial management of the schemes, which in turn can increase the ability of the schemes to cover operating costs and recover investments.
- They can help to ensure good quality design, realistic sizing, and construction by the same firm that will subsequently operate the system.

- BOTs can prevent disputes after construction about the quality of the infrastructure, which often occur when the company responsible for operating the system is not the same as the one carrying out construction.
- BOTs can save time in the contracting process.
- Compared with typical community management approaches, BOT contracts can help ensure a more professional approach to O&M after construction is completed.

A.4 Assessing the Willingness-to-Pay

The possibility of using such an approach in Bangladesh—involving partial matching grants to mobilize community financing, private financing and management, and O&M costs covered by user fees—received a major boost with the publication in 2003 of a willingness-to-pay study, focused on the rural areas of the country (Ahmad et al., 2003).

Because of its apparent positive endorsement of consumer readiness to pay cost-reflective tariffs, the study played a pivotal role in triggering a long process of BOT experimentation. When many of those experiments were not successful because of what turned out to be an unwillingness of households to connect or stay connected to the schemes, some observers looked back at the 2003 study and identified it as the beginning of problems. A 2010 report by the World Bank's Water and Sanitation Program (WSP) noted that because the discrepancies between the study findings and actual demand were "so great," two conclusions were inescapable: "..willingness to pay studies should be viewed with some scepticism; and more study should be carried out on how rural consumers behave when faced with actual, not hypothetical choices" (WSP, 2010, 13).

In fact, the study's conclusions regarding the connection between the desire for piped water and the desire for arsenic-free water revealed a somewhat more fragile willingness-to-pay dynamic than some later accounts have suggested. Most of the respondents in the willingness-to-pay survey were not aware of the serious health implications of consuming arsenic-contaminated water. Only about 35 per cent of households in the sample had directly encountered arsenic contamination, and of those 41 per cent were still using arsenic-contaminated shallow tube wells. Of all the water supply technologies asked about in the survey, the respondents' overwhelming preference was for deep tube wells and piped systems (89 per cent). But the main reason for the preference was convenience rather than arsenic-free water.

About 70 per cent of respondents perceived convenience to be the main advantage of these systems, presumably because piped systems most closely matched the desirable service levels of shallow tube wells and hand pumps. Respondents in the sample area expressed a willingness-to-pay about 1.9 per cent of their monthly income for O&M charges associated with domestic piped water connections, and approximately 3.2 per cent of their annual incomes for the connections. But the desire for arsenic-free water was only a minute share of the overall desire for piped water. The study calculated that respondents were willing to pay only 0.2–0.3 per cent of their income for arsenic-free water.

The study was ultimately encouraging about the willingness-to-pay for piped water in the sense that the average willingness-to-pay was a small percentage of mean household income, and seemed adequate to cover the recurring operational costs of such schemes, as well as a reasonable share of capital costs.[2] Based on these findings, the study concluded that piped water supply systems might well be affordable in many rural areas in Bangladesh. But the demand was based on an overwhelming desire for convenience rather than desire for arsenic-free water. Demand (and willingness-to-pay) would likely remain strong as long as piped systems came close to matching the reliability, convenience, and water quality (smell, taste, and appearance) of shallow tube well hand pump systems. However, if piped systems did not actually perform in that manner, many households were willing to seek other sources of safe water or even return to unsafe shallow wells, because they did not fully understand or recognize the health risks of arsenic-contaminated water.

A 2006 survey conducted in one of the country's arsenic-prone areas found that adoption of arsenic avoidance measures correlated with higher education levels, but not with exposure to information campaigns about the dangers of arsenic. So, efforts by the government and its development partners over the years to communicate warnings about the hazards of arsenic exposure have had little effect, at least through the mid-2000s, possibly suggesting that such campaigns may have been poorly designed or under-resourced. The survey concluded that, among poorly educated rural households, if access to safe drinking water seemed inconvenient or water quality seemed poor, households would drink arsenic-contaminated water instead (Aziz et al., 2006).

A.5 The Bangladesh BOT Program

A.5.1 First Field Test of the Model

The first World Bank-funded project that attempted to test the findings of the willingness-to-pay study was the Bangladesh Arsenic Mitigation Water Supply Project (BAMWSP), which was implemented from 1998 to 2006. The project involved a US$44 million credit, focused mainly on providing arsenic-free water to severely affected villages and municipalities, and raising public awareness of the arsenic problem.

To test the willingness-to-pay for safe water in rural areas, BAMWSP began a pilot activity to construct 13 rural piped schemes using a BOT model. Local private sponsors were engaged to build, partially finance, and operate the schemes (after a 15-year operating period management would be turned over to the communities). This BAMWSP model required investor-operators (referred to as "sponsors" because most were non-government organizations (NGOs) rather than private companies or individual entrepreneurs) to provide 40 per cent of the investment costs. The investment would be recouped over 15 years of operations through tariff collections that would also pay for O&M costs. The community would make an upfront 10 per cent capital cost contribution, and BAMWSP would provide the remaining 50 per cent as a subsidy paid out on a performance basis, using GPOBA funding, with sponsors reimbursed for outputs achieved and confirmed by independent audits.

[2] The study noted that beneficiaries of water supply projects in developing countries were often asked to contribute 10 per cent to capital costs and meet the entire O&M costs. In the early 2000s, India was using these guidelines to implement a rural drinking water program targeting about 70 million people. The Bangladesh WTP study indicated that poor households were willing to pay 13 per cent of the capital costs for a domestic piped water connection; non-poor households were willing to pay 22 per cent (Ahmad et al., 2003, xiv).

Implementation of the BAMWSP project experienced severe delays that evaluations assumed were caused by management problems resulting from a lack of regional support for project activities by the government's DPHE. Because of problems on previous World Bank projects, the BAMWSP's project management unit (PMU) had been set up separately from DPHE, which was the main government agency charged with planning, designing, and implementing water supply and sanitation throughout the country (with the exception of the three largest urban areas). DPHE had implemented 90 rural piped water schemes, and had historically been the default government location for all PMUs established to manage rural water projects funded by development partners. DPHE had an extensive regional network of offices that could assist with water project implementation virtually anywhere in the country.

By the end of the BAMWSP project in 2006 (the project had been extended for one year), only one of the pilot schemes, for 1,100 households, was largely completed and the others were not yet under construction. This led to a US$5 million grant cancellation and reintegration of the PMU into DPHE. Because the slow rollout of BOT schemes was considered a function of poor program management, rather than flaws in the design of the BOTs, the model still seemed promising.

A.5.2 Second Field Test

A second early World Bank-supported project that also focused some of its resources on testing the BOT model for rural piped water supply was the Social Investment Program Project (SIPP-1), which was implemented from 2003 to 2007, and later extended to 2011 to help cope with the aftermath of the floods and cyclone of 2007. SIPP-1 was intended to use an International Development Association (IDA) credit of US$18.4 million to develop financial and institutional arrangements for improving access to local infrastructure services and implementing small community-driven social assistance programs. The SIPP-1 project was managed by the newly created Social Development Foundation (SDF), a community development organization established under the Ministry of Finance.

Six rural piped water schemes were implemented in the two districts, using the BOT model. The target number of total households was about 3,600. SDF signed contracts with six sponsors (all NGOs) requiring them to contribute 40 per cent of BOT project costs and source 10 per cent from local communities. SDF would contribute 50 per cent of total costs using its funds. Tariff revenues would cover all O&M costs. Sponsors were expected to select their BOT project sites (usually villages or growth centers), then design and construct the systems, and operate them for 15 years in order to recover their costs.

As with the BAMWSP project, SIPP-1 also experienced very slow implementation, and program management was again cited as the main problem. But program management had been strengthened for SIPP-1. Implementation delays were now more clearly the result of the fact that the complicated and fragile nature of BOTs had been underestimated. The requirement to carefully evaluate the skills and integrity of private sponsors and their proposed BOT projects, was of course essential for any kind of PPP project. But this necessary due diligence led to a design and approval process that was long and complicated. Construction was expected to begin immediately on contract signing, but in practice was delayed by issues relating to land acquisition, the routing of pipelines, and the collection of the 10 per cent community contributions for capital investment. Schemes were scheduled to be completed within 12 months, but SIPP-1 data shows that completion times actually varied between 14 and 60 months, with an average of 36 months (Kamruzzaman et al.,

2012). The long completion periods subjected the schemes to cost escalations and, as a consequence, discouraged households from connecting.

Delayed completion times presented serious problems because, when most of the systems were completed, relatively few households had been connected. A 2014 review of the six BOT projects completed by SDF showed that the schemes never achieved more than 66 per cent of their targeted connections. This of course had a knock-on effect in terms of scheme viability. A basic assumption of the BOT approach, was that water tariffs would be sufficient to cover O&M costs, electricity bills, operator wages, sponsor service charges, and also meet equity return requirements. But SIPP-1 data shows that of the six schemes completed, only two were successful in generating adequate revenues to cover operating costs (one scheme stopped operation in 2010). The remaining schemes struggled to cover O&M expenses, much less service charges, investment returns, or depreciation expenses. Poor revenue collection efficiency (averaging 88 per cent) exacerbated problems with revenues (SDF, 2014).

A.5.3 The First Attempt to Scale-Up the Model

BAMWSP's unfinished schemes were transferred to the Bangladesh Water Supply Program Project (BWSPP), which began with an IDA grant of US$40 million for work over the period, 2005–9 (later extended to 2010). BWSPP had been in planning as a way to dramatically scale-up the BOT model ever since the start of the BAMWSP pilots in 2003, and was already under implementation before BAMWSP actually reached completion. As a consequence, relatively little was known about the strengths and weaknesses of the BOT model. Clearly it worked in some pilot situations, but scaling-up the model in hundreds of villages at the same time was a vastly different and resource-intensive type of exercise. This was especially true considering the complicated nature of BOT project preparation, which was only just becoming apparent as the BAMWSP field test was concluding.

In addition to components focusing on non-piped water supply and ways of improving the response to natural disasters, BWSPP's original design called for it to rapidly scale-up the BAMWSP BOT model by using it to construct piped water schemes in 300 villages. BWSPP would provide technical assistance and 50 per cent capital grants to support private sponsors to design, construct, and operate piped schemes for 15 years. (After 15 years, a community organization was supposed to take over management from the private sector sponsor.)

Sponsors would provide 40 per cent of the investment as equity and would collect an additional 10 per cent from the local community. A performance-based output-based aid (OBA) approach was to be used in paying out the 50 per cent subsidy, with sponsors reimbursed for outputs achieved. Because the OBA approach required sponsors to pre-finance investments for which subsidies would ultimately be paid, as well as raise their own equity contributions for the schemes, BWSPP also intended to develop some kind of financing mechanism, such as a partial credit guarantee, to interest local banks in making long-term loans to sponsors to help cover these pre-financing costs. As with SIPP-1, BWSPP used a very thorough process for evaluating and recruiting sponsors to carry out the planning, implementation, and operation of the rural piped schemes.

By the time the mid-term review of BWSPP began in 2007, its implementation had come to a standstill. Again, official evaluation documents attributed the lack of progress to poor program management. But unlike the two earlier projects involving BOTs, BWSPP's PMU had been moved back into DPHE at the start of implementation in order to take advantage of DPHE's regional and authoritative presence in the rural water sector. But this had not helped, as the BWSPP implementation completion report later acknowledged.

The PMU was still unable to recruit capable sponsors fast enough to make expected progress on hundreds of individual BOT projects. The length of time needed to develop the BOT schemes before construction could begin continued to surprise BWSPP managers, even though this had been a problem with both of the earlier field test exercises. To go from a signed Memorandum of Understanding (MoU) to a grant agreement required a median of three years for the 21 schemes (with one scheme taking four and a half years). The fact that the individual BOTs were complicated, poorly designed, commercially and technically fragile, unattractive to local businessmen, and of not much interest to government counterparts was still not acknowledged as key barriers to implementation.

As a result of the mid-term review, BWSPP was restructured, the original US$40 million credit was reduced to US$18.5 million, and many of the original performance targets were cut back or removed. Activity on rural piped water supply was trimmed from the initial target of 300 villages to 21 villages (13 of which were the original schemes initiated under BAMWSP, seven years earlier). The number of targeted household beneficiaries was decreased from 100,000 to 25,000. Sponsor equity requirements per scheme were lowered from 40 per cent to 20 per cent and the total subsidy per scheme was increased to 70 per cent. (The requirement that communities contribute 10 per cent was retained.) The process of developing a financing mechanism for system sponsors never really began and was dropped at the time of BWSPP restructuring.

When BWSPP ended, the revised target of 21 piped schemes had been met, with NGOs rather than local businesses making up most of the sponsors contracted to construct and operate the schemes. Construction on all the schemes had started, several had also begun operations, but only two had track records of longer than three years. For those in operation, the duration of service delivery was about six hours a day. Approximately 10,000 households ultimately benefited from this component, as against the revised target of 25,000.

A.5.4 Designing a Second Attempt at Scale-Up

In 2012, two years after the completion of BWSPP, the World Bank implemented a second attempt at scaling-up the BOT model, the Bangladesh Rural Water Supply and Sanitation Project (BRWSSP). This was a US$75 million IDA credit for work to be undertaken from 2012 to 2017. The focus remained on rural areas and included three components, including rural sanitation, non-piped water, and piped water BOT schemes. The BOTs were to be implemented in approximately 125 areas where shallow tube wells were significantly affected by a combination of problems, including arsenic contamination, salinity, iron contamination, and low water tables.

Each scheme was expected to achieve between 600 and 1,200 domestic connections. As long as the schemes proved to be technically and financially viable (using a minimum number of consumers as the threshold for viability) each would cover single or multiple villages depending on the density and number of households. Private sponsors would be selected competitively to construct and operate the schemes on behalf of the local governments, which would own the assets. The sponsors would receive OBA subsidies for most of the BOT project costs based on performance (measured via certified achievement of BOT project milestones), but would still be responsible for significant levels of investment as well as the cost of long-term operation and maintenance of the facilities. All of these sponsor costs would have to be recovered from revenues.

BRWSSP was expected to build on the lessons learned from BWSSP as well as recent global experience rural piped water schemes. In various ways, BRWSSP incorporated modifications to the BOT model as it was used in earlier World Bank projects. Key differences are outlined in the following subsections.

BOT projects

The BOTs developed under earlier World Bank projects tended to be unattractive to entrepreneurs or businesses because of the way in which subsidy support was structured. Sponsors were required to pre-finance 90 per cent of the BOT project capital costs and collect the other 10 per cent from communities. Of this amount, 50 per cent would eventually be reimbursed, based on certified achievement of construction milestones. The credit facility, expected to be implemented under the previous World Bank project, was intended to help secure financing for the entrepreneurs. But the facility was never established. Moreover, sponsors struggled to get households to make good on their commitment to contribute 10 per cent of the scheme capital costs. Even when it was paid, the household share was almost never contributed upfront, adding to the financing pressure affecting sponsors.

To make the BRWSSP BOTs more attractive to private sponsors, the subsidy level per scheme was increased to 70 per cent from BWSPP's original level of 50 per cent. Although still output based, the subsidies were mostly to be provided on achievement of construction milestones rather than service delivery ones, so sponsors would be reimbursed for their investments earlier in the process than had been the case on earlier World Bank projects. Finally, in recognition of the difficulty in connecting households to these systems, BRWSSP was designed to allow sponsors full subsidy payment disbursements for achieving 70 per cent of system connections rather than 100 per cent as in BWSPP.

It was also decided that sponsors would no longer handle some key BOT project selection and preparation tasks. DPHE, with support from a World Bank-funded engineering consultancy firm, would be responsible for feasibility studies and for the design and supervision of construction, as well as for scheme site selection. This meant in effect a partial abandonment of the classic BOT model that depended on sponsor involvement in design and construction to help facilitate familiarity with operational systems and sustainability during implementation.

Sponsors

When BOT schemes were tendered under earlier World Bank projects, potential private sponsors typically showed interest in bidding, at least at first. But by the time of bidding, most private businesses and entrepreneurs concluded that full cost recovery was too difficult if not impossible, and as a result they did not participate in the tenders. This left most of the schemes to NGOs, many of which were actively engaged in seeking shares of the considerable amounts of donor funding available in the early 2000s for arsenic-related activities. A number of the NGOs involved in the early BOTs may have misunderstood the difference between typical donor-funded arsenic mitigation work and the commercial intention behind the BOTs. Whatever their understanding, most of these NGOs demonstrated more of a philanthropic approach to their operations than a commercial one. They focused primarily on providing a community service, rather than recovering their capital investment. This mind-set was reflected in the fact that monthly O&M estimates by the scheme managers covered only routine costs, and did not include reserves for replacements and repairs, much less capital investment.

Under BRWSSP, tougher bidding requirements were adopted in order to increase the involvement of commercially oriented enterprises and entrepreneurs as private sponsors, instead of the NGOs that dominated earlier tenders. But the schemes were also batched into clusters of multiple villages in an effort to offer sponsors more attractive BOT commercial opportunities that took advantage of economies of scale. This was also expected to reduce the number of procurement actions needed by BRWSSP. Prospective private sponsors would receive training prior to bid submission so that they could comply fully with tougher procurement requirements designed to ensure that sponsors were competent and commercially oriented.

Customers

Under previous World Bank projects, services offered by BOTs were never extended for more than about six hours per day, instead of the required 12 hours. This reduction in service was done to cut back on costs, in line with lower revenue collections. The tariffs charged for water services seemed affordable as a percentage of average income, but not enough households were connecting to the systems, so total scheme revenues typically could not reach cost-recovery levels. When customers did connect, they often lobbied successfully to have tariffs lowered from originally agreed rates. AS BRWSSP started implementation, there was still no compelling evidence to confirm expectations regarding the willingness and ability of rural households to cover O&M costs of the schemes, much less meet a significant share of capital costs.

BRWSSP was designed based on the assumption that potential customers would be willing and able to pay for services, as long as the schemes met expectations regarding quality and service levels. By more carefully designing and siting schemes, and implementing a more rigorous sponsor selection process, it was assumed that service quality and reliability would be higher and, as a consequence, customers would connect and pay their bills. By ensuring that the schemes installed metered connections, the sponsors could more accurately measure usage and allow customers to manage their own demand.

Regulation

As the earlier World Bank projects were implemented, there had been no government regulator for rural piped water supply and no formal mechanism for regulating BOT contract compliance except via the contracts themselves. However, this approach (known as "regulation by contract") works best when the contracting parties are clearly identified and contractual relationships straightforward. But in Bangladesh's rural water sector this was not the case. Since the early 2000s, the government had been developing a policy to decentralize service delivery to the local level in order to ensure a more demand-driven, cost-effective, and sustainable approach in the water sector. The policy was eventually formalized with the Union Parishad Act of 2009, which assigned responsibility for owning, maintaining, and operating water delivery assets in rural areas to the Union Parishads (UPs), the lowest level of elected rural local councils. If fully implemented, this policy would have established local level "public" partners for the piped water BOTs in rural areas.

However, even after the Act was passed, the national-level water agency, DPHE, remained the sole governmental entity with technical capacity and authority in the rural water supply sector, because the UPs did not yet have the technical capacity to lead this subsector. This meant that a national agency would continue to play the key role in designing, supervising, and contracting out rural water supply schemes until such time as the UPs were able to fully assume that function. In effect, this left a regulatory void within which the BOTs would have to operate. Community groups were expected to monitor BOT contract compliance, but they typically lacked the skills and resources to do this effectively and received little assistance from DPHE.

Because the 2009 Act formally recognized UPs as owners of rural water assets, and no other formal regulator had been established for the subsector, BRWSSP recognized UPs as the de facto regulators of the rural water BOTs. BRWSSP therefore added a technical assistance component that would: (i) develop an institutional and regulatory framework to cover private sector participation in rural water supply; (ii) support increased delegation of responsibility to the UPs so that they could carry out their regulatory responsibilities; and (iii) facilitate the benchmarking of scheme operations to introduce accountability.

Technical Support

The previous World Bank project (BWSPP) had provided some capacity building and technical support to various BOT actors, but by the end of the project it seemed that more assistance was required than had been initially planned under the project. Sponsors generally lacked the capacity to prepare their bids, design their BOT schemes, or do water quality assessments. In many cases, it was apparent that they needed help in understanding how to operate their schemes commercially. The PMU also lacked capacity in many of these areas. Local communities needed help in dealing with sponsors and monitoring contracts. Higher-level officials in DPHE were willing to explore innovative solutions, but DPHE was still far from a consensus view that the BOT model was more than one option among several under consideration. (One manifestation of this lack of commitment to the BOT model was the absence of efforts by the government to play more of a role in supporting involvement in the BOT projects by rural private sponsors, local governments, and community organizations.)

World Bank staff assumed that these kinds of issues could be addressed effectively if a stronger effort was made to help government counterparts understand the model and its potential benefits, and play a more active role in attempts to roll it out. Technical support to DPHE's PMU was to be significantly upgraded in order to achieve stronger program management, but also to ensure that DPHE could provide technical support to other actors in the process. To monitor service capacity and quality, the UPs would receive technical support from DPHE and its consultants.

Monitoring and Evaluation

As BWSPP concluded there were still aspects of BOT implementation that were not well understood. This was partly a result of the fact that by the time BWSPP was restructured in 2008, its monitoring and evaluation (M&E) framework had not yet been developed. With the cutback in activity levels, plans for the framework were also scaled back. Normal performance information was not collected by the system, and key design features associated with the rural piped water schemes were not evaluated.

The M&E system for BRWSSP was designed in specific detail, including plans to monitor sponsor performance through annual audits and community surveys. The surveys were to be conducted by external evaluators to obtain information about the performance, progress, outcomes, and impacts of BRWSSP activities, including the piped schemes. Financial audits would confirm sponsor compliance with the terms of the service agreements. Annual or semi-annual benchmarking would be done to compare performance across sponsors. (Notably, the previous BWSPP project had conducted only one performance audit, which took place when the project ended.)

A.5.5 Results of the Second Scale-Up Attempt

The February 2015 Mid-Term Review showed that, as with the forerunner World Bank projects, BRWSSP had also encountered significant problems resulting in severe delays. After 34 months (just over half of the project period), only 7.4 per cent of the funding had been disbursed. Of the 125 targeted BOT contracts, none had been completed. Eight schemes had been awarded and, of those, only one—developed with grant support prior to BRWSSP—was 70 per cent complete. With the exception of the latter, the Mid-Term Review estimated that no schemes would be completed before the end of 2016, roughly six months before the BRWSSP's planned closing date.

As a consequence of this lack of progress, BRWSSP was restructured to reduce the targeted number of schemes from 125 to 35, and the beneficiaries of piped schemes from 550,000 to 154,000. At least 90 schemes were cancelled, 75 of which DPHE estimated had already been discussed with and approved by local communities. In addition, the IDA allocation for the piped water component was reduced by US$20 million. The end date of BRWSSP was also extended from June 30, 2017 to December 31, 2017, to facilitate the achievement of revised project objectives.

BRWSSP's final implementation report noted that 37 piped water schemes had been constructed by the end of 2017 (World Bank, 2018). But according to the last BRWSSP status report, 33 of those schemes were completed in the last nine months of 2017 (most during the six-month extension period). This had to have been a surprising achievement, considering that this total number of completed BOTs in six to nine months was larger than the total number of all BOTs completed since this work began 14 years earlier. And among other things, this meant that BRWSSP could not meet its original objective of supervising and evaluating the commercial operation of each scheme for at least six months after the completion of construction (World Bank, 2017). BRWSSP's management unit remained in place until June 2018, to deal with the "operational issues" that were emerging at the time of project termination. However, to date there has been no published follow-up evaluations that assess how many of these schemes were operated commercially for any length of time (a 2015 evaluation of BWSPP found that after six years of operation, only four of the 21 schemes were likely to recover their investment—see section A.5.6).

While program management shortcomings were again blamed as primary causes of implementation delays (abetted by civil and political unrest in the country), project documents suggest that fundamental problems with the design and implementation of the BOT model were much larger than program management could have been expected to deal with.

BOT Projects

Once the technical assistance support team started to prepare pre-feasibility and feasibility studies, they realized that the process was more complicated and time-consuming than anticipated. Problems with site selection and scheme design were still compromising BOT project sustainability. In some cases, needed treatment plants were left out of scheme designs to accelerate preparation and reduce capital and operating costs. When BOT schemes were prepared, many were not strongly commercial, as DPHE reported in the Mid-Term Review. This was due to the need for a 20 per cent equity stake and the challenges associated with recouping this investment over the 12-year operating period. DPHE thus requested that the OBA grant contribution be increased to 90 per cent per BOT project, which would have been more consistent with prevailing government policy and similar to the subsidy levels on other government-sponsored rural water projects. DPHE believed that the additional subsidy would make it easier to attract sponsors. DPHE also noted that the cost-recovery potential of the schemes was further undermined by the need for sponsors to pay for electricity at commercial rates, which were three times the level of irrigation rates. As electricity costs could be as much as 60 per cent of total scheme operation costs, particularly if water treatment was involved, these higher rates were particularly damaging to the commercial viability of the schemes. The Mid-Term Review however did not recommend changes to the cost-sharing structures of the schemes because bidding for 29 schemes had already started.

Sponsors

Prospective sponsors continued to be unenthusiastic about BOT offerings, with many of the schemes failing to attract bidders. The PMU seems not to have done as much as expected in terms of market sounding or in promoting the schemes once target areas were selected, much less encouraging the participation of more technical and commercial bidders. Taking away sponsor responsibilities for decisions on scheme location and design may have improved the technical viability of some schemes, but may also have made them less attractive to bidders and probably increased the involvement of sponsors who were less knowledgeable about, and not as well known to, local communities. In addition, the batching, or packaging of multiple schemes, designed to attract bidders with economies of scale, was not permitted by the PMU. "Sociopolitical reasons" were cited, presumably meaning that the PMU did not want to give the impression that they were favoring certain regions over others. Whatever the reason, the inability to package multiple schemes increased development costs and offered bidders smaller and less attractive BOT project opportunities. Sponsors who actually bid for schemes tended not to be the larger commercial enterprises or smaller, competent private entrepreneurs that the BRWSSP was hoping to attract. The Mid-Term Review therefore recommended that pre-bid market surveys be conducted in each district to determine if there was enough interest among private businesses to warrant a bid process. In other words, it was no longer assumed that all the schemes identified and developed by the PMU would automatically attract private sector interest.

Customers

With no schemes in operation at the time of the Mid-Term Review, it was impossible to judge customer willingness and ability to pay for water distributed by the schemes. However, based on all of the attempts to roll out the BOT model to date, it was becoming clear that even when communities agreed to the 10 per cent equity contribution they were expected to make, that amount was almost never fully paid up front. It was clear that community contributions in the range of 5 per cent were more achievable.

Regulation

Slow government decision making prior to sponsor recruitment meant that it took roughly two years to contract and mobilize DPHE's key technical assistance support team that was supposed to build internal capacity, carry out crucial BOT preparation activities, and work on the regulatory and institutional framework. Work on regulation had not yet started by the time of the Mid-Term Review and it was subsequently cancelled. The Mid-Term Review concluded that during the first half of BRWSSP, the DPHE PMU had provided neither the support nor the regulatory oversight needed for the sustainable roll-out of the BOTs. And because most of the training and capacity building for DPHE's PMU had not started by the time of the Mid-Term Review, 44 per cent of this funding was subsequently cancelled, essentially guaranteeing a continuation of DPHE underperformance in terms of its oversight responsibilities.

M&E. With none of the schemes likely to be in operation before the end of 2016, the plans for financial audits, community surveys, and sponsor performance benchmarking were also cancelled.

A.5.6 Postscript: BWSPP Monitoring Report

Because in 2005 BWSSP had been the first World Bank project to attempt a scale-up of the BOT model, the Bank's Water and Sanitation Program (WSP) initiated a monitoring program to assess progress of the 21 schemes set up by the project (13 of which had actually started development under the earlier project, BAMWSP) (WSP, 2015). The report was issued in January 2015, far too late to be of any benefit in designing BWSSP's successor project (the report was issued just a month before the Mid-Term Review of the successor project, BRWSSP).[3] All 21 schemes were under construction or in operation when BWSPP ended in 2010. But at that stage, the majority of the schemes had not yet established meaningful operational track records. In addition, BWSPP's own M&E system had never really started functioning. This meant that when planning for a renewed scale-up of the model under BRWSSP was initiated in 2012, there was limited knowledge about the actual performance of these schemes.

Accordingly, the 2015 WSP monitoring report represents the first and only comprehensive, published accounts of performance by these early BOTs. The report drew the following conclusions:

- **Sustainability.** Six of the 21 schemes were not operating for various reasons including equipment breakdowns and theft, iron contamination (in cases where no treatment unit had been installed), and non-payment of water bills by users. Of the six, three schemes had never started operation because of technical design problems.
- **Management quality.** Of the 15 operational schemes, the WSP report concluded that four were poorly managed.
- One scheme lost its treatment plant because of flood damage, but continued to sell untreated water to community customers, who in turn did not pay bills regularly due to the poor quality of service.
- A second scheme also had water quality problems. In addition, weak system pressure meant that more distant households often did not receive water.
- A third scheme similarly had water quality problems and many households had started using their own tube well water or water treated and sold by local venders.
- A fourth scheme had pipeline design problems—many users could not access water because of poor system pressure. Tariff collection was also poorly managed. After a dispute over tariffs with the local community water committee, the sponsor abandoned the scheme, leaving it under the management of the local government (the UP), which struggled to keep the system operating.

[3] Two earlier reviews had been conducted by WSP, but the reports had not been formally issued and are no longer publicly available.

- **Service levels.** Supply hours typically ranged from three to six hours per day rather than the original target of 12 hours. This was because connection coverage of most schemes was limited to 50–60 per cent, resulting in lower than anticipated demand and lower than expected revenues. Many potential customers expressed the view that because so much grant funding had supported the capital costs of the schemes, grants should also pay for household connections. Others were unhappy with the water quality and poor service standards.
- **Network expansion.** Connections declined in eight of the 15 functional schemes, mainly because customers either voluntarily disconnected due to inferior services (pressure failures in the supply lines or poor water quality), or were disconnected for non-payment of water bills (again, frequently due to dissatisfaction over weak water pressure or poor water quality). The WSP report established that no marketing or motivational programs had been undertaken to increase household connections by sponsors in any of these 15 schemes. Some of the sponsors attempted to access loan funding from commercial banks in order to finance system expansion, but found that local banks did not recognize small water operators as acceptable borrowers.
- **Metering.** While a number of household meters had been installed when the schemes were first constructed, most of them had stopped working or had been stolen in the years since. Metered bills had never been produced by any scheme. None of the sponsors had ever attempted to install new household meters to manage demand and increase income.
- **Capital investment.** No additional capital investments for system expansion or installation of additional facilities were ever made by any sponsor. Only three schemes maintained funds for major repairs or equipment replacement. Most sponsors lacked the technical capacity to rehabilitate or repair their own schemes, and generally were reluctant to make any further investments for repairs or to meet rehabilitation costs. Typically, this unwillingness to invest additional funds was a contributory factor in the closing of those schemes that were no longer operational.
- **Tariff rates and collections.** As a consequence of increased operating costs (including electricity charges that were much higher than anticipated), tariffs increased for almost all of the schemes. Electricity charges typically represented 40–50 per cent of total operational expenses, and even more if treatment plants had been added to the schemes. But none of the tariff increases were sufficient to meet capital investment requirements. Substandard service and poor water quality were cited as the main reasons for low collection rates. As a result, the average collection rate across the operational schemes was unpredictable, with the FY2012–13 rates at 84.3 per cent, jumping to 92.1 per cent the following year.
- **Profitability.** Of the 15 functioning schemes, seven were operating at a loss, mainly because of low tariffs, poor collections, high electricity costs, and/or high water treatment costs. The average return on sponsor equity was only 2.75 per cent. WSP projected that only four schemes would be able to recover their original 30 per cent sponsor investments over the 18-year contract period. But the report noted that the

NGO sponsors operating most of these operational schemes were not doing so with commercial intentions.

- **Other commitments.** As per the BOT contracts, the sponsors had agreed to maintain proper accounting systems, including separate depreciation accounts, but none of the schemes were found to be in compliance with these requirements. DPHE had not conducted any of the agreed-on performance or financial audits of the scheme accounts. Only two of the 15 schemes had met their commitments to regularly test water quality.

A.6 The International Experience

As the Bangladesh BOT program was unfolding, research was already demonstrating that the potential for private participation in the water sector was often overestimated when it came to profits and investments. Studies by Sirtaine et al. (2005), Gassner et al. (2009), Marin (2009), and Estache and Philippe (2012) have been cited in earlier chapters of this book. These four research studies focused on large, mostly urban water PPPs that were not set up initially with large amounts of subsidy funding. These studies demonstrate that the large PPP projects that stimulated interest in water PPPs in the 1990s were not as profitable as assumed at the time. These PPPs also did not generate the kind of private investment that was frequently cited as their principal benefit. If the larger urban PPPs could not meet these expectations, it is not so surprising that smaller rural PPPs would have difficulties consistently demonstrating profitability and increased private investment, even with partial capital subsidies.

When the BWSPP Monitoring Report was issued in 2015, there was also a growing body of research literature on the use of modestly subsidized BOT contracts for rural piped water delivery, as mechanisms for solving problems associated with community management models.

Kleemeier (2010) conducted a desk-top study that reviewed 24 piped water projects, about half in Africa, and examined the experience of private water supply management in very small rural settlements. The review found that the projects often had problems finding competent private operators, and frequently could not generate sufficient revenues even when a private operator could be recruited. In addition, governments and their development partners failed to provide professional support to local communities to enable them to interact with and regulate these private operators. Accordingly, a flaw in the design of these projects was the assumption that rural private operator initiatives could make competent government institutions unnecessary. Instead it was clear that government would need to play an ongoing role in the regulation, training, and professional support required by these schemes if they were to have a chance of succeeding.

However, Kleemeier found that evidence was lacking on the financial sustainability of privately managed rural piped water schemes. Recordkeeping on these projects was typically not adequate enough to support that kind of analysis. Evaluations were not carried out to collect and analyze data, and the studies that were done were not widely disseminated. While Kleemeier found cases of profitable BOT contracts in Burkina Faso and Paraguay, and viable community and private management schemes in Niger and Senegal, she concluded that even if the private operator approach appeared promising, the sustainability of the model was "not yet proven" (Kleemeier, 2010, 28).

Foster (2012) supported most of Kleemeier's findings several years later in a second desk-top study. Foster found that over a quarter of rural piped schemes in Benin, Burkina Faso, Mali, Niger, Rwanda, and Senegal were privately operated. But Foster's review demonstrated that only a few isolated cases existed of private operators who invested their own money in schemes with the expectation of recouping full capital costs via user fees.

While he saw potential value in using BOT contracts to make possible the sustainable operation of rural water facilities, he noted that some kind of substantial subsidy would be essential to attract private involvement. He also agreed with Kleemeier that even if a vibrant rural water market could be established in a country, there still would be a need for competent government institutions to be involved in monitoring and regulating these projects, setting tariffs, managing contracts, and administering subsidies.

Finally, Foster concluded that little real evidence existed regarding the financial or technical performance of private operators, and he questioned "the viability of rural water businesses" (Foster, 2012, 4).

Sy, Warner, and Jamieson (2014) reviewed data and reports from three countries—Bangladesh, Benin, and Cambodia—and arrived at conclusions about the potential opportunities for domestic private investments in water and sanitation in poor countries. The authors found that, by 2025, about 20 million people in the three countries would need to access water from rural piped water schemes, i.e., ten times the 2014 number. But the authors also identified commercial and policy factors that tended to constrain the expansion of private schemes, including the following:

- **Weak demand.** Demand for water by poor households was not high enough for private operators to expand their system capacity, or even make full use of existing capacity. According to international health guidelines, poor households in these countries should have been consuming more water, but because of tariffs and connection fees that they perceived to be high they were discouraged from doing so, especially given the quality of water being sold when compared to alternatives (e.g., rainwater, wells, springs, and boreholes). If operators could supply water that seemed to be of good quality, demand for piped water might increase.
- **Lack of viable business models.** For privately managed schemes to be viable they must achieve "size" economies of scale, with levels of sales and prices that are adequate to cover all of the system's costs. But governments and development partners struggled to find business models that could achieve this kind of scale.
- **Investment philosophies.** In Bangladesh and Benin, where system designs were determined in a top-down fashion by the governments and their development partners, most of the investments that private operators were supposed to make were expected to cover repairs or maintenance. However, many firms are not profitable, and sponsors were reluctant to invest in the systems that they were operating. This was apparently due to doubts about the cost-recovery potential of their businesses. In Cambodia, most enterprises were planning investments in network and water production expansion, with half of them contemplating investments in new schemes. Their biggest concern however was access to finance. In all three countries, firms interviewed by the authors said they believed that water was too expensive for poor people and that few incentives existed to increase access by the poor.

- **Unsupportive policies and institutions.** Government policies in all three countries limited access to investment in the water sector. In Bangladesh, tariff levels were not high enough to allow cost recovery, much less ensure a return on investment. Investment was therefore dependent on access to government or donor financing. In Benin, government design of overly large systems were a barrier to system expansion. In Cambodia the legal framework for semi-urban water supply was limiting the types of investments that firms are willing to make.

The study by Sy, Warner, and Jamieson (2014) concludes with recommendations for action mostly by governments and development partners in three key areas: (i) stimulating the demand for network services by the poor; (ii) improving business viability and business models by removing policy and other impediments to efficient behavior by private firms; and (iii) improving the investment climate and the incentives to invest in challenging markets.

Gero et al. (2014) conducted a systematic review of recent literature (164 studies) on factors affecting the success of water sector engagement by micro, small, and medium private enterprises. The main constraints to business viability identified were limitations on demand, lack of business and technical skills, and financial challenges (especially limited access to credit), as well as policy and governance constraints. In terms of benefits for the poor resulting from enterprise management in the sector, the authors found that the provision of accessible and affordable water services in poor rural areas was challenging for these private businesses. As a result, such service was not usually a priority for these enterprise managers, who tended to gravitate to customers who can pay their water bills. The evidence suggested that poor households who were unwilling or unable to pay for connections or water tariffs often turned to unsafe water supplies. The authors concluded their review of engagement by small private enterprises in the water sector by noting: "First, that matching and bringing together demand and supply is much more complex than might meet the eye, and requires greater attention from practitioners and analysts alike" (Gero et al, 2014, 340).

A.7 Emerging Hybrid Projects in the Rural Water Sector

Water schemes involving private operation continue to show promise if key elements are in place such as strong private partners, knowledgeable consumers, subsidy support, and clear regulatory regimes, and government ownership and support. In many instances, interest in private sector participation has grown as the shortcomings of traditional community management schemes have become increasingly evident. But in most LICs, including Bangladesh, those key elements are not in place, and efforts to move beyond a handful of PPP projects have not been successful. Because of that lack of success, the rural water sector is rapidly moving beyond a binary debate about the merits of classic PPP operations vs. traditional community management schemes.

Research by groups like the International Water and Sanitation Centre (Moriarty et al., 2013) suggests that the emerging service delivery model in this subsector, which is most responsive to user demands and government mandates and constraints, may lie somewhere between PPP approaches and traditional community management schemes. This combination of the characteristics of both approaches results from the realization that the community management model is reaching the limits of what can be realistically achieved using an approach based on informality and voluntarism, and that sustainable achievement of desirable levels of service delivery do not always result from this approach. A combined or hybrid approach involves a continuation of community management principles, but with a stronger degree of professionalism and external support to community owners of schemes. In some cases, this may mean contracting important aspects of service provision to private operators, but with asset ownership and final decisions on service levels and tariffs remaining with communities or local government. In effect, private participation would be carried out on the basis of traditional kinds of contracting, like consulting or service contracts rather than PPP contracts. These are rural forms of the hybrid management contracts discussed earlier in Chapter 6.

In some countries, these hybrid arrangements in the water sector are referred to as "professionalization contracts." They have been developed in India for mid-sized urban water utilities, but might be adaptable for smaller rural schemes in a country like Bangladesh. In India, these contracts involve private firms contracted to help municipal water utilities implement standard operating procedures for each functional area of the utility, such as network management, commercial functions, administration and finance, and capital planning and management. The contractor would also advise on billing systems, asset management, leak detection, and maintenance. The contractor would then provide training and ongoing management advice. Actual management control of the utility would not change hands (Ehrhardt, Mugabi, and Kingdom, 2015). These are not PPP arrangements, so private contractors cannot be expected to cover any of these costs—funding for these contracts, and for any needed capital investments, must be sought elsewhere.

Perhaps rural areas in Bangladesh should be left to an enhanced community management model that builds on existing efforts undertaken by the government and its development partners, with more emphasis on professionalization of services, contracting out operations, and long-term sustainability. The management of rural piped water schemes using PPP-like approaches could be reserved for reasonably well capacitated local governments in rural areas. Experience in Bangladesh suggests that private participation in infrastructure services might be much more sustainable in urban or even peri-urban environments due to higher population densities, better informed and more affluent customers, and more interested, competent small local businessmen acting as operators.

A.8 Conclusions

The Bangladesh BOT program illustrates many of the themes of this book. PPP models were pressed into service as part of an urgent response to a national crisis, the arsenic contamination of groundwater in rural areas. The BOT model must have seemed like a natural solution to World Bank staff because it was already being strongly recommended, under structural adjustment lending programs, as a mechanism for improving the management and financing of infrastructure services in regions like SSA, where the model was enlisted to help deal with the financial crisis triggered by mismanaged SOEs.

But as with infrastructure service delivery in Africa, there was very little evidence on which to base expectations that PPPs would be successful models for the commercial delivery of rural piped water in Bangladesh. The BOTs were launched without a clear understanding of the challenges associated with these kinds of projects. An assessment of total family incomes suggested that most households could afford to pay for these water services. But their willingness-to-pay had the potential to sharply decrease as they weighed the costs involved against the quality of the water, the reliability and convenience of service, and the availability of alternative water sources. The 2003 willingness-to-pay study demonstrated that concern over arsenic contamination was not the main reason for preferring piped water schemes, and was not a deterrent that would keep households from accessing unsafe alternative sources of water if the convenience and quality (e.g., taste and appearance) of piped water were deemed unsatisfactory. When the reliability and convenience of the BOT schemes did not meet expectations, many prospective customers refused to connect to the networks, or if they connected, then refused to pay and were disconnected.

Before the results of the field testing were clear, efforts to scale-up the use of the model in hundreds of locations were initiated, and two attempts at scale-up failed. The entire effort exhibits a kind of unshakable, almost ideological, faith in the fundamental viability of the BOT model, despite an almost constant flow of evidence pointing to its dysfunctionality in rural areas of such a poor country. Program evaluations were repeatedly surprised by the length of time needed to prepare individual BOT projects and blamed project management weaknesses for what seemed like preparation delays. Today, with the accumulation of evidence about the shortcomings of PPPs in developing countries, it would be unthinkable to propose doing 300 rural piped water BOT projects over a four-year period. Of 425 projects targeted by the 15-year BOT program, only 56 reached some kind of conclusion, and many of these, probably most, will not prove to be commercially sustainable (Table A.1).

Like the structural adjustment lending programs in SSA, which used the offer of MDB sector loans to incentive the reluctant acceptance of infrastructure PPPs for SOE utilities by host governments, the BOT program in Bangladesh was an MDB creation. It was backed by incentives in the form of sector financial support of various kinds. As with many African countries, the PPP approach was clearly not the Bangladeshi government's idea of a solution to the problem of delivering safe water to rural end users, but the government reluctantly accepted it.

Throughout the Bangladesh BOT process, managed by the World Bank, other development partners active in the country remained unconvinced that the BOT model was capable of being scaled up as intended. UNICEF, DANIDA, AusAid, and UNDP all supported community-managed rural piped water projects that generated some positive outcomes (see DANIDA, 2005). These organizations continued to support more conventional models of water service delivery, including community management approaches. As a result, the Bangladeshi government was faced with conflicting recommendations from its development partners. For example, as the WBG's first attempt at scaling-up the BOT model under BWSPP were concluding in 2009, the Asian Development Bank's Independent Evaluation Department offered the following comments about the water sector in Bangladesh:

> Support for reforms has not been coordinated well enough, and was sometimes misguided (support for private sector-based solutions in rural water supply, which in the context of Bangladesh are premature). (ADB, 2009, 45)

In terms of almost every important evaluation category discussed in Chapter 2, the Bangladesh BOT program reflected the shortcomings that have plagued PPPs in developing countries worldwide, particularly LICs:

- **PPP Prevalence.** As mentioned earlier, neither the government nor the private sector had any familiarity with PPPs or any particular interest in using them in the water sector. Nothing happened during the BOT program to change these views.
- **Costs and profits.** The costs of these BOT systems were relatively high—deep tube wells needed to be dug, pipes installed for household delivery, and treatment added in many cases. The local private sector had no experience with PPPs, but local businessmen could see that covering these costs, much less making a profit, by selling water to rural households would be extremely difficult. This is the principal reason

Table A.1 The Bangladesh BOT Project Track Record

World Bank-supported Projects	Dates	Initial Targets	Revised Targets	End-of-project Results	Comments
Designing and testing the BOT model:					
1. Bangladesh Arsenic Mitigation. Water Supply project (BAMWSP)	1998-2006	13 BOTs	-	1 under construction, none operational	The 13 schemes later included in BWSPP's revised target of 21
2. Social Investment Program Project (SIPP-I)	2003-2011	6 BOTs	-	6 under construction, none operational	By 2014, only 2 schemes covering costs
First attempt to scale up the BOT model:					
3. Bangladesh Water Supply Program Project (BWSPP)	2005-2009	300 BOTs	21 BOTs	Most under construction, several operational	By 2015, 6 BOTs cancelled, only 4 likely to recover investment
Second attempt to scale up the BOT model:					
4. Bangladesh rural Water supply & Sanitation Project (BRWSSP)	2012-2017	125 BOTs	35 BOTs	37 constructed, some operational	34 schemes completed in last 9 months of the project; sustainability of schemes not yet clear

Source: World Bank, 2003, 2004, 2007, 2011a, 2011b, 2012, 2018.

why local businessmen mostly opted not to compete for these BOT projects. Most of the BOTs were managed by NGOs will little commercial business experience.

- **Project preparation.** The preparation costs of these BOT projects were much higher (in both time and money) than anyone expected. The initial view seems to have been that hundreds of BOTs could be rolled out in assembly-line fashion, but this turned out to be impossible. Each BOT required careful location and design; due diligence was required on every sponsor. The fact that program managers so badly misjudged the length of time needed to adequately prepare these small BOT projects suggests that the BOT mechanisms being promoted was not well understood.
- **Finance and investment.** Because the schemes were not strongly commercial in nature, neither sponsors nor end users were enthusiastic about contributing to BOT capital costs as expected by World Bank staff. The use of performance-based subsidies to reimburse sponsors for initial investments only after output achievement was independently certified, placed sponsors under financial strain and increased transaction costs. Sources of finance for small businesses in Bangladesh were difficult to identify or access, making the initial required investments difficult.

- **Poverty impacts.** As with many PPPs in developing countries, it was assumed that the BOT schemes would have some pro-poor impacts simply because they were located in rural areas. But because the schemes were only marginally commercial, sponsors were incentivized to increase the number of connections to generate cost-covering revenues. As the BRWSSP implementation completion report admitted, this led the schemes to focus on customers who were able to afford services and pay their bills: "formal incentives were not built into the model to ensure poorer households were served and supported" (World Bank, 2018, 25).
- **Governance issues.** Finally, in terms of governance, as noted, this program was not the government's idea and the government did not take ownership of it. The government did little to even support the BOT program with financing, regulation, or technical assistance for the rural schemes or local government bodies charged with overseeing the schemes. As the BOT program rolled out, the government, supported by other development partners, continued to install fully subsidized tube wells across the country, so residents in BOT service areas frequently had other, cheaper, options for safe water.

As the failures of the BOT program mounted, program managers began to compromise on some PPP characteristics. BRWSSP took site selection and BOT project design away from the private sponsors, increased subsidy levels, reduced some of the performance objectives, increased technical assistance, and tried to recruit more commercial sponsors. But program managers were apparently determined not to abandon the basic PPP approach by exploring the use of hybrid models that combined PPP elements with features of other kinds of contracts, as well as with community management approaches that were already widely in use in Bangladesh.

Unfortunately, the cost of maintaining the integrity of the PPP model may have been the failure to find more effective ways of connecting Bangladesh's rural poor to safe sources of water. The arsenic problem has not gone away. A 2013 national survey of drinking water in Bangladesh found that millions of households in rural areas were still consuming water with arsenic concentrations well above levels considered safe. A 2016 report by Human Rights Watch argued that the government is mismanaging the arsenic response by, among other things, allowing local officials to use political considerations in positioning deep tube wells, rather than prioritizing areas of severe contamination (Human Rights Watch, 2016). The authors of that report urged the government and its development partners to redouble efforts to find an effective service delivery model to help deal with this problem. But after 15 years of experimentation at least we now know that BOTs are not the solution.

References

Ahmad, J., B.N. Goldar, S. Misra, M. Jakariya. 2003. *Willingness to Pay for Arsenic-Free, Safe Drinking Water in Bangladesh*, WSP South Asia Series, Delhi: Water and Sanitation Program.

Argos, M. 2010. "Arsenic Exposure from Drinking Water, and All-Cause and Chronic-Disease Mortalities in Bangladesh (HEALS): A prospective cohort study," *The Lancet* 376(9737): 252–8.

Asian Development Bank (ADB). 2009. "Urban Sector and Water supply and Sanitation in Bangladesh: An Exploratory Evaluation of the Programs of ADB and Other Aid Agencies," Independent Evaluation Department, July.

Augenblick, M., B.S. Custer. 1990. "The Build, Operate, and Transfer ("BOT") Approach to Infrastructure Projects in Developing Countries." Policy, Research, and External Affairs Working Paper WPS 498, Washington, DC: World Bank (August).

Aziz, S.N., K.J. Boyle, M. Rahman. 2006. "Knowledge of Arsenic in Drinking-Water: Risks and Avoidance in Matlab, Bangladesh," *Journal of Health, Population, and Nut*rition 24(3), 327–35.

DANIDA. 2005. "Water Supply and Sanitation Sector Programme Support (WSSPS) Phase II, HYSAWA Project, Project Document," Government of Bangladesh, Ministry of Foreign Affairs, Denmark, October.

Ehrhardt, D., J. Mugabe, W. Kingdom. 2015. "Professionalization Contracts for Small Municipal Water Service Providers in India: Business Model Development," Final Report prepared for the World Bank, June.

Estache, A., C. Philippe. 2012. "The Impact of Private Participation on the Performance of Infrastructure in Developing Countries: Summary of the academic evidence," IFC Economics Notes, No. 2, April.

Foster, T. 2012. *Private Sector Provision of rural Water Services: A Desk Study for Water for People*, Denver, CO: Water for People.

Gassner, K., A. Popov, N. Pushak. 2009. *Does Private Sector Participation Improve Performance in Electricity and Water Distribution*? PPIAF Trends and Policy Options, No. 6, Washington, DC: World Bank.

Gero, A., N. Carrard, J. Murta, J. Willetts. 2014. "Private and Social Enterprise Roles in Water, Sanitation and Hygiene for the Poor: A systematic review." *Journal of Water, Sanitation and Hygiene for Development* 4(3): 331–45.

Human Rights Watch. 2016. *Nepotism and Neglect: The Failing Response to Arsenic in the Drinking Water of Bangladesh's Rural Poor*. Human Rights Watch, ISBN: 978-1-6231-33399 (April 4). Accessed at: https://www.hrw.org/report/2016/04/06/nepotism-and-neglect/failing-response-arsenic-drinking-water-bangladeshs-rural

Kamruzzaman, A.K.M., I. Said, O. Osman, M. Hasmori, E. Hossain. 2012. "Water Business—Public–Private Partnership in Rural Bangladesh," Proceedings of the 3rd International Conference on Business and Economic Research, Bandung, Indonesia, 12 March.

Kleemeier, E. 2010. *Private operators and rural water supplies: A desk review of experience*. World Bank Water Papers. Washington, DC: The World Bank.

Leigland, J., A. Motaleb, W. Islam. 2015. "Private Sector Delivery of Rural Piped Water Services in Bangladesh: A Review of Experience, 2003–2015." Water and Sanitation Program Working Paper, Washington DC: World Bank. Accessed at http://documents.worldbank.org/curated/en/372701468014378850/pdf/106256-WP-P149962-PUBLIC.pdf:

Marin, P. 2009. *Public–Private Partnerships for Urban Water Utilities: A Review of Experiences in Developing Countries*, PPIAF Trends and Policy Options, No. 8, Washington, DC: World Bank.

Moriarty, P., S. Smits, J. Butterworth, R. Franceys. 2013. "Trends in Rural Water Supply: Towards a service delivery approach," *Water Alternatives* 6(3): 329–49.

Sirtaine, S., M.E. Pinglo, J.L. Guasch, V. Foster. 2005. *How Profitable are Infrastructure Concessions in Latin America? Empirical Evidence and Regulatory Implications*, PPIAF Trends and Policy Options, No. 2, Washington, DC: World Bank.

Social Development Foundation (SDF). 2014. "Rural Piped Water Pilot Project," Presentation to the World Bank, 25 March.

Sy, J., R. Warner, J. Jamieson. 2014. *Tapping the Markets: Opportunities for Domestic Investments in Water and Sanitation for the Poor.* Directions in Development, Private Sector Development, Washington, DC: World Bank.

Water and Sanitation Program (WSP). 2010. "Learnings from Bangladesh: Experience in Private Provision of Rural Piped Water," Field Note, December, Washington, DC: World Bank.

Water and Sanitation Program (WSP). 2015. "Monitoring Report on 21 Rural Piped Water Schemes under Bangladesh Water Supply and Program Project (BWSPP)," Bangladesh SSDPSP—Water Project, Washington, DC: World Bank.

World Bank. 2003. Project Appraisal Document on a Proposed Credit in the Amount of SDR 13.5 Million (US$18.24 Million Equivalent) to the People's Republic of Bangladesh for a Social Investment Program Project, Washington, DC: World Bank.

World Bank. 2004. Project Appraisal Document on a Proposed Grant in the Amount of SDR 27.6 Million (US$40.0 Million Equivalent) to the People's Republic of Bangladesh for a Water Supply Program Project, Washington, DC: World Bank.

World Bank. 2007. Implementation Completion and Results Report (IDA-31240 SWTZ-21082) on a Credit in the Amount of SDR 24.2 Million (US$44.4 Million Equivalent) to Bangladesh for Arsenic Mitigation Water Supply, Washington, DC: World Bank.

World Bank. 2011a. Implementation Completion and Results Report (IDA-H1010) on a Grant in the Amount of SDR 27.6 Million (US$40.0 Million Equivalent) Subsequently Reduced After Restructuring to the Amount of SDR 11.8 Million (US$18.6 Million Equivalent) to the People's Republic of Bangladesh for a Water Supply Program Project, Washington, DC: World Bank.

World Bank. 2011b. Implementation Completion and Results Report (Cr. 3740) on a Credit in the Amount of SDR 13.5 Million (US$18.4 Million Equivalent) to the People's Republic of Bangladesh for a Social Investment Program Project, Washington, DC: World Bank.

World Bank. 2012. Project Appraisal Document on a Proposed Credit in the Amount of SDR 48.4 Million (US$75 Million Equivalent) to the People's Republic of Bangladesh for the Bangladesh Rural Water Supply and Sanitation Project, Washington, DC: World Bank.

World Bank. 2017. Implementation Status and Results Report: BD Rural Water Supply and Sanitation Project (P122269). Washington, DC: World Bank (November 17).

World Bank. 2018. Implementation Completion and Results Report (IDA-5075) on a Credit in the Amount of SDR 30.3 Million (US$41.04 Million Equivalent) to the People's Republic of Bangladesh for the Bangladesh Rural Water supply and Sanitation Project, Washington, DC: World Bank.

World Health Organization (WHO). 2002. "Arsenic—Mass Poisoning on an Unprecedented Scale." Accessed at www.who.int/features/archives/feature206/en/#

Index

Note: Tables, figures, and boxes are indicated by an italic "*t*", "*f*", and "*b*", respectively, following the page number.

For the benefit of digital users, indexed terms that span two pages (e.g., 52–53) may, on occasion, appear on only one of those pages.

The manufacturer's authorised representative in the EU for product safety is Oxford University Press España S.A. of el Parque Empresarial San Fernando de Henares, Avenida de Castilla, 2 – 28830 Madrid (www.oup.es/en or product.safety@oup.com). OUP España S.A. also acts as importer into Spain of products made by the manufacturer.

www.ingramcontent.com/pod-product-compliance
Lightning Source LLC
LaVergne TN
LVHW011821200926
848484LV00005B/1268
* 9 7 8 0 1 9 8 8 6 1 8 2 9 *